ECOTOURISM

Tourism, Hospitality and Leisure Titles Available from Thomson Learning

Andersen & Robinson: *Literature & Tourism*

Arnold: *Festival Tourism* (forthcoming)

Aronsson: *The Development of Sustainable Tourism*

Baker, Huyton & Bradley: *Principles of Hotel Front Office Operations* 2/e

Ball, Jones, Kirk & Lockwood: *Hospitality Operations*

Baum: *Managing Human Resources in the European Tourism & Hospitality Industry*

Bray & Raitz: *Flight to the Sun*

Brown: *Tourism & the Olympics* (forthcoming)

Buhalis & Laws: *Tourism Distribution Channels*

Bull & Church: *Tourism in World Cities*

Carmouche & Kelly: *Behavioural Studies in Hospitality Management*

Clark, Riley, Wilkie & Wood: *Researching & Writing Dissertations in Hospitality & Tourism*

Clark: *Interpersonal Skills for Hospitality Management*

Clift & Carter: *Tourism & Sex*

Clift & Grabowski: *Tourism & Health*

Clift & Page: *Health and the International Tourist*

Clift, Luongo & Callister: *Gay Tourism*

Collins: *Becoming a Tour Guide*

Cooke: *The Economics of Leisure & Sport*

Cullen: *Economics for Hospitality Management*

D'Annunzio-Green: *HRM in Tourism & Hospitality*

Deegan & Dineen: *Tourism Policy & Performance*

Diamantis: *Ecotourism*

Doolan: Applying Numbers: *IT for Tourism & Leisure*

European Tourism University Partnership: *Resort Management in Europe*

Fattorini: *Managing Wine & Wine Sales*

Foley & Lennon: *Dark Tourism*

Foley, Lennon & Maxwell: *Hospitality, Tourism & Leisure Management*

Forsyth: *Maximizing Hospitality Sales*

Go & Jenkins: *Tourism & Development in Asia*

Godfrey: *The Tourism Development Handbook: A Practical Approach To Planning & Marketing*

Goldsmith, Nickson, Sloan & Wood: *HRM for Hospitality Services*

Hall & Jenkins: *Tourism & Public Policy*

Hall & Page: *Tourism in the Pacific*

Horner & Swarbrooke: *Marketing Tourism, Hospitality & Leisure in Europe*

Howie: *Managing the Tourist Destination*

Hudson: *Cities on the Shore*

Hudson: *Snow Business*

Huyton & Baker: *Principles of Hotel Front Office Operations* 2/e

Ingold, McMahon-Beattie & Yeoman: *Yield Management*

Ioannides: *Mediterranean Islands & Sustainable Tourism*

Johns & Lee-Ross: *Research Methods in Services Industry Management*

Jones & Lockwood: *The Management of Hotel Operations*

Jones & Merricks: *The Management of Food Services Operations*

Jones & Newton: *Hospitality & Catering: A Closer Look*

Jones: *An Introduction to Hospitality Operations*

Julyan: *Sales & Service for the Wine Professional*

Knowles, Diamantis & El-Mourhabi: *The Globalization of Tourism & Hospitality* 2/e

Kotas: *Hospitality Accounting*

Kotas: *Management Accounting for Hospitality & Tourism*

Law: *Urban Tourism*

Laws & Prideaux: *Managing Tourism & Hospitality Services*

Laws & Prideaux: *Researching Tourism & Hospitality Services*

Laws et al.: *Tourism in the 21st Century* 2/e

Laws: *Improving Tourism & Hospitality Services*

Laws: *Tourism Marketing*

Laws: *Tourist Destination Management*

Leask & Yeoman: *Heritage Visitor Attractions: An Operations Management Perspective*

Lee-Ross: *HRM in Tourism & Hospitaltiy*

Lennon: *Tourism Statistics*

Lockwood & Jones: *People & the Hotel & Catering Industry*

Lockwood: *The Management of Hotel Operations*

Lumsdon: *Tourism Marketing*

MacLellan & Smith: *Tourism in Scotland*

Mawson: *The Fundamentals of Hospitality Marketing*

Morgan: *Resort Management in Europe*

O'Connor: *Using Computers in Hospitality & Tourism* 3/e

Page, Brunt, Busby & Connell: *Tourism: A Modern Synthesis*

Pender: *Travel Trade & Transport*

Raitz & Bray: *Flight to the Sun*

Robinson et al.: *Sports Tourism* (forthcoming)

Ryan: *The Tourist Experience* 2/e

Seaton & Bennett: *Marketing Tourism Products*

Shackley: *Managing Sacred Sites*

Shackley: *Wildlife Tourism*

Shone & Parry: *Successful Event Management* 2/e

Stokowski: *Leisure in Society*

Thomas: *Management of Small Tourism Firms*

Tribe: *Corporate Strategy for Tourism*

Van Der Wagen & Davies: *Supervision & Leadership in Tourism & Hospitality*

Verginis & Wood: *Accommodation Management*

Webster: *Environmental Management in the Hospitality Industry*

Wood: *Working in Hotels & Catering*

World Tourism Organization: *National & Regional Tourism Planning*

Yeoman & McMahon-Beattie: *Revenue Management & Pricing*

Yeoman & McMahon-Beattie: *Sport & Leisure Operations Management*

Ecotourism

Management and Assessment

Dimitrios Diamantis

THOMSON

Australia • Canada • Mexico • Singapore • Spain • United Kingdom • United States

THOMSON

Ecotourism: Management and Assessment

Copyright © Dimitrios Diamantis 2004

The Thomson logo is a registered trademark used herein under licence.

For more information, contact Thomson Learning, High Holborn House; 50-51 Bedford Row, London WC1R 4LR or visit us on the World Wide Web at: http://www.thomsonlearning.co.uk

British Library Cataloguing-in-Publication Data
A catalogue record for this book is available from the British Library

ISBN 1-84480-047-4

Published by Thomson Learning 2004

Typeset by YHT Ltd, London
Printed in Croatia by Zrinski d.d.

Contents

Part A Theoretical Outline

Part B Case Studies Outline

Preface

Note from the World Tourism Organization (WTO)

The International Year of Ecotourism (IYE) 2002 has been an excellent opportunity for a collective reflection, with participation of all types of stakeholder related with this particular tourism segment, on the ways ecotourism should be developed, managed, regulated and monitored in order to be an effective contributor to sustainable development. At the intergovernmental level, the United Nations gave a mandate to the World Tourism Organization (WTO) to take responsibility for the IYE, with support from other agencies. In this context, in the preparation of and during the international year, WTO aimed at involving all the actors in the field of ecotourism, with the following four objectives in mind:

1. Generate greater awareness among public authorities, the private sector, the civil society and consumers regarding ecotourism's capacity to contribute to the conservation of the natural and cultural heritage in natural and rural areas and the improvement of standards of living in those areas.
2. Disseminate methods and techniques for the planning, management, regulation and monitoring of ecotourism to guarantee its long-term sustainability.
3. Promote exchanges of successful experiences in the field of ecotourism.
4. Increase opportunities for the efficient marketing and promotion of ecotourism destinations and products on international markets.

In order to reach these objectives, WTO carried out various activities at both international and national levels, the results of which were reported to the UN General Assembly in 2003.

First, WTO recommended its member states to set up special programmes and strategies for ecotourism, to establish national and/or local committees, involving all the stakeholders relevant to this activity, to provide support for the creation and operation of sustainable small and medium sized ecotourism enterprises and to set up compulsory and/or voluntary regulations regarding ecotourism activities, particularly in what refers to their environmental and socio-cultural sustainability. Many countries have followed WTO recommendations and were involved intensely in ecotourism activities and policies, most of which continued throughout 2003 and beyond.

Second, in order to exchange experiences, examine problems, promote cooperation nationally, regionally and internationally, and identify future challenges in ecotourism, WTO organized a series of regional or thematic seminars and conferences. These conferences were held in all main regions of the world and also through the Internet. The experiences and results from all these meetings were used as a base of discussions at the World Ecotourism Summit in Québec. The latter was successfully held in Québec City, Canada from 19 to 22 May 2002, with the participation of nearly 1200 delegates from 132 different countries. The main outcome of the summit is the Québec Declaration on Ecotourism, which has to be considered as a base document for every future discussion on ecotourism and for practical action.

Third, WTO prepared, and in some cases contributed to, a number of special publications for the IYE. First, with the purpose of learning about the trends in the main ecotourism generating markets, the World Tourism Organization conducted research and published seven pioneer country reports on the following markets: Canada, France, Germany, Italy, Spain, the UK and the USA. Second, with a view to contributing to the dissemination of sustainable ecotourism practices worldwide and the recommendations related to ecotourism already existing, specific guidelines and compilations of good practices were produced and disseminated. A guide on sustainable tourism in natural protected areas was also published.

The progress made during the IYE was substantial in terms of both understanding the complexity of this segment of the tourism industry and disseminating good practices. The time has come now for an intensive utilization of the results of the IYE, by national and local governments, by NGOs involved in this field and especially by tourism companies of all sorts and sizes. WTO is encouraging its 140 member states to apply those recommendations of the Québec Declaration that appear more relevant to their own national characteristics and conditions. This is the only way to make the IYE a lasting success.

Ecotourism: Management and Assessment is in line with these objectives. First, it contributes to the enrichment and the diffusion of analysis and guidelines on ecotourism, dealing with different specific aspects, such as global policy, visitor management, monitoring, certification, etc. Second, it gives concrete examples of ecotourism practices from different parts of the world, in different geographic and climatic contexts and for different social organizations. Thus, it permits local entrepreneurs, communities and authorities among others, to get a clearer idea of what ecotourism should be and what they can adapt from other existing ecotourism experiences.

Finally, it is useful to reaffirm that, as a pioneer segment, ecotourism has a double responsibility which is simultaneously ethical and environmental and which impinges on economic viability. It should be used in each country, and particularly in developing countries, as the spearhead of the entire tourism industry. Ecotourism can become the paradigm of how to satisfy the growing desire to fill our spare time with innovative activities, in different places, but contributing to the enhancement of peoples and nature.

Eugenio Yunis
Sustainable Development of Tourism, WTO
Madrid, March 2003

Note from the Business Enterprises for Sustainable Travel (BEST)

Travel and tourism is the world's largest industry, generating approximately one-half a trillion dollars a year in economic activity. In 2000 698 million individuals travelled to another country, two-thirds of them for vacation or leisure. That number is expected to reach one billion by 2010. As environmental and social concerns have moved higher up the development agenda, we are acutely aware of the powerful impact that we as travellers have on the natural environment, especially on our seacoasts, freshwater resources, high mountain areas, forests and fragile ecosystems.

In the face of the potentially negative effects of travel, there *is* good news. Travellers' environmental concerns are growing. The Geotourism Study issued in March by the Travel Industry Association of America, funded by the National Geographic Society and supported by Business Enterprises for Sustainable Travel (BEST), showed that the majority of the travelling public (71%) indicates that it is important to them that their visits to a destination not damage its environment.

As United Nations Secretary-General Kofi Annan pointed out recently: 'We now perceive a more complex relationship between human society and the natural environment that recognizes the potential of the planet's privileged 20 percent to benefit the balance of humanity.'

BEST, a programme of The Conference Board, which was formed in 2000 in partnership with the World Travel and Tourism Council (WTTC), must make the most of every opportunity to maximize all efforts to raise the bar of sustainability in the travel and tourism industry. To this end, BEST documents travel and tourism practices that benefit destinations worldwide. Our database now includes more than 500 such efforts from 80 countries around the world (*www.sustainabletravel.org*).

It is encouraging to learn that travel-related enterprises are increasingly becoming positive forces in sustainable development. Such businesses are documented in Dimitrios Diamantis's edition *Ecotourism: Management and*

Assessment. These exemplary efforts can help restore the natural environment, as well as contribute to social and economic development and the preservation of traditional cultures.

We all are members of a new tourism movement. If we lead the way in cultural and environmental stewardship, our future generations will be able to continue to enjoy the earth's riches.

Michael Seltzer
Business Enterprises for Sustainable Travel
New York, March 2003

Note from UNESCO

The 2002 UN International Year of Ecotourism (IYE) helped draw the international community's attention to the challenges and opportunities associated with ecotourism development. Based on a number of interesting case studies from around the world, this current volume contributes to advancing further the critical examination of ecotourism that was embarked on during the IYE. An examination that undoubtedly will help decision makers around to world to reinforce management instruments, policies and institutional frameworks in favour of 'true' ecotourism.

For decades, UNESCO has been studying the cultural, environmental and socioeconomic impacts of tourism using a multidisciplinary approach. Several of these studies have focused on some of the 425 sites in 95 countries that make up the UNESCO World Network of Biosphere Reserves. Biosphere reserves are sites established by countries participating in the UNESCO Man and the Biosphere (MAB) Programme to promote biodiversity conservation and sustainable development based on local community efforts and sound science. As these sites are also increasingly being targeted for tourism, including ecotourism operations, they constitute, in our opinion, privileged areas for the academic, as well as the policy community to gain additional fruitful insights on sustainable tourism, including ecotourism. We are therefore very much encouraged that chapters in this book, which take the readers on such a fascinating journey, do assess ecotourism-related experiences in biosphere reserves and we invite other researchers to enhance practices with this focus.

Peter Bridgewater
UNESCO, Director Division of Ecological Sciences;
Secretary Man and the Biosphere (MAB) Programme
Paris, March 2003

Introduction

During the last decade ecotourism was seen as a concept that was situated at the centre of tourism's new research paradigm reflected by the search for new forms of tourism products. In these days, with resorts raising and falling in popularity as well as with the global threats within the society, ecological areas are of paramount importance both for domestic and international visitors.

For any ecological area, however, to maintain its attractiveness and character different management and assessment tools are needed. With the rationale to contribute to the body of knowledge of ecotourism, this book aims to focus the discussion of ecotourism on management and assessment of sites, destinations, communities and resources. As a result, the 19 chapters in this volume can be used both as theory and case studies which can be utilized as a full course of study into ecotourism management and as a source of reference. To this effect, at the beginning of each chapter *four learning objectives* are provided and at the end of each chapter *four questions are posed* which relate to the learning objectives. More specifically, the book is divided into two parts, one on the theory, the second on case studies:

- *Part A, the theoretical outline*, covers the basic structure of ecotourism, with emphasis on management and assessment. Here, seven chapters are presented which aim to provide an overview of issues and concerns.
- *Part B, the case studies*, provides 12 case studies of different issues of ecotourism management and assessment. The case studies range in length so that they can be used as classroom exercises and/or for project work. The case studies also cover different themes, which can be seen in the outline provided within the section. At the end of this section, websites are provided in order to assist the readers in commencing their research.

As such, the editor wishes to thank the contributors for their efforts in providing the chapters and expertise. Special thanks are due to Sue Geldenhuys from the University of Technology in South Africa as she assisted with ideas and constructive feedback for putting the volume together. Thanks are also due to Jennifer Pegg and Laura Priest at Thomson, project manager Penelope Allport and copy editor Helen Baxter, for their fine job on the book.

Last, but not least, thanks go to the readers of this volume who will assist the concept of ecotourism as to whether or not it can provide its rewards to the economy, society and environment in a symbiotic manner.

Dimitrios Diamantis

Author Profiles

Dimitrios Diamantis is an MBA course manager and the research coordinator in Les Roches, Switzerland. Prior to that he worked at Bournemouth University in the UK, where he also completed his PhD on the area of consumer behaviour and ecotourism. He is currently involved in ecotourism management and assessment projects in various destinations.

Part A: Theoretical

Dimitrios Diamantis
Les Roches, School of Hotel Management, CH-3975, Bluche, Valais, Switzerland
dimitriosdiamantis@yahoo.co.uk
www.les-roches.ch

Sue Geldenhuys
Department of Tourism Management, University of Technology, Private Bag X680, Pretoria 0001, South Africa
geldens@techpta.ac.za

Pamela A. Wight
Pam Wight & Associates, 14715–82 Ave, Edmonton, Alberta, Canada T5R 3R7
pamwight@superiway.net

Edward W. (Ted) Manning
President, Tourisk Inc., Sustainable Destinations, 1980 Saunderson Drive, Ottawa Ontario, Canada K1G2E2
tourisk@rogers.com
www.tourisk.org

Xavier Font
Centre for the Study of Small Tourism and Hospitality Firms, Leeds Metropolitan University, Calverley Street, Leeds LS1 3HE, UK
X.Font@lmu.ac.uk

Margot Sallows
Department of Earth and Environmental Sciences, University of Greenwich at Medway
Central Avenue, Chatham Maritime, Kent ME4 4TB, UK
margot.sallows@virgin.net

David A. Fennell
Department of Recreation and Leisure Studies, Brock University, St Catharines,
Ontario, Canada L2S 3A1
david.fennell@brocku.ca

Richard Butler
Professor of Tourism, School of Management, University of Surrey, Guildford, Surrey
GU2 5XH, UK
R.Butler@surrey.ac.uk

Stephen W. Boyd
University of Otago, Department of Tourism, Level 4, Commerce Building, PO Box 56,
Dunedin, New Zealand
sboyd@business.otago.ac.nz

C. Michael Hall
Professor and Head, Department of Tourism, University of Otago School of Business,
University of Otago, PO Box 56, Dunedin, New Zealand
cmhall@business.otago.ac.nz

Part B: Case Studies

David Weaver
Department of Health, Fitness and Recreation Resources, George Mason University
Prince William 1 (Room 312, Mail Stop 4E5), 10900 University Bvld, Manassa, VA
20115, USA
dweaver3@gmu.edu

Ginger Smith
College of Professional Studies, Associate Professor and Associate Dean of Tourism
Studies, School of Business and Public Management, The George Washington
University, 805 21st St, NW, Washington, DC 20052, USA
smithg@gwu.edu

Alvin Rosenbaum
International Institute of Tourism Studies, The George Washington University, 8781 Preston Place, Chevy Chase, MD, USA
arosen@gwu.edu

Tazim B. Jamal
Department of Recreation, Park and Tourism Sciences, Texas A&M University College Station, TX 77843–2261, USA
tjamal@tamu.edu

Andrew N. Skadberg
Texas Cooperative Extension, Department of Recreation Park and Tourism Sciences, Texas A&M University College Station, TX 77843–2261, USA
a-skadberg@tamu.edu

Kim Williams
9501 State Route 170, Rogers, OH 44455, USA
riley@raex.com

Atsuko Hashimoto
Department of Recreation and Leisure Studies, Brock University St Catharines, Ontario, Canada L2S 3A1
Atsuko.Hashimoto@Brocku.ca

David Telfer
Department of Recreation and Leisure Studies, Brock University St Catharines, Ontario, Canada L2S 3A1
David.Telfer@Brocku.ca

Tim Knowles
Principal Lecturer in Hospitality Management, Manchester Metropolitan University, 94B Aintree Road, Little Lever, Bolton BL3 1ER, UK
timknowles@msn.com

Christian Felzensztein
International Marketing Lecturer, Universidad Austral de Chile, Valdivia, Chile, South America

Carlos Costa
SAGEI, University of Aveiro, 3800 Aveiro, Portugal
ccosta@egi.ua.pt

Colin Johnson, PhD

Professor and Chair, Department of Hospitality Management, San Jose State University, USA

cjohnson@casa.sjsu.edu

Anna Spenceley

Institute of Natural Resources, University of Natal, 67 St Patricks Road, Private Bag X01, Pietermaritzburg 3209, South Africa

SpenceleyA@nu.ac.za

Harold Goodwin

International Centre for Responsible Tourism, University of Greenwich at Medway, Central Avenue, Chatham Maritime, Kent ME4 4TB, UK

harold@haroldgoodwin.info

Bill Maynard

209 Jalan Ara, Bangsar Baru 59100, Kuala Lumpur, Malaysia

WBMaynard@aol.com

Yvette Johansson

Les Roches, School of Hotel Management, CH-3975, Bluche, Valais, Switzerland

yvettejohansson@hotmail.com

Ralf Buckley

Director, ICER, Griffith University, PBM 50, Gold Coast Mail Center, Queensland 9726, Australia

R.Buckley@mailbox.gu.edu.au

Ross K. Dowling

School of Marketing, Tourism and Leisure, Faculty of Business and Public Management, Edith Cowan University, Joondalup WA 6027, Australia

r.dowling@ecu.edu.au

List of Figures

List of Tables

xix

A Theoretical Outline

ECOTOURISM MANAGEMENT: AN OVERVIEW

ECOTOURISM ASSESSMENT: AN OVERVIEW

PRACTICAL MANAGEMENT TOOLS AND APPROACHES FOR RESOURCE PROTECTION AND ASSESSMENT

INDICATORS AND RISK MANAGEMENT FOR ECOTOURISM DESTINATIONS

ECOTOURISM CERTIFICATION CRITERIA AND PROCEDURES: IMPLICATION FOR ECOTOURISM MANAGEMENT

THE POLAR FRAMEWORK AND ITS OPERATION IN AN ECOTOURISM SETTING

ECOTOURISM POLICY

1 Ecotourism Management: An Overview

Dimitrios Diamantis

The four main objectives of this chapter are to:

- Outline the definitional perspective of ecotourism
- Overview the components of ecotourism
- Discuss the ecotourism impacts (economic, social, environmental)
- Explain the marketing, demarketing and practitioners' aspects of ecotourism

Introduction

The popular appearance of ecotourism in the late 1980s was treated as a panacea to all tourism-related problems in the destination areas. Its popularity (Blamey, 2001; Orams, 2001) claimed to be associated with the:

- general search for natural attractions during a holiday
- eagerness to achieve sustainable development by any means
- potential employment opportunities in natural areas
- shift towards planning in protected areas.

This popularity has also been translated into an increase of visits for ecotourism-related purposes, which, it is claimed, accounts for around 20% of total tourism arrivals (WTO, 1998). At the recent ecotourism summit in Québec in Canada, numerous issues were discussed that reflect the importance of the concept both at the national and local levels (see Chapter 7). There are, however, a number of pitfalls with ecotourism, most of which are associated from its position within the tourism spectrum, its similarities with other 'green' tourism products as well as its effective application (Orams, 2001).

For the purpose of this volume, ecotourism is treated both as a sub-component of alternative tourism and as natural-based tourism, being part of the concept of sustainability. In addition, other sustainable products (i.e. agrotourism, wine tourism, rural tourism) claim to have similarities with ecotourism as well as being part of both nature-based and alternative tourism (Jaakson, 1997; Diamantis, 1999; Diamantis and Ladkin, 1999; Blamey, 2001; Orams, 2001).

On the other end of the spectrum, both mass tourism and other forms of tourism such as cruise tourism and business tourism are searching for a sustainable ethos in their practices and as such are placed outside the sustainability borders. Ecotourism characteristics are opposite those of mass tourism, especially the experiential aspects of both concepts. For instance, ecotourism activities depend on the natural and cultural environment whereas mass tourism activities depend mostly on the built environment (see Figure 1.1).

Furthermore, looking at the definitions of ecotourism, the majority of them share a similarity of lack of precise focus over their components.

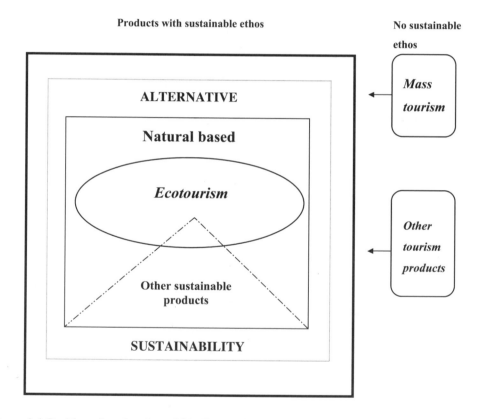

Figure 1.1 Position of ecotourism within the tourism products spectrum

Conceptual definitions of ecotourism

There are numerous conceptual definitions of ecotourism, all of which try to identify the meaning of the concept. Orams (1995) suggests that the majority of ecotourism definitions lie between the passive position (i.e. concentrates solely on ecotourism development, not enhancing the antagonistic impacts or the ecotourist's need to be satisfied) and the active position (i.e. actions of protecting the environment and the behavioural intentions of ecotourists).

More specifically, ecotourism was first defined as 'traveling to relatively undisturbed or uncontaminated natural areas with the specific objective of studying, admiring, and enjoying the scenery and its wild plants and animals, as well as any existing cultural manifestations (both past and present) found in these areas' (Ceballos-Lascuráin, 1987: 14).

In a similar vein, other researchers elaborated this definition by emphasizing certain aspects of it (see Table 1.1). For example:

- Ziffer (1989) highlighted the *conservation, natural-based, economic and cultural components* of ecotourism.
- Boo (1991) viewed ecotourism not only from *natural and conservation components, but also the economic and educational elements*.
- Forestry Tasmania (1994) emphasized the *nature-based, educational, social and sustainability components of ecotourism* by distinguishing between ecotourism and nature-based tourism.
- Blamey's (1995) dimensions of ecotourism included four main components: *nature-based, environmentally educated, sustainably managed and distance/time*.
- Lindberg and McKercher's (1997) definition highlights the *natural-based and sustainability* components of ecotourism.

A comparison of these definitions indicates that ecotourism tends to have three main components: *natural-based*, *educational* and *sustainable management* that includes *economic*, *social*, *cultural* and *ethical issues*. Although these themes are more or less clear, limitations arise by attempts to express all these components with a single definition that is applied in all circumstances and in all ecotourism research settings (Diamantis, 1999; Diamantis and Ladkin, 1999). Unlike tourism definitions, there is no one *established* conceptual and technical definition of ecotourism.

As a guiding *conceptual* principle, however, ecotourism can be said to be that which occurs in natural settings (protected and non-protected) with an attempt to increase benefits to the economy, society and environment through sustainable educational practices from locals to tourists and vice versa.

In measuring ecotourism at the destination level this definition is still restrictive. It seems that it is better to operationalize the *technical* aspects of it based on trade-off scenarios of its themes.

Table 1.1 Conceptual definitions of ecotourism

1. Ecotourism is a form of tourism inspired primarily by the natural history of an area, including its indigenous cultures. The ecotourist visits relatively undeveloped areas in the spirit of appreciation, participation and sensitivity. The ecotourist practices a non-consumptive use of wildlife and natural resources and contributes to the visited area through labor or financial means aimed at directly benefiting the conservation of the site and the economic well-being of the local residents. (*Ziffer*, 1989: 6)

2. Ecotourism is a nature tourism that contributes to conservation, through generating funds for protected areas, creating employment opportunities for local communities, and offering environmental education. (*Boo*, 1991b: 4)

3. Nature-based tourism that is focused on provision of learning opportunities while providing local and regional benefits, while demonstrating environmental, social, cultural, and economic sustainability. (*Forestry Tasmania*, 1994: ii)

4. An ecotourism experience is one in which an individual travels to a relatively undisturbed natural area that is more than 40 km from home, the primary intention being to study, admire, or appreciate the scenery and its wild plans and animals, as well as any existing cultural manifestations (both past and present) found in these areas.

5. An ecotourist is anyone who undertakes at least one ecotourism experience in a specified region during a specified period of time. (*Blamey*, 1995: 24)

6. Ecotourism is tourism and recreation that is both nature-based and sustainable. (*Lindberg and McKercher*, 1997: 67)

Trade-off technical definitions of ecotourism

Looking at the technical trade-off definitions of ecotourism, four different approaches can be devised ranging from very weak to very strong (see Table 1.2):

- In the *very weak definition*, the core emphasis could be given to the natural-based component. For example, a definition could be implied on measuring the basis of ecotourism practices in both protected and non-protected areas.
- In the *weak definition*, the core emphasis could be given mainly to the natural-based component and to a lesser degree on the educational and sustainability components. Here, a definition could stress the measurement of the basis of ecotourism practices in both protected and non-protected areas, which generates a low level of education/conservation/economic/social/cultural benefit to the destination.
- In the *strong definition*, all three elements should be considered equally. For instance, a definition could stress the measurement of the basis of ecotourism practices in both protected and non-protected areas, which generates a high level of education/conservation/economic/social/cultural benefit to the destination.
- In the *very strong definition*, all three elements should be equally considered, but with less emphasis on the economic aspects of ecotourism. In this case, a definition could stress measurement of the basis of ecotourism practices in both protected and non-protected areas, which generates a high level of education/conservation/social/cultural benefit and a low level of economic reward to the destination.

Table 1.2 Trade-off technical definitions of ecotourism

Definition	Elements
VERY WEAK	*Core emphasis:* **Natural-based component:** protected and non-protected areas
WEAK	*Core emphasis:* **Natural-based component:** protected and non-protected areas *Less emphasis:* **Educational component:** interpretation and training programmes **Sustainability component:** economic and/or social-cultural elements
STRONG	*Core emphasis:* **Natural-based component:** protected and non-protected areas **Educational component:** interpretation and training programmes **Sustainability component:** equal emphasis on economic and social-cultural elements
VERY STRONG	*Core emphasis:* **Natural-based component:** protected and non-protected areas **Educational component:** interpretation and training programmes **Sustainability component:** emphasis on social-cultural elements rather than on economic elements

The benefit of creating these kinds of definition is that they coincide with different types of sustainability (Hunter, 1997; Blamey, 2001). For ecotourism to be close to its main principles, only the strong and very strong definitions can be operationalized. The very weak and weak definitions, however, do not represent 'true' ecotourism practices but can be applied in specific circumstances, i.e. mass tourism destinations starting to practise ecotourism. Having said that, for the trade-off technical definitions to be operated, an understanding of the different management issues embodied within the components of ecotourism is required.

Components of ecotourism

The natural-based component

All the ecotourism definitions, regardless of their perspective, include the natural-based component. As ecotourism initially developed in tropical regions, the natural-based experiences have been seen to take place in a protected area (Barnes, 1996), which is 'an area dedicated primarily to the protection and enjoyment of natural or cultural heritage, to maintenance of biodiversity, and/or maintenance of ecological life-support services' (IUCN, 1991 in Ceballos-Lascuráin, 1996: 29).

Apart from protected areas, other attractions include national parks, wildlife and biological reserves, coastal and marine areas, which are simultaneously used by both natural-based tourists and ecotourists. Thus, it was claimed that the setting in which ecotourism operates includes the 'legally protected areas' as they offered a guarantee of their long-term attractivity (Ceballos-Lascuráin, 1996). The attractivity of these protected areas, however, remains in some cases an illusive goal. For instance in Central America, Asia and Africa protected areas are facing serious internal and external problems. Some of the issues related to protected areas are habitat fragmentation, negative impacts from development including activities from ecotourism and illegal activities within protected areas such as poaching and deforestation.

Meanwhile, according to Goodwin (1996), managers of protected areas could turn nature tourism into ecotourism, based on the motivation of their consumers, in other words at *the point of consumption* or based on a sound management strategy both in terms of numbers and activities.

In general terms, natural-based tourism has been claimed to contain three main components (Valentine, 1992: 109):

- *First*, the nature of experience which is nature dependent, containing attributes such as intensity of interaction with nature and social sensitivity.
- *Second*, the style of this experience, where different product elements such as willingness to pay, group size and type, and length of stay are considered to be of significance.
- *Third*, the location of the natural-based tourism experience, such as accessibility, ownership of location and the fragility of the resources used.

In light of these suggestions, natural-based tourism has inevitably generated certain similarities with ecotourism, in terms of the natural common setting used by both forms of tourism. However, the initial setting of ecotourism (protected areas) has been criticized from the sense that it is too restrictive, on the platform that ecotourism promotes mainly the conservation and environmental issues of non-protected areas (Blamey, 1997). Nowadays, however, it is believed that ecotourism could take place both in protected and non-protected areas, but with a strong emphasis on conservation and educational components (Blamey, 1997, 2001).

Activities of ecotourism in a natural setting

The activities of natural-based tourism can be distinguished into three main categories (Valentine, 1992: 110):

- activities dependent on nature (e.g. birdwatching)
- activities enhanced by nature (e.g. camping)
- activities where the natural setting is incidental (e.g. swimming).

For instance, in a discussion concerning the classification of water recreational activities, Smarton (1988) lists four generalized types of recreation activity:

kinetic, *situation based*, *harvest based* and *substitution based*. It was claimed, that because ecotourism would discourage a consumption use of natural resources, the harvest-based experience does not apply to activities such as hunting and the collection of flora and fauna. The other three forms mentioned can be claimed to be included in ecotourism activities (Smarton, 1988):

- kinetic experiences were non-mechanically powered activities such as hiking, diving, swimming
- situation-based experiences entail a strong association with the destination as a unique characteristic
- a substitution or aesthetic experience includes observation of natural phenomena, for example birdwatching.

In addition, Duffus and Dearden (1990) treated activities in terms of human and wildlife interaction. They suggested that the continuum of human and wildlife interaction could be treated in terms of consumptive use to non-consumptive use. The non-consumptive use activities are those in which the organism is not affected by human interaction (e.g birdwatching, whale watching, nature walks and natural photography). Contrariwise, consumptive use activities impose certain purposefully intended impacts on the organism such as forms of hunting and fishing (Duffus and Dearden, 1990: 215–16). They further added low consumptive use activities, which are those related to observation purposes in certain attractions such as zoos, animal parks and scientific research.

In comparing all the last mentioned approaches, the emphasis on ecotourism related to activities focused on educationally oriented recreation activities and on the enhancement of knowledge through non-consumption usage of the natural resources. In addition, all the activities are assessed as to whether or not they enhance and/or protect the environment. In all cases, the natural-based component of ecotourism is based on the biological, physical and cultural features both in protected and non-protected environments, in which the sustainability and/or conservation elements should signify its practices.

Sustainability component

One of the significant aspects of ecotourism is sustainability (see Chapters 4 and 5). In the late 1980s, through increased awareness of global environmental issues, sustainability began to emerge as a key component in the world, expanding not only into the tourism sector but also to all other sectors within the economy (Archer and Cooper, 1994; Godfrey, 1996). In 1987 the World Commission on Environment and Development defined sustainable development as 'growth that brings benefits to people today without damaging resources or prospects for future generations'](Wood, 2002).

Sustainable management concerns resource management. It recognizes that the world's resources are limited and they are being used up every day without consideration of replenishing or protecting them (Godfrey, 1996). Tourism's interest in sustainable development becomes therefore very logical, considering this industry sells the environment and the resources it provides as its product (Murphy, 1994). For local inhabitants, sustainable development concentrates on promoting the well-being of people through the stipulation of healthy and supportive economic and social conditions. Sustainable tourism development concerns not only developing new environmentally friendly products, but also those aspects of the industry that make all stakeholders more resource conscious (Godfrey, 1996).

Planning for sustainability regarding the tourism sector involves not only the host community but also the government on both regional and national levels. All need to work together for this goal to be achieved. The responsibility for conserving the natural environment in an area should not be the responsibility of the locals working on their own. All stakeholders need to be involved, this includes the locals, the private sector, the government and visitors (Gurung and De Coursey, 1994). A government's planning and policymaking body, especially regarding environmental regulations, plays a major role in assisting sustainable ecotourism practices. Governments around the world have realized the economical benefits that can be derived from ecotourism and are therefore becoming more involved in its development. 'The significance of government planning in regards to sustainability is highlighted by the various national strategies for ecologically sustainable development implemented throughout the 1990s in many countries around the world' (Wearing and Neil, 1999: 25).

The concept of sustainability is closely interlinked with the theory of carrying capacity. This relates to predetermined limits to development, population pressure and infrastructure in a particular area. Three main areas that are subject to these limits are the environment, the society and the economy. Different stakeholders regularly convey different views on carrying capacity management. In environmental settings, the concept applies to the maximum number of people who can utilize a location without an unacceptable decline in the quality of the experience gained by visitors. From a community viewpoint, carrying capacity (see Chapters 2 and 6) relates to a destination's ability to absorb tourism before the community feels negative effects. The carrying capacity for the economy concerns employment and revenue earned, among others, and as long as these are positive and the host community benefits from tourism, the predetermined level is correct. In early stages of tourism development, the control within a destination is locally based. However, as a destination grows international companies move in, taking a large amount of the revenue earned out of the destination (Stadel, 1996). 'A primary means of maintaining sustainability is by limiting tourist numbers and therefore the possibility for environmental degradation' (Wearing and Neil, 1999: 23).

Local issues

One of the most vital elements of ecotourism is the involvement of the host community. Tourism needs to be incorporated into the social and economic life of the community (Gunn, 1994). This involvement should be in a direct form, such as share of the revenue generated, employment and, most importantly, control in development and implementation of ecotourism. Tourism can also create improved social welfare, education and infrastructure (Cater, 1994). The local population is often dependent on natural resources provided by the environment, therefore any changes regarding the environment should come from within the communities (Wearing and Neil, 1999). Part of the involvement of the local population can come in the form of empowerment: the community is given the responsibility to make decisions or, at least, to be part of the decision-making process. 'There are at least five areas where local people can help to bring about nature tourism activities: information gathering, consultation, decision making, initiating action and evaluation' (Brandon, 1993: 140). The local community needs to be involved from the beginning of the project to establish the area as a ecotourism destination. If this is not done properly, the most likely outcome is that the population feels powerless in the face of the development and does not have the strength to influence the development (Brandon, 1993).

By having local involvement the economy of the host community thrives as well. The multiplier effect increases through improved employment and higher earnings of the local population. Import leakages decline and revenue earned by expatriate workers also diminish (Cater, 1994). Care must be taken so the local population is not actually being *exploited* by introducing ecotourism to the area. In several destinations, the indigenous population is promoted as a major attraction, they are used as guides and provide accommodation in traditional villages and houses (Boyd and Butler, 1996). The provision of local guides has a number of benefits for the local community, negative impacts on the environment are reduced, environmental awareness of the local community is increased and, of course, it provides employment for the population (Ross and Wall, 1999).

Before the implementation of ecotourism, the local population should be educated through a 'public participation programme' as to what the benefits and potential hazards are that will be derived from introducing ecotourism to the community (Addison, 1996). Public participation regarding the community planning process is vital for quality sustainable tourism development (see

Chapter 3). Local and regional values and culture needs to be taken into consideration when implementing ecotourism.

Educational component

Considering the fact that ecotourism seeks to promote responsible travel, then education and interpretation have to be the foundation and this should aim to include the local community and both domestic and international travellers (Ross and Wall, 1999). Ecotourism appeals to people who wish to interact with the environment and, to varying degrees, develop their knowledge, comprehension and appreciation of it. The aim of ecotourism is to educate the visitor about the value of natural environments (Wearing and Neil, 1999).

One part of the learning process is to provide onsite educational programmes at the destinations (see Chapter 2). Ecotourism operators are in an incomparable position to offer environmental and cultural interpretation. This type of information can be provided during and after the event in the form of brochures, videos, local guides and through walk and talks. Prior to the trip information can be made available to the ecotourist regarding the special concerns for that particular destination (Ross and Wall, 1999).

The visitor will encounter different learning experiences during an ecotourism journey, the main focus is the natural environment but also, where indigenous people are involved, their traditions and culture will be part of the learning process (Hawkins, 1994). 'Ecotourism is primarily concerned with an individual search for learning and for the associated personal development, and no specific level of social contact is required to make the experience worthwhile' (Eagles, 2001: 7).

Providing education and interpretation as a part of the experience makes the visitor aware of the environment and how their actions can contribute to the conservation of the same. This is especially the case when visiting fragile resource sites – greater caution will arise from the visitor. Environmental education, if utilized successfully, can fortify environmental consciousness, concern and dedication through an amplified comprehension and appreciation of nature. 'Through interpretation and education, ecotourists can gain a better understanding, awareness and appreciation of the natural and cultural environment' (Black, 1999: 1).

This third criterion is interlinked with the second, concerning sustainability. In the desire to understand and appreciate the natural attractions of a destination lies a desire to ensure that those attractions are not destroyed but sustained for future visitors (Weaver, 2001). The local population in a community will also take part in this learning process; by having educational programmes set up for the visitors they will also be encouraged to take part of the knowledge. By working together, the visitors and the host community will strive together for conservation and to achieve sustainability of the environment.

Ecotourism management considerations: impacts perspective

Governments and non-governmental organizations around the world are developing and promoting ecotourism in protected areas to benefit local communities and to help preserve the environment and different ecosystems (Pleumarom, 1995). However, as with all forms of tourism, impacts of both a positive and negative nature do follow. One of the important aspects of ecotourism is the involvement of the local community. This only includes participation in the decision-making process and employment, among other elements, but also a complete understanding of what ecotourism actually means, the consequences that it will have on the society as a whole, including knowledge of all impacts that might follow (Walker, 1995).

To reinforce the positive impacts of ecotourism, it is necessary for the inhabitants to be integrated in the planning and development of ecotourism projects at an early stage (Shores, 1999). In order for locals to contribute wholly in the planning process, they must be both attentive to the impacts and supportive of the development. In addition, it is important that local populations have a crucial level of awareness of the prospective benefits and costs of tourism to contribute effectively in the planning process (Walker, 1995; Wood, 2002). The challenge any ecotourism operator faces is reducing any negative impacts, which ultimately is one of ecotravel's goals, while presenting economic incentives to local people and businesses (Beeh, 1999).

Evaluation of the knowledge of ecotourism impacts can be considered by understanding the host community's sensitivity of the positive and negative environmental, economical and social impacts of ecotourism (Walker, 1995).

Through a survey conducted in two communities in Mexico, San José and Alta Cimas, both involved in ecotourism, the importance and effects of a community organization programme (COP) were identified. The objective of the COP was to develop social, economic and conservation projects, not necessarily to inform locals concerning the positive or negative impacts that might occur. The residents of Alta Cimas were involved in a COP for two years and the conclusion of the survey was that the inhabitants were more conscious of the positive environmental, negative economical, positive social and negative social impacts than San José citizens. However, San José had a higher realization of the negative environmental impacts. Both communities were likewise responsive to the positive economic impacts of ecotourism. It can be concluded from this example that community programmes are beneficial for increasing the awareness of ecotourism development and should be encouraged in any community that is planning to develop ecotourism (Walker, 1995; Addison, 1996).

When identifying and analyzing the different impacts that ecotourism can have on a society, either positive *or* negative, three characteristics are acknowledged: economic, environmental and social. It is not possible to identify which of these three impacts are the most important as 'they are all vital to the successful introduction, operation and perpetuation of ecotourism' (Wall, 2002: 114).

Economic impacts

The impacts of ecotourism, or any economic activity, can be classified into three categories: direct, indirect and induced. Direct impacts are those arising directly from tourist spending, indirect impacts are those such as when a restaurant is purchasing supplies in order to cater to tourists and, last, induced impacts are those such as when an employee who works in a restaurant buys goods and services from wages earned (Lindberg, 1996; UNEP, 2003).

One main advantage of ecotourism is that expenditure by ecotourists is, in general, greater that that of the average tourist. An operation that has incorporated the main components of ecotourism, and especially local community participation, implies that a large part of the revenue gained will stay within the region. When well managed, ecotourism can assist in redistributing income to local people and generate other indirect earnings within local areas (Israngkura, 1996).

Ecotourism can play an important role in remote regions where development is slow to progress. The revenue that is gained can be used for various development projects, infrastructure and to ensure long-term sustainability of local areas. Employment, even in small numbers, does make a positive impact on the economy. In protected areas, ecotourism also plays a significant role as it raises political and financial awareness and support for conservation, which is one of the goals of ecotourism (Lindberg, 1996; Schaller, 2002). Revenue will be generated for resource conservation management, either directly through a percentage of (for example) the entrance fee to a national park or by donations from the general public (Dowling, 2001).

Due to the fact that visitor numbers are usually very low in ecotourism resorts or lodges, operators need to be careful not to become involved in the financial gain of the business. Should this happen growth in the direction of mass tourism is likely to occur. Other areas of concern would be to make sure that the owner of or investor in the ecotourism operation does not take the majority of the profits out from the region but reinvests the revenue locally (Simmons, 2001; Wood, 2002). Despite the tendency of the ecotourism operator to purchase supplies locally, some leakages will, however, occur when importing goods or services from outside the region (Weaver, 1998).

Environmental impacts

The environment is the natural asset that ecotourism thrives on; if it is not developed and managed properly ecotourism can result in negative environmental impacts which would undermine the whole concept of sustainability (Anonymous, 2002b). The timing and duration of an ecotourist's visit to a sensitive area, and the nature of use impact relationship, implies that ecotourism can be very challenging to environmental resource systems (Simmons, 2001). However, most ecotourism operators have recognized the value of sustainability and conservation and are changing their business practices to preserve their natural resources and improve the environment. The same goes for the ecotourist; they can support this development by educating themselves more about the environmental impacts that can arise from ecotourism and by tourism in general, also by selecting their travel choices to those that support and protect conservation and preservation of the natural wonders of the earth (The International Ecotourism Society, 2002).

Environmentally, ecotourism is anticipated to offer motivation and incentives for preservation of natural areas and regions. The positive impacts that are expected to arise from ecotourism come in both financial and physical form. Natural conservation, maintenance against environmental degradation, improvement and protection of biodiversity are a few examples of what ecotourism strives to achieve for the area in which it operates. For the visitor, ecotourism will help to raise environmental awareness and ethics which they will take back with them to their home destination (Israngkura, 1996; Anonymous, 2001a).

Ecotourism is usually concentrated in sensitive and unique environments, which may have limited capability to resist use pressures and ultimately will cause negative impacts on the environment (Simmons, 2001). One issue of concern, especially for ecotourism lodges in a wildlife area, is the harassment of animals. Tour guides and their drivers may leave established tracks to find rare animals such as lions and rhinos and in so doing disturb the natural settlement of all the animals in the area (Anonymous, 2001a; Anonymous, 2002c). Excessive amounts of litter and tramping in sensitive areas are also a concern that needs to be considered very carefully. Introducing raised boardwalks, however, can reduce tramping (Hvenegaard and Dearden, 2002). Other negative impacts include damage to plants, forest clearance, soil compaction, pollution (water, noise and air) and marine resource destruction such as coral damage and over-fishing (Israngkura, 1996).

As such the efforts of different practitioners have been targeted to overcoming such negative practices, mainly by creating methodologies for indicator assessment and certification programmes (see Chapters 4 and 5).

Social impacts

Social impacts occur everywhere when people from different cultures and societies meet and especially when tourism development takes place it becomes more noticeable. Indigenous people are regularly the core attraction for ecotours visiting remote and scenic natural areas, such as the Amazon, Africa and remote places of the Far East. In order for them not to become exploited and their communities broken up, it is important that the local community is involved in all instances of the planning and development of ecotourism (Anton and Gines, 2002). 'To benefit local communities and be socially sustainable, ecotourism must foster environmental and cultural understanding, appreciation and conservation' (Zeppel, 1997).

There are different factors that influence the socio-cultural impacts of ecotourism, including the following: scale of tourism development – this concerns the number of tourists in relation to the host population. In many ecotourism destinations the number of visitors is small, but so is the number of permanent residents (Zeppel, 1997; Simmons, 2001); economic level of host community – in many locations, the residents of the Third World are visited by people from highly developed countries. They bring with them hard currency and spend it without thinking that the local population does not have the same chances or opportunities (Israngkura, 1996; Zeppel, 1997; Hvenegaard and Dearden, 2002); a third aspect is cultural differences between host and guest – when tourists arrive at their destination, they bring with them different beliefs, values and behaviours that will influence the contact they have with the host population (Zeppel, 1997; Honey, 1999; Anton and Gines, 2002; Rátz, 2002).

There are several positive impacts that do arise from encounters between visitor and host population. New facilities and services become accessible to the host population as these are developed for tourists, the creation of unique jobs which require the expertise of local people and resources and funds to re-establish local arts, traditions and cultural activities. Ecotourism can also encourage the local community to value its natural and cultural assets and take pride in its heritage (Zeppel, 1997; Anonymous 2001a; Hvenegaard and Dearden, 2002; Wood, 2002).

'Social impacts cause more immediate changes in a local community's social structure and way of life while cultural impacts cause longer-term changes in community norms and standards, social relationships and cultural practices' (Zeppel, 1997). Due to this it becomes important to protect the host population from negative socio-cultural impacts. Examples of these impacts could be changes in value systems, traditional lifestyles, family relationships and individual behaviour or community structure, to name but a few (Israng-kura, 1996; Honey, 1999; Rátz, 2002; Anonymous, 2001a; Anton and Gines, 2002; The International Ecotourism Society, 2002).

Ecotourism management considerations: a marketing perspective

In order fully to understand exactly what marketing for ecotourism involves and represents, a basic definition on the subject will be given. According to USDA, marketing is 'the process of planning and executing the conception, pricing, promotion, and distribution of ideas, goods, and services to create and maintain exchanges that satisfy individual, organisational, and societal goals in the systemic context of a global environment' (2001: 5).

When an organization is established, the objectives of the enterprise are discussed and written down and from these the marketing objectives are drawn. By looking at one of the primary objectives of ecotourism, sustainability with protection of the environment, already confusion sets in. Namely, most organizations strive for a profit and then the question arises: can sustainability and profitability go hand in hand? The same goes for long-term versus short-term goals. There are many examples of destinations that have been 'used up' and then the developers move on, for example, in the south of Spain. Developers come and bring in often needed capital and resources to the area but after the area has been saturated and overdeveloped they move on, leaving the destination behind to pick up the pieces (Wearing and Neil, 1999). By going for short-term profit, once the environment has been destroyed the tourists will move away and no longer pay for coming to the area. Therefore it is more important to go for a longer-term approach, with products that work with the environment in order to maintain sustainability (Eccles, 2002).

Most of the marketing provided for products or services are demand led, meaning that if a demand is there from the general public then the products or services will be provided to fill this gap in the market. The same goes for tourism-related products or services: if there is an increase in tourism arrivals to an area, new hotels and resorts will be established; and, of course, the opposite, should a destination lose favour among travellers then, most likely, the large operators will draw away and find new and more interesting locations. Having a supply-led marketing approach means that products and service are provided but not overused – the operators control the market. By introducing a supply-led approach when it comes to marketing ecotourism destinations, the environment and local communities are given priority over profit. As indicated by Wearing and Neil 'to establish the best methods for marketing an ecotourism destination it is important to stress the necessity of marketing to be holistic enterprise, working with community groups, indigenous and other private voluntary organization programmes' (1999: 107).

Much of today's ecotourism marketing is related to ecological and social marketing. Definitions of these two alternative forms of marketing are as follows. Ecological marketing is 'the study of the positive and negative aspects of marketing activities on pollution, energy depletion and nonenergy resource depletion' (Polonsky, 2002: 2). 'Social marketing seeks to influence social behaviours not to benefit the marketer but to benefit the target audience and the general society' (Kotler and Andreasen, 1996: 389). By looking at what ecotourism tries to do in society in a very positive manner, we can see how these two alternative approaches are related to one another when it comes to ecotourism marketing (Wearing and Neil, 1999). As ecotourism continues to grow throughout the world it is important that all parties involved maintain a supply-led marketing approach and not to forget why ecotourism was developed in the first place.

Generally when we address marketing, the Four Ps – product, place, price and promotion – play an important role of the promotion of an organization and these four aspects will now be examined in further detail. One of the main difficulties concerning ecotourism products and services is that there is no set definition of the word ecotourism. As long as this is the case, everyone can apply the term 'eco' to a destination and claim they are practising and promoting ecotourism (Simmons, 2001).

Considering this fact, that there is a lack of understanding of what ecotourism is and what it includes, it makes it difficult in talking about the product in an established way. Instead, it has been suggested by Wearing and Neil (1999) that we emphasize that the experience within ecotourism should be highlighted in order to attract true ecotourists to a destination. The product can also be looked at as the place, region and area as all this contributes to the finished product.

The second consideration is place, since, when talking about ecotourism, place becomes synonymous with distribution and is essentially concerned with how the organization can reach its market and how customers can buy the products on offer. There have been many discussions concerning where a traveller should be able to purchase an ecotour or a vacation at an ecotourist resort. It has been suggested that they should not be available in ordinary travel agencies but in more specialized sectors. This can also be considered one way to control the demand for the product and keep it a supply-led market. By selling their products to certain travel agencies, the ecotourism operator's marketing efforts will be limited and not 'wasted' on the general masses (Wearing and Neil, 1999).

Price is another major consideration for an ecotourism operator. The price a

18

visitor is charged will ultimately define what the profit will be for the organization and is therefore considered one of the most important decisions taken in marketing. Price and sales volume are thereby linked due to the fact that the more an operator can sell the more profit the organization will earn (USDA, 2001). However, this leads back to the question we posed earlier in the chapter: can profitability and sustainability go together? In keeping the price high, an operator will be assured of attracting only 'true ecotourists'. By formulating higher prices ecotourism supply will remain controlled. In having controlled prices the carrying capacity of an area is not exceeded as well and the environment and the local community will not face such a great impact on their daily lives. Higher prices are not necessarily considered a negative aspect by the consumer, but could be perceived as equal to higher quality (Wearing and Neil, 1999).

With promotion comes the different communication tools that are available to a marketer, such as advertising, sales promotion, direct marketing, word of mouth and personal selling to name a few (Wilson and Gilligan, 1997). Ecotourists are known for being well informed about the area they are going to visit, therefore the information they receive prior to a vacation is of great importance (Black, 1999).

There are different media available to the marketer to reach these visitors, the most common being special interest magazines and direct mail. By using media such as these, instead of having a large advertising campaign on national television or in daily newspapers, the marketer will reach only a smaller, defined market instead of the wider general public (Wearing and Neil, 1999). The most beneficial and cost-effective communication tool is considered to be word of mouth and the advantages that can be reached by it are far more credible and trustworthy than any advertising campaign (USDA, 2001). Therefore, keeping past visitors informed about the ecotourist destination they have visited is of great importance, as this will make them tell friends and family about the vacation they experienced.

Ecotourism management considerations: a demarketing perspective

Demarketing and ecotourism is a relative new concept (Beeton, 2003). Groff (1998) gives three classifications of demarketing:

1 *General demarketing*: required when an organization wants to shrink the level of total demand.
2 *Selective demarketing*: required when a company wants to discourage the demand coming from certain customer classes.

19

3 *Ostensible demarketing*: involves the appearance of trying to discourage demand as a device to actually *increase* it.

When it comes to ecotourism, the general idea is to obtain the appropriate level of demand in such a way that the destination can remain attractive both naturally and economically. For example, in Canada a recommendation has been made to the minister of national parks that the parks should be demarketed and the so-called 'shoulder season' marketing campaign should be stopped. The minister accepted these recommendations (to be implemented in the year 2003) (Wilkinson, 2003, private communication).

As such, the key to an effective demarketing of ecotourism destinations is that of visitor management tools (see Chapter 3) as well as that of environmental education (Beeton, 2003). The aim of creating an educational programme relating to ecotourism (see Chapter 2), both at the national and local levels, assumes that the consumers will generate not only a better understanding of ecotourism but also why it is important not to overutilize the destinations.

Therefore, the suggested management strategies (Parks Victoria, 2000; Beeton, 2003) that correspond with demarketing and ecotourism include:

• discouraging, through education, feeding of wildlife
• providing safe wildlife observation areas to channel visitor movements
• reducing traffic congestion by introducing lower speed limits
• reducing the maintenance of certain walking tracks to encourage use by experienced walkers only
• develop a 'park full' strategy to encourage use of other destinations
• limit the overall capacity of camping and accommodation facilities to 4000 visitors
• maintain the ballot system
• require commercial operators to record and present sufficient information about their operations to allow more accurate monitoring
• develop the interpretation and education centre to best practice levels.

For any demarketing strategies to be successful, however, a collaboration of ecotourism operators is needed. Here, the management teams of an ecotourism operation, whether it is a resort or a national park, have certain guidelines that need to be followed for the area to be classified as an ecotourism destination.

Ecotourism management considerations: a practitioner's perspective

The ecotourism organizations and operators play a key role in following the set standards that have been established by various organizations, such as the

International Ecotourism Society based in Vermont, USA, and governments around the world. Michael Lee, the Federal Minister for Tourism in Australia made the following statement concerning the importance of making use of best practice methods for conserving the environment: 'Good environmental practices benefit a company's bottom line and meet the needs of discerning international and domestic markets. In other words good environmental practice is good business practice' (1995).

Australia is one of many countries that have developed a guideline for minimizing energy and waste usage, in order to assist ecotourism and nature-based operators to achieve best practice of these areas (Office of National Tourism, 2002). However, before establishing best practice methods most operators perform an environmental impact assessment prior to development of an area. The usage of an environmental impact assessment can have several different objectives: in determining the impact on a specific ecology or a single species, financial implications should something become damaged, comparing different sites for development or elevate the profile of environmental issues (Cooper et al., 1999).

As part of the best practices programme that Australia has developed, a Code of Practice for ecotourism operators has been established (see Table 1.3 and Chapter 3).

Table 1.3 Code of Practice for ecotourism operators

- Strengthen the conservation effort for and enhance the natural integrity of the places visited.
- Respect the sensitivities of other cultures.
- Be efficient in the use of natural resources (water, energy).
- Ensure waste disposal has minimal environmental and aesthetic impact.
- Develop a recycling programme.
- Support principals (i.e. hotels, carriers etc.) who have a conservation ethic.
- Keep abreast of current political and environmental issues, particularly of the local area.
- Network with other stakeholders (particularly those in the local area) to keep each other informed of developments and encourage the use of this Code of Practice.
- Endeavour to use distribution networks (e.g. catalogues) and retail outlets to raise environmental awareness by distributing guidelines to consumers.
- Support ecotourism education/training for guides and managers.
- Employ tour guides well versed in and respectful of local cultures and environments.
- Give clients appropriate verbal and written education (interpretation) and guidance with respect to the natural and cultural history of the areas visited.
- Use locally produced goods that benefit the local community, but do not buy goods made from threatened or endangered species.
- Never intentionally disturb or encourage the disturbance of wildlife or wildlife habitats.
- Keep vehicles to designated roads and tracks.
- Abide by the rules and regulations of natural areas.
- Commit to the principle of best practice.
- Comply with Australian Safety Standards.
- Ensure truth in advertising.
- Maximize the quality of experience for hosts and guests.

(Source: Anonymous, 2002a)

These 20 different points discuss the role of ecotourism in society, how the environment should be protected, the education that should be provided to managers and guides and maintaining the provision of a quality experience for both hosts and guests (Anonymous, 2002a).

In Canada something similar has been developed in order to enhance the understanding and managing of park tourism, called the Visitor Activity Management Program. 'This program develops a profile of each outdoor recreation user group for management planning' (Eagles, 1995: 15). Looking at ten different criteria, for example, natural resource impact, risk management and market expectations, the programme has assessed different outdoor recreation activities and has been of remarkable support in raising the profile of visitor management within agencies and then providing a structure for management (Eagles, 1995).

Providing specific guidelines for both the organization and visitors, such as the Code of Practice drawn up in Australia, will help reduce any negative impacts that might occur. According to Blangy and Epler Wood guidelines are 'a fundamental communications tool to reduce visitor impacts' (1993: 32). Guidelines can become one of the most cost-effective management tools available to an operation. By introducing guidelines, the local community will feel part of the operation as well, as their say will have a large influence on any directives drawn up (Blangy and Wood, 1993).

By adhering to different standards that have been developed, such as carrying capacity, codes of best practice and visitor activity management process, the natural and cultural heritage can be protected. Not only do they help protect the area and ensure sustainability, they also ensure that the local community can live on and prosper in the way they have done in the past before tourism development began (Wearing and Neil, 1999).

Other management issues concerning an ecotourism operator can be identified by looking at the different components of ecotourism, namely involvement and participation of the local community where the operation exists and the level of education provided by the organization to hosts and visitors alike. Seeing that local involvement is one of the key issues in ecotourism, this is one area the management team needs to focus more concertedly on. The more involved they become in the organization the more beneficial the tourism development will become for them (Cater, 1994).

There are several different factors that need to be under management control in order to protect and conserve the area and with the purpose of ensuring the quality experience visitors are expecting to gain (Chapters 3, 4, 5). Examples of this could be tourist infrastructure and development, visitor levels – referring to the carrying capacity of the area – souvenirs and access to the area to name a few (Wearing and Neil, 1999).

It is vital that the impact of visitors, socially, environmentally and economically, is monitored and evaluated in order to minimize and overcome it. Monitoring is done for a wide range of purposes, including to keep track of progress, results and to encourage participants. It needs to be an ongoing management process and evaluation of the results needs to follow in order to ensure that the objectives of the ecotourism operation are being met (Masberg and Morales, 1999).

Conclusion

Research within the area of ecotourism still appears currently to be at its development stage. There are a variety of definitions of ecotourism, each reflecting a range of paradigms and perspectives. The view that this chapter utilized is that a single definition of ecotourism is not really necessary if the discussion focuses on developing different trade-off definitions. Hence, it seems that ecotourism definitions could range from a very weak to a very strong stance, incorporating its three components (natural-based, sustainability and education). Within these components, both benefits and costs exist and in some circumstances there is disequilibrium towards greater costs. The marketing and the practitioner's perspective of ecotourism management is also well developed at the destination level, with cases pointing to good ecotourism practice. Of considerable interest is the new perspective of ecotourism research known as 'demarketing', carried out in an attempt to safeguard the more sensitive landscapes. This is a development in ecotourism research that will be interesting to watch over the coming years. Fundamentally, for ecotourism to continue to be a rigorous concept, in terms of both theory and practice, a commitment towards the fundamental principles of sustainability is required and a deep understanding of the issues of management and assessment in the setting in which it is practised.

Questions

1 Describe the components of ecotourism.
2 What are the benefits of practising the trade-off definitions of ecotourism?
3 Examine the main factors that will influence the marketing strategy of ecotourism at the destination level.
4 Pick a case study from this volume and suggest three factors that will help ecotourism practitioners in devising better management strategies.

References

Addison, L. (1996). 'An approach to community-based tourism planning in the Baffin region, Canada's Far North'. In Harrison, L.C. and Husbands, W. (eds) *Practicing Responsible Tourism*. New York: John Wiley & Sons, 296–312.

Anonymous (2001a) 'What is ecotourism?' (Available at *http://www.mssrf.org.sg/aeis*.)

Anonymous (2001b) 'International centre for ecotourism research'. (Available at *http://www.gu.edu.au*.)

Anonymous (2002a) 'Code of practice for ecotourism operators'. (Available at *http://www.bigvolcano.com.au*.)

Anonymous (2002b) 'Opportunities and impacts of ecological tourism'. (Available at *http://www.tumennet.mn*.)

Anonymous (2002c) 'UN-NGLS voices from Africa'. (Available at *http://www.unsystem.org*.)

Anton, D. and Gines, C. (2002) 'Tourism, biodiversity, and culture: toward a sustainable ecotourism strategy'. (Available at *http://www.idrc.ca*.)

Archer, B. and Cooper, C. (1994) 'The positive and negative impacts of tourism'. In Theobald, W. (ed.) *Global Tourism, The Next Decade*. Oxford: Butterworth-Heinemann, 73–91.

Barnes, J.L. (1996) 'Economic characteristics of the demand for wildlife-viewing tourism in Botswana', *Development Southern Africa*, 13 (3), 377–97.

Beeh, J.E. (1999) 'Adventure vs. ecotourism'. (Available at *http://www.findarticles.com*.)

Beeton, S. (2003) 'Demarketing: a new ecomanagement tool?' La Trobe University, PO Box 199, Bendigo, Victoria, Australia 3552 (*s.beeton@latrobe.edu.au*).

Black, R. (1999) 'Ecotourism and education'. (Available at *http://lorenz.csu.edu.au*.)

Blamey, R.K. (1995) *The Nature of Ecotourism*. Bureau of Tourism Research, Canberra, Australia.

Blamey, R.K. (1997) 'Ecotourism: the search for an operational definition', *Journal of Sustainable Tourism*, 5 (2), 109–130.

Blamey, R.K. (2001) 'Principles of ecotourism'. In Weaver, D. (ed.) *The Encyclopedia of Ecotourism*. Oxford: CABI, 5–22.

Blangy, S. and Epler Wood, M. (1993) 'Developing and implementing ecotourism guidelines for wildlands and neighboring communities'. In Lindberg, K. and Hawkins, D.E. (eds) *Ecotourism: A Guide For Planners and Managers*. North Bennington, USA: The Ecotourism Society, 32–54.

Boo, E. (1991) 'Ecotourism: a tool for conservation and development'. In Kusler, J.A. (comp.) *Ecotourism and Resource Conservation, A Collection of Papers*, Vol 1. Madison: Omnipress, 54–60.

Boyd, S.W. and Butler, R.W. (1996) 'Seeing the forest through the trees'. In Harrison, L.C. and Husbands, W. (eds) *Practicing Responsible Tourism*. New York: John Wiley & Sons, 380–403.

Brandon, K. (1993) 'Basic steps towards encouraging local participation in nature tourism projects'. In Lindberg, K. and Hawkins, D.E. (eds) *Ecotourism: A Guide For Planners and Managers*. North Bennington, USA: The Ecotourism Society, 134–151.

Cater, E. (1994) 'Ecotourism in the third world – problems and prospects for sustainability'. In Cater, E. and Lowman, G. (eds) *Ecotourism A Sustainable Option?* Chichester: John Wiley & Sons, 69–86.

Ceballos-Lascuráin, H. (1987) 'The future of ecotourism', *Mexico Journal*, January, 13–14.

Ceballos-Lascuráin, H. (1993) 'Ecotourism as a worldwide phenomenon'. In Lindberg, K. and Hawkins, D.E. (eds) *Ecotourism: A Guide For Planners and Managers*. North Bennington, USA: The Ecotourism Society, 12–14.

Ceballos-Lascuráin, H. (1996) *Tourism, Ecotourism, and Protected Areas*. Gland: IUCN.

Diamantis, D. (1999) 'The concept of ecotourism: evolution and trends', *Current Issues in Tourism*, 2 (2 and 3), 93–122.

Diamantis, D. and Ladkin, A. (1999) 'The links between sustainable tourism and ecotourism: a definitional perspective', *The Journal of Tourism Studies*, 10 (2), 35–45.

Dowling, R.K. (2001) 'Oceania'. In Weaver, D.B. (ed.) *The Encyclopedia of Ecotourism*. Oxford: CABI, 139–54.

Duffus, D. and Dearden, P. (1990) 'Non-consumptive wildlife-orientated recreation: a conceptual framework', *Biological Conservation*, 53, 213–31.

Eagles, P.F. (1995) Key issues in ecotourism management. Invited paper for State of Western Australia Annual Tourism Conference, Perth, Australia, June.

Eagles, P.F.J. (2001) 'Understanding the market for sustainable tourism'. (Available at *http://www.ecotourism.org*.)

24

Eccles, G. (2002) 'Marketing, sustainable development and international tourism'. (Available at *http://www.emeraldinsight.com*.)

Forestry Tasmania (1994) *Guided Nature-Based Tourism in Tasmania's Forests: Trends, Constraints and Implications*. Hobart, Australia: Forestry Tasmania.

Godfrey, K.B. (1996) 'Towards sustainability?' In Harrison, L.C. and Husbands, W. (eds) *Practicing Responsible Tourism*. New York: John Wiley & Sons, 58–79.

Goodwin, H. (1996) 'In pursuit of ecotourism', *Biodiversity and Conservation*, 5 (3), 277–91.

Groff, C. (1998) 'Demarketing in park and recreation management', *Managing Leisure*, 3, 128–35.

Gunn, C.A. (1994) *Tourism Planning, Basic Concepts Cases*. Washington, DC: Taylor & Francis.

Gurung, C.P. and De Coursey, M. (1994) 'The Annapurna conservation area project : a pioneering example of sustainable tourism?' In Cater, E. and Lowman, G. (eds) *Ecotourism A Sustainable Option?* Chichester: John Wiley & Sons, 177–94.

Hawkins, D.E. (1994) 'Ecotourism: opportunities for developing countries'. In Theobald, W. (ed.) *Global Tourism, The Next Decade*. Oxford: Butterworth-Heinemann, 261–73.

Honey, M. (1999). 'Definition of ecotourism: how to know ecotourism when you see it'. (Available at *http://www.lohasjournal.com*.)

Hunter, C. (1997) 'Sustainable tourism as an adaptive paradigm', *Annals of Tourism Research*, 24 (4), 850–67.

Hvenegaard, G.T. and Dearden, P. (2002) 'Ecotourism in Northern Thailand'. (Available at *http://www.idrc.ca*.)

International Ecotourism Society (2002) 'Environmental impacts of tourism'. (Available at *http://www.ecotourism.org*.)

International Ecotourism Society (2001) 'Statement on the United Nations International Year of Ecotourism'. (Available at *http://www.ecotourism.org*.)

International Ecotourism Society (2000) 'Ecotourism statistical fact sheet'. (Available at *http://www.ecotourism.org*.)

Israngkura, A. (1996) 'Ecotourism'. (Available at *http://www.info.tdri.or.th*.)

Jaakson, R. (1997) 'Exploring the epistemology of ecotourism', *Journal of Applied Recreation Research*, 22 (1), 33–47.

Klemm, M.S. and Martin-Quirós, M.A. (1996) 'Changing the balance of power'. In Harrison, L.C. and Husbands, W. (eds) *Practicing Responsible Tourism*. New York: John Wiley & Sons, 126–44.

Kotler, P. and Andreasen, A.R. (1996) *Strategic Marketing for Non-Profit Organisations*. New Jersey: Prentice Hall.

Lee, M. (1995) 'Best practice ecotourism'. (Available at *http://www.isr.gov.au/sport_tourism/*.)

Lindberg, K. (1996) 'The economic impacts of ecotourism'. (Available at *http://ecotour.csu.edu.au*.)

Lindberg, K. and McKercher, B. (1997) 'Ecotourism: a critical overview', *Pacific Tourism Review*, 1 (1), 65–79.

Lozada, H.R. (2002) 'Ecological sustainability and marketing strategy'. (Available at *http://www.sbaer.uca.edu/Research*.)

Mader, R. (2001) 'Exploring ecotourism in the Americas'. (Available at *http://www.planeta.com/ecotravel/*.)

Masberg, B.A. and Morales, N. (1999) 'A case analysis of strategies in ecotourism development', *Aquatic Ecosystem Health and Management*, 2, 289–300.

Murphy, P.E. (1994) 'Tourism and sustainable development'. In Theobald, W. (ed.) *Global Tourism, The Next Decade*. Oxford: Butterworth-Heinemann, 274–90.

Office of National Tourism (2002) 'Best practice ecotourism'. (Available at *http://www.isr.gov.au*.)

Orams, M.B. (1995) 'Towards a more desirable form of ecotourism', *Tourism Management*, 16 (1), 3–8.

Orams, M.B. (2001) 'Types of ecotourism'. In Weaver, D. (ed.) *The Encyclopedia of Ecotourism*. Oxford: CABI, 23–36.

Parks Victoria (2000) *Wilsons Promontory National Park Draft Management Plan*. Australia: Parks Victoria.

Pleumarom, A. (1995) 'Eco-tourism or eco-terrorism?' (Available at *http://www.untamedpath.com*.)

Polonsky, M.J. (2002) 'An introduction to green marketing'. (Available at *http://egj.lib.uidaho.edu*.)

Rátz, T. (2002) 'The socio-cultural impacts of tourism'. (Available at *http://www.geocities.com*.)

Ross, S. and Wall, G. (1999) 'Ecotourism: towards congruence between theory and practice', *Tourism Management*, 20, 123–32.

25

Schaller, D.T. (2002) 'Indigenous ecotourism and sustainable development: the case of Río Blanco, Ecuador'. (Available at *http://www.eduweb.com*.)

Shores, J.N. (1999) 'The challenge of ecotourism: a call for higher standards'. (Available at *http://www.planeta.com*.)

Simmons, D.G. (2001) 'Eco-tourism: product or process?' (Available at *http://www.landcare.cri.nz/conferences/manaakiwhenua/*.)

Smarton, R.C. (1988) 'Water recreation in North America', *Landscape and Urban Planning*, 16 (2), 127–43.

Stadel, C. (1996) 'Divergence and conflict, or convergence and harmony?' In Harrison, L.C. and Husbands, W. (eds) *Practicing Responsible Tourism*. New York: John Wiley & Sons, 445–71.

UNEP (2003) 'About ecotourism'. (Available at *http://www.uneptie.org/pc/tourism/ecotourism*.)

USDA (2001) 'Tourism and natural resource management: a general overview of research and issues'. (Available at *http://www.fs.fed.us/pnw/pubs/gtr506.pdf*.)

Valentine, P.S. (1992) 'Review: nature-based tourism'. In Weiler, B. and Hall, C.M. (eds) *Special Interest Tourism*. London: Belhaven Press, 105–127.

Walker, S. (1995) 'Measuring ecotourism impact perceptions'. (Available at *http://www.mtnforum.org*.)

Wall, G. (2002) 'Ecotourism: change, impacts, and opportunities'. (Available at *http://www.yale.edu*.)

Wearing, S. and Neil, J. (1999) *Ecotourism Impacts, Potentials and Possibilities*. Oxford: Butterworth-Heinemann.

Weaver, D.B. (1998) *Ecotourism in the Less Developed World*. Oxford: CABI.

Weaver, D.B. (2001) 'Ecotourism as mass tourism: contradiction or reality?' (Available at *http://www.hotelschool.cornell.edu*.)

Wilson, R.M.S. and Gilligan, C. (1997) *Strategic Marketing Management, Planning, Implementation and Control*. Oxford: Butterworth-Heinemann.

Wood, M.E. (2002) *Ecotourism: Principles, Practices and Policies for Sustainability*. Paris: UNEP/TIES.

World Tourism Organization (1998) 'Ecotourism now one-fifth of market', *World Tourism Organization News*, 1, 6.

Zeppel, H. (1997) 'Ecotourism and indigenous people'. (Available at *http://ecotour.csu.edu.au*.)

Ziffer, K.A. (1989) *Ecotourism: The Uneasy Alliance*. Washington, DC: Conservation International and Ernst & Young.

2 Ecotourism Assessment: An Overview

Sue Geldenhuys

The four main objectives of this chapter are to:

- Outline the assessment concepts of carrying capacity (CC), recreation opportunity spectrum (ROS) and limits of acceptable change (LAC) and explain their significance
- Present the tourism opportunity spectrum (TOS) and suggest the indicators to be measured and monitored if the opportunities are to be sustained over time and explain its strengths and weaknesses
- Discuss visitor impact management (VIM), visitor activity management process (VAMP) and the tourism optimization management model (TOMM) as proactive, flexible and conceptual frameworks that contribute to decision-making practices
- Examine different tools for managing the visitation to ecotourism sites and the nature of educational programmes

Introduction

Growing public concern about the decline of natural rainforests, loss of endangered species and global warming has brought conservation issues to the forefront of public debate. An emerging dissatisfaction with mass tourism has led to increased demand for nature-based experiences of an alternative kind. At the same time, less developed countries have begun to realize that nature-based tourism is providing a less destructive use of resources than alternative such as agriculture and logging and that it offers a means of earning foreign exchange. Research on the environmental impacts of tourism has demonstrated that it can be as destructive as other industries, if left unchecked and despite its environmentally benign image even ecotourism can induce substantial ecological changes in protected areas (Wall, 1997).

Until recently, the main purpose for the establishment of protected areas in developing countries, and to some degree also in developed countries, was to preserve important natural features and unique habitats, which would otherwise have been at risk of disappearing. Globally, there are approximately 8500 protected areas that cover 5.17% of the earth's land surface and the growth in the designation of protected areas provided opportunities for people's recreation and enjoyment, as it was acknowledged that income derived from activities within protected areas could provide a positive secondary income. As protected areas became increasingly popular as tourism destinations, management focus shifted gradually in the direction of visitor management to protect the resources from excessive human impacts. The gravity of these problems led professionals to stress the importance of providing protected areas with appropriate management tools that can be used effectively to address a range of issues associated with the environment, visitors and local people. Today it is recognized that park officials need the infrastructure and management capability to maximize visitor enjoyment while minimizing negative impacts to natural and cultural resources and to local people.

Ecotourism assessment

Numerous planning and management frameworks have been developed to assist managers in preventing, combating or minimizing the effects of recreational use on natural environments. The assessment concepts of carrying capacity (CC), the recreation opportunity spectrum (ROS), tourism opportunity spectrum (TOS), limits of acceptable change (LAC), visitor impact management (VIM), visitor activity management process (VAMP) and the tourism optimization management model (TOMM) are examples of visitor management and assessment frameworks, intended to complement existing decision-making processes (see also Chapter 3).

Carrying capacity

The first sustainable management technique is the determining and implementation of carrying capacity (CC). Carrying capacity is a term borrowed from wildlife ecology and widely discussed in recreation management (see Chapter 6). The central idea is that 'environmental factors set limits on the population that an area can sustain. When these limits are exceeded, the quality of the environment suffers and ultimately, its ability to support that population' (Stankey, 1991: 12). Because of the origins of the term in the natural sciences it was believed that biological studies could determine the capacity of an area's natural resources, establishing how much use the environment could endure and regulating access to the resource (Stankey, 1991: 11). However, this scientific basis suggests an objectivity and precision, but this is not the case when used in planning involving *human* systems.

Carrying capacity has also been applied to landuse planning and growth management and other aspects of human activity and the definition of carrying capacity has been extended to include the many variables inherent in man-made systems. Shelby and Herberlein (1986) subdivided carrying capacity as follows:

- *Ecological capacity* (ecosystem parameters) – to quantify the type and degree of disturbance that an animal community is receiving from visitors. Ecological capacity is reached when changes in wildlife behaviour are observed or when species begin to disappear or other changes such as soil erosion become obvious (Clark and Gilad, 1989).
- *Physical capacity* (space parameters) – physical carrying capacity is the level beyond which visitor satisfaction drops as a result of overcrowding. Biologists arrive at a figure that respects the ecological limitations of a site by placing a limit on the number of visitors' days permitted in order to preserve the integrity of a natural resource base. Many East African national parks exceed this by a large margin, causing dissatisfaction and loss of business to less crowded parks in southern and southwest Africa.
- *Facility capacity* (development parameters) – accommodation carrying capacity is fixed by bedspace and transport carrying capacity by the number of passengers who can be transported.
- *Social capacity* (experience parameters) – host social carrying capacity is the level beyond which unacceptable change will be caused to local cultural stability and attitudes towards tourists. Governments of host countries often have a more flexible approach and less scientific way of establishing carrying capacities. Their maximum figures may reflect the need to maximize short-term foreign exchange earnings even if this destroys the resource base in the long term.

Carrying capacity can, therefore, vary according to the season but also as a result of factors such as behavioural patterns of tourists, facility layout and management, the dynamic nature of the environment and the changing attitudes of the host community. The combination of these factors will affect the determination of carrying capacity.

The most accurate and complete definition of carrying capacity for tourism is 'the maximum level of visitor use an area can accommodate with high levels of satisfaction for visitors and few negative impacts on resources' (McNeely and Thorsell, 1989). To calculate this figure it is necessary to establish maximum use estimates. In order to do this, many planners rely on defining a 'tolerable level' of visitation which can be sustained over time. It is insufficient merely to estimate the carrying capacity of the park or protected area in terms of visitor days. The maximum sustainable capacity of an area will determine the placement of geographically separated access points and tourists facilities to avoid excessive contacts between different groups visiting the park at the same time. Factors linked to seasonality should be incorporated within both animal and human communities. The WTO recommended the following formula (Parks Canada, 1991) for estimating tourist carrying capacity:

$$\text{Carrying capacity} = \frac{\text{Area use by tourist}}{\text{Average individual standard}}$$

The denominator is usually expressed as persons/metre^2 which is carefully defined for each case by evaluating psychological and ecological capacity. From this one can derive the total daily visits:

$$\text{Total daily visits} = \text{Carrying capacity} \times \text{Rotation coefficient}$$

Where:

$$\text{Rotation coefficient} = \frac{\text{No. of daily hours open for tourism}}{\text{Average time of visit}}$$

In order to determine environmental factors it is necessary to take note of the following:

- *Size of the area* – some areas may be inaccessible and therefore not usable.
- *Fragility of environment* – the fragility of soils varies widely, with loose sand being the most vulnerable.
- *Wildlife resources topography and vegetation cover* – wildlife resources will vary in distribution and diversity according to the season of the year. Topographic factors also affect capacity as thick bushes can conceal both animals and people, whereas visitor concentration is much more noticeable on open savannah.
- *Behavioural sensitivity of certain species to human visits* – some species are especially vulnerable to the presence of visitors.

A further list of variables exists which determine social carrying capacities and include:

- *Viewing patterns* – visitors are never evenly distributed across an area. Studies of Amboseli suggested that the majority of visitors use a small percentage of the area at specific times of the day.
- *Tourists' viewing choices* – these are determined not only by the availability of species but also the tourists' interest. The main attractions for tourists are mating, dying, feeding and hunting.
- *Visitors' opinions* – views on present crowding can be obtained from surveys. They can also be utilized to improve the provision of information and interpretation facilities.
- *Available facilities* – can be obtained from other quantifiable variables such as available bedspaces.

Information such as this can assist management increase of carrying capacity by designing new viewpoints, tracks or trails and dispersing visitors over a wider area or by reducing conflicts between competing uses by zoning.

Once management has established the objectives for social and environmental conditions, carrying capacity can be used as a tool for management planning and the avoidance of animal disturbance. Some aspects of carrying capacity can be modified, such as the physical carrying capacity by fencing or walkway construction. The physical carrying capacity depends on many factors and in order to generate a successful management plan, it is necessary to know in what situation the park or wilderness area was before visitors arrived.

Carrying capacity has, however, not been as useful a tool as anticipated. A major problem in the capacity literature is that impact and evaluation often become confused. An example is the concept of resource damage. All human use has an *impact*, but is it *damage*? The term damage refers to a change (an objective impact) and a value judgment that the impact exceeds some standard. It is best to keep these two separate. There are various types of impact, among them human impact. An example of this will be where the presence of a certain number of hikers leads to a certain degree of soil compaction. This is a change in the environment, but whether it is damage depends on management objectives, expert judgments and broader public values. Most carrying capacity conflicts do not revolve around resource questions but rather around value questions (Shelby and Herberlein, 1986). Lime and Stankey (1971: 182) observed: 'Determining carrying capacity ultimately requires the consideration of human values. Because of the subjectivity of the values, it is essential that managers carry on an active dialogue with a variety of publics.'

Canada recognized the concept's deficiencies and went on to develop more broad-based concepts such as the recreation opportunity spectrum (ROS).

Recreation opportunity spectrum (ROS)

ROS is a framework for determining carrying capacities and managing recreational impacts and can be used as a comprehensive planning approach for regional planning and management. As a framework it promotes recreational diversity that provide a broad array of recreational opportunities for users. The ROS has been in use by the US Forest Service and the Bureau of Land Management since the 1970s (Clark and Stankey, 1979; Driver et al., 1987; Nilsen and Taylor, 1997).

According to Nilsen and Taylor (1997) outdoor recreational opportunities present people with choices that include the activities they would like to participate in, the setting they deem appropriate to carry out these activities and the kind of recreational experience they wish to obtain. ROS defines a recreational opportunity as: 'the opportunity to participate in a desired recreation activity within a preferred type of setting to realize desired and expected experiences' (Driver, 1990).

When analyzing the definition, it becomes evident that a recreation opportunity consists of three components: activity, setting and experience. A recreation setting is a combination of the biophysical, social and managerial conditions that characterize a given place and would include:

- Natural qualities such as scenery, vegetation and landscape which would then be the biophysical setting.
- Recreation use qualities, such as the levels and types of use constituting the social setting.
- Conditions provided by management that may include facility development, patrols, roads and regulations, constituting the managerial setting (Clark and Stankey, 1979).

The ROS define four to six setting categories of landuse management, from urban to pristine. These categories form the focus of recreation resource planning and management. This tool helps managers to gain an understanding of the physical, biological, social and managerial relationships. The most effective way to ensure quality in outdoor recreation is through provision of a diverse set of opportunity classes or zones and this is one of the basic assumptions underlying ROS. It also enables managers to accommodate the recreational needs of a larger public while at the same time protecting the resource by providing a range of opportunities that corresponds to resource capabilities and constraints. One of the cornerstones for social equity is the management of diversifying recreational opportunities at international, national and local levels (Parks Canada, 1991). The absence of such diverse opportunities may lead to favouritism, elitism and discrimination.

Land management and planning based on ROS can form the basis for different use intensities and levels of visitor management. Normally, visitor management practices are more prevalent and visible in intensive use zones. These services may include well-structured facilities to provide information (visitor centres), easy access to natural features (paved trails, scenic overlooks) and general visitor services (food services, restrooms). The emphasis is on maximizing use while limiting further impacts on areas already impacted. In zones or opportunity classes that are more extensive or have lower visitor density, the management influence is less evident and limited facilities are provided. The emphasis is on maximizing the nature experience while minimizing impacts on the resource.

The ROS is a regional planning process that was adapted to tourism because of concern about growing tourism demand and limited resource supply. The planned and incremental growth of tourism generally continues through various developmental stages, from underdeveloped rural area to human-built urban environments (Murphy, 1985; Mathieson and Wall, 1987; Gunn, 1994). The TOS is an instrument that makes it possible to describe this continuum (see following section) and by so doing helps to identify consequences of development and preserve ever decreasing opportunities for ecotourism. The lack of comprehensive planning for a wide array of tourism opportunities spanning longer periods of time is of concern since the distribution of tourism opportunities is changing through a shift towards higher development levels, away from less developed tourism opportunities.

Tourism opportunity spectrum (TOS)

The need for a comprehensive planning approach that considers a wide array of tourism opportunities over time has led to the adaptation of the ROS to the TOS. The TOS constitutes a continuum ranging from primitive and undeveloped conditions to an urban environment which is intensively developed and consists of a human-built environment. The proposed TOS shown in Table 2.1 list five categories, which are not equally distributed along the TOS continuum, but they were chosen as illustration of this concept and adapted by Dawson (2001: 48–51) from the ROS literature. Because of the exceptions and differences between tourism areas, and the wide variety of tourism situations, the goals and setting characteristics in the TOS constitute general conceptual guidelines and not hard and inflexible rules. The characteristics of the five reference points could be expanded to include other characteristics such as available infrastructure, acceptable social behaviour and so forth.

Adapted from the ROS, TOS and RCOS literature (Clark and Stankey, 1979; Driver et al., 1987; Butler and Waldbrook, 1991; Robertson et al., 1995; Boyd and Butler, 1996) the management goals and the six setting characteristics are used in the TOS to classify the tourism category settings (see Table 2.1). The six settings characteristics underpin the formulation of specific indicator variables and standards. The standards are the quantifiable aspects of the indicator variable that are the baseline against which existing conditions at the site are judged as either acceptable or unacceptable (Stankey and McCool, 1990).

The first step to implement this would be to define the tourism setting type, on which different levels of opportunities provided for visitors and the characteristics and indicators to monitor the provision of those tourism opportunities at the current or proposed position of the site or area on the TOS can be determined. To develop the site at a new position, a comparative study can be made of alternative TOS positions along with the consequences. The identification of positive and negative regional, social, environmental and economical conditions, each position on the TOS's alternative consequences can be evaluated for a specific site. Planners and managers can then make more informed decisions:

- to continue to provide the tourism opportunities planned for visitors at a particular ecotourism site or area
- or to increase the level of development and change the tourism opportunities planned.

Table 2.1 A proposed tourism opportunity spectrum and examples of setting characteristics

Setting characteristics	Ecotourism	Nature-based tourism	Rural tourism	Rural–urban tourism	Urban tourism
Management goals	Preservation and protection of the resource	Conservation and resource management	Resource management and some development	Resource management and economic development	Economic development and enterprise
Accessibility factors (difficulty, access type, means of conveyance)	Very difficult or controlled access, mostly by trails or water routes; may be very remote from human habitation	Difficult or controlled access, mostly by trails, water routes and secondary roads	Moderately accessible on secondary and primary roads	Accessible on secondary and primary roads: some public transportation	Easy access on highways and roads by vehicles and public transportation
Visual characteristics (acceptability of visitor impacts)	No readily apparent changes to the natural environment or very minimal localized user impacts	Primarily a natural-appearing environment and landscape, but some human impacts are evident	Mix of natural and managed environment and landscape with evidence of human habitation	Moderately managed environment and landscape with evidence of human habitation	Extensively modified and man-altered landscape and environment for human habitation and enterprise
Visitor environmental impact factors	Very minimal user impacts and some concentrated user impacts (e.g. hiking trials and scenic vistas) but with few users	Minimal user impacts and localized to recreation activity areas and facilities (e.g. boat launch sites, campgrounds but with low numbers of users)	User impacts that are prevalent in small areas due to site development and management, plus some concentrations of users (e.g. marinas, motels)	Moderate user impacts due to site development and management, plus moderate volume of users (e.g. full service resorts, developed attractions)	High degree of user impacts due to extensive site development and management, plus high volume of users (e.g. theme parks, retail store complexes)
Onsite management factors (existing infrastructure)	Very limited infrastructure (e.g. hiking trails); most supporting infrastructure is off site but within the region	Minimal infrastructure to support visitor activities on site	Some infrastructure and commercial development	Moderate infrastructure and commercial development	Extensive infrastructure and commercial development
Social interaction factors	Infrequent user–user or group–group interactions; managers expect highly ethical behaviour to other users and environment	Some user–user or group–group interactions; managers expect highly ethical behaviour to other users and environment	Moderate user–user or group–group interactions; managers expect highly ethical behaviour to other users and environment	Frequent user–user or group–group interactions; managers expect highly ethical behaviour to other users and environment	Extensive user–user or group–group interactions; managers expect highly ethical behaviour to other users and environment
Visitor management factors (acceptable regimentation)	Managed for non-motorized users and non-consumptive recreational activities	Managed for non-motorized users and some motorized users and non-consumptive and consumptive recreational activities	Managed for motorized and non-motorized users and non-consumptive and consumptive recreational activities	Managed for motorized and non-motorized users and more consumptive recreational activities	Managed for motorized and non-motorized users and more conspicuously consumptive recreational activities

(Source: Dawson, 2001: 49)

Measures to mitigate or minimize changes to the characteristics can also be considered. It is imperative to make an analysis of the tourism opportunities in an area, as this will provide an outline or overview of the distribution of the tourism opportunities currently available and suggest where there is market competition, where market niches could be developed and what types of new tourism development will be compatible with existing opportunities. The guiding concept for this process is the development of a rational and comprehensive planning approach for regional planning and management that provides a broad array of tourism opportunities for users that are appropriate to the regional social, environmental and economic conditions.

The advantages of using a TOS are that:

- It constitutes a planning and management matrix approach that is both rational and comprehensive.
- It indicates what tourism opportunities are already provided or sustained.
- It links supply with demand in a practical planning process.
- It provides a framework to evaluate the regional tourism alternatives and consequences of changing development levels.

One of the challenges of the TOS analysis approach is that it requires managers and planners to accept all the tourism setting types and characteristics unanimously. Lack of general consensus or agreement can affect the entire regional planning process. Onsite managers and planners should specify and accept indicators and standards to monitor the process over time.

The TOS is a conceptual approach to a tourism planning tool (Butler and Walbrook, 1991) that enables a rational and comprehensive overview for assessing the tourism opportunities provided within an area. Issues pertaining to the sustainability of tourism opportunities can be addressed, along with the indicators that need to be monitored to measure the experience and resource conditions. As the demand for natural resource increases to keep pace with world populations, TOS can help planners to understand how ecotourism, nature-based tourism and other types of tourism relate to one another and make a major contribution to preservation and conservation movements that seek to increase appreciation for the natural environment and educate users. An understanding of where ecotourism and nature-based tourism fall within a continuum of tourism development opportunities and careful management and long-term planning may make ecotourism one of the most effective weapons in the arsenal of the contemporary conservationist.

Limits of acceptable change (LAC)

The rapid increase in recreation use of US national parks in the 1950s and 1960s led to Wight's (1964) suggestion to apply the concept of carrying capacity (CC) to recreation management. As previously noted the CC concept was originally used in biological models to determine appropriate levels of animal use of forage resources. Attempts were made to adapt the CC concept to recreational settings and gave birth to the recreation carrying capacity (RCC). RCC is defined as 'the maximum number of people who could use a resource without damaging the social or biological conditions stated in the area's objectives' (McCool, 1990). Practical attempts to establish RCC in wilderness and wild river areas in the USA met with considerable failure and this led to the emergence of LAC (Frissel and Stankey, 1972). The main difference between the RCC and the LAC is that in the LAC process, the focus is shifted from the number of users involved to the degree of change which is acceptable in each specific zone or ROS class in a given protected area.

The LAC planning system consists of eight steps, namely:

- identification of concerns and issues
- definition and description of opportunity classes
- selection of indicators of resource and social conditions
- specifying standards for the resource and social indicators
- identification of alternative opportunity class allocations
- identification of management actions for each alternative
- evaluating and selection of an alternative
- implementation of actions and monitoring condition (Stankey et al., 1985).

The LAC framework offers more scope for public participation which is conducive to a consensus-based planning approach to natural area management. However, to date it has not been implemented with any great success, due to a lack of political and economic support from stakeholders (McArthur, 1997b). LAC systems also require considerable resources to establish inventories of resource and social conditions. The LAC system is a technical planning system that provides a systematic decision-making framework that helps acceptable resource and social conditions and prescribes appropriate management actions (Stankey, 1991: 14). Conflict between recreation, tourism and conservation can be resolved through the LAC framework. Furthermore, it defines the impacts associated with different levels of environmental protection and allows environmental change consistent with, and appropriate and acceptable to, different types of recreational opportunities (Stankey, 1991: 13). The establishing of specific indicators and standards related to conservation values, in conjunction with close monitoring, makes it possible to define what impact levels are admissible before management intervention become necessary (Stankey, 1991: 12).

It is important to note that the LAC system does more than develop and extend the ROS framework. It also represents an important reformulation of key elements of the CC concept (Prosser, 1986: 8). Instead of concentrating on the question 'How much recreation use is too much?', it focuses on desired conditions. In doing so, the LAC approach sidesteps the use/impact problem. The LAC emphasis is on management of the impacts of use, thereby recognizing that the resource and social conditions of an area are the most important (Lucas and Stankey, 1988).

Visitor impact management (VIM)

Over the past 20 or 30 years the sharp recreational increase and the use of natural areas for such activities has led to the emergence of visitor impact management (VIM) with elements of both the ROS and LAC. VIM is a planning framework that incorporates resource and visitor management to reduce and control adverse impacts on outdoor recreational areas and opportunities. The National Parks and Conservation Association initiated a study which resulted in VIM and the initial objectives were:

- to study existing literature dealing with recreational carrying capacity and visitor impacts
- and to apply this resulting understanding by developing a plan to manage visitor impacts (Graefe, 1990; Nilsen and Taylor, 1997).

The goals underlying the study were:

- to control or reduce unwanted visitor impacts by providing a variety of types of information and tool to assist planners and managers
- to understand the nature and causes of visitor impact to avoid a repetition of past problems in management programmes
- to develop a consistent process to deal with impacts to natural environment as well as impacts to the quality of visitor experience (Nilsen and Taylor, 1997).

In order to understand the nature of recreational impacts, VIM defines five sets of considerations namely:

- *Impact interrelationships* – biophysical and social impacts do not occur in isolation, but are continuously interacting.
- *Use impact relationships* – the amount of use in relation to the amount of recorded impacts although this relationship need not necessarily be linear.
- *Varying tolerance to impacts* – different habitats and user groups respond differently to the same amount of use.
- *Activity-specific influences* – specific activities result in specific types of impact.
- *Site-specific influences* – the time of year and the condition of the site will determine the amount and type of impacts (Nilsen and Taylor, 1997).

Like all other frameworks, VIM recognizes that effective management involves both scientific and subjective considerations (Stankey et al., 1985; Shelby and

Heberlein, 1986). The framework addresses three basic key issues that are inherent to impact management:

- identification of problem conditions
- determination of potential causal factors affecting the occurrence and severity of the unacceptable impacts
- selection of potential management strategies to mitigate unacceptable impacts (Graefe, 1990).

These issues are operationalized in an eight-step sequential process:

- The timely identification of unacceptable changes occurring as a result of visitor use and development of management strategies to keep visitor impacts within acceptable levels.
- The integration of visitor impact management into existing agency planning, design and management processes.
- Ensuring that visitor impact management is based on the best scientific understanding and situational information available.
- Fixing management objectives that identify the resource condition to be achieved and the type of recreation experience to be provided.
- The identification of visitor impact problems by comparing standards for acceptable conditions with key indicators of impact at designated times and locations.
- Ensuring that management decisions to reduce impacts or maintain acceptable conditions are based on knowledge of the probable sources of and interrelationship between unacceptable impacts.
- Addressing visitor impacts using a wide range of alternative management techniques.
- The formulation of visitor management objectives, that incorporate a range of acceptable impact levels to accommodate the diversity of the environments and experience opportunities present within any setting (Graefe et al., 1990).

It is evident that the VIM process consists of a combination of legislation and policy review, scientific problem identification (on social as well as natural levels) and analysis and professional judgement (Payne and Graham, 1993; Wearing and Neil, 2000).

Indicators and standards form the basis of both LAC and VIM frameworks to define impacts deemed unacceptable. Furthermore, they situate carrying capacities within the broader managerial context. However, whereas VIM refers to planning and policy and includes identification of probable causes of impacts, LAC focuses on defining opportunity classes (Graefe et al., 1990; Payne and Graham 1993).

Visitor activity management process (VAMP)

VAMP, an extension of VIM, shifts the emphasis back to the user of the resource. This differs from ROS and LAC, where the emphasis is on managing the resource instead of the user. VAMP involves the development of activity profiles which connect activities with:

- the social and demographic characteristics of the participants
- the activity setting requirements
- trends affecting the activity (Wearing and Neil, 2000).

The main advantage of VAMP is that it can contribute to a more integrated approach to management of protected areas since it is designed to operate in parallel with the natural resource management process. VAMP is a proactive, flexible, conceptual framework that facilitates decision making related to the planning, development and operation of park-related services and facilities (Nilsen and Taylor, 1997). It has the potential to develop better information about customary users, stakeholders, visitors and non-visitors and decisions about access and use of protected areas. Furthermore, it can assist with the management of visitor programmes by putting into consideration the parks' objectives, natural resource features and values. It also incorporates a format for assessing the effectiveness in meeting public needs and expectations (Graham, 1990).

VAMP also provides a framework to ensure that visitor understanding, appreciation and enjoyment of the resources is considered just as carefully and systematically as the protection of the natural resources. This is done by incorporating social science data and integrating that into the park's management planning process. The VAMP concept of visitor management follows the traditional approach to planning, but emphasizes throughout each stage the understanding of park visitors (Taylor, 1990). VAMP's proactive approach to profiling visitor activity groups, suggesting target messages and evaluation before the development of interpretive programmes, may lead to more effective interpretation and environmental education programmes.

Tools for managing visitor use of ecotourism sites

Managing the visitor use of ecotourism sites can be a complex process. As such, different tools have been created in order to minimize the negative impacts that ecotourism can create and to protect the resources. The most important tools are now examined.

Restricting the amount of use

Impacts can be limited with relative ease by reducing use. In order for this to be applied successfully, it is not necessary either to have an understanding of the real cause of the problems or to get involved in more direct and active management problems. This technique cannot be used in instances where supply is greater than the demand for available recreational opportunities. It should only be implemented after other possible techniques have proved ineffective, as it conflicts with the objectives of maximizing satisfaction through providing opportunities for recreation. Various tactics can be adopted to limit the amount of use:

- Restrict entry to an area but allow visitors free choice to move about and change their routes and activities.
- Issue a restricted number of permits for specific campsites, zones or itineraries within the area. This option prevents spontaneous movement because visitors are required to stick to destinations they agreed to before entering the area. However, this method has relatively high administrative costs because rangers must patrol more widely to make sure that visitors comply.
- Require reservation: this is the most frequently used tactic in protected areas and can be done by mail, telephone or in person. It is generally accepted and helps those who are able to plan ahead. The use of a reservation system in conjunction with a first-come first-served technique (queuing) will benefit those who live nearby and those who can freely dispose of their time.
- Issue a restricted number of permits sold through a lottery system, which will benefit those who examine probabilities for success at different areas.
- Restrict the size of groups: this tactic can be especially effective to avoid social conflicts. Large groups can dominate recreational facilities and may contribute to crowding problems (Clark and Stankey, 1979). Large parties are likely to create larger disturbed areas simply because they must spread out over larger areas. Apart from affecting a larger area, they can also disturb an area in a much shorter time than a small group.
- Fines and recourse to legal action are necessary management techniques to deal with parties that deviate from the agreed itineraries.
- Restrict duration of stay by limiting the amount of time visitors may spend in any one area. Duration of stay limits can be placed on time spent both in the entire recreation area and at specific sites within the area. This discourages parties from settling in and occupying any specific site for as long as they want and allows access to more parties, particularly in highly developed recreation areas. In terms of ecology, the most important place to restrict the length of stays is lightly used places. In these areas, dispersal forms part of the ongoing management policy.

Dispersal of use

Ecological impact caused by human activity is often the result of high levels of use concentration in popular places. The answer may be to disperse use at such sites and can be achieved by:

- dispersing visitors on the same site with more distance between them
- dispersing visitors on more sites with or without more distance between them
- dispersing visitors in time (increasing off-season use) with or without changing spatial distribution.

These techniques can be achieved through the use of:

- education
- set itineraries
- access control through the use of a quota system
- requiring that visitors be accompanied by guides (Roggen and Berrier, 1981).

Concentration of use

Management concentration of use (Cole et al., 1987) is a technique frequently used in campsites and other intensive use areas:

- Without changing the number of sites, the distance between parties can be changed.
- Instead of using undisturbed areas, a few designated developed areas are used to concentrate campers, swimmers, boaters and so forth. Tent pads are usually used in campsites to identify spaces for camper to erect their tents.
- Concentration of use in time.

The main principle of managing developed recreational areas as a way of limiting impacts on resources is the use of spatial concentration of use.

Seasonal limitations on use

Recreation should be prohibited or limited in seasons when wildlife is vulnerable and soil is water-saturated and prone to disturbance. It is therefore common for recreation to be prohibited or restricted during such periods.

Zoning

Zoning may also be employed to control different uses and separate various types of density of use, allowing for lower density in areas where more resource protection is desired or prohibiting particularly destructive users from using parts of the area. This is a multidimensional technique that is based on ecological data to juggle the demands of protection and use in determining the most appropriate levels of use for specific areas within the area. Perhaps the most important outcomes of this is to ensure that 'activities in one zone do not impinge on the planned functions of another' (Buckley and Pannell, 1990: 29).

However, zoning is not commonly used in ecotourism, as ecotourism involves low-impact travel which requires few facilities and minimal disturbance to the environment and other wilderness users.

Trail system design

Yet another indirect management action is trail system design which may be effective not only in the redistribution of use, but may also improve the quality of the visitor experience and stimulate 'modes of behavior which enhance the environmental quality of the site' (McNeely and Thorsell, 1989: 37). For eco-tourists, the trail provides an experience in itself and it is not regarded merely as a route to the attraction. The design of the trail in itself can contribute to improving the quality of the experience. Visitor actions, and not only visitor numbers, can contribute to negative impacts on the environment. It is the few uninformed, unskilled and careless groups and not the many typical parties that cause most of the damage (Lucas, 1984).

Low-impact education

It is important to realize that impact management will remain recreational in nature without educated and caring users. Illegal, careless, unskilled and uninformed actions can be addressed by education. The prerequisites for a successful education programme are a focused message, an identified audience and a well-selected communication method (Fazio and Gilbert, 1986). There are various ways of educating the public, such as use of signs, written material and use of resource and cultural interpretation. Some direct management techniques, such as length of stay restrictions and group size, could be explained more effectively by educational programmes.

Qualifying requirements

This measure will benefit those visitors who are willing to invest the time and effort in order to demonstrate possession of a certain amount of skill/knowledge before they can obtain a permit.

Visitor fees and charges

As natural areas have become more popular for recreational use, visitor fees and charges have been gaining increased consideration. There is a range of each and they constitute methods to capture revenue that can be channelled back to implement conservation objectives:

- *Visitor fees* – including park admission fees and trekking fees are levied on users of an area or facility.
- *Concessions* – the permission to operate within a location to provide certain services to visitors are usually levied on groups and individual visitors and are called concessions.
- *Sales and royalties* – these fees are levied on a percentage of earnings that have been

derived from activities or products at the site – examples are crafts, photographs or postcards and so forth.

• *Taxation* – this is an extra cost imposed on goods and services that are used by tourists.

Information and interpretive services

No protected area can succeed without the support and goodwill of its visitors. Managers could address much of what they would like to communicate about their protected areas through information and interpretation. The following information collated in a package could go a long way to addressing this problem:

• reasons for the existence of the protected area
• behaviour in protected areas
• what there is to see
• where to see what you want
• what visitors are looking at
• what prompts visitors to came back again (MacKinnon et al., 1986).

Information dissemination has emerged into the most important indirect management technique used to minimize visitor-induced impacts in natural areas.

Ecotourism educational programmes

It was claimed that there two main types of environmental education within the protected and non-protected areas (Blamey, 1997):

• First, education in terms of species and genetic diversity which takes the form of simple observation and in-depth learning. Here, there is some form of gazing, either in terms of intensive interaction with certain species, or simply observing certain species. Although it was claimed that this type of gazing in the natural settings is different from in-depth learning about certain subjects (i.e. geology, ecology), it includes a form of onsite educational experience, all reflecting the needs of the consumers.
• Second, education in terms of ecosystems' diversity and how to minimize the conflict of environmental functions derived from tourism activities. This type of educational experience can be seen as including both general information about the ecology as well as certain codes of conduct; in turn there was a claim that these codes of conduct refer to those individuals who least need it. In addition, different responses emerged from individuals before the tour and during the tour, as code utilization did not allow ecotourists to become more environmentally committed.

In particular, for ecotourism purposes a situation-specific model appeared to take place in three phases (Forestell, 1993: 271–5):

• pre-contact

- contact
- post-contact.

The focus of the *pre-contact interaction* tended to be skill-oriented programmes focusing on the anticipation and apprehension of the participant. During the *contact interaction*, the provision of specific scientific information about the species, genetic and ecosystems diversity was provided in such a manner that it facilitated the participant's ability to observe the different relationships between organisms, rather than having these identified by the guide. During the *post-contact phase*, the emphasis was placed on the enhancement of the participants' ecologically sensitive behaviour patterns, by providing a number of programmes to further ecotourists environmental goals (membership of certain groups, volunteer programmes, signing a petition, etc.) (Forestell, 1993).

Although this model represents one of the first attempts in ecotourism settings, Orams (1995) argues that not all ecotourism programmes can be designed in these three stages, in that there is a need to utilize a range of strategies or techniques for increasing the effectiveness of interpretation. In turn, he suggested that interpretation should enhance some elements of the cognitive learning theory, that of cognitive dissonance, affective domain, motivation/incentive to act, opportunity to act and the evaluation and feedback (Orams, 1995: 87–90). These techniques should then be offered as a 'menu' from which certain strategies can be implemented (Orams, 1995). In all the cases, he pointed to the lack of interpretation programmes in ecotourism, especially regarding the empirical effectiveness of such techniques (Orams, 1995).

Others however, brought to light certain issues concerning the effectiveness of the planning process, by suggesting that there is a need to integrate an external needs assessment (Masberg, 1996). Here, the argument is that the current interpretation programs of ecotourism concentrate on the input of internal sources or providers of a particular organization. Hence, Masberg's study showed that by utilizing a regular assessment, based on the needs of the professionals, the public and the recreation providers, ecotourism interpretation programmes can be effective as they espouse a regular customer input (1996: 48–50). This input can be utilized in order to assist with the development of the programmes, identifying content needs of specific visitors groups or as a tool to formalize decision-making procedures (Masberg, 1996: 49).

Conclusion

Simply theorizing about sustainable tourism is no longer sufficient. There is a need to contribute some practical tools towards realizing tourism in a sustainable development context. In the past carrying capacity has not been as useful as anticipated. While reducing use is certainly an appropriate strategy for certain problems or situations, carrying capacity is only one of many tactics within this strategy. Other strategies are also available, each with its own tactics. Tools such as TOS, VIM and VAMP offer more flexible application. They focus not only on managing use but also on managing the resource, the visitor and the impact. LAC recognizes the diversity of visitor expectations and preferences. Although LAC has been modified for wider application it needs further refinement to apply to more intensely used areas. VAMP, intended for both front- and backcountry application, requires modification if it is to be used outside park settings. VIM is a flexible process, suitable for smaller scales than LAC and adaptable to wilderness, rural or densely populated areas. All these tools have evolved over time and are likely to continue to do so.

None of these tools presented should be seen as a panacea for tourism and resource management problems. However, they do provide valuable frameworks within which decisions can be made about acceptable conditions, priorities and resource management in a region or more specific context.

Questions

1 Describe the meaning of carrying capacity.
2 Choose one site from the case studies in this volume and apply the ROS and LAC models.
3 Select one case study from this volume and apply the VIM and VAMP models.
4 Using one site from the case studies in this volume, design an educational programme for ecotourism.

References

Blamey, R.K. (1995) The elusive market profile: operationalising ecotourism. Paper presented at the Geography of Sustainable Tourism Conference, University of Canberra, ACT, Australia, September.
Blamey, R.K. (1997) 'Ecotourism: the search for an operational definition', *Journal of Sustainable Tourism*, 5 (2), 109–30.
Boyd, S.W. and Butler, R.W. (1996) 'Managing ecotourism: an opportunity spectrum approach', *Tourism Management*, 17 (8), 557–66.
Buckley, R. and Pannell, J. (1990) 'Environmental impacts of tourism and recreation in national parks and conservation reserves', *Journal of Tourism Studies*, 1 (1), 24–32.
Butler, R.W. and Waldbrook, L.A. (1991) 'A new planning tool: the tourism opportunity spectrum', *Journal of Tourism Studies*, 2 (1), 2–14.
Clark, B.D. and Gilad, A. (1989) *Perspectives on Environmental Impact Assessment*. Dordrecht: Reidel.
Clark, R.N. and Stankey, G.H. (1979) The recreation opportunity spectrum: a framework for planning, management, and research. General technical report PNW-GTR-98. US. Department of Agriculture, Forest Service, Pacific Northwest Forest and Range Experiment Station, Portland, OR.
Cohen, E. (1997) 'The impact of tourism on the physical environment', *Annals of Tourism Research*, 2, 215–37.

Cole, D.N., Petersen, M.E. and Lucas, R.C. (1987) Managing wilderness recreation use: common problems and potential solutions. General technical report INT-230. USDA Forest Service, Ogden, UT.

Dawson, C.P. (2001) 'Ecotourism and nature-based tourism: one end of the tourism opportunity spectrum?' In McCool, S.F. and Moisey, R.N. (eds) *Tourism, Recreation and Sustainability Linking Culture and the Environment*. Wallingford, UK. CABI, 41–53.

Driver, B.L. (1990) Recreation opportunity spectrum: basic concepts and use in land management planning. In Towards Serving Visitors and Managing our Resources. Proceedings of a North American Workshop on Visitor Management in Parks and Protected Areas. Tourism Research and Education Centre, University of Waterloo, 159–84.

Driver, B.L., Brown, P.J., Stankey, G.H. and Gregiore. T.G. (1987) 'The ROS planning system: evolution, basic concepts, and research needed', *Leisure Sciences*, 9, 201–212.

Fazio, J.R. and Gilbert, D.L. (1986) *Public Relations and Communication for Natural Resource Managers*. Kendall: Hunt Publishers.

Forestell, P.H. (1993) 'If leviathan has a face, does gaia have a soul? Incorporating environmental education in marine eco-tourism programs', *Ocean & Coastal Management*, 20 (3), 267–82.

Frissel, S.S. Jr. and Stankey, G.H. (1972) Wilderness environmental quality: search for social and ecological harmony. In Proceedings of the 1972 National Convention, Hotsprings, AZ.

Graefe, A.R. (1990) Visitor impact management. In Towards Serving Visitors and Managing our Resources. Proceedings of a North American Workshop on Visitor Management in Parks and Protected Areas. Tourism Research and Education Center, University of Waterloo, 213–34.

Graefe, A.R., Kuss, F.R. and Vaske, J.J. (1990) *Visitor Impact Management: The Planning Framework*, Vol.2. Washington, DC: National Parks and Conservation Association.

Graham, R. (1990) Visitor management and Canada's national park. In Graham, R. and Lawrence, R. (eds) Towards Serving our Visitors and Managing our Resources. Proceedings of the First Canada/US Workshop on Visitor Management in Parks and Protected Areas, Waterloo, Ontario, Tourism Research and Educational Centre, University of Waterloo and Canadian Parks Service, Environment Canada.

Gunn, C.A. (1994) *Tourism Planning: Basics, Concepts, Cases*, 3rd edn. Washington, DC: Taylor & Francis.

Lime, D.W. and Stankey, G.H. (1971) Carrying capacity: maintaining outdoor recreation quality. Forest Recreation Symposium Proceedings. Northeast Forest Experimental Station, Upper Darby, 174–84.

Lucas, R. (1984) 'The role of regulations in recreation management', *Western Wildlands*, 9 (2), 6–10.

Lucas, R. and Stankey, G. (1988) *Shifting Trends in Wilderness Recreational Use*. Missoula, MO: United States forest Service.

MacKinnon, J., MacKinnon, K., Child, G. and Thorsell, J. (eds) (1986) *Managing Protected Areas in the Tropics*. Gland: IUCN.

Manning, R.E. (1979). 'Strategies for managing recreational use of national parks', 4 (1), 13–15.

Masberg, B.A. (1996) 'Using ecotourists to assist in determining the content for interpretation', *Journal of Park and Recreation Administration*, 14 (2), 37–52.

Mathieson, A. and Wall, G. (1987) *Tourism: Economic, Physical and Social Impacts*. New York: John Wiley & Sons.

McArthur, S. (1997a) Beyond the limits of acceptable change – introducing TOMM. In Proceedings of Tread Lightly on the World Conference, Coffs Harbour, NSW.

McArthur, S. (1997b) Growth and jobs in Australia's ecotourism industry. In Australian Ecotourism Guide 1997/98, Ecotourism Association of Australia, Brisbane, 33–4.

McCool, S.F. (1990) Limits of acceptable change: evolution and future. In Towards Serving Visitors and Managing Our Resources. Proceedings of a North American Workshop on Visitor Management in Parks and Protected Areas. Tourism Research and Education Centre, University of Waterloo, 185–94.

McCool, S.F. (1991) Limits of acceptable change: a strategy for managing the effects of nature-dependent tourism development. Paper presented at Tourism and the Land: Building a Common Future, Whistler, 1–3 December 1990.

McNeely, J.A. and Thorsell, J. (1989) *Jungles, Mountains and Islands: How Tourism can help Conserve Natural Heritage*. Gland: IUCN.

Murphy, P.E. (1985) *Tourism: A Community Approach*. New York: Methuen.

Nilsen, P. and Taylor, G. (1997) A comparative analysis of protected area planning and management frameworks. In McCool, S.F. and Cole, D.N. (eds) Proceedings of the Limits of Acceptable Change and Related Planning Processes: Progress and Future Directions, Missoula, Montana 20–22 May. General technical report INT-GTR-371, US Department of Agriculture, Forest Service, Rocky Mountain Research Station, Ogden, UT, 49–57.

Orams, M.B. (1995) 'Towards a more desirable form of ecotourism', *Tourism Management*, 16 (1), 3–8.

Parks Canada (1991) Visitor activity concept. VAMP Technical Group, Ottawa, ON: Parks Canada, Program Headquarters, 16.

Payne, R. and Graham, R. (1993) 'Visitor planning and management'. In Dearden, P. and Rollins, R. (eds) *Parks and Protected Areas in Canada: Planning and Management*. Toronto: Oxford University Press.

Prosser, G. (1986) 'The limits of acceptable change and introduction to a framework for natural area planning', *Australian Parks and Recreation*, 22 (2), 5–10.

Robertson, R.A., Dawson, C.P., Kuentzel, W. and Selin, S.W. (1995) Trends in university-based education and training programs in ecotourism or nature-based tourism in the USA. In Thompson, J.L. et al. (eds) Proceedings of the Fourth International Outdoor Recreation and Tourism Trends Symposium and the 1995 National Recreation Resource Planning Conference, St Paul, Minnesota, 14–17 May. University of Minnesota, College of Natural Resources and Minnesota Extension Service, St Paul, MN, 460–66.

Roggen, J.W. and Berrier, D.L. (1981) 'Communication to disperse wilderness campers', *Journal of Forestry*, 79, 295–7.

Shelby, B. and Heberlein, T.A. (1986) *Carrying Capacity in Recreation Settings*. Corvallis: Oregon State University Press.

Stankey, G.H. (1991) Conservation, recreation and tourism: the good, the bad and the ugly. In Miller, M.L. and Auyan, J. (eds) Proceedings of the 1990 Congress on Coastal and Marine Tourism – A Symposium and Workshop on Balancing Conservation and Economic Development, National Coastal Resources Research and Development Institute, Newport, OR.

Stankey, G. and McCool, S. (1990) 'Managing for appropriate wilderness conditions: the carrying capacity issue'. In Hendee, J.C. et al. (eds) *Wilderness Management*, 2nd edn. Golden, CO: Fulcrum Press, 215–39.

Stankey, G.H., Cole, D.N., Lucas, R.C. Peterson, M.E. and Frissell, S.S. (1985). The limits for acceptable change (LAC) system for wilderness planning. United States Forest Service general technical report INT-176. United States Department of Agriculture, Ogden, UT.

Taylor, G. (1990) Planning and managing visitor opportunities. In Graham, R. and Lawrence, R. (eds) *Towards Serving our Visitors and Managing our Resources*. Proceedings of the First Canada/US Workshop on Visitor Management in Parks and Protected Areas, Waterloo, Ontario, Tourism Research and Education Center, University of Waterloo and Canadian Parks Service, Environment Canada.

Wall, G. (1997) 'Is ecotourism sustainable?', *Environmental Management*, 21, 483–91.

Wearing, S. and Neil, J. (2000) *Ecotourism Impacts, Potentials and Possibilities*. Oxford: Butterworth-Heinemann, 39–56.

Wight, P.A. (1994) 'Limits of acceptable change: a recreational tourism tool for cumulative effects assessment'. In Kennedy, A.J. (ed) *Cumulative Effects in Canada: From Concept to Practice*. Papers from the Fifteenth Symposium held by the Alberta Society of Professional Biologists, 13–14 April, Calgary, 159–78.

3 Practical Management Tools and Approaches for Resource Protection and Assessment

Pamela A. Wight

The four main objectives of this chapter are to:

- Analyze the integrative planning approaches
- Introduce different examples of protected area planning in Canada
- Discuss the methods available for stakeholder involvement
- Identify different tools for ecotourism planning

Introduction

Sustainable tourism needs to be viewed in the context of sustainable development. Sustainable development is not a fixed state; it is 'a *process of change* in which the exploitation of resources, the direction of investments, the orientation of technological development, and institutional change are made consistent with future as well as present needs' (WCED, 1987: 9). Sustainable development is not a destination, rather, it is a journey. By now, the need to incorporate social, economic and environmental dimensions in sustainable tourism is relatively well known (see Chapter 1). But actually, sustainable development includes five interrelated components:

1 *Economic*: dealing with wealth creation and improved conditions of material life.
2 *Social*: measured as well-being in nutrition, health, education and housing.
3 *Political*: pointing to such values as human rights, political freedom, security, participation and some form of self-determination.
4 *Cultural*: in recognition of the fact that cultures confer identity and self-worth to people.
5 *Ecological*: recognizing the primacy of conserving the life-giving natural resources and processes on which all progress depends.

Developments have always tended to stress the first two conditions, particularly the economic. Environmental impact assessment (EIA) has tended to stress the fifth. Protected areas (PAs) focus on environmental systems, but they cannot realistically exist in an operational vacuum; most environmental systems coexist with economic development and address the needs and aspirations of society in this mixed system and cultural and political components may well shape social and economic conditions and values. This requires an integrative approach by all players. We need to consider *all five* dimensions mentioned to contribute most effectively to sustainable development and sustainable tourism.

Sustainable tourism is not equivalent to sustainable development; it is only part of the whole idea of sustainable development (Wight, 1996). 'Sustainable tourism' has become a form of shorthand for tourism that attempts to adhere to sustainable development principles.

Not all tourism has been or is sustainable; neither has it always conformed to these principles. Sustainable tourism involves a challenge to develop quality tourism products without adversely affecting the natural and cultural environment that maintains and nurtures them, taking into account the political context of the community/society. As such, the following sections present some of the practical management tools in managing resources protection and planning protected areas.

Integrating human use and protection goals in protected area planning and management

Canada's natural and wilderness areas feature an unequalled inventory of pristine environments, unique wildlife, spectacular scenery and distinct aboriginal cultures. Growing demand for these features make many of these areas tourism destinations in waiting. For such places, Hinch and Butler (1996) suggest that the 'spread of tourism has been driven in part by a perpetual search for new destinations, and in part by an increasing interest in and marketing of things natural or unspoiled'.

To understand all the dimensions of tourism in an area, planners and strategists must recognize that tourism is part of an interdependent system of causes and effects (McIntosh et al., 1995). A truly sustainable tourism plan requires that all parties contribute towards achieving a shared set of outcomes – a vision that reflects their shared values.

Integrative planning approaches required

More than 20 years ago, Mathieson and Wall (1982) pointed out the need 'to integrate the analyses of social, economic and environmental effects of tourist development to derive an overall assessment of the desirability' of tourism development. Later, Getz (1987) called for a 'process, based on research and evaluation, which seeks to optimise the potential contribution of tourism to human welfare and environmental quality'. Different tourism planning models have evolved and include different traditions and perspectives (Table 3.1).

Table 3.1 Traditions and perspectives of tourism planning models

Tradition	Perspective
Boosterism	Tourism is good and should be developed
Commercial	Tourism is a business that should provide a financial return to its investors
Economic	Tourism creates employment and attracts foreign revenue
Environmental	Tourism has an impact on resources, so should have an ecological basis. Tourism is a spatial phenomenon
Community based	Tourism is neither good nor bad. Its development should be guided by local wishes

(Source: McVetty, 1997, adapted from Getz, 1987)

With the exception of *boosterism*, which is not a rational approach, each tradition represents responsible tourism planning from a single perspective. Taken alone, these perspectives cannot address the range of tourism impacts that an integrated approach requires. As McVetty and Wight (1998) point out, traditional tourism planning perspectives fail to address tourism impacts in all its dimensions. In general, these approaches seek to maximize or minimize tourism impacts from a single perspective and tend to oversimplify. There is need for an integrated approach where the decision-making framework incorporates community values, appropriate scales and broad-based public involvement in management and monitoring. The integrated approach is summarized in Box 3.1.

Box 3.1 Summary of integrated tourism

Integrated tourism is part of a complete system that includes the environment, community, industry, economy and the legislative environment. Its planning should be democratic and integrated with related planning processes. Its planning should help tourism to contribute to a community's well being. (McVetty, 1997)

The tourism optimization management model (TOMM) recently evolved in Australia from the limits of acceptable change (LAC) model, because LAC could not accommodate the perspective of those who sought an overall quality of life in the community (Manidis Roberts, 1997). It is essentially an integrative approach. It involves developing a realistic set of tourism scenarios for a destination, including their benefits and disbenefits, and working with stake-holders to develop a set of outcomes for tourism and visitor use, together with realistic and measurable indicators. When implemented, these indicators are monitored and may trigger a management response. TOMM as a management tool is consistent with the principles of integrated tourism planning and addresses the broad set of tourism benefits and impacts based on community values, tourism assets and realistic market opportunities. It was designed to operate at a regional level, rather than at a single site; to serve a variety of stakeholders, rather than a single agency; and to help foster a sustainable tourism industry, rather than focus on minimizing negative impacts (Chapter 2).

Integrative planning in practice: protected area planning in Canada

Aulavik National Park

Aulavik National Park was established in 1992 on Banks Island in Canada's Arctic. The island's 140 residents are all clustered in Sachs Harbour, an Inuvialuit Hamlet about 250 km south of the park boundary (two hours by plane and two or more days by land or water). The Inuvialuit retain rights to traditional subsistence activities within park boundaries.

The park's establishment agreement directed that services and facilities would be developed in response to *market demand*. But Parks Canada recognized that not only does demand vary over time, it is also affected by the very establishment of a park. They also realized that demand would be further affected by the character of any facilities or services and by marketing and packaging. They commissioned a visitor market analysis using an integrated tourism planning approach, to help managers and stakeholders understand the influences and impacts of park-related tourism – in all its dimensions – and to develop a system to achieve those objectives (Pam Wight & Associates, 1998a). The approach included:

1 *A situation analysis*: this included an information review; community and stakeholder consultations; Parks Canada interviews; commercial trends review (including a travel trade survey); and legislative and policy environment review. By addressing the social, economic, environmental, cultural and political/legislative concerns, it ensured all the interrelated components of sustainable development were considered. The analysis found significant park-related tourism potential, but found the network of legislation, agreements and administrative bodies was, in some cases creating barriers to the very outcomes that they were put in place to support.

2 *Developing a shared vision*: This vision represents a set of desired outcomes for tourism and visitor use that are very similar for community residents, regional stakeholders and

Parks Canada. Overall, the shared vision for tourism was summarized as a: 'sustainable tourism industry based on renewable resources and on cultural experiences, which is compatible with traditional values and activities, and where the community is enabled to participate optimally'.

3 *Alternative visitor use scenarios*: These scenarios are based on the area's commercial realities and regulatory environment and were not based on growth, but on visitor type and intended to optimize tourism outcomes. Outcomes investigated were: no substantial change – no commercial operations in the park; enabling outside companies to operate in the park; partnerships (between local and outside operators) to optimize tourism outcomes.

The TOMM approach revealed that key stakeholders were unaware that their separate initiatives had produced minimal visitor use. Certainly, there had been few negative impacts, but there were even fewer benefits. These early stages of integrated planning helped Parks Canada and stakeholders to address this quandary in ways that support the shared objectives of the park and its stakeholders. Integrated tourism planning has shown potential to bring Parks Canada and its local stakeholders together to manage their activities in ways that support a well-researched, realistic and shared set of desired outcomes. Park managers then started planning the next phase in the TOMM/integrated planning process – developing an integrated suite of indicators for a monitoring and management programme to bring together the expertise of several disciplines. Without this integration into existing plans and policies, the efficacy of a single partner's efforts would be limited.

Gwaii Haanas National Park Reserve/Haida Heritage Site

Gwaii Haanas is a rugged and remote wilderness area located on the Queen Charlotte Islands/Haida Gwaii (The Islands) of Northwest British Columbia. Parks Canada and the Council of the Haida Nation cooperatively co-manage this protected area, which adds a layer of complexity to management. Previous tourism planning for Gwaii Haanas failed, because of: community division; a strong resource extraction industry; low awareness of sustainable tourism; and a feeling that the planning process was being driven by 'off-Islanders'.

Parks Canada has more recently been working with the tourism industry to refine tourism marketing for The Islands. In a search for alternatives to traditional tourism planning models, the integrated approach was selected. Baseline research came from Parks Canada visitor surveys and focus groups and was analyzed through market research and tourism opportunity analysis (Pam Wight & Associates, 1999a). Research included: a review of attitudinal information (both of residents and visitors); a review of summer visitors to The Islands; a review of Vancouver and Calgary focus group results; research on ecotourism, culture and aboriginal tourism markets; product evaluation; and issues evaluation. This baseline research forms the basis of the tourism planning process and the results are used by Gwaii Haanas managers, local communities and the tourism industry.

The integrated planning approach helped to focus this complex research exercise, so information collection and presentation was designed to address many of the issues. The research examines Gwaii Haanas at a series of levels (the total Islands' community, the regional level and the global tourism industry). The Islands' experience is also reviewed from the visitors' perspective. The report identifies for the Islands' communities the shared values, shared concerns, opportunities and gaps in service and current and potential visitor information. The research shows that different groups of visitors have different benefits and costs, which enabled park management to develop plans to move into the next phases of their integrated planning process. Local management feel that the integrated approach at an early stage helped them better to understand their visitors and the dynamic outcomes of their visits. It might also be useful for future research to consider an inverse approach – that of stakeholder articulation of *undesired* outcomes, which are to be avoided by the planning process.

Protected area management – a range of approaches

There are a number of management approaches available to PAs, each of which could be used in isolation or in a complementary, integrated fashion. Wight (1999a) characterizes the approaches from 'hard' to 'soft' (Figure 3.1). However, there has tended to be a high emphasis on the hard, command and control approach in PAs.

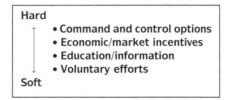

Figure 3.1 A range of management approaches

PA managers have a range of mandates, with a prime duty often being enshrined in legislation that is oriented towards protection and conservation. However, PAs often have intrinsic values for all people and by designation as a protected area, their very attractiveness has ironically been shown to increase.

Depending on the type of natural area, other thrusts may include scientific research, education, enjoyment or general recreation. They may have to restrict access to sites, due to the fragility of the resource, for cultural or other reasons and protection and conservation may have to take precedence. This has an impact on tourism operators, who may find that they only have access to markets at certain seasons, weekends, holidays, etc. However, the protected area manager has other priorities, related to long-term sustainability of the resource. In addition, they may also need to provide visitor facilities, have repeat visitation, interpret the area, manage the impacts of visitors and manage their relationship with the surrounding communities and commercial operators (Wight, 1999b). Thus there may be many tensions which arise, due to their own mandates and their feeling that operators do not understand their perspectives. PA managers are searching for tools for sustainability.

The tourism industry is primarily driven by private enterprise and profitability is a prime inducement to undertake any activity. These businesses will be concerned with market demand, competitive advantage, life expectancy, investment requirements, marketing advantage, operational requirements and time required to return a profit. These concerns operate in an often volatile marketplace. Tourism operators experience tensions related to their need to operate profitably, the long lead times required to foster markets, their ongoing costs particularly in remote areas, the need to support and educate visitors and the long lead times in obtaining approvals to operate in protected areas, as well as the frequently changing regulations. They feel that PA managers do not adequately understand their perspectives.

Further tensions may arise when one takes into account local communities' and visitors' perspectives. Most parties fail to understand each others' perspectives. To succeed in the challenge of moving towards a more sustainable tourism industry, better stakeholder involvement processes are needed, as well as better partnerships and collaborations between the various players. In particular, partnerships are needed between tourism operators, who are often delivering the tourism experience, and PA managers, who control the use of the resources.

Informing and involving stakeholders

Steps to involve stakeholders in planning and management

Protected area managers should not have the only voice in planning and management of these areas. Planning processes represent a blend of technical expertise, public and indigenous knowledge, and it is imperative that managers seek *all* these perspectives. While the actual numbers of potential stakeholders for any one destination may seem overwhelming, they may be more easily understood in terms of the following categories:

1 *Technical*: comprising protected area managers and experts.
2 *Public*: comprising tourism operators (interested in maintaining profitability of operations and ensuring legal mandates are respected); visitors and users (for whom protected area facilities and programmes are developed); and society at large including local communities (which often designate the PA, indicate its values and develop management expectations).

Phase 1 **Early consultation**	• Consult informally to determine the major issues raised • Estimate level of public interest and the most likely stakeholders • Identify key individuals
Phase 2 **Initial planning**	• Chart agency's decision-making process – thought to prepare a programme • Identifying stakeholders and public • Determine information exchange needs • Clarify public involvement objectives
Phase 3 **Development of a** **public involvement** **programme**	• Choose detailed methods of stakeholder involvement • Establish internal agency communications • Commit resources • Schedule and assign work
Phase 4 **Implementation** **of programme**	• Carry out initial work • Monitor the public involvement programme • Evaluate the results of involvement
Phase 5 **Post-decision** **public involvement**	• Develop post-decision requirements (at the least notify public of decision and how their comments were used) • Implement as required

Figure 3.2 Steps in developing and implementing a stakeholder involvement programme

A key to success is the ability to integrate the public and technical streams of input to management agency activities. Successful involvement of all groups' perspectives throughout the decision-making processes, enabling each to contribute constructively, results in a better plan, with more ownership, more consensus and greater 'buy-in' to management activities.

This consensus building is needed for acceptance and subsequent resource allocation for implementation. Therefore, developing a stakeholder involvement programme will be an important element of success. Figure 3.2 illustrates the major steps for involving the various public bodies. The participation programme should be designed to fit the unique needs of the situation.

Select the appropriate approach and techniques for stakeholder involvement

In order to maximize credibility, it is important to provide meaningful opportunities for stakeholders to contribute, which usually is related to the participation programme developed. Table 3.2 shows a range of select public involvement techniques as a continuum. While it is easy to assume that there is only one consensus-building technique appropriate to a particular situation, in fact, during the course of stakeholder involvement, it may be desirable to use a wide variety of techniques. It is important to note that the views of the various stakeholders are often in conflict, making it critical that stakeholders know which protected area management objectives are paramount and why.

Table 3.2 A continuum of stakeholder involvement approaches and selected techniques

Approach	Description	Selected techniques	Message to the public
Public information education	*Knowledge about a decision*	• Advertising • Newspaper inserts • Posters	*You want them to know and understand about it*
Information feedback	*Being heard before the decision*	• Briefs • Focus groups	*You want them to understand and support your programme*
Consultation	*Being heard and involved in discussions*	• Community meetings or gatherings • Conferences • Workshops/problem-solving meetings	*You want to understand them and value their views and input*
Extended involvement	*Having an influence on the decision*	• Advisory groups • Taskforces • Charettes	*You seriously expect to implement most of their advice*
Joint planning	*Agreeing to the decision*	• Consultation • Mediation • Negotiation	*You are fully committed to using the results in all but the most extenuating circumstances*

Managing protected areas and ecotourism destinations

Protected area management challenges

Park systems are often represented as having the difficult task of meeting two goals: enjoyment and protection of parks. It is relatively easy to characterize parks as constantly having problems in attempting to meet the two often contradictory objectives – providing protection/conservation, as well as opportunities for understanding, appreciation and enjoyment and recreation. This sometimes divisive debate does not acknowledge historic realities (Wight, 2001). The Canadian Parks Service has existed since 1885 and there has been an evolution of reasons why parks were created. For example, in Banff National Park, tourism was the driver, whereas new Arctic parks are much more biological preserves, while some PAs (e.g. Gwaii Haanas) have strong natural *and cultural* landscape protection functions. Thus, as protected areas have evolved, we have seen the building of a diverse 'product line' (e.g. tourism, conservation, recreation) representing different states of the ideological balance over the years. Additionally, once infrastructure is created in a park, it is essentially 'cast in stone'. This presents an even greater and complex challenge for management agencies.

It is all too easy to target certain vulnerable PAs for criticism, for example, by saying that a park is being 'loved to death' by its visitors. This perspective, however, is beginning to be viewed by Parks Canada in terms of supply and demand management (Figure 3.3), rather than in terms of conflicting objectives. For instance parks may have a limited supply of access/accommodation in some highly attractive areas, which may have excess demand. The latter is usually due to a combination of pressures of visitation and lack of application of the full range of direct and indirect management tools to deal with this. This echoes the need to manage supply, demand *and* impact.

Although there is a new move to examine and incorporate a range of hard and soft management approaches, it is fair to say that it is still common to find a 'limits'-based perspective high in the list of management tools that are being

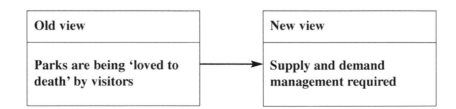

Old view	New view
Parks are being 'loved to death' by visitors	Supply and demand management required

Figure 3.3 Views about parks: old and new

RESOURCE PROTECTION AND ASSESSMENT

adopted in PAs – a command and control approach. Supply and demand management can move beyond command and control approaches (the 'hard' end of management approaches), to incorporate many of the other tactics and tools available. Softer management approaches need more emphasis. It is not the purpose here systematically to discuss all management tools available for PAs. However, it is useful to note that the range of tools employed could focus very much more on those which manage the demand, and the visitor, specifically.

Problems related to human use and impact

A number of authors have recognized that many environmental problems are common in wilderness, parks or protected areas that are related to tourism activities. In addition, the use of adjacent land may impact the protected area (Table 3.3).

In the face of such actual or potential problems in and adjacent to PAs, one of the commonest management responses is to put a limit on use. This often

Table 3.3 Problems common in wilderness/natural areas

Negative impacts of visitors on the environment

• Trail creation (and deterioration)	• Habital loss
• Campsites (and deterioration)	• Emissions and air pollution
• Litter	• Firewood collection
• Crowding	• Visual and noise impacts
• Packstock impacts	• Over-fishing undersized fishing catches
• Solid and human waste problems	• Impacts on vegetation
• Weeds, fungi and exotic species	• Damage to sand dunes/reefs
• User conflicts	• Soil compaction or erosion
• Water pollution (physical or biological)	• Increased fire risk
• Overdevelopment	• Damage to archaeological sites
• Tracks and ORVs	• Cultural vandalism
• Boats damaging banks	• Wildlife disturbance, habituation or impact
• Changed watercourses	• Trampling (human or horse)
	• Souveniring (flora, fauna, other)

(Sources: Cole, Petersen and Lucas, 1987; McNeely and Thorsell, 1989; Buckley and Pannell, 1990; Dowling, 1993; Wight, 1996)

takes the form of limits to commercial or FIT activities through such means as limits on numbers of visitors, facilities, licences, group size or use quotas. This is a relatively easy approach. However, it is also simplistic and may well be inappropriate (in that visitor use is one of the goals of many areas) and also it may be inappropriate in terms of the best solution to problems.

In a similar way, the literature has presented numerous calls for tourism carrying capacity to be determined, in order to appropriately plan, manage and control the direction and consequences of tourism and other activities (e.g.

McNeely and Thorsell, 1989; International Working Group on Indicators of Sustainable Tourism, 1993; Consulting and Audit Canada, 1995). However, while the *concept* of carrying capacity is appealing, it has had limited success outside the field of wildlife management (where it was originally developed) and cannot deal with the complexity and diversity of issues associated with recreation and tourism (McCool, 1991; Bianchi, 1994; Wight, 1994, 1996, 1998a; Hall and McArthur, 1998). Some of the problems inherent in attempting to determine carrying capacity include:

- *unrealistic expectations* (e.g. that there is a technique which can provide a magic number, limit or threshold)
- *untenable assumptions* (e.g. that there is a direct relationship between visitor use and impact; and that limiting use limits impact)
- *imprecise and varying parameters* (e.g. are we dealing with biophysical resources? the host community? visitors? what activities? how are they behaving?)
- *historic patterns do not necessarily project* (science is based on historic patterns, not current patterns, which are unknown)
- *multiscale outcomes* (there are a multitude of scales in time and space in which outcomes may occur and a 'number' may not adequately address these)
- *there is no norm* (systems move on – whether natural or human – and at different speeds, whether or not one variable is held at a constant number).

Although attractive in *conceptual* terms, in *practical* tourism terms carrying capacity is not an applicable concept.

Management approaches and tools available

Management approaches

Research and programmes are now focusing on managing the *supply*, the *demand*, the *resource* and the *impacts*, rather than carrying capacity:

1 *Managing the supply* of tourism or visitor opportunities, e.g. by increasing the space available or the time available to accommodate more use.
2 *Managing the demand* for visitation, e.g. through restrictions of length of stay, or total numbers, or type of use.
3 *Managing the resource* capabilities to handle use, e.g. through hardening the site or specific locations or developing facilities.
4 *Managing the impact* by reducing the negative impact of use, e.g. modifying the type of use or dispersing or concentrating use.

Figure 3.4 illustrate these strategies, together with a number of tactical approaches related to each.

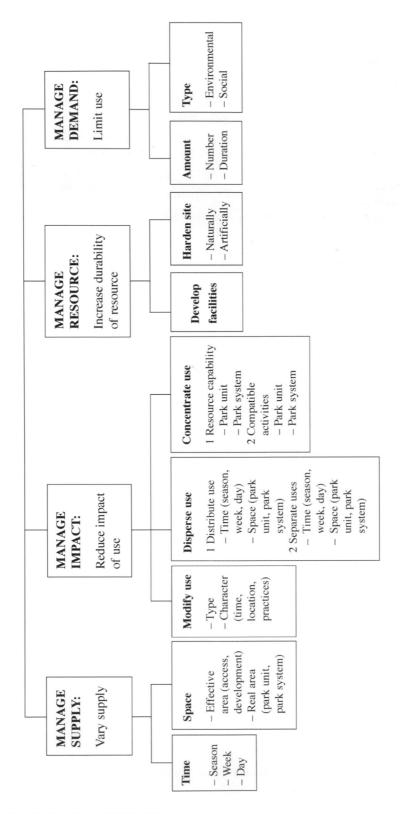

Figure 3.4 Strategies for managing protected areas
(Derived from Manning, 1979)

Management tools and tactics to respond to specific problems

With respect to addressing specific problems in destinations, such as those illustrated in Table 3.3, Cole et al. (1987) point out that there is a *range* of management strategies which may be appropriate (see Table 3.4). Each management strategy has a number of tactics, of which only one is a form of carrying capacity. In fact, Cole et al. indicate that they have always found other *more effective* means to deal with problems, than applying carrying capacity (which is a strong 'command and control' approach).

Table 3.4 (p.62) provides a helpful illustration of the various approaches to management, in the form of a practical decisions/choice menu. It gives a good visual summary of the range of techniques from which to select the optimum approach for any particular situation or problem in a specific area. As the table suggests, there are many ways of managing for sustainability. Each of the techniques described can be viewed as taking one of four different approaches: managing supply, demand, resources and impact. Although these tactics were developed for terrestrial systems, they may be modified for management of marine areas. It should be noticed that in terms of approach, the tools in this 'toolbag' range from hard to soft.

Sample management tools

Visitor management

Visitor management is an important aspect of any form of tourism in sensitive areas, whether in a PA or an adjacent region or communities (see Chapter 2). Examples of specific visitor management tools which could usefully be employed include those illustrated in Table 3.5 (Pam Wight & Associates, 1998b [SK Bird Trail]). It should be noted that although most of these tools address visitors *during* activities in the PA, some target the visitor *before* their arrival at the PA and effective tools will also affect visitors *after* they leave.

Voluntary approaches: codes and guidelines

Canada developed an excellent Code of Ethics and guidelines for sustainable tourism a decade ago (TIAC, 1992). Unfortunately, these had poor industry distribution and application. There have been strong moves over the last decade, to introduce more sustainable forms of tourism and to demonstrate to visitors this sense of responsibility. This has been found among countries, destination regions, cities, hospitality chains, groups of separate businesses

Table 3.4 Strategies and tactics for managing wilderness, natural and protected areas

Strategy	*Management tactics*
1 Reduce use of the entire wilderness/ protected area	1 Limit number of visitors in the entire wilderness/protected area (carrying capacity) 2 Limit length of stay 3 Encourage use of other areas 4 Require certain skills and/or equipment 5 Charge a flat visitor fee 6 Make access more difficult in wilderness/protected area
2 Reduce use of problem areas	1 Inform about problem areas and alternative areas 2 Discourage or prohibit use of problem areas 3 Limit number of visitors in problem areas 4 Encourage/require a stay limit in problem areas 5 Make access harder/easier to areas 6 Eliminate facilities/attractions in problem areas, improve facilities/ attractions in alternative areas 7 Encourage off-trail travel 8 Establish different skill/equipment requirements 9 Charge differential visitor fees
3 Modify location of use within problem areas	1 Discourage/prohibit camping/stock use 2 Encourage/permit camping/stock in certain areas 3 Locate facilities on durable sites 4 Concentrate use through facility design or info 5 Discourage/prohibit off-trail travel 6 Segregate different types of visitors
4 Modify timing of use	1 Encourage use outside peak use periods 2 Discourage/ban use when impact potential high 3 Fees in periods of high-use/high-impact potential
5 Modify type of use and visitor behaviour	1 Discourage/ban damaging practices/equipment 2 Encourage/require behaviour, skills, equipment 3 Teach a wilderness ethic 4 Encourage/require a party size and/or stock limit 5 Discourage/prohibit stock 6 Discourage/prohibit pets 7 Discourage/prohibit overnight use
6 Modify visitor expectations	1 Inform visitors about appropriate wilderness/protected area uses 2 Inform about potential conditions in wilderness/protected area
7 Increase resistance of the resource	1 Shield the site from impact 2 Strengthen the site
8 Maintain/ rehabilitate resource	1 Remove problems 2 Maintain/rehabilitate impacted locations

(Source: Cole et al., 1987)

Table 3.5 Examples of visitor impact management tools

VIM tools	Select examples
Target appropriate markets	Influence mix; attract specific types
Promotional tools	Agree where and when to promote a site; have alternatives
Educate and inform	Use tourism information centres and materials to educate before arrival on site, about expectations, behaviour, etc.
Interpret and motivate	Inform and interpret to give greater understanding about sensitivities
Direct visitors	Use signage to influence behaviour
Influence behaviour	Develop code, guidelines, directed at visitors, community, operators, etc.
Guides/stewards	Use on-site personnel to supervise, protect, inform, interpret positively
Involve community	Involve schools, groups, especially re maintenance and improvements
Involve community agencies	Involve agencies and individuals in developing code or guidelines for site and community

and individual businesses. One particular form of voluntary activity that has proliferated is guidelines or codes for visitors or operators.

One example in Britain is the Welsh Ceredigon Marine 'Heritage Coast', which was the first to have its boundary extended out to sea. It developed a Code of Conduct to encourage responsible use of the area (Figure 3.5). This is displayed on leaflets and interpretation boards and is included in the local tide tables.

The range of topic areas covered by the Welsh Code contrasts with a number of Canadian destinations that have tended to develop a *single*-focus code, such as for whale watching. An exception is on the west coast of Vancouver Island, where staff at Pacific Rim National Park Reserve collaborated with marine operators to develop an expanded range of voluntary guidelines (Wight, 2001) related to:

- shoreline wildlife viewing
- seabirds viewing
- pinnipeds viewing
- killer whales/orca viewing
- grey and humpback whale viewing
- Grice Bay wildlife viewing (a specific sensitive location).

The Pacific Rim guidelines covered not only wildlife viewing, but also getting into position; viewing; leaving the area; and even distance viewing and waiting.

Boats
• Operate with care and attention to safety of occupants and other sea users
Dolphins
• Maintain a steady speed and course or slow down gradually
• Don't chase, manoeuvre erratically, turn towards or attempt to touch or feed
Seals
• Don't interfere with seals or pups on beach
• Control dogs and keep away from seals
Birds
• When sailing, keep 100 m out from cliffs in breeding season (specified)
• Don't sail directly towards rafts of birds resting or feeding on the sea
• Avoid unnecessary noise close to cliffs
Fishing
• Don't discard tackle, take home for proper disposal
Jet skis
• Don't launch or operate in the area (heritage coast)
Divers
• Observe BSAC Code of Conduct
Beaches
• Take home all your litter
• Keep to dog bye-laws
• Replace shore rocks you move to keep alive the animals that live underneath

Figure 3.5 Welsh Code of Conduct covering diversity of topics

Education and interpretation

Visitor management tools are not only often neglected, but each one of them has a range of dimensions which it would be helpful to explore (Chapter 2). As only *one* example, interpretation is a sadly under-utilized management tool. Interpretation can and should achieve much more than simple transmission of educational information. In order to be used as a visitor management tool, interpretation has to affect visitors' behaviour and in order to do this, motivating them, through appeal to their emotions is very effective. Interpretation may have multiple objectives (Figure 3.6).

Learning	• What visitors learn/remember
	• This is commonest application of interpretation
Behavioural	• What visitors do
	• Helps focus on what you want visitors to do and how to use information given
Emotional	• Must occur first, to alter visitor behaviour or attitudes
	• Helps visitors remember the topic because of strong feelings created; helps feel surprise, anger, guilt, pride and other desired emotions

Figure 3.6 Interpretation objectives

It is the information/learning aspects of interpretation which have commonly had the greatest emphasis. However, in the context of resource management, behavioural objectives are most important, because they can help shape visitors' behaviour and thus lessen resource impact. Emotional objectives are also critical, because they motivate visitors to change their behaviour, and also help visitors to 'take away' important messages and values. In the context of the *independent visitor* to PAs who may not have access to commercial interpretive tours, it is important that there is adequate emphasis given to non-verbal interpretive messages. These may be *during* the visit (e.g. in interpretive displays or literature) or even *before* the visit (e.g. in tourism literature or on Internet websites).

Marketing as a demand management tool

One challenge for famous protected areas and ecotourism destinations is the impact of third-party media on tourism demand. The Gwaii Haanas research found that the visitors' image of the destination was being shaped through a number of outside sources: the provincial tourism agency, travel media, news media and conservation groups. The focus has been on traditional icons, particularly the World Heritage Site SGaang Gwaii (with an overused image of mortuary poles along the beach). This can create visitor expectations of seeing totem poles everywhere. Current research is looking at this more closely, to help stakeholders to work more closely with the media and tourism industry partners to shift the focus away from the traditional icons. Within the context of this new thinking, the brand for The Islands and Gwaii Haanas is being considered. The images for travellers need not be grand or dominating (like the Eiffel Tower or the Pyramids); they may be windmills, rickshaws, palm trees or penguins (Figure 3.7).

Old marketing view		New marketing view
The image of Gwaii Haanas and the Islands must focus around wilderness and the old Haida villages and poles	$\Rightarrow$	The Islands have many special characteristics that give a competitive advantage and that can be used as images

Figure 3.7 Shift in views about marketing Gwaii Haanas

Command and control approaches

A recent study has examined best practices in collaborations between PA managers' practices and those of eco-adventure operators, in terms of use of PAs and maintaining natural heritage integrity (Pam Wight & Associates, 2001). The objective was to generate a wide range of good collaborative practices for the tourism industry and for managers to choose from, since there has often been friction between these groups and a lack of understanding of other perspectives. It examines successful practices by both the parks agencies and also the tourism operators, in terms of planning, policymaking, relationship building, communications, administration, supporting ecological integrity, marketing and monitoring. It also presents suggestions for improvement.

It was found that the key *challenges* (those areas with the fewest successful collaborations and with the most issues) were in planning and particularly policy making. This is where rules, regulations, licensing and permitting procedures, quotas and standards tend to be imposed. These are usually command and control mechanisms. One typical suggestion for the future by one tourism operator was: 'protected area managers should change the paradigm from "us and them" to "we are partners in managing this resources and its visitors".' This reflects operator perspectives that collaboration is a better approach. The area where most *exemplary* practices were generated was in the stewardship of individual tourism businesses (including company goals to support sustainability; design and delivery of programmes, packages or facilities; resource protection and sustainability; and contributions to local communities). It is interesting to note that these are areas where operators have direct control. One of the most important *opportunity* areas of practice is communications – needed for improved relationships, information transfer, trust building and collaboration.

New technologies to manage the resource and human use

It is interesting to note that innovative management tools are emerging from new technologies. These may assist in managing both the visitors and the resource, with the combined effect of managing impact.

An area which is often *not* well addressed relates to visitor transportation, movement and management. It is in this area that many of sustainable tourism's greatest challenges and criticisms occur. This may be because the challenges are larger than the individual business or destination scale. Recently, there have been some exiting new developments in the field of software tools for management. One such is Archaeolink Interpretive Park in Scotland (Wight, 1998b).

Archaeolink is a 40-acre prehistory park in Scotland. It is a tourist attraction and educational venue for a range of visitors. It has an 'underground' interpretive centre in a huge sod mound, as well as an outdoor component, with Pictish farmstead, a Roman marching camp and hill fort. Indoor elements include interactive computer educational tools.

The computer software 'ArchaeoQuest' was tailor made for the site and has two elements: *ArchaeoBrowse* and *ArchaeoQuest*. The Browse feature allows visitors to look at all the sites in the region. Icons on the map represent various types and periods of archaeological site (e.g. stone circles, hill forts, the Picts or symbol stones). One can obtain further information about any site, via images, detailed information, a video display or a map. This allows visitors to determine which types of site are most interesting.

Quest is intended to assist the tourist in visiting the sites of interest to them. It allows the visitor to enter details and to respond to visitor interests as well as to site conditions. The categories of visitor question include:

- *Party size* – 1; 2; 3–4; 5–12; 13–20; over 20.
- *Level of fitness* – low, average, high.
- *Mode of transportation* – foot, bike, car, coach, public transportation.
- *Time available* – 1 hour, <3 hours, <6 hours, 1 day, more than a day.
- *Level of archaeological knowledge* – low, average, high.
- *Eventual destination today* – a series of regional options is presented for selection on the map.
- *Topics of interest* – a menu of choices is presented. Choices are the same as in Browse.

Once visitors answer these questions, the on-screen map shows an individualized proposed route. Part of the analysis includes site constraints (e.g. if there is *not* adequate parking for certain sizes of party, sites which would match in every other way are eliminated from the route selection). This allows the program to manage visitor parties, vehicles and resource constraints. It provides education, entertainment, information, improved visitors satisfaction and resource management functions.

This software has potential to be further modified to manage destinations at many scales. Whatever the destination, it would be possible to select which sites or attractions would feature on a software program, for commercial and/or environmental management or other purposes. This could have tremendous application for the most popular parks and PAs and computer terminals could be in multiple locations both inside and *outside* the PA, so as to assist in rerouting visitors and protecting the resource. It could also have application in historic sites and urban locations.

Spheres of influence as a tool in management

Protected areas may be impacted by many forces, including those which originate outside the PA. In order to solve problems that may affect the PA, managers need to understand the topics which are under the direct or indirect management control and those which are not, as well as those which may be subject to their influence rather than direct control. This understanding helps select the most relevant management tools under varying circumstances. Figure 3.8 shows the spheres of influence of protected area managers.

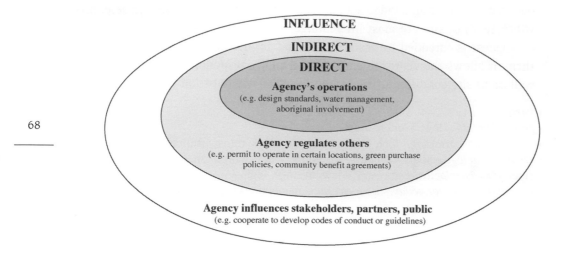

INFLUENCE

INDIRECT

DIRECT

Agency's operations
(e.g. design standards, water management,
aboriginal involvement)

Agency regulates others
(e.g. permit to operate in certain locations, green purchase
policies, community benefit agreements)

Agency influences stakeholders, partners, public
(e.g. cooperate to develop codes of conduct or guidelines)

Figure 3.8 Protected area manager's spheres of influence of tourism activities

The spheres of influence can be described as follows (and can apply in similar ways to protected area managers, destination managers, ecotourism operators, etc.):

1   *Direct*: At the core are the agency's own operations. It can have a *direct affect* on such operations and ensure there is minimal negative impact (e.g. by adhering to certain minimum standards for visitor centre or trail construction, by adhering to design or planning standards, by having certain hiring or operational policies).
2   *Indirect*: The agency may also have an *indirect impact* on the activities of others (e.g. it may require or prohibit private sector tourism operators from doing certain activities; or it may insist its partners or collaborators have certain operational procedures, such as green purchase policies).
3   *Influencing*: The agency may have no control over others, but may be able to *influence* them – whether individuals, agencies, communities, operators, public (e.g. it may be able to make constructive suggestions at interagency meetings, lead by example in hiring practices or inform and advocate in public forums).

It is likely that influencing has been given insufficient effort and attention as a management tool. For example, in areas outside parks, resource managers have no control, yet these may be important as buffer zones or for extending PA values and objectives. It may be that focusing on influence though, say, through collaborative and voluntary initiatives makes most sense to effect positive change.

Voluntary initiatives are becoming very common globally. These may relate to the operations of private sector tourism operators, to visitor codes or to all-embracing destination codes. They may be an initiative of a specific group or of a destination such as a protected area. Protected areas managers have the opportunity to work with stakeholders or potential partners, on issues of relevance to them all. Although the protected area manager may not *stipulate* actions, they may suggest, collaborate and contribute to initiatives. If this is done with an understanding of other stakeholders' perspectives, there may be successful outcomes.

For example, as described previously, Pacific Rim National Park Reserve managers had little control over commercial tourism operators, because the area is not a gazetted park. Staff could only provide other commercial tourism operators with recommendations and guidelines. However, in order to solve or prevent potential problems, they took a collaborative approach with operators in developing guidelines and codes. The industry agreed, because they had ownership in the outputs (Wight, 2001). Not only that, but respect has been established between agency staff and operators, as well as better communications and learning experiences. This reflects an agency move towards more adaptive and collaborative management, where cycles of learning and action are taking place and stakeholders decide together on actions.

It is particularly important for a protected area agency and individual staff to develop exceptional communication skills, to build good relationships and to influence or persuade other stakeholders to cooperate for the benefit of the resource as well as their own interests.

Conclusion

A number of interrelated components are involved in sustainable development – economic, social, political, cultural and ecological. All these dimensions need to be considered in order to contribute effectively to sustainable tourism. A new generation of tourism plans is evolving to help destinations realize more of tourism's benefits while avoiding its range of potential pitfalls.

In PAs there have tended to be many distinct and often different points of view, but those with weight have tended to be the resource manager. Other perspectives are often missing – those of local communities/cultures, tourism operators and visitors. Tourism in destination areas must be able to meet the needs of industry, the local community, the tourism resource and the visitor. The voice of stakeholders needs to be built into planning and management.

Most tourism destinations are conscious of the need not only to *develop*, but also to *manage* for sustainable tourism. This presents a special challenge in PAs, particularly those where the ecological integrity of the destination may be of prime consideration. A common response to visitor or resource problems in PAs has tended to be 'command and control' oriented (a classic example being the call for 'determining the carrying capacity', an impractical approach). Reasons for this 'hard' approach may possibly be because it is simpler, particularly in times when managers themselves are struggling with a lack of resources, ranging from staff, to time, to funding. However, it has been shown to be the area of greatest tension between PA managers and eco-adventure operators.

PAs have given less consideration to 'softer' management approaches, yet there are many under-utilized management strategies and tactics. For example, visitor impact management tools have tremendous potential, including voluntary and collaborative approaches, as demonstrated in Pacific Rim NP Reserve, or Wales' Marine Heritage Coast. These require good cooperation and communication between resource managers and commercial operations and mutual understanding of perspectives.

Other useful management approaches focus on integrating the management of demand, visitors, impacts and the resource. In particular, educational approaches have excellent potential for influencing visitors, which is important since visitors themselves may be an active partner in accomplishing sustainable tourism. Much will depend on how well they are reached and 'touched', whether by natural area managers or by tour operators. Interpretation is a management tool which has tended to focus on information transfer, but has great potential to motivate and so to modify behaviour and attitudes. The benefits of a comprehensive visitor management approach include the ability to influence visitors *before*, *during* and *after* their visit.

In addition to the large range of strategies and tactics available for PA management, there are a number of specific tools that are emerging to assist in tourism management. For example, some software programs include great benefits to fulfil a number of PA management objectives: resource protection; visitor behaviour management; and visitor enjoyment and satisfaction, as illustrated at Archaeolink in Scotland.

The integrated approach to tourism *planning* aims to develop effective, sustainable tourism plans that reflect the shared perspectives of the stakeholders in the tourism system, the full range of potential tourism impacts and the realities of the marketplace. The integrated approach to tourism *management* uses the full range of command and control, incentive, educational and voluntary approaches and selects appropriate strategies and tactics. It aims to bring all parties on side by engaging or collaborating with visitors and commercial operators and can actively contribute to resource protection.

A main message is that there are many tools in the PA manager's toolbag. The challenge is to move from the status quo, to integrate other stakeholder perspectives and to apply those tactics and tools collaboratively, in a manner appropriate to the place, the community and the visitor.

Questions

1 Why is the integrated planning approach required in managing ecotourism destinations?
2 Discuss the main factors that influence ecotourism planning in the two national parks given as examples from Canada.
3 Choose one site from the case studies in this volume and apply the stakeholders' analysis model.
4 Select one case study from the book and design a strategy for managing the protected areas.

References

Bianchi, R. (1994) 'Tourism development and resort dynamics: an alternative approach'. In Cooper, C. and Lockwood, A. (eds) *Progress in Tourism and Hospitality Management*, Vol. 5. Chichester John Wiley & Sons.

Buckley, R. and Pannell, J. (1990) 'Environmental impacts of tourism and recreation in national parks and conservation reserves', *Journal of Tourism Studies*, 1 (1), 24–32.

Cole, D.N., Petersen, M.E. and Lucas, R.C. (1987) Managing wilderness recreation use: common problems and potential solutions. Gen. Tech. Rep. INT-230, USDA Forest Service, Ogden, UT.

Consulting and Audit Canada (1995) *What Tourism Managers Need to Know*. Spain: World Tourism Organization.

Dowling, R.K. (1993) 'Tourism planning, people and the environment in Western Australia', *Journal of Travel Research*, 31 (4), 52–8.

Getz, D. (1987) Tourism planning and research: traditions, models, and futures. In Proceedings of the Australian Travel Research Workshop, hosted by the Western Australia Tourism Commission, 5–6 November, Bunbury, Western Australia.

Hall, C.M. and McArthur, S. (1998) *Integrated Heritage Management: Principles and Practice*. London: The Stationery Office.

Hinch, T. and Butler, R. (1996) 'Indigenous tourism: a common ground for discussion'. In Butler, R. and Hinch, T. (eds) *Tourism and Indigenous Peoples*. London: International Thomson Business Press.

International Working Group on Indicators of Sustainable Tourism (1993) Indicators for the Sustainable Management of Tourism. For the Environment Committee of the World Tourism Organization, Industry, Science and Technology Canada, and International Institute for Sustainable Development: Winnipeg. February.

Manidis Roberts (1997) Developing a tourism optimisation management model (TOMM). Final Report, South Australian Tourism Commission, Adelaide.

Manning, R. (1979) 'Strategies for managing recreational use of national parks', *Parks*, 4, 13–15.

Mathieson, A., and Wall, G. (1982) *Tourism: Economic, Physical, and Social Impacts*. London: Longman.

McCool, S.F. (1991) Limits of acceptable change: a strategy for managing the effects of nature-dependent tourism development. Paper presented at Tourism and the Land: Building a Common Future conference, 1–3 December, Whistler, BC.

McIntosh, R., Goeldner, C. and Ritchie, J.R.B. (1995) *Tourism: Principles, Practices, Philosophies*. Toronto: John Wiley & Sons.

McNeely, Jeffrey A. and Thorsell, James W. (1989) 'Jungles, mountains, and islands: how tourism can help conserve the natural heritage', *World Leisure and Recreation*, 31 (4), 29–39.

McVetty, D. (1997) Segmenting Heritage Tourism Party-Visits on Dunedin's Otago Peninsula: A Strategic Approach. Masters's thesis, University of Otago, Dunedin, New Zealand.

McVetty, D. and Wight, P. (1998) Integrated planning to optimise the outcomes of tourism development: the case of Aulavik National Park and Banks Island, NWT. Presentation to Revving the Engines . . . Making Profitable Destinations, TTRA Canada Conference, 4–6 October, Toronto.

Pam Wight & Associates (1998a) 'Visitor market analysis for Aulavik National Park', *Canadian Heritage*, March.

Pam Wight & Associates (1998b) *Saskatchewan Bird Trail, Part 2: Community Planning Guide*. Regina: Saskatchewan Wetland Conservation Corporation.

Pam Wight & Associates (1999) Market analysis for Gwaii Haanas National Park Reserve/Haida Heritage Site. Prepared for the Archipelago Management Board, March.

Pam Wight & Associates (2001) *Best Practices in Natural Heritage Collaborations: Parks and Outdoor Tourism Operators*. Ottawa: Canadian Tourism Commission.

Tourism Industry Association of Canada (TIAC) (1992) *Code of Ethics and Guidelines for Sustainable Tourism*. Ottawa: TIAC and National Round Table on Environment and the Economy.

Wight, P.A. (1994) 'Limits of acceptable change: a recreational tourism tool for cumulative effects assessment'. In Kennedy, A.J. (ed.) *Cumulative Effects in Canada: from Concept to Practice*. Fifteenth Symposium held by the Alberta Society of Professional Biologists, April 13–14. Calgary, Alberta, 159–78.

Wight, P.A. (1996) Planning for Success in Sustainable Tourism. Presentation to 'Plan for Success' Canadian Institute of Planners National Conference, Saskatoon, Saskatchewan, 2–5 June.

Wight, P.A. (1998a) 'Tools for sustainability analysis in planning and managing tourism and recreation in the destination'. In Hall, C. Michael and Lew Alan A. (eds) *Sustainable Tourism: A Geographical Perspective*. Harlow: Addison, Wesley Longman.

Wight, P.A. (1998b) Innovative visitor management and movement tools: economic, environmental and marketing benefits. Presented to Moving the Economy, an International Sustainable Transportation Conference organized by Transportation Options, 9–12 July, The Green Tourism Association and City of Toronto.

Wight, P. (1999a) Planning for Resource Protection and Tourism Management in Protected Areas: A Practical Perspective. Presentation to University of Waterloo Geography/Recreation course; subsequently published in Wall, G. (ed.) (2003) *Tourism: People, Places and Products*, Department of Geography occasional paper 19.

Wight, P. (1999b) Characterizing Sustainable Tourism: Perspectives, Definitions, and Beyond, for Tourism in Natural Areas. Invited presentation to NAFTA Dialogue on Sustainable Tourism in Natural Areas in North America, Commission on Environmental Cooperation, Playa del Carmen, Mexico, 27–28 May.

Wight, P. (2001) Integration of biodiversity and tourism: Canada case study. Invited paper presented at the International Biodiversity Protection and Tourism Workshop, 29–31 Mar, UNEP/UNDP/BPSP/GEF, Mexico City.

World Commission on Environment and Development (1987) *Our Common Future*. WCED. New York: Oxford University Press.

4 Indicators and Risk Management for Ecotourism Destinations

Edward W. (Ted) Manning

The four main objectives of this chapter are to:

- Discuss the risks to ecotourism destinations
- Evaluate how indicators can be used to help define risks and responses
- Clarify how participatory procedures can aid in the mobilization of key stakeholders for ecotourism destinations in their planning and management
- Illustrate some of the solutions which can be used to minimize negative effects and capture positive ones from ecotourism

Introduction

Ecotourism depends on the sustainable use of the world's most ecologically and culturally fragile destinations (see Chapter 1). Without good information regarding the assets and attributes of these destinations, those who would sustain and protect the destinations are, in effect, unarmed. How can the planners and managers of tourism and of impacted destinations obtain the information that they require to build and maintain sustainable forms of tourism?

Beginning in 1992 the World Tourism Organization (WTO) has been the catalyst for work to improve the information for managers of tourism destinations from those catering to mass tourism to those serving limited numbers in remote ecosystems and isolated villages. The stimulus for this initiative was the growing interest worldwide in sustainable development and an appreciation that tourism was often unsustainable and damaging to the resource base on which it depends. While tourism was identified at the Rio conference in Agenda 21 (United Nations, 1992), as a potential response to resource depletion in traditional resource sectors and as a means to diversify human activity in mountain environments, little attention was given to the role of the tourism industry itself – as a catalyst for both positive and negative changes in ecological and cultural environments.

Tourism is a unique industry, inextricably linked to the resources it uses and sensitive to any disruptions or changes. Those who devise and deliver tourism experiences need an early warning system of unacceptable changes and undesired impacts. Yet tourism managers, particularly in destinations where there is little organization or formal management (e.g. remote communities, wilderness areas) have little ability to anticipate problems and take preventive action. These types of destination are the focus for what is advertised as ecotourism – tourism which, in effect, targets the unique and fragile.

Whether or not the actual tourism experience is managed in a way that is sensitive to the vulnerabilities of the destination the very act of tourism carries with it risks both to the industry and to its targets. The tourism industry is very volatile; tourists can suddenly disappear, reacting to perceived problems of damage to key tourist assets, risks to their person or economic chaos. Civil unrest can cause immediate cancellations. The European tour company that had booked the entire property for the next two weeks called to cancel. A simple television documentary on clear-cutting of timber in one valley of western Canada in 1994 caused hundreds of calls from tour operators and tourists in Germany inquiring whether there were any trees or wildlife left to see. In 1998 publicity regarding hostilities towards tourists in the Chiapas area in eastern Mexico caused a downturn in rural and village tourism throughout the country, even in the peaceful hills of Nayarit thousands of kilometres away. The tourism industry is volatile and managers need early warning signals if they are to be able to respond effectively to changes that place their industry or its destinations at risk. One practical answer lies in the use of indicators.

As such, the main objectives of this chapter are addressed within the context of the WTO initiative to develop indicators of sustainability for tourism destinations and in case examples including those from studies done in Peninsula Valdes Argentina (Manning and Manning, 1995) Mexcaltitan, Mexico and Kukljica, Croatia (Manning et al., 2001) which illustrate the use of indicators as a catalyst for planning ecologically and culturally fragile destinations. It should be noted that ecotourism employed as a noun to describe a form of tourism product and ecotourism used as an adjective to define a destination are different. This chapter examines how the effects on ecotourism destinations (irrespective of what form of tourism they actually get) can be anticipated and, it is to be hoped, controlled.

Indicators for ecotourism destinations

The WTO initiative began as a response to known incidents of degradation to valuable attributes of tourism destinations (World Tourism Organization, 1996; Manning, 1999b). While many were recipients of mass tourism (beach degradation in the Costa del Sol, shore zone contamination in the Great Lakes, damage to built heritage sites in Cambodia, etc.) many of the incidents involved more localized impacts on ecosystems caused by a less concentrated form of tourism. Rangers were reporting erosion of trails in national parks, reef ecosystems from Queensland to Malaysia to Cozumel were showing damage from divers and snorkelling and reports were being received of changes due to tourism impact from the Galapagos and from the mountain reserves of the Monarca butterfly sanctuary. Clearly, a means of anticipating and preventing unacceptable impacts was required. Where ecological thresholds or fragile relic cultures are involved, the need for good means to document changes to key attributes becomes even more critical.

Ecotourism destinations at risk

Each destination is unique. At the same time, the stresses tourism brings to sites are also unique, as different types of visitor create different impacts. The impacts are related not only to numbers, but also to the means of access, the size of groups, the behaviour of the tourists, the levels of control and management of a site and to the specific sensitivities of the assets of the site to the types of activity (Manning, 1999a). Twenty photographers paddling quietly through the Danube Delta in search of rare birds have a significantly different impact from 20 drunken celebrants in five high-powered rubber boats roaring through the backwater habitats. The managers of ecologically and culturally valuable sites need a means to define key risks, to measure changes in the attributes at risk and therefore to react before a site is damaged or even destroyed.

The risks to ecotourism destinations include the following:

- *Heavy use levels*, particularly during the periods where the ecosystem may be most fragile (e.g. breeding season for delicate species) or the cultural experience may be most vulnerable (local festival, tribal ceremony).
- *Consumptive use* which damages the destination (collection of plant or animal life, hunting, diversion of water).
- *Alterations* to the destination due to other uses (clear-cutting of forests, building of access roads, construction of dams, weirs).
- *Environmental impact* from other uses (e.g. pollution of streams from agriculture, acid rain on lakes, noise from nearby highways).
- *Toxic tourism* – damage to sites and assets from the activities of insensitive tourists who

may damage wildlife, interfere in local cultures or contaminate sites with their own waste.

Those who wish to protect the assets of ecotourism destinations require tools to respond to these risks, ideally providing an early warning system so that action can be taken in time.

Indicators in the context of ecotourism

The development of indicators for impacted or potentially impacted destinations has particular cogence for those destinations suitable for the range of experiences commonly advertised as ecotourism. Both the attributes of the destination and the sensitivities of tourists to changes and deterioration in these attributes are likely to be more consequential than in other sites. A tourist visits Peninsula Valdes Argentina (see Manning and Manning, 1995) to see the southern right whale and the elephant seal colonies. If pollution, or overexploitation (including excessive chasing by excursion boats) diminishes the numbers or drives them away (there is some evidence that right whale breeding pairs have abandoned the gulf for the more protected waters on the northern side of the peninsula where there is no whale watching) the ecosystem and the ecotourism it can support is in peril. The management of risk to the destination and to the experiences it supports are therefore central to the overall protection of ecotourism destinations. The indicators are designed to help provide the information which will allow better management decisions to be taken.

Core indicators and ecosystem-specific indicators

The WTO process was designed to help tourism managers and managers of protected sites identify what information was key to their decisions and would help them reduce the risks to their enterprise and to the communities and environments they exploit (WTO, 1996). The WTO approach has been to help direct deliberations on indicators identification and selection in the following ways:

1 *Core indicators*: WTO has identified a small core indicators set which is likely to be useful in almost any situation; these indicators (Table 4.1) have been found to be useful in virtually all destinations in which they have been evaluated and constitute a minimal list that is fundamental to management and planning of destinations. They are not unique to ecotourism or to particular features of destinations. The indicators that relate to levels of protection, critical habitats, tourist densities and to the management of waste are particularly pertinent to *most* ecotourism sites.

2 *Ecosystem-specific indicators*: The core indicators are supplemented with additional indicators that have been found to be useful in particular ecosystems or types of destination, responding to the issues and impacts that are generally found in the type of

Table 4.1 Core indicators of sustainable tourism

Indicator	Specific measures
Site protection	Category of site protection according to IUCN** index
Stress	Tourist numbers visiting site (per annum/peak month)
Use intensity	Intensity of use – peak period (persons/hectare)
Social impact	Ratio of tourists to locals (peak period)
Development control	Existence of environmental review procedure or formal controls over development of site and use densities
Waste management	Percentage of sewage from site receiving treatment (additional indicators may include structural limits of other infrastructural capacity on site – e.g. water supply, garbage)
Planning process	Existence of organized regional plan for tourist destination region (including tourism component)
Critical ecosystems	Number of rare/endangered species
Consumer satisfaction	Level of satisfaction by visitors (questionnaire based)
Local satisfaction	Level of satisfaction by locals (questionnaire based)
Composite indices	
Carrying capacity	*Composite early warning measure of key factors affecting the ability of the site to support different levels of tourism
Site stress	*Composite measure of levels of impact on the site – its natural and cultural attributes due to tourism and other sector cumulative stresses
Attractivity	*Qualitative measure of those site attributes which make it attractive to tourism and which can change over time

* The composite indices are largely composed of site-specific variables. Consequently, the identification and evaluation of the indicators that comprise these indices require on-site direction from an appropriately trained and experienced observer. In future, based on the experiences in designing composite indicators for specific sites, it may be possible to derive these indices on a more systematic basis. In practice, these have proved unique to each site and to the mix of assets and risks present.
** International Union for the Conservation of Nature and Natural Resources.

destination. The 'ecosystem-specific' indicators are a list that has evolved in application – and specific sets have been compiled for each of:
• small islands (water supply, ratio of locals to visitors, capture of foreign exchange)
• beach destinations (e.g. erosion, sea or lake water quality, use densities)
• mountains (erosion, biodiversity, percentages of each ecosystem with different levels of protection, costs of rehabilitation of degraded sites)
• small communities and their cultural assets (social stress levels, measures of cultural integrity, levels of employment in tourism)
• fragile ecosystems (retention of species diversity, area degraded, measures of health of key indicator species, levels of use – often in specific seasons)
• built cultural sites (costs of repair)
• managed game parks (loss of species, poaching levels).
An explanation of these indicator sets and their application can be found in the manual

What Tourism Managers Need to Know (WTO, 1996). It should be noted that all these types of ecosystem or attraction are the focus for ecotourism – the types of asset targeted by those seeking ecotourism experiences.

3 *Risk scan*: The third, and possibly most important step is to ensure that a scanning process is carried out to identify the risks not necessarily covered by the aforementioned indicator sets. This process will often produce further indicators critical to the management of the particular site/destination and the unique assets or sensitivities that are found there. A participatory process, involving a range of stakeholders – local residents, local institutions, tourists and tourism industry representatives as well as planners, other key industries and a range of local and outside experts – has proved most effective in this procedure (Manning and Dougherty, 2000; Manning et al., 2001). In applications to impacted destinations, local knowledge is often critical in the identification of key assets and in the clarification of the dependencies related to them. Who is really employed in taking tours through the Bentota river mangrove (see Manning et al., 2000)? What are the real impacts of the motorcycle jungle tours at Tulum Mexico on habitat, local villages near the route, vegetation on the path?

What is a good indicator?

The problem with information is that it often overwhelms. With regard to the social, economic and environmental effects of the activities for which they are responsible, managers of impacted destinations typically have either no information on the key assets and their use or state or, conversely, too much, based on large studies that may have great detail on specific species or impacts. Indicators are those sets of information chosen because they are meaningful to real planning and management decisions. The indicators must also be supported in a way which gets the information to those who can affect the future of an ecotourism destination, in a useful form, when it is most needed. A good indicator is above all relevant. It must also be understandable, scientifically supportable and available when needed to make a difference to the decisions that tourism managers must make.

Participatory indicator development

The approach which the WTO international taskforce has developed for definition of indicators is based on a participatory process, directly involving the destination and the local community. The methodology features a participatory workshop process which, in itself, can produce benefits for the destination and for the participants. One of the tenets is that tourism cannot be planned or effectively managed outside the context of the communities and economic and ecological systems within which it is located; you cannot plan *tourism*, only *destinations*. The process is designed to be inclusive and access and use all the information available relating to the values, expectations and needs of stakeholders – including the tourists. Key steps are the following.

Identifying key stakeholders

The research phase involves collection of key information on the site, tourism conditions, stakeholders, past concerns and studies which can be used to support the definition and implementation of indicators. Contact is made with key local experts at the destination who may act as resources for the participatory process. It is also essential to clarify who are the current and potential users of the destination and the nature of their interests.

Defining the destination

In this stage, the destination's boundaries are clarified. This can be a complex step where the desire is to encompass the limits of habitats, tourism activity, jurisdictional boundaries and the units for which data may be available. While for island destinations like Cozumel, Mexico (Manning et al., 1999), or Ugljan-Pasman, Croatia (Manning et al., 2001), boundaries may be clear (although much tourism also involves visits to adjacent waters and nearby shores) in other cases, the clear definition of boundaries can be more problematic (see Manning et al., 2000, regarding Beruwala, Sri Lanka, or Manning and Clifford, 1999, with regard to Lake Balaton). Often data is difficult to obtain for the boundaries which encompass the destination. Where the destination is a park or heritage area, often there are good data for the managed park area but little for the periphery where much of the tourist activity takes place. In the Prince Edward Island case (Clifford and Dougherty, 1994), most tourism development occurred in unorganized areas adjacent to the national park which was the main attraction. There may be different destinations at different scales: the reef system is a distinct ecotourism destination within the larger destination of Cozumel. Precise definition of ecological boundaries may be the subject of controversy, particularly where the range of species has not been scientifically determined.

Identifying the destination's assets

What are the priority tourist use areas and current/potential attractions? Is the entire draw dependent on a single waterfall, picturesque villages or on access to viewing sites with rare fauna or flora? Assets are the key reasons why tourists visit a destination and they deserve, therefore, particular attention, both in indicator development and in subsequent planning and protection initiatives. Often such an asset must be separately defined and site specific indicators developed (e.g. Chankanaab reserve on Cozumel or the mangroves on the Bentota river in Sri Lanka). Assets may be seasonal (the butterflies are in the Monarca reserves in the Sierra Madre only in the winter months, the piping plover breeds in the dunes of Prince Edward Island National Park in May and June).

Gaining participation

Any approach that does not involve the full range of those with interest in the destination (not just its tourism) will miss key information and may create future problems. Those who know the destination most intimately tend to be those who live within or in close proximity to the destination or who are current users. As these stakeholders often have clear insights into which indicators are practical, their support and participation in providing information to assist in key issues identification and indicators selection is invaluable. In particular, local authorities, planners and the tourism industry are important. In the studies done at Peninsula Valdes, Argentina, and Prince Edward Island, Canada, local conservation officials and non-governmental organizations were critical sources of information on both the assets and their fragility. Because local communities have their own perspectives on their own key values and on current or anticipated impacts, their active participation has also been sought – both from those who are involved directly in tourism and those concerned more broadly with the community or region or with the protection of the environmental or cultural assets.

Identifying key values

All stakeholders will have their own views on which assets are important and why. Their participation is essential to determine which assets are critical to the needs of both tourists and local residents. How sensitive are these to changing demands by the tourism industry and to the impacts of other changes which can alter their attractiveness to tourists? Will the tourist still come if the water is dirty, the crocodiles no longer visible or the market closed? Furthermore, how sensitive are the values of local residents to the changes that tourism can bring? How crowded can the church or mosque get before the congregation closes its doors to tourists? It is often difficult to identify a commonality of values, as different groups, even in the smallest communities, may hold different views or be dependent on different aspects of the resources of the region. Proponents of tourism may speak of consulting the community – in reality there can be many different communities with different value sets, varying relationships to the site and different concerns regarding its use. Those who stand to gain as outfitters, guides or guesthouse managers may react differently from those who see no role for them in tourism and perceive the increased activity as adversely affecting their own activities. Some values may be negotiable (e.g. numbers, timing, price for access) while some may not be subject to negotiation (access to a sacred site or critical habitat).

Clarifying thresholds and system sensitivity

Risk may depend on levels of impact. Integral to the concept of sustainability is a recognition of the potential limits to use (or carrying capacity) of a destination (Manning, 1999a). Information documenting the biophysical and social dimensions of sustainability for the destination is useful. Studies may already exist which provide a scientific basis for species vulnerability, or document levels of stress. In some cases there are already known limits (e.g. water availability on an island like Cozumel) or standards (legislated or indicative) which can serve as benchmarks and can assist in identifying thresholds beyond which tourism may no longer be considered sustainable at that particular destination. For Peninsula Valdes, a past inventory of whales may serve as a baseline, while negotiated limits on numbers of vessels and distances they will maintain from whales are indicative benchmarks that can be used. The indicators initiative may stimulate an initial survey that can help to at least identify these sensitivities and, at a later date, can lead to the establishment of standards (e.g. no more than ten whale-watching boats in the bay at a time) or legislated/regulatory limits (current (2002) limits were maximum 74 tourists a day walking Canada's West Coast Trail or 52 per day on New Zealand's Milford Track).

Measuring current tourism

Documentation of current use and stresses may not be simple, particularly for new destinations where there has been no planning or access control. Who comes, when, where and for what purpose? What is the typical experience? What are the trends in tourism densities and concentrations? Can we identify different stakeholders among the tourist community with different interests and/or sensitivities (e.g. whitewater rafters vs photographers or birdwatchers vs users of off-road vehicles). Each may have very different needs and sensitivities. Most visitors to the Danube Delta travel quietly in small boats – with rowboat access to the most fragile sites – the objective is to see the most waterfowl possible. Recent addition of fast motorized rubber boats has opened many back canals to a new form of visitor – whose impact on wildlife is significantly greater and may deter the birdwatchers. All tourism is not equal.

Identifying management

Who has the mandate to deal with tourism issues and with the planning and management of the destination? For the islands of Ugljan and Pasman, Croatia, despite their small size and function as a single destination, jurisdiction is split between five municipalities and broad planning authority rests at the county level. In Prince Edward Island, Canada, the national park was found to have a good management plan for the seashore, but little influence over the park periphery which was in private hands and in a region without a strong local municipal or regional planning capacity (Clifford and Dougherty, 1994). In Beruwala, Sri Lanka, there was no organized planning agency and only a loose relationship to the municipality bordering the heavily used destination (Manning et al., 2000). One of the effects of participation by many different stakeholders in the indicators' development process has been the clarification of need for some coordinating body that can deal with multi-sector issues at the level of the overall destination. The measurement of level of control and management for the site can itself be a key indicator relative to the ability to manage impacts on the destination.

Identifying issues

The core of the indicator process is a participatory workshop, with local and visiting experts seeking agreement on the principal social, economic, cultural and ecological risks to the destination and to the tourism which it supports. Discussion typically focuses on the values and expectations that both tourists and local residents hold concerning the destination. With this knowledge, it then becomes possible to identify and prioritize the risks to tourism and to the other values of stakeholders associated with trends and proposals that may impact the destination. These risks may be either within the management purview of the tourism industry (e.g. control of pollution of the ecosystem from the tourists themselves) or beyond its ability to affect (e.g. climate change, major changes in accessibility due to new highways). A key issue in Cozumel was cruise ship concentration – most arrived on Tuesdays (second day out from Miami, Houston, Tampa, New Orleans) providing significant stress on infrastructure and heavy concentrations of snorkelling on the fragile Paraiso reef (Manning et al., 1999). This became an important focus for risk/indicator development reflecting the levels of visitation on peak days and therefore level of stress on local resources.

For indicator development, an initial assessment is sometimes done in advance by experts to form the basis for a focused discussion. A practical issue for many non-specialist participants may be their difficulty in understanding scientific information. In the small community applications done to date, care has been taken to seed some experts into each small group to provide support in understanding such information. Similarly, local expertise is also dispersed among groups to ensure local context and knowledge is respected.

Matching risks to indicators

Once there is agreement on what the key risks are (and which are priorities) a further participatory procedure (usually in small, heterogeneous groups) is used to define a longlist of possible indicators that might be of use in understanding the issues/risks and in helping to manage them. What are the pieces of information needed to allow managers at the destination level and at the site-specific level to understand the changes that may affect the key assets and the industry as a whole? In the Ugljan-Pasman case, three working groups addressed different issue areas which related to a range of risks and opportunities defined for the destination. The mix of expertise, ranging from local officials and politicians, industry participants, academics, consultants with studies in the region, national-level officials, experts from many countries and specialists brought a range of perspectives that led to a good dialogue reflecting many complementary areas of knowledge. The longlist was intended to be as complete as possible – defining what would be an ideal response to all the important risks. At this stage, no potential indicator is eliminated – even those which may be very difficult to collect (e.g. breeding success for whales, percentage of tourists who see key species, expenditure per tourist to visit the site, level of resentment by locals related to tourism activity).

Selection of priority indicators

The identification of priority indicators for the destination is done in small groups charged with assessing each candidate indicator. A review template is typically used to assist the working groups to assess each potential indicator relative to five criteria: relevance, feasibility, credibility, clarity and comparability (i.e. potential to be used for comparison over time and between destinations). Participants can also consider both the long-term and short-term utility of the indicators and urgency of their implementation. Ultimately, a priorization is done using a star rating system (one to five) to assign priorities to the indicators, based on these and other considerations related to the key issues of the site. A central consideration is the practicality of the indicators; facilitators ask 'Who will use it and for what purpose?'

The selection and evaluation of the indicators is undertaken according to the following criteria:

- *Relevance* of the indicator to local decision-making strategies and goals, including key regional trends – does the indicator respond to the key risks and issues and provide information which will aid in their management? (If it is not relevant, stop here.)
- *Feasibility* of obtaining and analyzing the needed information – how can the information be obtained? Is it already available or will it require special collection or extraction?
- *Credibility* of the information and reliability for users of the data – is the information from a reputable/scientifically sound source, is it considered objective, will it be believed by users?
- *Clarity and understandability* to users – if they receive the information will they be able to understand it/act on it?
- *Comparability* over time and across jurisdictions or regions; can the indicator be used reliably to show changes over time, relative to standards or benchmarks, or relative to other destinations?

(For a more detailed description of these, see Manning et al., 2001).

Indicator elaboration

Once a list of key indicators has been agreed on, each remaining indicator is reviewed relative to the logistics of implementation. The key issues are: who will use the information, who will provide it, how it will be treated/analyzed and how detailed, how often, how accurate and how current must the information be to affect decisions? Key considerations are whether data are relevant, reliable and valid and where they can be obtained on an ongoing and affordable basis. (Note: this can also result in some of the priority indicators being dropped or deferred.) In practice, it has been found that this exercise is best done by a small working group after the participatory phase is completed. A key to success is the consideration of alternatives where the most desirable information is unavailable or too expensive. In Villa Gesell, Argentina, measurement of beach erosion was considered critical. In the absence of air photography, it was agreed that simple measurement in key locations from a fixed point (end of the dock) once a month at high tide would be a simple yet clear alternative – and it could even be done as a class project by the local school (Manning and Manning, 1995). In practice, the indicator development process is very much one of sub-optimization – getting what is practical and establishing a process to get the information to those who can make the best use of it.

In each of the case studies and workshops done for the WTO, it has been found that the key to implementation is *commitment*. Ideally, the indicators become part of a planning process for the destination, helping to define what is important and ultimately used to develop performance measures for the planning and management of the destination. The workshop process can be a key building block in development of the group which will have to support the implementation stage. Ultimately, the indicators can be the basis for ongoing public reporting on risks, achievements and remaining challenges – a form of state of the environment reporting for destinations and for key sites within them.

Indicators and the planning process

Indicators are not an end in themselves. The objective is to support a more robust planning process for destinations. A stronger process will help to sustain the key social, economic and ecological values shared by stakeholders. As well, where there are incompatibilities between the values held by stakeholders and their perceptions of sensitivity and risk associated with change, the indicator development process is a catalyst for open deliberation of the trade-offs – helping to identify the different perceptions of what is acceptable and what are the desired limits of acceptable change. Often, the users and managers of eco-tourism destinations, and the local community who rely on the same resources, have never met, lacking a forum for open debate over what it is important to sustain. While participatory planning is a laudable objective for all destinations, it is particularly important where there is risk of damage; that is, the destinations most favoured for ecotourism experiences. In each of the cases, the indicators process has served to bring together stakeholders, many of whom had never before met to discuss shared problems. In the Lake Balaton application in Hungary, water managers and environmentalists who participated in the same discussion groups began to realize that they shared the same perceptions of many of the issues and were not adversaries but, rather, potential allies in dealing with water quality issues (Manning and Clifford, 1999). In Cozumel, the workshops initiated a public debate on how many tourists were *too* many, providing a focus for input into an island-wide planning process. When applied to the emerging ecotourism destination of Peninsula Valdes, Argentina, the indicator development process served to show gaps in baseline data that would be essential as the fragile habitat for the southern right whale and several other species attains World Heritage status.

In the fall of 2000 the author participated in an application of the indicator approach as part of a graduate course presented at the University of Nayarit. The case study chosen for the programme was the tiny island of Mexcaltitan, located in a large coastal swamp in western Mexico. The tiny island appears to be a perfect circle from the air, with streets radiating from the central square like bicycle spokes. The 2000 residents obtain their living from shrimp fishing, and have done so for thousands of years. The island legends support the idea that the Aztec civilization began here before migrating to central Mexico and there is enough artifactual evidence (2000-year-old ruins, mounds, relics) to lend credence to the legend. The island is inundated with water in the wet season. The island has a unique culture and economy. It has no infrastructure to support tourism (five hotel rooms and two small shrimp restaurants). It is surrounded by one of the richest and densest concentrations of birds on the continent. It has just been featured in two major tourist magazines and busloads of tourists from Puerto Vallarta and Mazatlan are beginning to arrive.

The indicators initiative, with background research done by teams of students, was a class project and involved a workshop discussion on the island with key islanders and local officials. The meeting was the first discussion by the islanders of the possible impacts of tourism and how they might begin to consider what tourism they wanted. Work to involve outside help in the planning process has begun, stimulated by the indicators – as a catalyst for community involvement. The exercise helps each stakeholder to be more explicit regarding their values and what they consider needs to be sustained.

Management of ecotourism in response to risk

The approach discussed in this chapter is very much a form of risk assessment, as well as a means to raise awareness of risks to an ecotourism destination. The next step is the alteration of planning and management so as to reduce or mitigate the risks. Many tools exist that can assist those concerned with the preservation of the key assets of ecotourism sites. While a more comprehensive discussion of these tools can be found in the publication *Governance for Tourism in Impacted Destinations* (Manning and Prieur, 1998), some of the applications to ecotourism destinations are highlighted briefly here. The range of management tools extends from those that close or limit access (zoning, fencing, built access points, hardened routes), reduce demands (pricing, lotteries, pre-qualification) to a range of methods to reduce the impact of each user of the destination (use of guides, educational approaches, behavioural modification). The challenge for managers of ecotourism destinations lies in the fact that enforcement may be very difficult, as tourism may occur in small dispersed groups, requiring a more innovative and participatory form of management and control (Manning and Dougherty, 1998). The indicators approach can help to identify what is most critical to protect and can help stimulate discussion of both the limits to acceptable change and the means to foster participation in any management procedures.

Conclusion

While the indicators process has proved very useful to direct data collection and to focus management actions where there is a planning and management body charged with destination management, the process of development of the indicators is at least as important as any specific result, particularly where there is no plan in place. The indicators development process itself is a critical building block in creating sustainable destinations – which respect the values of residents and tourists alike. The indicators act as a catalyst for the identification of what is at risk, for the discussion of solutions, for the identification of partners in solutions and, ultimately, as the means to measure success. While every destination is unique, in fact, ecotourism destinations attract tourism *because* they are unique. The indicators process has proved versatile in helping ecotourism destinations to define and act to sustain that which is most important.

Questions

1   What indicators do you use on a regular basis to support your management decisions? Do these respond to the key characteristics that are used in the WTO process?
2   What are the most important risks to the ecotourism site or destination with which you are most familiar? Pick a case from the book.
3   Choose one site from the case studies in this volume. How much could it change before you could no longer obtain the experience that you most value? Would all other users react the same way?
4   How can a local community best become involved in the planning and management of ecotourism destinations? What means do they have to best influence the planning process to protect the issues that are most valuable to them? Pick a case from the book.

References

Clifford, G. and Dougherty, T.D. (1994) Pilot study on indicators for the sustainable management of tourism (Prince Edward Island Canada). Consulting and Audit Canada.

Manning, E.W. (1999a) 'Capacidad de carga: perspectiva del desarollo de un turismo sustentable (carrying capacity for sustainable tourism)'. *Catedra Sobre Turismo*. Cd. De Mexico: Fundacion Miguel Aleman, 99–110.

Manning, E.W. (1999b) 'Indicators of tourism sustainability', *Tourism Management*, 20 (2), 179–82.

Manning, E.W. and Clifford, G. (1999) Workshop on Sustainable Tourism Indicators for Eastern and Central Europe, Keszthely (Lake Balaton) Hungary, February 1999. World Tourism Organization, Madrid.

Manning, E.W. and Dougherty, T.D. (1998) 'Planning tourism in sensitive ecosystems'. In Singh, T.V., *Tourism Development in the Critical Environments*. Lucknow, India, Centre for Tourism Research and Development, 1–21.

Manning, E.W. and Dougherty, T.D. (2000) 'Planning sustainable tourism destinations', *Journal of Tourism Recreation Research*, Jubilee Volume, 25 (2), 3–14.

Manning, E.W. and Manning, M.E. (1995) Pilot Study on Indicators for the Sustainable Management of Tourism: Villa Gesell and Peninsula Valdes, Argentina, Sec de Turismo, Buenos Aires, Argentina and Centre for a Sustainable future, Ottawa, Canada.

Manning, Edward W. and Prieur, S. (1998) *Governance for Tourism: Coping with Tourism in Impacted Destinations*. Toronto: Foundation for International Training.

Manning, E.W., Hanna, M., Vereczi, G. and Manning, M.E. (1999) *Taller Sobre Indicadores de*

Turismo Sostenible para el Caribe y Centroamérica: Informe Final, Cozumel, Mexico, Mayo 1999
Madrid: Organizacion Mundial del Turismo.

Manning, E.W., Clifford, G. and Manning, M.E. (2000) *Indicators for the Sustainable Management of Tourism: Beruwala, Sri Lanka*. Madrid: World Tourism Organization.

Manning, E.W. Clifford, G., Klaric, Z. and Vereczi, G. (2001) Workshop on Sustainable Tourism Indicators for the Islands of the Mediterranean, Kukljica, Island of Ugljan, Croatia, 21–23 March 2001, Final Report. World Tourism Organization, Madrid.

United Nations Conference on Environment and Development (1992) Agenda 21. Proceedings of the Earth Summit, Rio de Janeiro, Brazil.

World Tourism Organization (1996) *What Tourism Managers Need to Know: A Practical Guide to the Development and Use of Indicators of Sustainable Tourism*. Madrid: World Tourism Organization.

88

Websites

UNEP sustainable tourism: *www.uneptie.org/pc/tourism/policy/principles.htm*
World Tourism Organization: *www.world-tourism.org.htm*

5 Ecotourism Certification Criteria and Procedures: Implication for Ecotourism Management

Margot Sallows and Xavier Font

The four main objectives of this chapter are to:

- Overview the certification process and examine how it relates to ecotourism
- Outline of the meaning of ecotourism certification and the benefits from a stakeholder's perspective
- Discuss how the ecotourism industry is engaging in the certification debate
- Provide evidence that well-managed ecotourism certification in a favourable context can be beneficial to the planning and management of a tourism destination

Introduction

This chapter provides an overview of how ecotourism certification has the potential to be a powerful tool in the management and planning of ecotourism. When reading this chapter, it is important to establish a conceptual ground of the principles of ecotourism and sustainable tourism (see Chapter 1). There is a wide variety of literature available that outlines such principles, including Wight (1993), Fennell (1999), Goodwin (1996), Mowforth and Munt (1998) and Honey (1999). As such, for the ease of understanding in this chapter, the following set of principles for sustainable ecotourism, proposed by Wallace and Pierce (1996), provide a useful summary:

- Ecotourism entails the type of use that does not degrade the resource and minimizes negative social and environmental impacts.
- Ecotourism increases awareness and understanding of an area's natural and cultural characteristics and how visitors engage within the system.
- Ecotourism contributes to the conservation and protection of natural areas.
- Ecotourism maximizes the participation of local people at all stages of the decision-making processes that determine the amount and type of tourism development in a place.
- Ecotourism should complement rather than overwhelm or replace traditional practices of

a community (for example, fishing, farming and social structures) and bring about direct economic and other benefits to local people.

Page and Dowling (2002) refine these points to identify five core principles considered fundamental to ecotourism, namely that ecotourism should be nature based, ecologically sustainable, contain environmental education, be locally beneficial and generate tourist satisfaction.

Much debate has taken place over the potential and merits of ecotourism certification as a tool to help attain these principles. Over the last decade, programmes to certify environmental performance and activity have been introduced within the tourism industry, mainly in Europe and linked to accommodation provision, with more recent efforts to certify ecotourism in southern hemisphere countries. In a recent report published by the World Tourism Organization (WTO, 2002) on voluntary initiatives in sustainable tourism and ecotourism, some 104 programmes were identified, ranging from detailed and complex systems that demonstrate environmental performance, to those used merely as a promotional umbrella such as awards. In all, some 59 programmes globally could be classified as certification programmes, although only a handful of these are specifically designed for ecotourism. Certification programmes, regardless of whether they address sustainable tourism or eco-tourism, however, lack common baseline standards, procedures, criteria and exposure, creating customer confusion and with limited marketing value and limiting their effectiveness in promoting positive environmental and social benefit.

The tourism product offered by ecotourism relies on geographic and cultural diversity – the celebration of local differences – yet, at the same time, the tourism industry tends to expect a degree of standardization of the physical presence, operational procedures and staff-customer interaction to ensure consistency of service delivery (Burns and Holden, 1995). This is further exacerbated by the western markets and political processes, that require tour operators to meet certain standards to meet western legislation requirements. This often makes it difficult to apply western ideals in the very countries that rely most heavily on ecotourism, i.e. developing countries.

Thus, there are challenges in setting global sustainability standards. First, there are disparities in the priorities of the tourism industry in the north and south hemisphere countries, just as the economic, political, social and environmental situations in these countries differ (Font and Sallows, 2002). Despite most efforts for a participative process, some sectors of the tourist industry, particularly at the smaller scale, which is most often ecotourism operations, are less likely to be represented in the discussions, therefore rendering one of the very principles of ecotourism – local participation and consultation – void. Additionally, most certification programmes are operational in the developed world, leaving many parts of the world that rely on ecotourism for income generation often without access to certification, even if they would want to enter the process. Reasons for this lack of access can be attributed to lack of local skills in certification and costs associated with certification where it does exist – few programmes cater for the SME sector, which is, more often than not, the size of ecotourism operations. Thus the argument that certification is the only way forward in achieving sustainable tourism and ecotourism is a tenuous one and it could be asked where the demand for certification is coming from. Mowforth and Munt (1998) use the term 'neo-colonialism' – in this light it could be argued that certification demand is coming from the developed world, as they see it as a tool to control negative impacts on the environment and culture of a place, therefore placing western values on other cultures. Honey and Rome (2001) support this concept in suggesting certification standards prescribed by developed countries may be used as protectionist strategies, which will, in effect, preserve the business interests of the developed countries at the expense of the relative prosperity in developing countries.

The year 2002 represented a significant time for ecotourism, with the declaration of the United Nations International Year of Ecotourism (IYE, 2002). This special designation provided some impetus to consult more widely on the potential for certification as a tool to assist ecotourism planning and management. This chapter will outline part of the consultation with the ecotourism industry during the IYE 2002 events organized by the International Ecotourism Society (TIES) late 2001 and early 2002 in Central America (Belize), South Asia (India), Andean South America (Peru) and Southeast Asia (Thailand). These events included workshops to assess the perceptions of stakeholders in ecotourism on the feasibility of ecotourism certification and accreditation.

Ecotourism certification

There has been increasing interest in ecotourism certification in recent years, which has been reported on by numerous commentators (Honey, 1999; Epler Wood and Halpenny, 2001; Font and Buckley, 2001; Issaverdis, 2001; Sasidharan et al., 2002). There remains considerable confusion over what certification actually means and how it links into a global set of guiding principles. Further publications like the ones mentioned will contribute to reduce confusion and show the key challenges that ecotourism certification faces. Despite growing interest, acknowledgement of its potential benefits and many examples of good practice, published sources and practice acknowledge that ecotourism certification cannot be unquestionably accepted as 'the thing to do' and become a widespread requirement to trade (see the conclusions of Epler Wood and

Halpenny, 2001, for a useful list of reasons why ecotourism certification is not more widespread). At this point it is pertinent to examine what is meant specifically by the term ecotourism certification and the terminology associated with it.

Ecotourism certification terminology and procedures

The processes and terminology of conformity assessment are important to set the scene of ecotourism certification standards (Toth, 2000; Font, 2002; Honey, 2002). Importantly, it must be recognized that the terminology extends beyond just the tourism industry. The certification industry is global and certifies a virtually endless selection of products and processes to a large number of agreed standards. Key words to be understood include standard, process based, performance based, environmental management system (EMS), assessment, verification (first, second and third party), certification body, accreditation body and eco-label.

Tourism *standards* are found in a variety of forms and may consist of company internal standards, industry codes of practice, guidelines, awards and certification programmes, as well as some more general international 'agreements' and proclamations. Since the early 1990s there has been a huge growth in the number of tourism standards, with some 104 eco-labels, awards and self-commitment-styled standards identified by WTO (2002). The basic prerequisite for something to be called a standard is that is it documented and established as set of rules, conditions or requirements (Font and Bendell, 2002). Some standards can be as simple as an expression of principles, without establishing any systems for implementation, monitoring or verification of compliance. In general internal standards, industry codes of practice, guidelines and awards would fall into this category. Certification programmes, by way of contrast, are monitored and/or assessed. This is the process of examining, measuring, testing or otherwise determining the conformance of a person, organization or group of organizations with the requirements specified in the standard. This can be done in three ways:

1 first-party or self-assessment, where the organization makes its own assessment of its conformance
2 second-party assessment, where the purchaser (the organization buying the service from another person or organization) assesses the performance of the seller (the person or organization selling the service)
3 third-party assessment, where an external third party assesses the performance of an organization and verifies its conformance with the standard.

Certification is the process by which third-party assessment is undertaken, written assurance is given that the product, process, service or management system conforms to the standard. There are very few true tourism certification programmes of the 104 voluntary initiatives identified by the WTO and the majority of these focus on accommodation certification (Font and Bendell, 2002; WTO, 2002).

Recent developments in tourism certification

The origins of certification within international industries date back to 1993 when manufacturing standards were set by the European Commission and recognized through the Eco-Management and Audit Scheme (EMAS). This model, based on environmental management systems could be applied only in some fields with an application to the service sector limited to local authorities. A wider set of standards, applicable to any industry, was prepared by the International Standards Organisation in its manual *ISO 14001* (see Sheldon and Yoxon, 2001, for an example of an implementation manual).

The tourism industry, including ecotourism, however, is characterized by a large number of small firms and cannot easily apply EMAS and ISO systems, tailored only for large companies. The sole references for the industry were codes of practice, industry manuals, awards and finally eco-labels, mainly focused on demonstrating environmental efficiency (Synergy, 2000).

Eco-labels, as a result of certification, are subjected to proof of standard requirement management by a third party and to periodical re-examination. Acknowledgement for the success of tourism certification eco-labels has taken some time as many programmes have had to fight against disapproval for being expensive and time consuming, that they are too focused on hotels, do not assess performance and have a limited influence on marketing competition (Synergy, 2000).

Nevertheless, eco-labels and certification programmes seem to be the best method to communicate to ecotourists about environmental issues. However, the excessive fragmentation and confusion that arise need to lead to the creation of strategic alliances to have a stronger voice in the international market and greater market penetration (currently less than 1% of all tourism operations worldwide are involved with certification), especially in terms of economies of scale (Kahlenborn and Dominé, 2001). Within these developments the necessity for credibility is taking on more importance with the need of accreditation of certifiers and regulation of sub-sectors. This will increase the cost of certification and a revision of the current status of certification schemes but, contrariwise, it can assure transparency.

Increasingly, countries and NGOs are supporting new, mainly ecotourism certification programmes. These range from EU programmes such as the WWF Arctic and the Ecotourism Society of Sweden, to Latin American programmes such as in Brazil and Peru, to the Fair Trade through Tourism Network in Africa. At the same time current programmes are looking for commonalities, with Green Globe entering into a working agreement with the Nature and Ecotourism Accreditation Program (Ecotourism Association Australia), when the International Ecotourism Standard was launched at the World Ecotourism Summit in Québec as part of IYE 2002. The debate as to whether ecotourism certification can and should be a market-based mechanism or requires subsidizing will not be solved here, but it is interesting to note that the great majority of ecotourism certification programmes currently only survive for as long as there is an injection of cash through donors or external funding. Font and Bendell (2002) found that a large proportion of programmes rely on government or NGO funding, and Epler Wood and Halpenny (2001) comment on the impossibility of running ecotourism certification programmes that are self-financing. Some programmes, such as the Fair Trade for Tourism Network decided not to certify operators due to the cost and difficulties in verification and the fact that funds could be used more effectively elsewhere (Patricia Barnett, personal comment).

Issues covered by tourism certification programmes

Tourism certification programmes criteria for meeting a standard are *process based* or *performance based* or a combination of both. Those that follow accepted processes and procedures that can be justified for the location and characteristics of the organization are process-based management standards that focus on a company's ability to make year-on-year (continuous) improvements. Generally, these programmes are based on an environmental management system (EMS). With this approach, a company makes a commitment not to reach a certain 'level' of performance, but to make an improvement in the way in which it manages identified issues, according to its own resources and capacity. By their very nature, process-based certification programmes are self-updating, as year-on-year improvement is an integral aspect of conforming to the standard. Some critics argue that process-based certification programmes are no guarantee of sustainability (Synergy, 2000; Honey and Rome, 2001). Furthermore, process-based criteria to meet standards might not be applicable here to assess firms that have little ability or incentive to keep paper records of actions taken.

Criteria that are entirely based on processes are justified to have such criticisms and yet it is justifiable to combine process and performance criteria, as found in the WTO report (2002) that surveyed 59 tourism certification programmes. Over 40% of the individual criteria used to measure conformity to a standard related to management actions and systems being in place to deal with sustainability, therefore emphasizing that the role of management is considered vital for a successful tourism certification programme. The global nature of tourism as an industry is fuelling process approaches, not only due to the increasing number of multinational companies aiming to use the same processes across the board, but also due to the international nature of travelling, which favours international recognition.

Performance-based ecotourism certification programmes, however, require every company to reach a threshold level and reach a pre-specified targets, guaranteeing a minimum level of performance. Performance-based standards are complex and require detailed context-specific adaptation (see Table 5.1). For example, what is considered appropriate consumption of a natural resource in one region is not necessarily the same in another. Thus any effort to set international standards based on performance and reaching set targets inherently requires regional adaptation or else very broad and basic standards which have the potential to lose meaning and impact. With widespread criticism that certification programmes are already too expensive, there are some questions over whether performance-based standards are achievable, as they inevitably increase the cost of the certification process due to a lack of streamlining.

The trend is to develop programmes that combine process-based mechanisms with performance measures, so as to ensure sound management practices within an actual performance-based framework. This approach has the added benefit of allowing for subsector specific criteria to be developed, such as for accommodation, tour operators, transport providers, tourist attractions and so on, as each sub-sector has different priorities. In terms of ecotourism, this is important as different aspects of an operation can be taken into consideration.

Another key issue is the need for phased participation in ecotourism certification programme, also referred to as 'stepped versus one-level certification'. There is some debate that phased participation, say from bronze, to silver to gold level encourages more companies to become involved in ecotourism certification programmes, as it is perceived as tangible to enter at a low level, with the aim of striving for the high level. It could be argued that the difficulties with managing a phased tourism certification programme are too great; that the management costs become unmanageable; and the consumer is sent a confused message about what is 'good' and what is 'bad'. However, phased participation does have a benefit in that it can encourage greater participation from those companies that might want to become more sustainable in their operations, but feel the need to start 'small' and aim for the top over a longer period of time. Some companies decide they will never proceed to the higher level, however, which can degrade the perceived quality of the programme, as other companies question the point of striving further if others are not – why should they bear the cost burden?

Table 5.1 Performance criteria for ecotourism certification

Environmental
- Waste: solid and water (consumption, reduction, recycling, disposal)
- Energy (consumption, reduction, efficiency)
- Water (consumption, reduction, quality)
- Hazardous substances (reduction, handling, use of nature-friendly cleaning products)
- Noise (reduction)
- Air quality (quality improvement)
- Transport (public transport green alternatives provided)
- Specific standards for impacts specific to diving, golf, beaches and other subsectors

Economic
- Creation of local employment
- Supply chain management through green and sustainable purchasing policies
- Creation of networks of 'green businesses' within a given destination
- Use of locally sourced and produced materials and food
- Use of organic food

Social accountability
- Community (relations, welfare)
- Community (participation, organization, involvement)
- Personnel: fair treatment

Cultural
- Emphasis and conservation of local/regional culture, heritage and authenticity
- In keeping with aesthetics of physical development/architecture

Quality
- Customer satisfaction
- Health and safety
- Services and facilities provided (environmentally friendly and/or for environment/wildlife observation/ enjoyment)
- Employee capacity building/education/qualifications
- Overall business competence

Destination resource protection
- Habitat/ecosystem/wildlife maintenance and enhancement
- Environmental information/interpretation/education for customers
- Overall environmental protection

(Source: Font and Bendell, 2002)

Involvement in tourism certification programmes

The WTO report (2002) identified that despite the large number of tourism (including ecotourism specific) programmes that exist globally, there is still negligible impact of the programmes on changing industry behaviour to be more sustainable and a low number of certified companies per programme. At best a programme will have 5% of the market share of companies for a tourism sub-sector in a given destination, with the exception of the Blue Flag programme, which has a large market share due to its niche market nature for beaches and marinas only. However, most schemes acknowledge they are running to resource capacity and would not be able to cope with an increased number of companies as the fees would not cover the costs.

Certification of sustainable tourism and ecotourism is perceived as providing competitive advantage (Mihalič, 2000) and this is one of the key reasons for industry interest in the proposed Sustainable Tourism Stewardship Council. Competitive advantage is, however, relative to the share of competitors meeting those standards and any efforts to increase the number of applicants for certification should consider at which point they need to promote benefits other than marketing competitiveness as their selling point. Also competitive advantage is relative to the customer's perceived link between sustainability, or environmental quality, and the core of the product being purchased. Currently less than 1% of the world's tourism industry is involved with certification, which does not indicate there is a competitive advantage associated with certification. Nevertheless, ecotourism companies are more likely to show an interest in proving their sustainability than more generalist tourism businesses that rely less directly on environmental quality of destinations.

Voluntary standards in ecotourism are a valid method to show best practice and industry leadership. They provide a range of capacity-building benefits on environmental management, eco-savings and support to green marketing claims. There is no data to suggest whether ecotourism businesses perceive the internal benefits (eco-savings and environmental management) are greater than the external benefits (green marketing), but this would provide evidence to suggest the potential for expanding the current standards across the industry. WTO (2002) shows that certification schemes are struggling to increase the perception of benefits from certification beyond the committed few and this is a costly and time-consuming exercise. Government incentives to introduce voluntary standards are required for a more meaningful share of the industry take-up.

Thus the question of effectiveness of such a large number of relatively small programmes must be asked – is the fact there are so many programmes in fact contributing to the lack of *effectiveness* on a broader scale? How could this current situation be resolved, so as to increase consumer recognition of ecotourism certification and positively influence consumer choice of holiday product or service for a more sustainable option? It is now pertinent to examine the role accreditation could play in improving the current low take-up rate of tourism certification programmes.

Current issues and problems with certification

Industry issues

It is mainly accommodation providers, such as hotels in the mainstream tourism industry, and eco-lodges in the ecotourism industry, that have been targeted for their overall quality and also environmental quality issues, since it is easier to manage a single 'operation'. Accommodation providers working towards certification are generally doing it with eco-savings as the incentive, although it is fair to say many eco-lodges do so out of a drive to provide an environmentally responsible tourism product. In countries such as Costa Rica, several lodges have become certified through the (CST) programme. The Serena Group operates eco-lodges and larger hotels throughout Kenya and Tanzania and is using the Green Globe programme to certify their properties. These are, however, exceptions, and in the Costa Rican example the application and verification process is subsidized.

The market

Eco-labels are meaningless in the majority of cases and tourists perceive that certified products are more expensive. The most successful campaign is the Blue Flag, since they have linked environmental quality with health and safety in such a way that tourists can see the benefits to themselves as individuals. The majority of other programmes are not widely recognized or understood by the average tourist. Similarly, there has been a reluctance by the tour operators to become involved in certification as many see it as too cumbersome and expensive to implement within their organizations. Instead, the Tour Operators Initiative for Sustainable Tourism Development, a UNEP/UNESCO/WTO initiative, has determined corporate social responsibility as a more suitable path.

Governments

Some governments have introduced programmes of certification as a voluntary initiative tool, to generate interest and create industry leaders. The WTO data show that 20 out of 59 programmes are led by government agencies and 38 out of 59 have some government involvement (Font and Bendell, 2002). The possibility of an international accreditation body might help governments become more involved, since a variety of governments that do not have a national system at present might consider developing one. Maccarrone-Eaglen and Font (2002) conducted a survey of WTO government members and the 26 governments responding were positive to the benefits of certification and accreditation, although for some southern hemisphere governments this was not a priority.

Non-governmental organizations (NGOs)

NGOs have used self-created certification systems to reward pilot projects for conservation programmes, but these are usually small scale and do not make a difference to the market unless they take a product or destination cluster. NGOs are more likely to be involved in ecotourism programmes than governments and also NGO programmes tend to be in developing countries. Often the programmes operated by NGOs are seriously under-funded and under-resourced. Once the initial funding grant to develop a certification programme dries up, the NGOs are left with a system to administer and manage but without the necessary ongoing financial support to make it successful. The main interest from NGOs revolves around ecotourism and fair trade tourism, rather than eco-efficiency. Of particular note is the launch and expansion of the Fair Trade Through Tourism initiative under the auspices of Tourism Concern. Again, just as with the tour operators, there is some concern that certification might not adequately meet the goals of fair trade, so it is more than likely the corporate social responsibility model will take precedence as the programme rolls out. This network folded in September 2002 when external funding dried out and could not continue as a self-financing programme.

North–south divide

From a geographical/economical perspective, eco-labels in northern countries tend to be run by governmental or quasi-governmental organizations focusing on eco-savings as the key issues in their criteria, mainly around energy and water conservation, while eco-labels operating in southern countries are run by NGOs focusing on a mix of social and environmental issues. Seen in this context, setting international standards on environmental and social performance can be seen by the countries of the south as another method for countries of the north to attach conditions to trading agreements that limit their economic and social development (Font and Sallows, 2002).

Results of the IYE 2002 consultation

Widespread consultation was undertaken as part of the IYE 2002 preparations. Essentially, consultation consisted of preparatory meetings and it was during these that breakout sessions were held to concentrate on certification issues. This paper uses the results of four workshops out of a longer list of consultation methods, available at the Rainforest Alliance's website for the Sustainable

Tourism Stewardship Council's feasibility study. The workshops reported in this chapter include:

- Mesoamerica – Belize City, Belize
- Andean South America – Lima, Peru
- East Africa – Nairobi, Kenya
- Southeast Asia – Chiang Mai, Thailand.

Mesoamerica

There were 23 participants at the Mesoamerica workshop, representing countries such as Belize, Costa Rica, El Salvador, Guatemala, Honduras, Mexico, Nicaragua and Panama.

The perception from the participants in Central America is that certification is not an effective tool for generating consumer demand, that consumers are not aware of certification and that in those cases where certification is known, this is perceived to make the facilities more expensive or cheaper. Certification does play a role in consumer choice, with price, convenience and an overall perception of quality being more important. Although environmental and social certification is quality, this is not a message that is meaningful to the consumer and the way that the message is packaged to the consumer should be reviewed. Without a product differentiation that is meaningful to the consumer, the certified tourism provider cannot justify a higher price. It is believed (or rather hoped) that some tourists such as the European market are more sensitive to the certification message than the American.

For industry, certification is a source of criteria of sustainability and quality standards, in the form of manuals and advice. Certification is also perceived as a method to differentiate the quality of the service or product, and to differentiate it from the traditional tourism packages (Central America). It is hoped that this differentiation will mean access to government incentives, particularly for microfirms.

In Central America there were divided opinions about the type of benefits that the government should provide to certified companies. For example, the Costa Rican government runs marketing activities specifically promoting the companies certified by the CST. Those against this considered that funds raised through taxes should be used to benefit all taxpayers equally. An underlying issue around this point is the fact that different companies will not all have the same access to knowledge and potential to become certified, hence the perception of imbalance. Those in favour thought this is an incentive to improvement and therefore those companies that have made an investment to become certified should be rewarded. It was perceived that governments in Central America are only introducing what they see it is done elsewhere as a fashion, not through real conviction.

Issues arise in the certification of community-based ecotourism development programmes, which not only will not have the economies of scale to apply for certification, but possibly will not be making profits or these will be invested back into community. This is the case of the Guatemalan Green Deal programme. Proposals for a certification programme in the Dominican Republic, called Kiskeya Alternativa, have been abandoned due to the low efficiency of resources that certification supposes as opposed to other methods of community development.

Andes

There were 90 participants from Colombia, Venezuela, Ecuador, Peru and Bolivia. The Andean region is familiar with a wide variety of certification processes, although it can be assumed that Ecuador and Peru are the most familiar with all of the issues, while Bolivia, Colombia and Venezuela had the least experience. This is possibly due to the current activity in both Ecuador and Peru to develop suitable certification programmes. The private sector was underrepresented at the meeting, which was largely comprised of representatives from NGOs, academics and the community.

Community issues loom very large in this region. Amazonian areas of all the Andean countries represent vast ecotourism potential, however communities in these regions have little access to good educational systems and capacity building for community-based tourism projects has been sparse, although highly significant in certain areas. Communities in this region are very interested in being part of the ecotourism economy. They are justly concerned about being left out of national planning and development process. Certification could be viewed as just one more way to disenfranchise these communities, as they will have difficulty taking part in certification projects without a great deal of technical assistance.

The industry members that were present came with a strong interest in certification and understood the need for accreditation. They want to use certification to help them compete in the market, as currently they are competing against their Central American counterparts, many of whom are actively involved in certification. The major concern expressed was cost and feasibility of certification in the region, which links to concerns outlined in the literature earlier in this chapter.

However, several certification programmes are being launched in the region, mainly with government support. An overriding concern is how certification might engage SMEs and communities, as there is a perception that these organizations and individuals will be excluded to an extent. Also, there is a question mark over the potential success of certification in the region, as there are a large number of businesses operating without financial buffer and how will certification be seen as a priority business issue when there are so many other financial and business concerns. This can lead to larger firms affording the cost and time to work towards certification and rewarding larger firms as ecotourism flagships.

It was felt that any certification programme should not be politicized and that it should maintain neutrality. A clear system of norms for all certification programmes needs to be established to ensure a level playing field and that all sectors of society can participate. In particular, this region is concerned that ecotourism certification could become part of the system of political favours and corruption that is typical of their experience with government projects. In addition, there is considerable concern that the market for certified products might not be present and they consider that the market should be prepared for certification. Furthermore, for certification to be successful in the region, there is a strong need for training of personnel that will be auditing against the standards set.

East Africa

The workshop consisted of 30 participants from Kenya, Tanzania and Uganda. This region has a mixed level of awareness about certification and the role it can play in delivering sustainable ecotourism. This is of interest, given that a large percentage of the total tourism product within the region is ecotourism. Kenya has a much greater knowledge of certification, but this is due to a major study undertaken by the Kenya Ecotourism Society into the potential to develop a Kenyan ecotourism certification programme. Thus, at a national level, there is greater understanding and many consider the international realm is not relevant to their own situations. Interestingly, there is a high awareness of the role of national standardization and normalization bodies (bureaux of standards), which indicates that there is some acceptance of a more regulatory approach to certification.

However, a number of challenges were recognized in the region. First, there is an absence of regulatory systems on the whole. Second, there is a lack of criteria for ecotourism certification, as well as a lack of financial and technical resources (including a skilled labour force of auditors and managers) properly to implement any form of ecotourism certification. Third, the political situation in the region is such that there is no legislation to cover certification and environmental performance/social accountability and without this there are no powers of enforcement, rendering certification impossible, as tourism operations will not participate without being forced to.

Nevertheless, the time may come in the near future where this reluctance turns into business imperative. There is a sense that all stakeholders demand certification – consumers, donor agencies, investors, governments and tourism operators. However, until there is a demonstrated awareness at the consumer level and better marketing of ecotourism certification, it is unlikely the situation will change. Should this situation arise, there are a range of costs and benefits which could be brought to the region through ecotourism certification, namely:

Benefits
- Environmental and social improvement
- improved efficiency
- developing product goodwill through marketing of certification
- access to better markets of tourism
- improved sustainability – social, environmental and economic
- development of consumer-friendly products
- credibility.

Costs
- Enormous financial costs in terms of technology and technical expertise
- need for capacity building
- developing reliable, effective baseline data
- establishment of an auditing framework
- limitations to the size of the ventures, reducing the amount of revenue from certification
- time required for implementation.

One key issue raised was the potential inequities between SMEs and larger businesses, as the latter, with their substantive revenue bases, could benefit from certification more than SMEs.

In terms of accreditation, East Africa saw a range of benefits, primarily due to the different pace of development and priorities among countries in the region, however, and due to the transmutability of the border at certain points, there needs to be cross-border policies applied to different types of tourism products. The diverse range of organizations involved in certification would also benefit from a system that would allow comparison between different certification programmes, in terms of consistency, objectivity, transparency, credibility and acceptability. However, such a system would have to be provided with very minimal bureaucracy and financial input. There should, however, be coordination between countries/regions and international systems to ensure regional sustainability, profitability and benefit sharing, while at the same time, enhancement of the social, cultural and natural environments.

The implications of the results are such that there is widespread consensus within East Africa that certification and accreditation are useful tools in encouraging a triple bottom-line approach to sustainable ecotourism management. There are a range of issues that still need to be resolved in terms of land tenure, competition for resources and human–wildlife conflicts, however, given that the tourism product in the region is essentially ecotourism based, the potential for certification to act as a management tool is great.

Southeast Asia

The Southeast Asian workshop was held with 18 participants from Cambodia, China, Indonesia, Laos, Malaysia, Myanmar, Thailand and Vietnam. The level of knowledge of ecotourism certification was variable, largely correlating to the level of development in place, that is, newly industrialized countries (NICs) such as Malaysia and Thailand versus that of less-developed countries including Cambodia and Laos. What participants did agree on is that process and performance-oriented standards were useful.

However, there are some significant challenges facing the region in terms of implementing widespread ecotourism certification, including cost and the time needed to implement certification. Other challenges that were raised by the participants included the need to maintain standards and some kind of monitoring system in place to ensure that this remains so when the standards have been established. As well, standards need to be continuously rising to match the improvements in performance and process to ensure that there is always a higher standard to be attained. There is a need to better educate the consumer and industry on what the performance indicators are and why they are in place, to ensure an overall appreciation of their value and acceptance.

Unlike other workshops, this one was interesting as there was a perceived market demand for ecotourism certification in terms of defining the quality or security of the product on offer. It was considered that the consumer will pay more for a guarantee that the tourism product is of a high quality (the term quality includes environmental quality), however, at this point the consumer and the tour operator alike are not adequately informed about certification and, consequently, it is difficult to charge higher rates. Another interesting point is that is was not felt SMEs were disadvantaged over larger enterprises, however, unlike in other regions, it was felt the governments need further training on the benefits of certification so they can help promote the development of regionally applicable programmes.

The costs and benefits of certification were recognized as including:

Benefits
- Consumers benefit by having a sustainable product offering
- represents the development of a new tourism market segment development
- fosters a good reputation for a business
- effective for branding tourism products
- promotes a higher value clientele.

Costs
- The benefits derived from current certification programmes come at too high a cost
- lengthy development and application in terms of training, process, systems, facilities, promotion and capacity building.

In terms of accreditation of certification programmes, there was a strong consensus that accreditation was important as it would allow for the development of common core standards and market certification. Importantly, it was considered that accreditation has the potential for further work with governments that may be encouraged to set up national certification products and policies, therefore contributing to the triple bottom line of sustainable tourism in the region.

Participants felt that accreditation will also have the added benefit of assisting protected area managers, local communities and tourism businesses. Thus overall, again considering the broad range of ecotourism products in the region, certification has the potential to aid planning, development and management of ecotourism.

Québec Declaration on Ecotourism

The World Ecotourism Summit in Québec, May 2002, was the culmination of the preparatory meetings. The workshops reported on in this chapter represent one subset of these preparatory meetings. The significant outcome of the Québec Summit was the Québec Declaration on Ecotourism. Several key recommendations made in the declaration refer specifically to ecotourism certification and include:

- **For national, regional and local governments**
  Use internationally approved and reviewed guidelines to develop certification schemes, ecolabels and other voluntary initiatives geared towards sustainability in ecotourism, encouraging private operators to join such schemes and promoting their recognition by consumers. However, certification systems should reflect regional and local criteria. Build capacity and provide financial support to make these schemes accessible to small and medium enterprises (SMEs). In addition, monitoring and a regulatory framework are necessary to support effective implementation of these schemes.
- **For the private sector**
  Adopt as appropriate a reliable certification or other systems of voluntary regulation, such as ecolabels, in order to demonstrate to their potential clients their adherence to sustainability principles and the soundness of the products and services they offer.
- **For intergovernmental organizations, international financial institutions and development assistance agencies**
  Develop or adopt, as appropriate, international standards and financial mechanisms for ecotourism certification systems that take into account the needs of small and medium sized enterprises and facilitates their access to those procedures, and support their implementation. (Québec Declaration on Ecotourism 2002)

While it is beyond the scope of this chapter to review the recommendations of the Québec Summit in any depth, it should be recognized that these recommendations have significant implication with regards to the use of certification as a tool to contribute to better planning and management of ecotourism.

Implications for ecotourism management and planning

There are roles for both the public sector and private sector to take on greater responsibility in planning ecotourism in such a way it can be managed in a sustainable way in perpetuity.

Overall, the workshops reviewed show there was a strong feeling that the public sector will have to absorb some of the costs to incentive companies to (1) invest to improve quality standards and (2) pay the price to be regularly verified as meeting those standards. The push for certification at national level needs to be an integrated system that not only gives the opportunity to be certified and the support to apply for certification through soft credit schemes, training and access to markets. Companies entering certification will require a startup subsidy in the form of grants to invest in capacity building, marketing and green technology to meet the standards in the first place or to have clear proof that the investment can be offset in a medium term through reduced operational costs coming from eco-savings. It was acknowledged that usually grants are for product development and upgrading, not marketing. However startup funds will have limitations in time and overall amount and this is desirable, since certification programmes need to become financially sustainable. Exactly how this will work is still an issue, but it is likely the solutions will vary between regions. As an example, the CST is currently subsidized by the Costa Rican government and the success of this programme has meant a growth in number of applications and therefore cost of running the programme.

The workshops also demonstrated a perception that the current organizations applying for certification are not doing it for marketing purposes and that certification will not solve the applicant's marketing problems. More needs to be done by certification programmes to market their seal and this must be done in conjunction with the certified companies. This is also where accreditation of certification could come into play, as an accreditation body could perform marketing and lobbying functions that would potentially benefit all certification programmes. Finally, a key underlying issue is the reduction of operating costs through eco-savings, which can be reinvested in paying for the process of certification, but this requires economies of scale to make it workable.

If certification becomes a source of competitive advantage, this might change the way in which ecotourism companies market themselves and, ultimately, their management. Two possible avenues are for governments to undertake specific marketing campaigns to promote certified producers and accreditation programmes to promote the use of certified suppliers as part of distribution channels' chains of supply. If either of these methods is effective, ecotourism companies might redirect some of their marketing efforts to showing how they meet certification criteria and, in effect, pass on part of their marketing work to other organizations. These are tentative thoughts and only time and examples will prove just how feasible they are.

Conclusion

The use of the words ecotourism and sustainable tourism should be limited to those products or services meeting the characteristics of the definition of either term. Unfortunately, there are no means to regulate their use and they are often used for greenwashing. In the short term governments, non-profit organizations and industry associations have started voluntary initiatives to identify those companies with high standards, but there are many difficulties in the process of managing processes to verify those companies that meet standards of ecotourism. This paper has reviewed the current literature and experiences of a variety of ecotourism certification programmes through the primary research collected during workshops organized as part of the preparatory meetings for the International Year of Ecotourism across a variety of locations in southern hemisphere countries with ecotourism operators and experts.

The conclusions from this chapter are that across the world there is an acceptance that ecotourism certification can be a beneficial tool and, if it could be implemented given the appropriate context, it could help in providing a level playing field for all businesses and governments in managing the impacts of ecotourism on the environment and community. The facts are less encouraging and when reviewing challenges on a region-by-region basis, it is clear that many of these challenges cannot be dealt with by certification and in some cases certification will only worsen current inequalities by promoting those who have the capacity to fulfil assessment requirements.

The success of and hope for ecotourism certification, however, relies on three key players: governments, the private sector and the international community such as intergovernmental organizations, international financial institutions and development agencies. The recognition that all these players need to be involved is of paramount importance, as, until the Québec Declaration, there was little or no recognition that the expansion and adoption of these programmes is the responsibility of all, not just the green movement. At this stage we would like to add a fourth player, the tourism distribution channels, which have a corporate social responsibility for promoting sustainable suppliers over non-sustainable ones, in absence of a market demand for sustainable products.

Acknowledgements

The authors would like to thank Rainforest Alliance for commissioning the research and to the International Ecotourism Society for organizing and conducting the consultation workshops.

Questions

1 Discuss the benefits of the certification process to ecotourism sites.
2 Outline the current status of the certification programmes.
3 Evaluate the implications of creating certification programmes in ecotourism settings.
4 Suggest four factors that will influence the success of the certification programmes in the future.

References

Burns, P. and Holden, A. (1995) *Tourism, A New Perspective*. Hemel Hempstead: Prentice Hall.

Epler Wood, M. and Halpenny, E. (2001) 'Ecotourism certification: progress and prospects'. In Font, X. and Buckley, R. (eds) *Tourism Ecolabelling: Certification and Promotion of Sustainable Management*. Wallingford: CABI.

Fennell, D. (1999) *Ecotourism: An Introduction*. London: Routledge.

Font, X. (2002) 'Environmental certification in tourism and hospitality: progress, process and prospects', *Tourism Management*, 23 (4), 197–205.

Font, X. and Bendell, J. (2002) *Standards for Sustainable Tourism for the Purpose of Multilateral Trade Negotiations: Studies on Trade in Tourism Service for the World Tourism Organization (WTO)*. Leeds: Leeds Metropolitan University.

Font, X. and Buckley, R. (eds) (2001) *Tourism Ecolabelling*. Oxford: CABI.

Font, X. and Sallows, M. (2002) 'Setting global sustainability standards: the Sustainable Tourism Stewardship Council', *Tourism Recreation Research*, 27 (1), 21–32.

Goodwin, H. (1996) 'In pursuit of ecotourism', *Biology and Conservation*, 5 (3), 277–91.

Honey, M. (1999) *Ecotourism and Sustainable Development: Who owns paradise?* Washington, DC: Island Press.

Honey, M. (ed.) (2002) *Setting Standards: The Greening of the Tourism Industry*. New York: Island Press.

Honey, M. and Rome, A. (2001) *Protecting Paradise: Certification Programs for Sustainable Tourism and Ecotourism*. Washington, DC: Institute for Policy Studies.

International Year of Ecotourism (2002) Quebec Declaration on Ecotourism, Madrid: WTO.

Issaverdis, J.P. (2001) 'The pursuit of excellence: benchmarking, accreditation, best practice and auditing'. In Weaver, D. (ed.) *The Encyclopedia of Ecotourism*. Wallingford: CABI.

Kahlenborn, W. and Dominé, A. (2001) 'The future belongs to international ecolabelling schemes'. In Font, X. and Buckley, R. (eds) *Tourism Ecolabelling: Certification and Promotion of Sustainable Management*. Wallingford, CABI.

Maccarrone-Eaglen, A. and Font, X. (2002) *Sustainable Tourism Stewardship Council Feasibility Consultation of World Tourism Organization (WTO) Government Members*. Leeds: Leeds Metropolitan University. *http://www.world-tourism.org/sustainable/STSC.htm*

Mihalič, T. (2000) 'Environmental management of a tourist destination: a factor of tourism competitiveness', *Tourism Management*, 21, 65–78.

Mowforth, M. and Munt, I. (1998) *Tourism and Sustainability: New Tourism in the Third World*. London: Routledge.

Page, S. and Dowling, R. (2002) *Ecotourism*. Harlow: Pearson Education.

Sasidharan, V., Sirakaya, E. and Kerstetter, D. (2002) 'Developing countries and tourism ecolabels', *Tourism Management*, 23, 161–74.

Sheldon, C. and Yoxon, M (2001) *Installing Environmental Management Systems: A Step-by-step Guide*. London: Earthscan.

Synergy (2000) *Tourism Certification: An Analysis of Green Globe 21 and Other Certification Programmes*. Godalming: WWF UK.

Toth, R. (2000) *Implementing a Worldwide Sustainable Tourism Certification System*. Alexandria, VA: R.B. Toth and Associates.

Wallace, G. and Pierce, S. (1996) 'An evaluation of ecotourism in Amazonas, Brazil', *Annals of Tourism Research*, 23 (4), 843–73.

Wight, P. (1993) 'Sustainable ecotourism: balancing economic, environmental and social goals within an ethical framework', *Journal of Tourism Studies*, 4 (2), 54–66.

WTO (2002) *Voluntary Initiatives in Sustainable Tourism*, Madrid: WTO.

Consultation workshops

Individual workshop reports at *http://www.rainforest-alliance.org/programs/sv/stsc-consultation-results.html*

Mesoamerica International Year of Ecotourism preparatory meeting, Belize City, Belize, November 2001

Andean South America International Year of Ecotourism preparatory meeting, Lima, Peru, 7 February 2002

East Africa International Year of Ecotourism preparatory meeting, Nairobi, Kenya, 23 March 2002

South East Asia International Year of Ecotourism preparatory meeting, Chiang Mai, Thailand, 8 March 2002

6 The POLAR Framework and its Operation in an Ecotourism Setting

David A. Fennell, R.W. Butler and S.W. Boyd

The four main objectives of this chapter are to:

- Discuss the concept and origins of carrying capacity
- Analyze the preformed planning and management frameworks
- Review the pros and cons of the POLAR framework
- Evaluate the steps of the POLAR framework

Introduction

The concept of carrying capacity is a relatively simple one and one that is intuitively acceptable to most individuals, namely, that there is an upper limit to the amount of use that is appropriate for a specific facility or resource (see Chapter 2). Humans accept such limits in their daily lives without great problems, for example, maximum numbers of seats in a stadium for a ballgame, a limited number of places on a train or airplane or space on a floppy disk in a computer. We have become accustomed to authorities in various areas setting what are, in effect, capacity limits for many elements in society. In the recreation context just noted, we are reconciled to the fact that most recreation facilities have an upper limit of use. In the case of stadia, this is normally the number of seats, although in the interests of safety a maximum number of occupants may be set which is below the seating level. Even in natural areas we may be faced with limits to the amount of use which is permitted, for example, it is normal in parks to have a set number of campsites and except for a very few occasions such as holiday weekends, to limit campground use to the number of parties matching the number of campsites. In other recreation areas numbers may not be limited directly but limits to use may occur, for example, on golf courses a maximum of four players per party is the norm and starting times of so many minutes between each party will in effect set a maximum number of parties that can be allowed to play each day. The actual numbers of players, as the actual numbers of campers, may vary from day to day, depending on average party size, but the principle of a maximum number of units is adopted. Similar restrictions on numbers occur with respect to fishing and hunting permits and with respect to numbers of guest passes being sold at private recreation facilities such as ski clubs or golf clubs. In the last cases, the key factor being considered is the quality of the recreation experience for owner/members, rather than the ecological limitations of the facility. In the case of campgrounds, the limits may represent what are perceived of as natural limits to further campground expansion or simply be the result of a lack of funds to develop further sites in the campground. In the case of hunting and fishing limits the intent is to keep use levels below the capability of the natural resource (the wildlife) to reproduce and maintain its numbers. In all these cases, the recreating public and managers of recreation areas have little difficulty in accepting the principle of carrying capacity and limitations on the level of use. However, as one moves towards non-consumptive use of natural resources, especially common resources such as forests, rivers and scenery, it becomes more difficult to select suitable limits to use and even harder to justify these limits to the recreating public.

Evolution of the concept of capacity

Concern over the number of users or the amount of use in a specific area is not new, even in the recreation field. An anonymous 16th-century English poet (writing in 1598) commented on the effect of excessive fishing on stocks in Elizabethan England:

> But now the sport is marred,
> And wot ye why?
> Fishes decrease,
> For Fishers multiply.

For centuries before this observation, those in power had been well aware of the effect of excessive use on stocks of game and other renewable resources and had gone to great lengths to protect their own resources, often by draconian measures. In those early days the primary purpose of limits to use was to maintain exclusivity of access, mostly from consumptive use related to survival rather than recreation purposes. It was not until the post-war period that recreation use of natural areas reached levels that began to threaten the quality of the resources of such areas. Until then, most recreation area managers had been more concerned with encouraging use of the areas for which they had responsibility than with restricting use. There was, therefore, very little knowledge existing about the operationalization of the concept of carrying capacity and very little concern over the issue, as numbers did not pose a threat to resource quality or to the quality of the recreational experience. Most of the literature that existed on carrying capacity in the early post-war years came from the field of range management and wildlife research and focused on the number of animals that an area could sustain without overuse of its resources. It is not surprising perhaps, that the first efforts at studying carrying capacity in a recreation context were related to trying to identify the maximum numbers of users an area could withstand without suffering ecological damage.

Ecological and social elements

Such was the intent in one of the most frequently quoted pioneer studies of carrying capacity by Wagar (1964), although when he had completed this study that author was forced to comment:

> The study ... was initiated with the view that the carrying capacity of recreation lands could be determined primarily in terms of ecology and the deterioration of the areas. However, it soon became obvious that the resource-oriented point of view must be augmented by consideration of human values. (Wagar, 1964: i)

It is clear that underlying much of the early research on carrying capacity was the assumption that the biological capacity of an area is a fixed value and that specific environments or areas have definite limits of use, beyond which ecological damage would occur. It is generally accepted now, however, that such an assumption is incorrect, because the carrying capacity of an area varies with a considerable number of variables, including seasons of use, soil and vegetation characteristics, the species of wildlife involved and the level and nature of management of the area (Shelby and Heberlein, 1986). There are, therefore, a number of capacities for an area, which may vary over time, and which certainly vary over space with the nature of use and the type of species (or user in a recreation context).

As noted by Wagar earlier, another and equally fundamental variable has to be taken into carrying capacity considerations, namely *human preference*. In the early stages of carrying capacity research this was often related to crowding, on the assumption that reaction to crowding was the most important aspect of user satisfaction. In the context of the areas in which such research was conducted this was not an unreasonable assumption, for almost all the early research was conducted in wilderness areas and one of the primary attractions of such areas was the absence of other recreationists. However, even in the early 1960s, Lucas (1964) demonstrated that numbers of people was not the only and not even necessarily the most important consideration to users with respect to perception of crowding and satisfaction, but that types of use and user were of equal or greater significance.

Whereas in many of the early studies of capacity the focus was on numbers of users permitted in an area, Stankey and McCool (1989) have commented that this previously popular principle that the key issue in management is that the number of persons involved is no longer accepted and note that a growing body of research clearly indicates that this is not the case. There are very few studies claiming to show a statistically significant relationship between measures of user satisfaction and measure of density, such as numbers of users or frequency of encounters. They go on to suggest several reasons for this, including the fact that, contrary to many of the earlier assumptions about satisfaction, solitude is not the only item of concern, but that there are number of motivations and needs which can be met by recreation use, even in wilderness surroundings. They also point out other factors which help explain the range of responses between varying levels of satisfaction and density. These include aspects of self-selection, i.e. users preselect areas which they assume from experience or knowledge will have acceptable density levels, the fact that dissatisfied users may not return to an area, and thus not show up in user surveys, the difficulty of measuring satisfaction, the saliency or importance of the setting and attributes of an area and the influence of expectations and preferences on perceptions (Stankey and McCool, 1989).

The early studies of carrying capacity of recreation areas were, for the most part, conducted in wilderness settings and were dominated by researchers working for or with the United States Forest Service. This tradition of leadership in capacity research continued through the 1970s and the research literature includes many works by US Forest Service employees, including Driver, Hendee, Lime, Lucas, Stankey, and Wagar. Research on carrying capacity has been a major theme in the recreation literature since the 1960s and has been recognized as such by many researchers. A review of the literature by Vaske has listed almost 3000 references on this topic and the number of articles and reports continues to grow. It is clear, however, that the nature and thrust of much of the research on this topic have changed greatly over the last decade and a half, in part because researchers have become more knowledgeable about the concept and its complex nature and in part because it has been realized that, like the Holy Grail, a magic capacity figure for an area does not exist.

Furthermore, Shelby and Heberlein (1986) suggest four types of capacity, namely ecological, social, physical and facility. The ecological capacity reflects the ability of the environment to withstand recreational use. Social capacity refers to the numbers of users an area can hold before the recreation experiences decline in quality for users. Physical capacity and facility capacity could be viewed as related, the former referring to the actual amount of space available for specific functions, e.g. camping, and the latter referring to the capacity of such man-made items as car parks and ferries. In both cases, it may be possible to increase the capacity by the application of technology and/or capital investment and thus, to some extent, they may both be viewed as modifiable. To these may be added a further element, which may be termed institutional capacity, which relates to levels of use that may be imposed by authorities for such reasons as safety, e.g. with respect to boats, licensed premises, stadia and the like. In most studies, however, discussions of capacity are limited to the aspects of ecological and social capacity.

114

Issues

It was recognized relatively early that there are a number of key components to carrying capacity and that these are closely interrelated (Lime and Stankey, 1971). Although they have been described in a variety of ways, they can be simplified as (a) the impacts of recreational use on the environment, (b) recreationist preferences and perceptions and (c) management and policy goals and objectives. To many researchers management is the key to carrying capacity, because the management policy provides the context in which the impacts of users and the preferences of users can be evaluated and their relative importance determined. A definition of carrying capacity such as 'the maximum amount of recreation use an area can withstand without suffering significant ecological damage and still provide an acceptable recreation experience', which was not uncommon in the 1960s and 1970s, is impossible to operationalize until 'significant' and 'acceptable' are defined in the context of the recreation area and the role it is to fulfil. Clearly, if the area under consideration is an urban park, built on reclaimed land, then 'significant ecological damage' has a different meaning from that which would be applicable for a national park, where the emphasis may be on ecological integrity and an absence of man-induced change. Similarly, if the area is used by wilderness campers the experience they will be looking for may be more dependent on level and type of use allowed than if the area were used by downhill skiers. The decisions on the role and purpose of the area and the type of use allowed within it must be made before levels of use can be determined and enforced. Thus management cannot be divorced from issues of capacity.

There are a number of general aspects of the concept of carrying capacity which have been clarified in the last decade. The first relates to the last point noted, namely, that the production of capacity limits are meaningless unless placed in the context of management objectives. A second point is that it is generally recognized that there is not a single measure of satisfaction which can be applied to use of an area, but that there may be multiple aspects of satisfaction. Related to this is the fact that dissatisfaction may well be a different element from satisfaction and may operate on a separate, if similar continuum. A third point on which there seems to be agreement, even if the problem is not solved, is that the implications of encounters between users vary according to a number of variables, including place, time, frequency and type. Another point is that the compatibility or tolerance of different user groups to one another also varies according to a range of circumstances. Finally, there is agreement that there is considerable variation in ecological impacts from recreation use in an area, along with a range of potential indicators of impacts.

While there may be general agreement on all or many of these points, there are not yet clear solutions to a number of important issues (Graefe, Vaske and Kuss, 1986). The relationship between use and impact is still problematic, i.e. the detailed linkages and reactions between crowding or density, satisfaction, type of use and environmental effects are not clear. There can be no general recommendation on whether management should be with a priority on use and satisfaction or on ecological conditions, i.e. whether the emphasis should be on recreation or protection. This inevitably becomes dependent on the specific role of the recreation area under consideration. There is no universal method to incorporate the preferences, expectations and satisfactions of potential or previous users into capacity considerations and this raises a number of problems related to equity, elitism and disenfranchisement. There is also no universally accepted way to limit numbers to an area once a use limit has been set, which will be viewed as acceptable by all elements of the population.

Preformed planning and management frameworks

As stated earlier, the growing interest and participation in outdoor recreation in the post-World War II era, especially on public lands, created many new problems for park managers. These, according to Payne and Graham (1993), can be loosely grouped as follows: (i) the presence of large numbers of visitors creating long-term damage to park resources; (ii) the increasing number of encounters between people and animals, especially large carnivores, producing unpleasant results for both; and (iii) different types of visitor with conflicting motivations. These types of issue, especially the increased human dimension in parks, proved to be challenging for parks managers, who maintained a traditional focus on park ecology issues and who had formal training as ecologists or resource managers (some would argue that this continues to be a constraint to comprehensive park management). As such, the knowledge and motivation effectively to understand and mitigate the conflicts that recreationists had on each other and the natural resources of the park was absent.

The response to these pressures was the creation of a number of preformed planning and management frameworks designed to interface human and resource dimensions through integrated means. Such frameworks began to appear in the 1970s and began to increase in number throughout the 1980s. The most frequently used frameworks appear to be the recreation opportunity spectrum (ROS) and the limits of acceptable change (LAC), with other models including the visitor impact management framework (VIM) and the visitor activity management process (VAMP) (see Chapter 2). These management tools are considered to be much more holistic in their attempts to manage recreational use and resource protection than more traditional resource-based park management schemes. The first two of these are now briefly considered.

Recreation opportunity spectrum

The recreation opportunity spectrum (ROS) was developed by the United States Forest Service in the late 1970s for the purpose of better managing the relationship between the setting, the activities and the experiences desired by those participating in various outdoor recreation activities (see Chapter 2). Inherent in the ROS framework is the notion that recreation must be viewed as a behavioural phenomenon, with the recreational setting defined as the combination of physical, biological, social and managerial conditions which give value to recreational activities. From the diversity of recreation settings possible, a framework was developed which focused on recreation opportunities that ranged along a spectrum between pristine wilderness to high-density urban settings. Six attributes were used to define the nature of recreational opportunities possible within each setting: access, other non-recreational resource uses, onsite management, social interaction, acceptability of visitor impacts and acceptable level of regimentation. Using these six factors, recreational opportunities are identified for a specific setting and subsequently controlled through management guidelines.

The ROS framework, although conceptual in nature, has a high degree of flexibility in integrating the resource (setting) with visitor issues in order to determine the supply of recreational opportunities. The spectrum offers managers the means to examine opportunity settings with respect to the capability of potential users to avail themselves of those opportunities which exist. The framework can also be used in concert with management plans to allow for the protection of environmentally sensitive environments and identify those settings where recreational activities can be promoted that are deemed suitable to meet the desired experiences of participants.

Limits of acceptable change

The limits of acceptable change (LAC) planning process, also developed by the United States Forest Service, was borne out of the recognition that issues concerning carrying capacity were ultimately based on the social judgement of managers and the need explicitly to outline a process to identify acceptable use levels (see Chapter 2). The purpose of the framework is to determine acceptable and appropriate resource and social conditions for recreation settings. The process is prescriptive in nature as it utilizes a set of management actions in order to achieve appropriate and acceptable conditions. Emphasis moved from how much use an area could tolerate to the type of conditions that were desired in an area. In essence, change in areas was accepted given that managers had control over this change. The LAC planning process is based on the following four major components:

1 specification of resource and social conditions
2 comparison of existing with desired conditions
3 identifying those actions necessary to achieve conditions
4 monitoring and evaluation of actions taken.

These four components are operationalized through a nine-step planning process.

A major strength of the LAC planning process is that it offers managers a easy step-by-step guide to control change within the setting. Also, the framework is prescriptive in nature which allows positive steps to be taken to control growth, rather than time being wasted on remedial measures to minimize any damage that has already occurred. Table 6.1 includes some of the key characteristics of the ROS and LAC models.

Table 6.1 Key characteristics of ROS and LAC frameworks

Characteristic	ROS	LAC
Purpose	Provision of settings to match with recreational activities	Setting use standards for wilderness areas
Focus	Modification, access, user interaction, and management	Identification of opportunities for recreational activities
Scope	Wide, regional	Narrow, site specific
Public involvement	Limited	Extensive
Information type used	Formal (e.g. survey)	Informal
Decision-making process	Technical	Consensual
Product	Identification of recreation settings through mapping and other planning devices	Management to minimize gaps between resource and social standards

The POLAR framework

A more recent addition to the family of preformed planning and management structures is the procedure for operationalizing limits for the administration of rivers (POLAR) framework, developed by Butler, Fennell and Boyd (1992) specifically to manage outdoor recreation on river environments. It is premised on the notion that all rivers are unique in their physiography and patterns of use. Consequently, although POLAR is a general model, it was designed to be applicable to any river environment or any other linear environment where recreational activity occurs. POLAR is a tool from which better to understand the relationship between settings, physical and social zones and measures of impact and recreational use. The operational procedures of POLAR are arranged in a series of stages and steps (see Figures 6.1 and 6.2), and the basic aspects of the framework are discussed in the following sections.

Rivers are dynamic environments which often flow for hundreds of miles through many different types of undeveloped and developed region, including mountains, plains, wilderness areas and both rural and urban regions. As such, rivers can be quite pristine and natural or they can be greatly transformed through chemical, mechanical or physical means. The introduction of changes to the physical and biological nature of a river are not site specific, but rather transitory. This means that the deposit of agricultural pollutants, industrial effluent and other toxins has a direct impact on regions downstream. Also, because of their linear nature, the type of management required for rivers is not necessarily the same as it may be for terrestrial natural areas. The setting of borders and other demarcations for the former is based on the physical nature of the river, perhaps in association with flood plains or other features. By the same token, terrestrial parks, which in the past have been internally oriented (see Dearden and Rollins, 1993), have established borders that are geopolitical in derivation.

Also, just like natural areas in general, river corridors are subject to the same types of recreational pressure from any number of motorized and non-motorized activities. These include jet skis, jet boats, motorboats for fishing, houseboats, white water rafts, angling, hiking, eco-challenges, canoeing, float planes, camping, tubing and do on. And while most of these are much more environmentally benign when compared with some other landuses, the recreational effects caused by water-based recreational use can be both direct (i.e. *observed* changes) and indirect (i.e. changes that are *not necessarily* observable) (see Hammitt and Cole, 1987). Even the reputedly benign ones, such as canoeing, can have impacts, especially when they allow humans to penetrate into some of the most pristine areas of a wilderness. Here, in these remote regions, humans introduce change. Furthermore, linking in with the previous paragraph, recreational use in terrestrial parks can be quite diffuse. Consequently, the

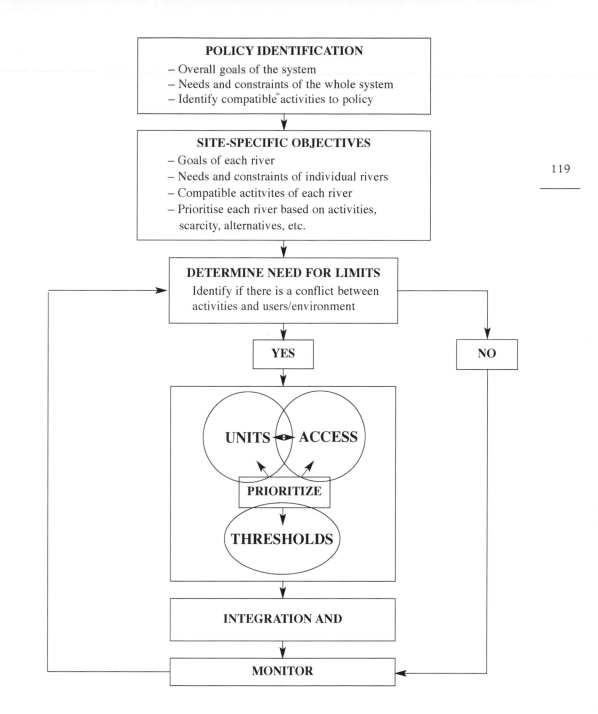

Figure 6.1 Framework of the procedure for operationalizing limits for the administration of rivers (POLAR)

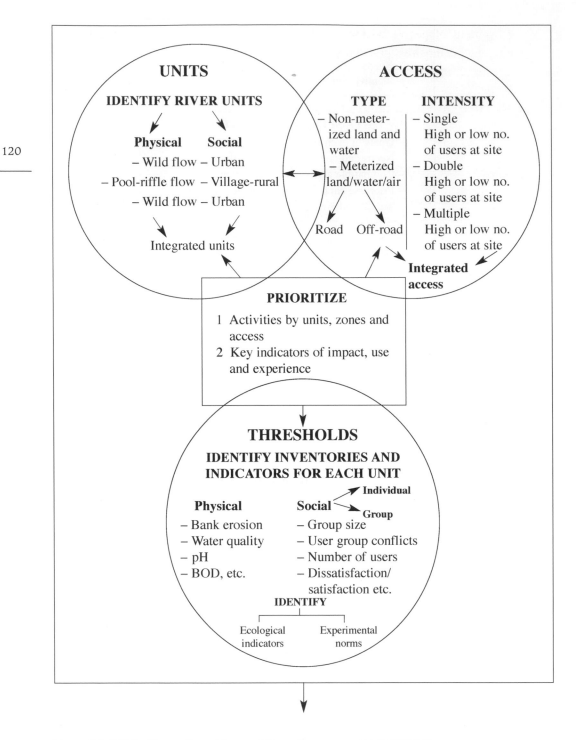

Figure 6.2 POLAR Stages Four, Five and Six: units, access and thresholds

movement of people within and between areas for the purpose of using, for example, campsites, has many possibilities. Not so in river environments where parties in specified areas must be managed in space and time. Three parties launching at the same time on a river must go the same way and compete for the same resources (e.g. choice campsites). This factor, among others, underlies the value of better understanding recreational access, space and time.

Stage One: policy identification

This framework recognizes that each river is a part of a broader regional or provincial management and classification plan and that the overall objectives and principles of that system have to be taken as the general guiding principles for each individual element in the system. The first stage therefore, requires an assessment of the applicability of the system-wide principles to the river under consideration and the identification of any constraints or requirements that may need to be imposed on the river in the light of the overall principles. In particular, current activities and level of use of those activities should be reviewed to ensure that they are compatible with the general system-wide objectives and principles, in order to identify existing or potential conflicts and incompatibilities.

Stage Two: site-specific objectives

In the context of the specific river, it is necessary to clarify the goals and objectives set out for the river. These may be contained and articulated in management plans or may not have been produced. It is necessary to have some goals and objectives defined for the river under consideration before an assessment of use limits can be made, for, as discussed earlier, there is general agreement that limits to use can only be meaningfully applied in the context of overall management objectives. Specific constraints and requirements should also be identified, e.g. the general characteristic of the river and the function it is intended to fill, such as providing wilderness river opportunities or a mix of backcountry and forecountry activities. Existing conflicts should be identified, including those between forms of recreation, those existing because of levels of use of forms of recreation and those existing because of the physical impacts resulting from the forms of recreation.

It is then necessary to prioritize the forms of recreation that currently exist and those that could be allowed on the river in the future, based on current considerations, and on activities engaged in on similar rivers in other areas. The procedure for this prioritization is a modification of that developed by Tivy (1973) in the United Kingdom. There are eight factors to be taken into consideration in this procedure and the goal is to arrive at a generalized score that will enable decision makers to compare the relative attributes of each potential activity against each of the others. It is not suggested that the activity with the highest score should automatically be ranked first and the one with the lowest score be ranked last. The procedure is not intended to make the decision, but rather to provide information (see Table 6.2).

Table 6.2 Evaluation of priority of recreational activities for the entire river

Activity Issues	Characteristic and score* (ranked as 3, 2, 1)
Specific activity	
Alternative opportunities in region	None, several, many
Quality of experience in region	High, medium, low
Proportion of visitors desiring activities	All, some, few
Relationship with other recreation activities	Complementary, compatible
Competitive	
Relationship with other resource activities	Complementary, compatible
Competitive	
Seasonality	Year round, seasonal
Proposed	
Permanence	Established, new
Proposed	
Change site characteristics	Negligible, some, great

* The higher the score, the higher the priority

The first step is to identify other opportunities in the region for the activity under consideration, that is, how many alternative opportunities exist in the region for visitors to engage in the recreation activity being considered. The region is left for the river manager to determine, it may be an administrative unit, it may be based on distance from populations centres providing the bulk of visitors to the river or some other basis. In the case of some recreation activities, the availability of opportunities may be so great that a small region may be sufficient, in the case of other activities, it may be necessary to consider a whole province as a region for this purpose. The results of this step should be entered into a matrix. The researcher has the choice of entering the raw data, i.e. specific numbers, or of categorizing the opportunities as 'none', 'several' or 'many'.

The second step is to evaluate the quality of experience offered by the river under consideration for the specific activity. It is not proposed that this should be done in great detail, but rather should be done on a comparative basis with other opportunities for that activity in the region considered in Step One. The quality of the experience should be categorized as 'high', 'medium' or 'low' and entered in the matrix.

The third step is a consideration of the proportion of all visitors to the river who desire to participate in the activity under consideration. If detailed user data are available then clearly these should be used, however, in the absence of such information, estimates will have to suffice. Again, the results should be entered in to the matrix, and the categories 'all', 'some' and 'few' should be used. Clearly, any activity for which there is no current or anticipated demand will not be considered.

In order to identify the relative compatibility of activities with one another, it is necessary to categorize the relationship between activities. For this purpose it is not necessary to take use levels into account. The researcher is required to categorize the activity on the basis of whether it is deemed 'complementary', 'compatible' or 'competitive' with other recreation activities. 'Complementary' is taken to mean that the activity under consideration has a mutually symbiotic relationship with other activities, 'compatible' in this context is taken to mean that the activity can coexist with other activities without difficulties, while 'competitive' implies that the activity has the potential for conflict with other activities because it competes for similar resources.

In step five a similar procedure is conducted for the activity in relation to non-recreational activities, for example, logging, mining, hydropower generation and transportation, in order to assess the exclusivity of the recreation activity. Identical categories to those in step four are to be used.

Step six relates to the seasonality of the activity. In those cases where an activity can be engaged in more than one season, but is primarily participated in during one only, then the predominant season should be identified. The purpose of this stage is to identify activities that have a limited season and therefore may be compatible for the river if their season of participation is different from that of another potentially incompatible activity. The categories 'year round', 'seasonal' (implying a recognized period of use) and 'limited', (implying a short and clearly defined period of use in that region or on that river) apply.

The seventh step relates to the existence of the activity on the river. The category 'established' means that the activity is an accepted one that has been conducted on the river for more than one season or year, whichever is applicable. 'New' applies to recreation activities that have only been engaged in on the river for the current year or a maximum of one year before. 'Proposed' is self-explanatory and refers to activities that have been or are being considered for the river.

The final step relates to the impacts the activity has on the physical environment of the river. At this stage it is *not* necessary to conduct detailed ecological research to complete the categorization, but merely to identify whether the activity has significant or insignificant environmental impacts. The categories to be used are 'greatly', implying there is considerable and serious impact from the activity, 'some', implying there are identifiable impacts from the activity and 'negligible', meaning that such impacts as do occur are not of significance.

For comparative purposes, only the categorizations can be scored, giving three points for a response in the first column, two points for a response in the second column and one point for a response in the third column. It must be emphasized, however, that the cumulative score needs to be regarded at best as an indicator. It is not a measurement of anything specific. The issues are not regarded as equal in significance and may vary in importance from one river to another. However, an activity which receives a high *may* be appropriate for a higher priority on the river than one which receives a low score. It should also be emphasized that only those activities that have been deemed compatible with the goals and objectives of *both* the system *and* the specific river should be considered in this procedure.

Stage Three: need for limits

At this point in the procedure, it is necessary to determine if the current and immediately projected uses of the river, and the levels of such use, present any conflicts or incompatibilities among the activities and users themselves, with the environment of the river or with the goals and objectives set out for the river. If the level and the type of use, both at present and for the immediate future, are both of such a nature that no such conflicts are apparent, then it is appropriate to move on to Stage Nine, which involves monitoring the use and effects of use. If conflicts or incompatibilities are identified or anticipated, then it is appropriate to proceed with Stage Four.

Stage Four: division of the river into units

This stage involves the division of the river into a number of river units in order to allow for more accurate delineation of limits to use. In the case of some rivers this step may have already been taken in some similar fashion to the one outlined here and those subdivisions may be utilized. There are two sets of criteria on which to delineate the river units, one set relates to the physical attributes of the river and the second to the social elements of the river and its surroundings. These criteria are similar to those derived by Manning (1980).

The first step is to identify significant changes in the physical characteristics of the river within the section which lies in the heritage river designation. Three categories have been selected, namely wild-flow, pool-riffle and steady and flat water and these pertain to the nature of the flow of the river itself. Given that flow is a major determinant of the quality of the recreation experience for canoeing and rafting, two of the major activities engaged in on recreational rivers, and also of considerable significance for other activities such as fishing, floating and swimming, which may also be engaged in on some rivers in the system, it was selected as the major variable to consider.

Wild-flow segments are those in which the water is flowing rapidly and in which there are rapids, waterfalls and white water. These last features are not a prerequisite of the wild-flow designation, but any section of a river with these features would certainly be designated as a wild-flow segment. Intermediate or pool-riffle flow segments are those sections of the river which are dominated by irregular patterns of flow, with an intermingling of pools and slow-flow areas with stretches of riffle flow and broken water. Steady-flow segments (consider also flat-water sections which include lakes), as the term implies, are those stretches of a river which are dominated by a regular consistent flow. It is intended that the river segments would be of an order of several kilometres in length, indeed, it may be that much or even all of a designated stretch of a river may fall entirely within one physical segment, although the expectation would be that in the majority of cases there will be several changes in the nature of the flow of a river and thus an equivalent number of physical segments. Specific features on their own do not automatically require delineation as a separate physical segment, particularly where they may be short in length. The physical segment is intended to represent the overall physical character of a stretch of the river.

A similar exercise is then to be undertaken for the settlement characteristics of the river. As with the physical elements, there are three categories involved. The first is urban, which is to be used when the nature of the area through which the river is flowing is dominated by human development, e.g. through a city or other urban area or in a landscape dominated by urban views. The village–rural category is to be used when the river is flowing through a landscape dominated by human activity or in which human activity is evident, but the nature of that activity is not predominantly urban, for example, through an agricultural area or an area showing evidence of forestry activity. The third category, and the one into which most of the heritage rivers will fall for most of their lengths, is backcountry, which implies that the area through which the river is flowing displays no or very little evidence of human activity and the area is essentially wild and undeveloped.

Once both the physical and settlement segments have been identified, it is necessary to combine these division to identify the river units. In the majority of cases this will be a relatively easy task, as the two types of segments are likely to be relatively exclusive with respect to boundaries. Settlement segments can be viewed in most cases as subdivisions within physical segments. The normal number of river units for a river would be one less than the total number of physical and settlement segments combined, although in a few cases where boundaries of both physical and settlement segments combine, the total number of river units could be less than this figure.

As an example, a river may begin in a wild-flow segment in a backcountry segment (river unit 1), change to pool-riffle flow in backcountry (river unit 2), continue as pool riffle into a village–rural segment (river unit 3) and change to steady flow in a village–rural segment (river unit 4) until it passes out of the river designation. The river units identified will, therefore, reflect both the physical and settlement characteristics of the river and its surroundings. As noted in the literature reviewed earlier, setting is a factor of considerable significance in determining the expectations and enjoyment of users. It should be noted that the river units should be evaluated periodically to determine if changes in the flow of the river, e.g. as a result of drainage alterations or in the nature of the surroundings, e.g. as a result of residential development, require a revision of the type of river unit designation or creation of new units.

In the original work by Butler, Fennell and Boyd (1992) it was acknowledged that there would be variation in size of the river units and that they were not meant to refer, under normal circumstances, to a specific feature, but rather to the general characteristics of a particular stretch of a river. It is not felt that this stage would present major problems in implementation to a 'normal' wilderness river.

Stage Five: access type and intensity

A similar exercise has then to be performed with respect to access to the river. Access points are of crucial importance in the context of management since they represent the best and, in some cases, the *only* locations at which use can be monitored and, if necessary, restricted. Furthermore, access points often represent major changes in use patterns, both with respect to levels of use and types of use. Above the initial access point to a river there may be very little use except for occasional fishing. From the access point downstream there may be a variety of water activities, until at least the next access point. There may also be a variety of land- and water-related activities at the access point itself, for example, camping, swimming, picnicking, outfitter bases, boat-launching sites and interpretive facilities. If an access point is not the initial one, such uses may significantly change the setting and the experience for users who joined the river upstream and had experienced backcountry settings until reaching the access point.

Access points are to be categorized on two types of criteria, one relating to the type of access, and one relating to the intensity of the access. The initial division is on the basis of type of access, whether this is motorized or non-motorized. The non-motorized access points should be further divided as to whether they offer access by land, by water or both. The motorized access points should be classified as to whether they offer access by land, by water or by air and, in the case of access by land, whether this is by road, or for off-road vehicles or some combination of these possibilities.

The second categorization is by intensity or level of access. This involves classifying the access by the nature of the type of user, whether there is access for only one type of user, for two types of user or for multiple types of user and, second, whether the number of users at an access point are high or low. The high or low measure has to be determined in the context of the overall level of use of the river, rather than being a preselected figure. Low numbers can be taken to imply that the level of numbers of users entering at that access point is measurably below the number expected if each access point on the river received an equal number of users. Thus if a river had five access points, the expected number of users at each access point can be taken to be 20% of all river users. A figure 25% or more below this level would be classified as low and a figure 25% or more above the expected level would be classified as high. (The 25% is an arbitrary figure and can be adjusted if felt appropriate.)

Once the access points have been classified by type of access and by intensity of access, they should be integrated to reflect the overall nature of access at each point. The following categorization is to be used:

Level 1: Non-motorized; single users, low level.
Level 2: Non-motorized; single users, high level or double users, low level.
Level 3: Non-motorized; double users, high level or multiple users, low level.
Level 4: Motorized; double users, high level or multiple users, low level.
Level 5: Motorized; multiple users, high level.

The different access levels are intended to reflect the probability of increasing conflict or problems arising as a result of the increasing numbers and types of user at the different levels.

Stage Six: prioritization

At this point, the first step is to prioritize activities and access for each of the river units identified in Stage Four. The process for prioritization of activities is the same as was utilized in Stage Two to prioritize recreation activities for the river as a whole and is illustrated in Table 6.3. In the context of the river units, however, the evaluation is conducted with reference to the river as whole and only for those activities that have been prioritized for the river as a whole. Thus, although for a river it may have been decided that canoeing and rafting may be acceptable in that order of priority, a different priority may be set for each individual river *unit*. If for example, there is only one suitable stretch of river for rafting, then this activity may be ranked first in priority in the river unit in which that particular stretch of river falls. Such a decision would have certain implications for the access points, since it would be necessary to ensure that suitable access was available at points above and below this river unit for users wishing to engage in the activities approved for that unit. At the river unit level it is considered essential to evaluate the potential environmental impacts of the specific forms of recreation and a procedure for doing this is shown in Table 6.4 (the second step). The six items listed pertain to characteristics of the unit and

Table 6.3 Evaluation of priority of recreational activities for each river unit

Activity Issues	Characteristic and Score* (ranked as 3, 2, 1)
Specific activity	
Alternative opportunities in region	None, several, many
Quality of experience in20region	High, medium, low
Proportion of visitors desiring activities	All, some, few
Relationship with other recreation activities	Complementary, compatible
Competitive	
Relationship with other resource activities	Complementary, compatible
Competitive	
Seasonality	Year round, seasonal
Proposed	
Permanence	Established, new
Proposed	
Change site characteristics	Great, some, negligible

* The higher the score, the higher the priority

Table 6.4 Significance of environmental impacts

Factor	Level of significance of impact* (ranked as 3, 2, or 1)
Activity's impact on the ...	
Uniqueness of site	High, medium, low
Vulnerability of site	High, medium, low
Reversibility of impact	High, medium, low
Severity of impact	High, medium, low
Spatial extent of impact	High, medium, low
Temporal extent of impact	Continuous, seasonal
Infrequent	

* The higher the number, the higher the impact

to the form of recreational activity being considered. As with the procedure for establishing priority of activities, the result of the process is not intended to provide a decision, but rather to provide comparative information on which a decision can be made.

The first element to consider is the *uniqueness* of the site, i.e. whether it has specific features such as vegetation or wildlife which is rare or endangered or represents an unusual or rare feature which could be impacted by the specific activity being considered. The second aspect is the *vulnerability* of the site, that is, whether it is particularly susceptible to the impacts created by the activity under consideration. For example, a steep rocky valley may well be almost impervious to ecological impact from canoeing, but a soft bank may be highly susceptible to use from power boats or erosion from the feet of users. The third element is an *assessment* of whether any impacts caused by the activity are permanent or could be reversed or removed. *Severity of impact*, the fourth element, refers to the level of impact caused by the activity and is a more subjective component. It refers to the nature of the impact, e.g. loss of ground cover is more serious than minor damage to mature trees. The *spatial extent of impact* refers to the amount of area affected by the activity, while the final aspect, the *temporal extent*, refers to the time over which an impact is likely to be experienced. The level of significance is to be indicated as 'high', 'medium' or 'low' and a score of 3, 2 or 1 assigned to each element. The maximum possible score would be 18, which would represent an activity having a high negative impact in all areas, while the minimum score is 6. Again, it should be stressed that the scores are only for comparative purposes. In any river unit it may be appropriate to decide that any one element is of such importance, for example, uniqueness of the unit, that any activity achieving a high score in this category is automatically ruled unacceptable in that unit.

After the activities have been prioritized it is necessary to determine the level of access to be permitted for each river unit (the third step of this stage), if applicable. In some cases, there may be no access points in a river unit, and thus this step is not necessary. Where access points exist, however, they should be reviewed to determine that the nature and intensity of access, including the types of activity, are appropriate for the mix of activities prioritized for the river unit and that conflicts and incompatibilities are not established or allowed to continue. Thus for a wild flow/backcountry river unit, with canoeing identified as the priority or perhaps even the only activity, it would not be appropriate to have a level 5 access point, which would almost inevitably result in other forms of use at higher levels than acceptable.

Stage Seven: *thresholds of maximum use*

In this stage, three steps are outlined that aim to structure limits on use levels for each river unit, based on the types and nature of recreation activity prioritized earlier and the susceptibility of the ecology of the river unit to impact. It is clear from the literature on carrying capacity that has been reviewed that setting a priori use limits is not realistic. The problem of ecological change being brought about by recreation use is often as much or more a function of the *type* of recreation than the actual *level* of use. It is necessary, therefore, to inventory and identify ecological indicators for each river unit and to ensure that environmental quality as revealed by these indicators does not decline as a result of recreation use (Table 6.5). Inventory implies that a measure will be made of the current quality or standard of each indicator used in a river unit and a minimum quality level or standard identified beyond which a decline is not acceptable.

The second of the three steps in this stage involves determining the setting which each river unit best represents and the mix of recreation users that will occur on that unit. It may be necessary to perform the exercise a number of

Table 6.5 Ecological indicators used to identify river units and amounts of use

Basic physical features	Soil characteristics
Width/length of river unit	Extent of trampling
Nature of flow (wild, pool, steady)	Extent of soil erosion
Water velocity	Soil compaction
Fluctuation of flow	Presence of slumping, heaving, creep
Seasonality (dry/frozen periods)	
Nature of streambed	**Biological indicators**
Presence of streambed material	Presence of algae
Dominant river pattern	Diversity/extent of aquatic plants
Extent of bank erosion	Fish type and diversity
Height of bank	Presence of waterfowl
	Land flora
Physical features/impediments to use	Game animals
Presence of ponds	Presence/diversity of birds
Still water	
Braiding of river	**Land use**
Presence of rapids, waterfalls, islands	% of unit in private/public land
Oxbow lakes	% managed by provincial/federal agencies
	% of unit protected
Water quality	Presence of historical sites
Degree of turbidity	% of unit in areas of general landuse
Water temperature	
Presence of bottom/floating solids	**Aesthetic elements**
Bacteriological conditions	Group size
Biological oxygen demand (BOD)	Conflict between user groups
Presence of pesticides/chemicals	Levels of satisfaction/dissatisfaction
Extent of eutrophication	Extent of crowding
pH level	Remoteness
Faecal coliform	Vandalism/extent of garbage
Transparency/productivity/phytoplankton quality	Scenic variety/uniqueness
	Noise levels

(Source: Chubb and Bauman, 1977)

times if there is seasonal variation in either the setting or the mix of users, as may well occur, especially on rivers with a variety of access levels.

At the same time, experiential norms, the third step, for each recreation activity should be selected, which also reflect the setting in which the activity is to take place, as research has shown that setting is significant in shaping enjoyment and satisfaction. A wide range of encounter norms, based on the literature reviewed, is contained in Table 6.6. The table reflects both activities, e.g. canoeing, and the setting, e.g. wilderness, as well as reflecting the groups with whom encounters may take place.

The end result of this stage should be a set of figures which represent the maximum number of users engaged in each activity in a specific setting in each river unit for particular periods or seasons, where applicable. These figures are not absolute capacity figures, but should be regarded as guidelines for maximum levels of use within specific conditions and are unique to each river unit. Thus it may be quite possible to have different use levels for the same specific activity in the same specific setting in different river units because of the

Table 6.6 Experiential norms for river recreation and backcountry experiences (number of parties)

Activities / Undefined rec.	General	Wilderness	Encounter levels for different settings / Semi-wilderness
Canoeing			
Tubers	0–2.3		
Canoeists	0–5.7		
Anglers	0–7.2		
Angling			
Floaters	0–6.5		
Boaters	0–5		
Anglers	0–25		
Bank anglers	0–13		
All river users	2–>25		
Floating			
Floaters	0–4	1.5	3.0
Jet boaters	0–10	1.5	
All river users	0–4	0–5	0–10
Rafting			
All river users	0–25		
Boating			
Boaters	11		
Commercial users	4–10		
Private users	5–25		
Jet boating			
Floaters	0–100	4.4	

different mix of users and/or the different ecological constraints of each of the river units.

Stage Eight: integration and implementation

It is necessary now to integrate the individual river units and the derived limits on use to produce *consistent limits* for the designated river or stretch of river. As each river unit has been examined in relative isolation, it is important to ascertain that inconsistencies and incompatibilities have not been built into the evaluation. As already noted, it is only at access points that users may enter and leave the river environment and, therefore, if certain uses are permitted on the river at a specific access point, in theory they can continue both upstream and downstream at least until the neighbouring access points. It is primarily at access points that limits to use can best be imposed and specific activities restricted or prohibited. Certain levels of access may make some restrictions extremely difficult to apply, unless strong enforcement is present. As certain levels of access may be unavoidable in some situations, for example, existing road access points, it may be necessary to institute limits of use lower than would otherwise have been the case for a specific river unit at an access point, because a downstream unit can only withstand a lower level of use for a specific mix of activities. It is for this reason that this stage is necessary. Once the river or designated stretch of river has been reviewed for internal consistency, then the limits on levels of use for the approved activities can be implemented.

Stage Nine: monitoring

The final stage in the procedure is the monitoring of use on the river. This is for two purposes. First, to ensure, through the use of the ecological indicators identified in Stages Six and Seven, that unacceptable change is not taking place in the environment of the river. Second, to ensure, through the use of the prioritization of activities and the encounter norms identified, that the quality of the experience of the users is not deteriorating through an inappropriate mix of uses or inappropriate levels of use. The level and frequency of monitoring can only be determined by the management body for the river and will inevitably reflect manpower and budgets available. Some monitoring of ecological change may be able to be accomplished with a minimum of field work if monitoring stations exist for such elements as water quality and other information may be able to be obtained from remote sensing, especially aerial photography. Monitoring of the quality of the recreation experience can only be done effectively through user surveys. Decreasing numbers of users may indicate dissatisfaction with the experience, although this is not certain. User surveys are the only way to obtain user opinions about their satisfaction and dissatisfaction with elements of their recreation experience, including such aspects as numbers and types of encounters and perception of environmental quality and setting.

If evidence suggests that there is a decline in environmental quality below the levels identified, or a decline in the quality of the user experience, then it may be necessary to adjust either the mix of uses or the level of use of specific river units or both. The emphasis in the model has been placed on setting limits to use which will safeguard the existing environment and recreation experiences, based on levels of use suggested in the literature. The peculiar and unique attributes of each river environment make it almost inevitable that, in some situations, general guidelines do not work as effectively as anticipated and adjustments are required.

In addition, if new uses are to be considered for a river at some time in the future, then the priorities and use limits will need to be reviewed. New access points or changes in the level of access points will also warrant a review of the priorities and use limits. So too would major changes in the provision of regional recreational opportunities.

Those rivers for which it was determined in Stage Three that no need for limits to use currently existed should be monitored on a regular basis to ensure that such a situation still exists. In such cases, where undesired or unacceptable environmental change is occurring, or where a decline in the quality of the recreation experience is recorded, then the POLAR model procedure Stages Four through Nine should be implemented.

Conclusion

The framework discussed in this chapter is a general one, aimed at meeting the need to determine use levels for rivers in a variety of different settings in order to safeguard the environments of these rivers and the quality of the recreation experience which they offer. As any general framework, it has its limitations. It will almost inevitably work better and be easier to apply in some situations than others. It is based on a reasonably comprehensive review of the literature on carrying capacity, river recreation and management and the many preformed planning and management frameworks which are currently in existence. Much of this literature pertains to the North American outdoor recreation perspective that may be different than other world regions in terms of setting and use preferences. One of the main strengths of the framework is the move away from a reliance on sophisticated datasets for decision making. In many cases, managers who have a good knowledge of the resource base and user groups can quickly make decisions about how to prioritize activities, in different settings, without a great deal of work. The framework is also easily modified to apply to other linear or corridor-based recreational activities, such as hiking, cross-country skiing and snowmobiling.

Although too lengthy to include here, the POLAR framework has been operationalized on two rivers in Saskatchewan: the Churchill River and the Clearwater River. In the latter case, the main issue was the interaction between canoeists and white-water rafters and the perceived need to allow more permits to operators (see Fennell, 1997). Here the issue was related primarily to level of use and not type, as the two groups are seen to be fairly compatible on the river. As such, canoeists showed concern if the level of rafting on the river exceeded their expectations, which was not necessarily the case for rafters. One of the key issues was campsite impact and the potential for conflict in the future. It was suggested that managers must be careful in trying to determine the appropriate level of use on the Clearwater. It should be understood that there is perhaps the belief that backcountry settings can never be underused, but can always be identified as being overused. The trick is to establish settings and use levels that provide maximum satisfaction to as many people as possible, without degrading the environment and the quality of the experience of the different groups of users.

Questions

1 Why is the carrying capacity of ecotourism destination so difficult to define?
2 What are the main benefits of applying the planning frameworks in an ecotourism setting?
3 What is the purpose of the POLAR framework?
4 Which of the main steps of the POLAR framework do you consider most difficult to implement?

References

Butler, R.W., Fennell, David A. and Boyd, S.W. (1992) *The POLAR Model: A System for Managing the Recreational Capacity of Canadian Heritage Rivers*. Ottawa: Environment Canada.

Dearden, P. and Rollins, R. (1993) 'The times they are a-changin'. In Dearden, P. and Rollins, R. (eds) *Parks and Protected Areas in Canada*. Toronto: Oxford.

Fennell, David A. (1997). Managing recreational use of the Clearwater River. Prepared for Saskatchewan Environment and Resource Management, Regina, Saskatchewan.

Graefe, A.R., Vaske, J.J. and Kuss, F.R. (1986) 'Resolved issues and remaining questions about social carrying capacity', *Leisure Sciences*, 6 (4), 497–507.

Hammitt, W.E. and Cole, D.N. (1987) *Wildland Recreation: Ecology and Management*. New York: John Wiley & Sons.

Jackson, E.L. and Burton T.L. (1989) *Understanding Leisure and Recreation: Mapping the Past, Charting the Future*. State College, PA: Venture Publishing.

Lime, D.W. and Stankey, G.H. (1971) 'Carrying capacity: maintaining outdoor recreation quality'. In Proceedings: Forest Recreation Symposium. Northeast Forest Experimental Station, Upper Darby, Pennsylvania, 174–88.

Lucas, R.C. (1964) 'Wilderness perception and use: the example of the Boundary Waters Canoe Area', *Natural Resources Journal*, 3 (3), 394–411.

Manning, E.W. (1980) River recreation use and analysis of carrying capacity. Water resources Research Center, University of Vermont, technical completion report.

Payne, R.J. and Graham, R. (1993) 'Visitor planning and management in parks and protected areas'. In Dearden, P. and Rollins, R. (eds) *Parks and Protected Areas in Canada*. Toronto: Oxford.

Shelby, B. and Heberlein, T. (1986) *Carrying Capacity in Recreational Settings*. Oregon: Oregon State University Press.

Stankey, G.H. and McCool, S.F. (1989) 'Carrying capacity in recreational settings: evolution, appraisal, and application', *Leisure Sciences*, 6 (4), 453–73.

Tivy, J. (1973) Recreational carrying capacity, Countryside Commission for Scotland: Battleby.

Wagar, J.A. (1964) 'The carrying capacity of wildlands for recreation', *Society of American Foresters*. Forest Service Monograph, 7:23.

7 Ecotourism Policy

C. Michael Hall

The four main objectives of this chapter are to:

• Identify the multi-scale nature of ecotourism policy
• Recognize the role of institutional arrangements in influencing ecotourism policy
• Appreciate the value of evaluation as a component of the ecotourism policy process
• Understand the complexity of the ecotourism policy process

Introduction

Given that 2002 was the International Year of Ecotourism and that the World Summit on Sustainable Development was held in Johannesburg in the August of that year it is perhaps not surprising that ecotourism reached a position on the national and international policy agenda that it has probably not reached before. Perhaps the summit of the international year was the release of the Québec Declaration on Ecotourism at what was entitled 'the first World Ecotourism Summit' held in Québec City in May. It was attended by over 1100 delegates and praise from senior personalities at conference as reported in the official World Tourism Organization (2002) press release was glowing:

> I have never witnessed such active participation at a summit on tourism ... We were expecting 500 to 600 delegates, and twice as many have shown up in Québec. Over 1,100 participants, including 40 ministers from foreign countries, as well as government and representatives from countries where tourism is still an emerging industry, constitute a very encouraging start for the future of ecotourism. (Honourable Judd Buchanan, Chairman of the Board of Directors of the Canadian Tourism Commission (CTC))

> I am convinced that the Québec Declaration on Ecotourism will become the point of reference for all future discussion and debate. This Summit, held in Québec City, and the Declaration are important steps, however, a lot of work remains to be done,

notably in the fight against poverty – a cause ecotourism can contribute to. (Dr David de Villers, Deputy Secretary-General of the World Tourism Organisation (WTO))

The impressive number of stakeholders and ecotourism practitioners that were able to participate in the Summit offers great hope for the full implementation of the Québec Declaration ... Through implementation of agreed guidelines, principles and standards, the follow-up regional consultations and concrete demonstration projects, the first-ever Ecotourism Summit has signaled that ecotourism, in practice, can contribute to poverty alleviation and environmental protection, the twin goals of the upcoming Johannesburg World Summit on Sustainable Development. (Oliver Hillel, Tourism Program Coordinator for the United Nations Environment Programme (UNEP))

The Québec Declaration signifies that from now on, ecotourism must be considered a privileged tool, leading the way and paving the road toward a tourism that is truly sustainable ... It is an expression of our belief that sustainable tourism can contribute to the more global effort of protecting the sustainability of our planet's resources. The debate and discussions of the past few days have allowed us to determine that Québec is on the right path. (Richard Legendre, Québec Minister responsible for Youth, Tourism, Recreation and Sport and Minister responsible for Wildlife and Parks)

Undoubtedly, the ecotourism summit along with the International Year of Ecotourism is of some significance. The conference did discuss a number of issues facing ecotourism particularly with respect to policy, planning, regulation, product development, marketing, promotion and monitoring. Reports on the conference were provided in the media throughout the world. However, in the discussion of ecotourism surrounding the conference it strikes the present author that something of an irony existed. Here was an international conference, carefully choreographed and managed, with a declaration developed over time through a strongly bureacratic and scheduled process, on a subject which, in its origins at least was meant to reinforce grassroots community involvement (if not ownership and control) of natural resources.

One of the most influential definitions of ecotourism was articulated by Ceballos-Lascuráin (1987 in Boo, 1990: xiv) as: 'Traveling to relatively undisturbed or uncontaminated natural areas with the specific objectives of studying, admiring, and enjoying the scenery and its wild plants and animals, as well as any existing cultural manifestations (both past and present) found in these areas.' While numerous variations of this definition exist, Ceballos-Lascuráin's original version captures the fundamental integration of natural and cultural elements within the ecotourism concept (see Chapter 1). Indeed, later definitions not only retained the original emphases but also reinforced the importance of serving or protecting the interests of the local destination population (e.g. Cater and Lowman, 1994). How is the seeming divergence between the international meeting in Québec and the original spirit of ecotourism to be reconciled or understood? Three responses can be provided. First, environmental issues along with the environmental effects of tourism are now a global concern. Second, because of international interest in the environment local tourism policymaking or activities can no longer be seen in isolation. Third, and related to the first two points, ecotourism policymaking is a complex multifaceted process.

These issues provide the context for the remainder of the chapter. This chapter initially provides a discussion regarding the nature of ecotourism policymaking. We then go on to discuss some of the institutional arrangements that have been established for ecotourism and the policy difficulties this has created. The chapter concludes by suggesting potential future directions for ecotourism and means to evaluate policy success.

137

Ecotourism policymaking: from the local to the global

Appropriate management of the environment is now widely recognized as a global responsibility. Concern over matters as diverse as global climate change, the ozone layer, acid rain, ocean pollution, whaling and natural heritage as led to the development of a host of international conventions and multilateral agreements. These environmental agreements will often affect tourism firms because of the legal responsibilities they may set governments in terms of the creation of legislation and regulation. However, concerns over issues surrounding ecotourism are widely dispersed at all levels of public governance. Several reasons can be put forward for this situation. First, there are often significant differences in how ecotourism is defined between different jurisdictions and between different stakeholders in ecotourism. Second, because of its character and difficulties in its definition a range of agencies will have interests in ecotourism within their jurisdiction. Third, because of the first two reasons, and particularly because of the manner in which ecotourism seeks to integrate conservation, development and marketing, different levels of public governance will also have different sets of interest in ecotourism.

Ecotourism policy may be defined, after Hall and Jenkins (1995), as whatever governments choose to do or not to do with respect to ecotourism. The definition of ecotourism policy covers the action, inaction, decisions and non-decisions of agencies and institutions that are concerned with public governance as it implies a deliberate choice between alternatives. Those alternatives arise out of the public policy process. Policy actors and stakeholders in the ecotourism policy process include pressure and interest groups, community leaders, lobbyists, bureaucrats, impacted individuals and others working inside and outside the 'rules of the game' established by government. However, these

ECOTOURISM POLICY

stakeholders influence and perceive public policies in significant and often markedly different ways. Therefore, ecotourism policies are the outcome of a policymaking process which reflects the interaction of actors' interests and values in the influence and determination of the tourism planning and policy processes (Hall, 2002).

The definition of ecotourism in different jurisdictions is an important part of the ecotourism policy process. After all, how can you effectively regulate, legislate or control something unless it can be defined effectively? Indeed, the difficulty in defining ecotourism may be one reason why there is very little ecotourism specific legislation. Instead, as will be further discussed later, ecotourism matters are often covered under more generic environmental, natural resource or tourism legislation. Nevertheless, the different policy definitions that may be used remain important because they help define the boundaries of the policy problem. For example, under the Australian Federal Government's 1994 national ecotourism strategy, ecotourism was defined as 'nature-based tourism that involves education and interpretation of the natural environment and is managed to be ecologically sustainable' (Department of Tourism, 1994: 3). Following a change of government, the replacement agency for the Department of Tourism, the Office of National Tourism (1997), defined ecotourism as 'nature-based tourism that involves interpretation of the natural and cultural environment and ecologically sustainable management of natural areas'. What is significant in both these definitions is that *ecological sustainability* is seen as a major driver for ecotourism, yet no mention is provided of cultural or social sustainability or even economic sustainability within the context of a definition. It is therefore perhaps of no surprise that such a definition meant that government programmes with respect to ecotourism focused on certain factors and not others in providing funding for ecotourism projects. Indeed, in commenting on the Australian national government's funding of tourism projects in rural and regional Australia, Jenkins (1997: 187) scathingly commented on the funding of 'dubious programmes which by their existence assume that the necessary frameworks for successful tourism and regional development are in place'.

Reasons for the eventual shape that ecotourism policy takes depends on the interaction of interests and their influence on government with respect to the policymaking process. Since World War II there has been a tremendous expansion in the number and scope of interest groups (also described as pressure groups) (Cigler, 1991). Up until the 1960s, interest groups were primarily business association based. However, since the early 1960s, there has been rapid growth in western nations in the number of citizen and public interest groups, particularly in the area of consumer and environmental concerns (Schlozman and Tierney, 1986).

Ecotourism policy has also been influenced by the growth in interest groups. Until the mid-1960s, tourism-related interest groups were generally confined to industry and professional associations. However, the growth of consumer and environmental organizations extended the number of groups having an interest in tourism issues, particularly as they related to aspects of tourism development at the local level. In the 1980s and the early 1990s the range of groups was extended still further as social issues, such as sex tourism and the fairness of international tourism trade became significant (Hall, 1999). Therefore, it is important to realize that groups with an interest in ecotourism go well beyond those that are part of the tourism industry and include a vast array of community, public and special interest groups, including those with a more general interest in environmental and social development (Hall and Jenkins, 1995). Table 7.1 provides examples of the range of interests groups that are involved in ecotourism policy.

Interest groups compete in their influence of policymakers at a range of different scales. However, their ability to influence policymaking are limited by a number of factors including financial resources, temporal resources, access to expertise, public relations skills and access to power. Many of these factors are hard for public interest groups to sustain over time. Therefore, in the wider tourism policymaking process it is often the case that corporate interests tend to dominate. However, in the area of ecotourism there are a large number of smaller industry stakeholders whose interests often coincide with those of conservation groups that are seeking to utilize ecotourism as a justification for the creation of reserves or the implementation of conservation measures. These interests may therefore form coalitions in attempts to influence government policy. For example, in the Australian situation the Ecotourism Association of Australia has been able to influence policy to the extent that a national eco-tourism strategy was developed by the Federal Government well before that of other forms of special interest tourism, while specific funding programmes were also established for ecotourism. It is notable that a country such as New Zealand, which has a very similar international market profile, set of national tourism policies, attitudes towards the environment, industry structure and use of nature-based tourism in international tourism promotion to Australia that there has been no attempt to develop a national ecotourism strategy. Arguably this relates in great part to the absence of a national interest group devoted specifically to ecotourism despite the existence of individual and often high-profile firms that are in the business of ecotourism. Increasingly, many governments and agencies involved in environmental management and ecotourism have been seeking to develop greater involvement with interest groups in the decision-making processes as a way to potentially improve the process through the incorporation of a wider range of views as well as assisting in the implementation of polices once they have been developed. Nevertheless, an effective institutional and regulatory system is also required in order to ensure that

Table 7.1 Interest groups in ecotourism policy

	Public governance organizations	Producer organizations	Non-producer organizations	Single-interest organizations
International	World Tourism Organisation World Heritage Committee	World Travel and Tourism Council	World Wildlife Fund Tourism Concern	Ecotourism Society
Supranational	APEC tourism working group Antarctic Treaty signatory meetings	Pacific Asia Travel Association Baltic Sea Tourism Commission International Association of Antarctic Tour Operators	Travel and Tourism Research Association	End Child Tourism in Asian Tourism (ECPAT)
National	Indonesian Directorate General Irish Tourist Board Countryside Commission	Irish Tourist Industry Confed	Australian Conservation Foundation National Trust	Ecotourism Society of Australia ECPAT (Australia)
Regional (including provincial and state)	Natal Parks Board Tourism British Columbia Scottish Tourism Board Tourism Alberta	Scottish Confederation of Tourism Shannon Development Coalition of Minnesota Business	Western Australian Conservation Council	Tasmanian Wilderness Society
Local	Tourism Vancouver Calgary Economic and Development Authority	Local chambers of commerce and industry associations	Ratepayers and residents' associations, e.g. Waikiki Improvement Association	Single-issue organizations such as a 'friends of a park' or a group that has been formed in order to prevent specific developments, such as a resort or an airport

ecotourism policies meet their desired ends and it is here that substantial issues emerge for ecotourism as 'policy making is filtered through a complex institutional framework' (Brooks, 1993: 79).

Institutional arrangements for ecotourism

The issue of definition has long been important for ecotourism as well as for policymaking and regulation. The main problem being how can you effectively manage or regulate something unless you can define it accurately? This issue has been a major issue for ecotourism and nature-based tourism for a number of years. While there are several management strategies that have been developed for tourism in natural areas there is little legislation or regulation which refers specifically to ecotourism. Instead, ecotourism is often managed through more generic limitations on activities that may be allowed or disallowed in certain identified areas.

Institutions are 'an established law, custom, usage, practice, organisation, or other element in the political or social life of a people; a regulative principle or convention subservient to the needs of an organized community or the general needs of civilization' (Scrutton, 1982: 225). Institutions are a set of rules which may be explicit and formalized (e.g. constitutions, statutes and regulations) or implicit and informal (e.g. organizational culture, rules governing personal networks and family relationships). Institutions order interrelationships between individuals or groups of individuals by influencing their behaviour (Hall and Jenkins, 1995). As a concept and as an aspect of ecotourism policymaking, institutions therefore act as both active and passive influences on the formation and implementation of ecotourism policy.

Institutions therefore 'place constraints on decision-makers and help shape outcomes ... by making some solutions harder, rather than by suggesting positive alternatives' (Simeon, 1976: 574). However, as the number of check points for policy increase, so to does the potential for bargaining and negotiation between interests. In the longer term, 'institutional arrangements may themselves be seen as policies, which, by building in to the decision process the need to consult particular groups and follow particular procedures, increase the likelihood of some kinds of decisions and reduces that of others' (1976: 575). For example, procedures for community participation and involvement in the policymaking process or even the adoption of environmental mediation procedures constitute institutional arrangements which are often significant for ecotourism. Similarly, new government agencies departments may be established as part of the changing activities and roles of government, particularly as new demands, such as environmental concerns, reach a high priority on the political agenda.

The establishment of new institutional arrangements specifically for ecotourism has been limited. Where this has occurred this has tended to be related to procedural matters, related to the adoption of consultative activities with local community interests and the undertaking of ecological impact studies. Although new private sector organizations have been established under the ecotourism label as part of the expansion of the market and the significance of ecotourism as a brand, no new specific ecotourism agencies have been established by the public sector. Instead, ecotourism has been incorporated into the activities of existing agencies which operate in the fields of conservation, national parks, tourism and regional development.

The role taken by agencies with respect to ecotourism depends on the relevant political context in different jurisdictions. For example, in some countries tourism departments have taken the lead on developing ecotourism policies, for example, as in British Columbia or Québec, while in others it has come more from national parks and conservation agencies, as in Western Australia. However, the integrative nature of ecotourism, in that it aims to integrate elements of conservation with that of tourism, also means that in policy terms it is related as much to conservation and environmental concerns as it is to those seeking tourism development. This situation has therefore led to the development of an extremely complex array of institutional arrangements for ecotourism which have had a dramatic affect on ecotourism policy development and implementation (Hall, 2002). For example, in the case of New Zealand at the national government level:

- The Department of Conservation is responsible for the Conservation Estate, those public lands on which national parks and reserves are based and which are the main areas in which ecotourism activities occur.
- Tourism New Zealand is the international marketing body responsible for promoting tourism, including ecotourism, internationally.
- The Ministry of Tourism develops tourism policy which so far has not been ecotourism specific although sustainability and the conservation of the natural resource base is an important component of the national tourism strategy.
- The Ministry of Economic Development has assisted in funding for regional development strategies which have highlighted the potential of ecotourism.
- The Ministry for the Environment assists in the setting of policy guidelines which affect environmental activities such as ecotourism.
- The Ministry of Research, Science and Technology has funded most of the large-scale research on ecotourism in New Zealand.

To illustrate the complicated nature of ecotourism policy further one also needs to consider the role of regional and local government which are also active promoters of ecotourism while also having a regulatory role in relation to regional planning activities as well as the implementation of onsite regulations (Hall and Kearsley, 2001). In addition to a potentially confusing set of institutional arrangements for ecotourism, the demands on government may also be paradoxical. For example, in a study of tourism operator attitudes towards sustainability in New Zealand, respondents expressed concern about government policy, usually in the context of compliance costs and border control issues, while at the same time concerns were expressed about the lack of government funding for environmental management and the Department of Conservation in particular (Kearsley, 1998). For a country with a brand as dependent on nature-based tourism as New Zealand, the varied responsibilities for ecotourism policy may seem surprising. However, it needs to be recognized that such a situation is typically the norm throughout the world. Rather than there being a single line agency responsibility tourism, and ecotourism in *particular*, permeates through the institutional structures of government and therefore creates a setting in which policymaking is inherently complex. This situation perhaps parallels that which existed for the environment as an area of policy concern in the 1960s. As an area of policy concern governments initially had substantial difficulties in addressing environmental issues as it cut across traditional government responsibilities. Yet, over time, specialist agencies were developed for specific environmental responsibilities while in some areas a 'whole-of-government' approach was generated in order to maximize attention of the many different components of government on 'solving' the environmental issue (O'Riordan, 1971). In the case of ecotourism, which ideally integrates marketing, development and conservation concerns, the problems of effective policy and administrative coordination are still being determined, although it needs to be recognized that typically there is no one perfect solution that will fit every jurisdiction. Instead, the structure of institutional roles and responsibilities for ecotourism will rest on the particular circumstances of the scale, location and values associated with public governance.

Evaluating ecotourism policy

Evaluation is a central component of the tourism policy process (Hall and Jenkins, 1995). Evaluation is the process whereby individual and public judgement processes are harnessed for reflection on action. Evaluation is the systematic, objective assessment of the effectiveness, efficiency or appropriateness of a programme or part of a programme. Evaluation tends to be more focused on determining performance for outcomes such as: impact assessment; justification; accountability; planning and resource allocation; improvement; and continued support (Hall and McArthur, 1998 after Cauley, 1993). Evaluation can be approached from many dimensions. One approach is from the product being evaluated, e.g. a policy. Another approach is from the timing of the evaluation relevant to the timing of the programme being evaluated, e.g. before, during and after the life of a policy or programme (Hall and Jenkins, 1995). Evaluation is a critical to assessing the success or value of a particular policy setting and more specifically, to determine whether:

• goals, objectives and strategies are appropriate to stakeholder needs and the public agency's vision
• objectives and strategies are being achieved
• resources are optimally allocated to achieve objectives and strategies
• resources are optimally used across objectives and strategies.

Ideally, policy and programme evaluation is largely oriented around assessing effectiveness and efficiency and, more specifically, to determine whether a programme's: objectives are being achieved; outcomes are appropriate to its objectives and stakeholder needs; resources are optimally allocated across programmes; and resources are optimally used within each programme. A policy evaluation and review must include: reassessment of the need for the programme; review and revision of program objectives to ensure appropriateness; review of the effectiveness, social justice and quality of service delivery; and assessment of efficiency and cost effectiveness of service delivery (Rose-Miller, 1993: 9). Unfortunately, there have been few published systematic evaluations of ecotourism policies and plans (e.g. James, 1991; Maguire, 1991; Liu, 1994; Ceballos-Lacuráin, 1996; Wallace and Pierce, 1996). Hall and MacArthur (1998) argue that there are a number of reasons why overall commitment to evaluation remains poor, including:

• a lack of financial resources and expertise
• misunderstanding of the nature and benefits of evaluation
• poor planning, leading to a near policy vacuum
• the absence of an evaluation culture.

This perception is deeply rooted among the constraints noted earlier, particularly a misunderstanding of the nature and benefits of evaluation. Hall and MacArthur (1998) observed that most heritage agencies, including those involved with ecotourism, spent less than 1% on evaluation. For example, in a survey of the major Australian park management agencies, respondents stated that evaluation was a low priority (Beckmann, 1988). The perceived cost of evaluation programmes was ranked as the major reason why they had not been adopted more readily.

Ecotourism agencies may also avoid the use of evaluation in order to remain totally flexible in their politically volatile climates as already discussed. Alternatively, they may be experiencing a policy vacuum. A vacuum may be caused by the absence of:

• an organized constituency of policymakers to whom the research is directed

- agreement among significant constituents on clear policy issues and identifiable research questions to be addressed
- consistent policy over a given area and hence clearcut policy options to be decided
- coordination among the independent agencies responsible for developing policies
- concrete ongoing operational programmes targeted to use the research findings (Hamilton-Smith and Mercer, 1991: 61).

Indeed, arguably, this characterization of reasons for a policy vacuum well describes the situation experienced in the ecotourism field in many jurisdictions. The lack of commitment to evaluation is also the result of an under-developed or absent evaluation culture (Amies, 1994). An evaluation culture may require:

- individuals and groups (including agency staff) to become genuinely interested
- critical debate about a programme, including debate by programme staff
- reflection in action by programme staff
- the impulse of programme staff and others to understand and make informed judgements and choices about the programme (Cauley, 1993).

The quality and utility of an evaluation can also be affected by the interests and priorities of those driving it: 'Evaluation results will have a far greater impact on decision making when administrators and other policy makers insist less on findings that are acceptable to them, and more on understanding those elements that determine program effectiveness' (Theobald, 1979: 175). This problem can be critical in instances where those evaluating ecotourism policies are the same ones that create them or support them. Unfortunately, the results of most evaluations of ecotourism policies, plans and programmes have not been published and have therefore generally not been available for others considering their own evaluation. Such a situation has substantial impacts on assessing the real value of ecotourism and the policy settings that surround it. Indeed, the following comments by Theobold (1979) regarding parks and recreation applies equally as well to the full spectrum of ecotourism programmes and policies:

> One of the major inhibiting factors to increasing the body of knowledge in recreation and parks is the lack of available information on such research as program evaluation ... Often, the sponsoring agency, as a condition of conducting the evaluation will swear the evaluator to absolute secrecy in regard to the study results. At other times, the design or procedures are so poorly conceived or carried out that the study fails to live up to the standards of good scholarship. (Theobald, 1979: 167)

The lack of published material is probably a reflection of practical restraints and the resistance to be 'judged'. It is difficult enough to secure sufficient human and financial resources to undertake an evaluation, let alone write it up in a manner that can be understood and considered by others in similar situations. Given general resistance to policy and programme evaluation, resistance to have an evaluation informally evaluated is to be expected. The result could be uncomfortable queries regarding the questions asked in the evaluation, criticism of the methods and results, or even vastly different conclusions and recommendations being suggested (McArthur, 1995). The end result of a lack of available material is that many efforts to develop and run evaluation programmes are dampened by the prospect of reinventing the wheel and typically fall back to being based around conducting research rather than considering policy and programme-specific problems and solutions (Hall and McArthur, 1998).

Conclusion

This chapter has discussed ecotourism in relation to three of the key concepts of public policy analysis: the nature of the policy process, the structure of institutional arrangements and role of evaluation. In all three of these areas ecotourism policy is noted to be highly complex and, in many ways, chaotic. However, it has also been argued that this is to great extent a function of the newness of the field and the manner in which ecotourism cuts across public agency functions. Arguably, it is also the result of little formal policy analysis (Fennell, 1999), a problem which permeates most of the tourism field, not just ecotourism specifically (Hall and Jenkins, 1995) and which, as discussed earlier, also reflects the absence of much formal policy evaluation. However, as Hall and MacArthur (1998) noted with respect to the broader field of heritage: 'A lack of evaluation often suggests a lack of strategic planning and a tendency for heritage management to be reactive rather than proactive, and to be heavily influenced by the values of individuals supporting it, often without an awareness of the impacts of those values on the management and ownership of heritage.'

This chapter commenced with several statements from the Ecotourism Summit, held in 2002 in Québec. These statements are highly enthusiastic. Yet such enthusiasm is possibly misplaced. At one time tourism in general was the likely panacea for areas undergoing economic restructuring. That has now been recognized as problematic and instead ecotourism has become the answer. However, the failings from the initial public agency enthusiasm for tourism are just as real for ecotourism. Tourism is a complex, dynamic, highly competitive and very fragmented industry that is notoriously difficult to control and set appropriate policy for. The issues of capacity and limiting its development are crucial to destination areas. The chances of conflict between tourism and other business and social activities are high, often because of the lack of understanding by policymakers and planners of the complexity of tourism. As Richter commented: 'Tourism policymakers have been far more ready to inventory sites than inventory the political factors that could support or strangle the industry' (1991: 191).

Effective ecotourism policymaking has been hampered by a lack of understanding of the political processes of planning and policymaking that include numerous stakeholders: government agencies at all levels, conservation groups, developers and local communities. The range of interests and conflicts has led to the advocacy of 'alternative', 'appropriate', 'soft' and 'sustainable' tourism policies, many of which have received little critical attention even though they tend to be long on vision and enthusiasm and short on implementation strategy. Increased focus therefore needs to be given to the formulation of the goals, institutional arrangements, instruments and evaluation of ecotourism policy if it is to become more effective in meeting the needs and aspirations of the local communities that it is meant to assist, rather than the consultants, policymakers and boosters who are often its uncritical proponents.

Questions

1 Discuss the implications of the ecotourism summit in Canada.
2 Evaluate the benefits of applying an ecotourism policy at the national level.
3 Critically appraise the limitations of applying an ecotourism policy at a national level.
4 What are the main obstacles of practising an ecotourism policy at the international level?

References

Amies, M. (1994) 'Program evaluation: a Commonwealth perspective – where are we now?', *Evaluation Journal of Australasia*, 6 (1), 31–42.

Beckmann, E. (1988) 'Interpretation in Australia – current status and future prospects', *Australian Parks and Recreation*, 23 (6), 6–14.

Boo, E. (1990) *Ecotourism: The Potentials and Pitfalls*, Vol 1. Washington, DC: World Wildlife Fund.

Brooks, S. (1993) *Public Policy in Canada*. Toronto: McClelland and Stewart.

Cater, E. and Lowman, G. (eds) (1994) *Ecotourism: A Sustainable Option?* Chichester: John Wiley & Sons.

Cauley, D.N. (1993) 'Evaluation: does it make a difference?', *Evaluation Journal of Australasia*, 5 (2), 3–15.

Ceballos-Lacuráin, H. (1996) *Tourism, Ecotourism and Protected Areas: The State of Nature-Based Tourism Around the World and Guidelines for its Development*. Gland: IUCN.

Cigler, A.J. (1991) 'Interest groups: a subfield in search of an identity'. In Crotty, W. (ed.) *Political Science: Looking to the Future*, Vol. 4 (*American Institutions*). Evanston: Northwestern University Press.

Department of Tourism (1994) *National Ecotourism Strategy*. Canberra: Commonwealth Department of Tourism.

Fennell, D. (1999) *Ecotourism: An Introduction*. London: Routledge.

Hall, C.M. (1999) 'Leisure and tourism organizations'. In Scarrot, M. (ed.) *Sport, Leisure and Tourism Information Sources: A Guide for Researchers*. Oxford: Butterworth-Heinemann, 197–231.

Hall, C.M. (2002) 'Institutional arrangements for ecotourism policy'. In Fennell, D. and Dowling, R. (eds) *Ecotourism: Policy and Practice*. Wallingford: CABI.

Hall, C.M. and Jenkins, J.M. (1995) *Tourism and Public Policy*. London: Routledge.

Hall, C.M. and Kearsley, G.W. (2001) *Tourism in New Zealand: An Introduction*. Melbourne: Oxford University Press.

Hall, C.M. and MacArthur, S. (1998) *Integrated Heritage Management*. London: The Stationery Office.

Hamilton-Smith, E. and Mercer, D. (1991) *Urban Parks and Their Visitors*. Melbourne: Board of Works.

James, B. (1991) 'Public participation in Department of Conservation management planning', *New Zealand Geographer*, 47 (2), 51–59.

Jenkins, J. (1997) 'The role of the Commonwealth Government in rural tourism and regional development in Australia'. In Hall, C.M., Jenkins, J. and Kearsley, G. (eds) *Tourism Planning and Policy in Australia and New Zealand: Cases, Issues and Practice*. Sydney: Irwin, 181–90.

Kearsley, G.W. (1998) Perceptions of sustainability in the New Zealand tourism industry. Paper presented at the Tourism and Hospitality Research Conference, 1988, Akaroa, Canterbury.

Liu, J.C. (1994) *Pacific Island Ecotourism: A Public Policy and Planing Guide*. Honolulu: Office of Territorial and International Affairs.

Maguire, P.A. (1991) 'Ecotourism development policy in Belitze'. In Veal, A.J., Jonson, P. and Cushman, G. (eds) Leisure and Tourism: Social and Environmental Change, Papers from the World Leisure and Recreation Association Congress, Sydney, University of Technology, Sydney, 624–30.

McArthur, S. (1995) 'Evaluating interpretation – what's been done and where to from here'. In Interpretation Attached to Heritage, Papers Presented at Third Annual Conference of Interpretation Australia Association, Interpretation Australia Association, Collingwood, 116–125.

Office of National Tourism (1997) *Ecotourism*. Tourism Facts No. 16, May (http://www.tourism.gov.au/new/cfa/cfa_fs16.html (accessed 31/12/97)).

O'Riordan, T. (1971) *Perspectives on Resource Management*. London: Pion.

Richter, L.K. (1991) 'Political issues in tourism policy: a forecast'. In: Go, F. and Frechtling, D. (eds) *World Travel and Tourism Review: Indicators, Trends and Forecasts*, Vol. 1. Wallingford: CAB, 189–93.

Rose-Miller, M. (1993) 'Evaluation in the Queensland public sector', *Evaluation News and Comment*, 2 (1), 9–13.

Schlozman, K.L. and Tierney, J.T. (1986) *Organized Interests and American Democracy*. New York: Harper & Row.

Scrutton, R. (1982) *A Dictionary of Political Thought*. London: Pan.

Simeon, R. (1976) 'Studying public policy', *Canadian Journal of Political Science*, 9 (4), 558–80.

Theobald, W.F. (1979) *Evaluation of Recreation and Park Programs*. New York: John Wiley & Sons.

Wallace, G.N. and Pierce, S.M. (1996) 'An evaluation of ecotourism in Amazonas, Brazil', *Annals of Tourism Research*, 23 (4), 843–73.

World Tourism Organization (WTO) (2002) Huge success for ecotourism – Québec Declaration on Ecotourism defines the basis for its international development, Québec City, 22 May 2002 (*http://www.world-tourism.org/newsroom/Releases/more_releases/May2002/EcotourismSummit2.htm*).

B Case Studies Outline

MANAGING ECOTOURISM IN THE ISLAND MICROSTATE: THE CASE
OF DOMINICA

KEY THEMES: IMPACTS, PRODUCT DEVELOPMENT

THE CASE FOR AN ECOTOURISM PEACE PARK AND CULTURAL HERITAGE
CORRIDOR IN THE KOREAN DEMILITARIZED ZONE

KEY THEMES: CULTURAL, POLITICAL

THE STATE OF NATURE TOURISM IN TEXAS: SUSTAINING THE RURAL
AGRICULTURAL FAMILY ENTERPRISE

KEY THEMES: SOCIAL, ENTERPRISES

CANADIAN ABORIGINAL ECOTOURISM IN THE NORTH

KEY THEMES: SOCIAL, MANAGEMENT

MARKETING ECOTOURISM: A FOCUS ON CHILE

KEY THEMES: BRANDING, PRODUCT DEVELOPMENT

MANAGEMENT OF THE ECOTOURISM DESTINATION THROUGH POLICIES OF
INVESTMENT: THE CASE OF THE PENEDA-GERES NATIONAL PARK,
PORTUGAL

KEY THEMES: INVESTMENT, RESOURCES

ECOTOURISM PLANNING CONSIDERATIONS IN EASTERN CENTRAL EUROPE

KEY THEMES: PLANNING, POLICY

RESPONSIBLE NATURE-BASED TOURISM PLANNING IN SOUTH AFRICA
AND THE COMMERCIALIZATION OF KRUGER NATIONAL PARK

KEY THEMES: MANAGEMENT, ASSESSMENT

DEVELOPMENT OF RESPONSIBLE TOURISM GUIDELINES FOR
SOUTH AFRICA

KEY THEMES: RISKS, GUIDELINES

ECOTOURISM IN THAILAND AND KENYA: A PRIVATE SECTOR PERSPECTIVE

KEY THEMES: IMPACTS, ENTERPISES

ECOTOURISM PLANNING AND DESTINATION MANAGEMENT IN VIETNAM

KEY THEMES: PLANNING, MANAGEMENT

AN ECOTOURISM DEVELOPMENT PLAN FOR THE ABROLHOS ISLANDS,
WESTERN AUSTRALIA

KEY THEMES: STRATEGY, INDICATORS

8 Managing Ecotourism in the Island Microstate: The Case of Dominica

David B. Weaver

The four main objectives of this chapter are to:

- Discuss ecotourism in Dominica
- Identify the status of ecotourism in the island
- Outline the impacts of ecotourism in the island
- Evaluate the current efforts of an ecotourism strategy in the island

Introduction

The Caribbean island of Dominica is often referred to as a prime example of a destination that focuses primarily, deliberately and *successfully* on ecotourism. But is this reputation justified? The major objective of this chapter is to assess this question by examining the current status of ecotourism on the island and the circumstances, both internal (i.e. tourism related) and external, that have given rise to this status. The future of Dominican ecotourism and the extent to which this case study can be extrapolated to other destinations will also be assessed. Of particular interest is its relevance to island microstates and other insular environments, which have emerged as a specialized focus of ecotourism research in the past decade (e.g. Weaver 1993, 2001a; Halpenny, 2001). The chapter begins with a brief description of Dominica's physical geography.

Cinderella of the Caribbean

Dominica, a 751-km^2 island of volcanic origin situated in the eastern Caribbean archipelago of the Lesser Antilles, is distinguished from other Caribbean islands by its exceptionally mountainous terrain and heavy forest cover. Its highest peak, Morne Diablotin, attains a height of 1730 m, while approximately 75% of its land area consists of closed forest cover that has been only minimally impacted by human intrusion. Precipitation levels that can exceed 10,000mm/ year support over 350 streams and, in combination with the extreme terrain, have given rise to at least six distinct vegetation communities (i.e. swamp forest, littoral forest, dry scrubland, deciduous forest, tropical rainforest, elfin woodland and montane rainforest) and a large number of waterfalls. The biodiversity of Dominica is also exceptional and includes 1600 recorded species of flowering plants and 166 native bird species. Notably, two species of bird – the red-necked and imperial parrots – are endemic to Dominica. That is, anyone wishing to observe these particular species in their native habitat can do so only on this particular island. With just 72,000 permanent residents, the island's population density of 96/km^2 is low by Caribbean standards.

This physical context is clearly advantageous to any government wishing to include ecotourism and allied forms of recreation in its development strategy. However, these same characteristics were long regarded by the Dominican government as a liability that inhibited the establishment of large-scale beach-based 3S tourism, a desired form of development that was pursued more or less successfully by Caribbean microstates such as Antigua, Barbados and St Lucia since the 1950s (Weaver, 1991). Most Caribbean governments at this time, including Dominica's, were influenced by what Jafari (2001) terms the 'advocacy platform' or the dominant view that sustained and unfettered mass tourism was the best means through which the economic development of poor countries could be facilitated. Yet, despite incentives comparable with those proffered by this type of destination, the pursuit of a similar 3S-based strategy in Dominica in the post-World War II era was fatally hindered by high precipitation, rugged terrain, the paucity of white-sand beaches, offshore waters with limited visibility and susceptibility to hurricanes (e.g. Hurricane David in 1979). Contributing 'human' factors included inadequate infrastructure and chronic socio-political instability (Honychurch, 1984). The tourism sector in Dominica prior to the 1970s can thus be described as 'circumstantial alternative tourism' (Weaver, 1991), in that it possessed a small-scale, locally controlled nature-based tourism industry characteristic of deliberate alternative tourism (Cazes, 1989), but this prevailed only because the island lacked the capacity to induce a more intensive level of tourism development. That is, by circumstances rather than design, Dominica remained stalled in the exploration or involvement stage of the destination lifecycle (Butler, 1980).

Nature island of the Caribbean

According to Weaver (1991), a consultant's report released in the early 1970s provided the catalyst for a new tourism philosophy in Dominica. This document, the 1971 Shankland-Cox Report, relied on unrealistic demand and supply projections to advocate a major expansion of the island's tourism facilities. The surrealistic nature of the report served as a 'reality check' that finally prompted the suspension of the long-held dream to establish a mass tourism industry in Dominica. The reorientation towards small-scale, 'local' tourism in the forest-covered mountains may have also been influenced by contemporary Caribbean academics and politicians such as James Mitchell of St Vincent, whose well-known phrase 'To hell with paradise' became a clarion call for regional critics of mass tourism. Such commentaries became increasingly common during the early 1970s and constituted the radical element of what Jafari (2001) calls the 'cautionary platform', which dominated tourism discourses throughout that decade. Henceforth, tourism strategy would focus on efforts to convert the rainforests and mountains of Dominica from tourism liabilities into tourism assets.

The new attitude was both reflected in and influenced by the 1975 release of the UN-sponsored Kastarlak Report (Kastarlak, 1975). This document concluded that the strength of the island's tourism potential was found in its interior and that marketing efforts were therefore required which focused on specialized market segments such as birdwatchers and environmentalists. A concurrent opportunity was provided by the formation of Morne Trois Pitons National Park, which placed under a high level of protection almost 10% of Dominica's land area and most of its active volcanic features, including the Boiling Lake and the Valley of Desolation. According to Weaver (1991), subsequent efforts to develop and promote the Dominican tourism product indicated a 'deliberate alternative tourism' approach – that is, the government appeared to support policies and actions that would foster a small-scale, locally controlled tourism industry, thereby deliberately 'freezing' the island in the involvement stage of the resort cycle. This is compatible with Jafari's (2001) description of the late 1970s and 1980s as the era of the 'adaptancy platform', when purportedly more appropriate forms of tourism such as 'alternative tourism', 'ecotourism', 'sanfter Tourismus', etc. were proposed in response to the critique of the cautionary platform.

Weaver's (1991) description of Dominican tourism during the late 1980s reveals a sector dominated by small, locally controlled hotels and guesthouses, a modest visitor flow relative to other Caribbean microstates, diverse market sources, a lack of clear seasonality and products that emphasize the natural environment and Dominican culture. The focus on nature was and continues to be embodied in the official slogan 'nature island of the Caribbean', which was used and continues to be used widely in its international promotion to identify and sanction a nature-based tourism product unique in the region. Although much of the accommodation supply and market was based in the capital city of Roseau and was business oriented, it is also justified to describe Dominica at this time as a rare example of 'comprehensive alternative tourism', wherein the entire destination is oriented to this form of tourism (Weaver, 1993). This contrasts with the 'regional' approach of most other islands, whereby small-scale tourism is promoted only in peripheral areas such as the Out or Family Islands (Bahamas), Barbuda (relative to Antigua) and Nevis (relative to St Kitts). At a policy level, the Dominican government encouraged comprehensive alternative tourism primarily through the indirect strategy of not expanding the island's two runways, thereby restricting the number of potential visitors.

Weaver (1993) actually refers to 'comprehensive *ecotourism*' rather than 'alternative tourism' in characterizing Dominican tourism in the late 1980s. However, in retrospect, it is perhaps more accurate to adopt the 'alternative tourism' label only, since whether 'ecotourism' as such was present in Dominica at that time is doubtful given the increased clarity in the eligible criteria of ecotourism that has emerged since the late-1990s (see Chapter 9). While the product was undoubtedly nature focused, there is little evidence of an accompanying formal educational or interpretive component or of an accreditation or specialized regulatory structure that would increase the likelihood of environmentally and socio-culturally sustainable outcomes. Hence, it may be more apt to describe Dominica during the late 1980s as a 'proto-ecotourism' destination – that is, one where the nature-based criterion is fulfilled, but not the educational and sustainability criteria that might be expected at a more mature stage of ecotourism development.

Current dynamics within tourism

New developments in the ten years since Weaver's 1991 analysis allow for an updated assessment of the Dominican ecotourism sector and its prospects. These new developments pertain firstly to the tourism sector itself (i.e. the 'internal environment') and then to the 'external environment'.

Overnight stayover tourism

Tourism-related developments include the continuing increase in international stayover visitors, which rose from 32,000 in 1988 (World Tourism Organization, 1989) to 60,000 in 1995 (TransAfrica Forum, 2000) and 75,000 in 2001. While reflecting a high rate of relative growth, the absolute numbers involved are not high by Caribbean standards (compare 250,000 stayovers for Antigua in 2001) and are compatible with an alternative tourism approach. Assuming an average visitor stay of seven days, the mean number of stayovers present on Dominica at any given time is less than 1500. This represents one tourist for every 48 Dominican residents or two tourists per square kilometre. Moreover, a substantial proportion of this traffic continues to consist of business travellers concentrated in Roseau, where the urban infrastructure is fully capable of accommodating this segment.

With respect to overnight facilities, the urban area of Roseau accounts for about 25% (i.e. about 150 units) of Dominica's 600 accommodation units. Another 250 units are found within beach-based hotels, including the 170-room Portsmouth Beach Hotel in the north of the island. Another 100 units are located within small, mainly seaside facilities that cater to divers and/or high-end visitors. While virtually all these establishments provide or offer access to tours of the interior, it is only the remaining 100 units (17% of Dominica's accommodation inventory) that potentially qualify as 'eco-lodges' or ecotourism-specialized facilities by merit of their interior location, size, appearance and activity as well as clientele descriptions. There are about 12 such facilities in Dominica, concentrated mainly in the hills between Roseau and Morne Trois Pitons National Park. While the location of these facilities clearly reveals a focus on natural attractions, there is still no evidence of any accreditation structure or formal interpretation that would indicate movement beyond the proto-ecotourism of the late 1980s. The recent formation of the Dominica Eco-tourism Association is an incipient attempt to institutionalize the ecotourism sector, but no information could be found in regard to its composition, mandate or activities. A potentially contentious issue is the foreign ownership of several of the lodges. While it is often argued that foreign ownership fosters dependency and revenue leakage, a counter-argument is that such participation increases the likelihood of an operation's financial sustainability by providing entrepreneurial expertise, investment capital and connections with the external tourism system (e.g. travel agencies and tour operators).

Cruise ship tourism

The overnight tourism situation in Dominica can be summarized as entailing a steady but non-threatening increase in arrivals and a broad tendency by almost all overnight facilities to provide client access to nature-based products. Nature-specialized facilities in the interior not only account for a relatively small portion of Dominican accommodations, but lack formal ecotourism accreditation or interpretation structures that qualify them as genuine ecotourism facilities. No comprehensive analysis of contemporary Dominican tourism, however, can proceed without considering recent developments in the cruise ship sector. The number of same-day cruise ship visitors in Dominica rose dramatically from under 7000 in 1985 to 132,000 in 1995 and over 250,000 in 2000. This rapid increase is attributed to a government decision in the mid-1990s to emphasize cruise ship tourism over stayover tourism as the best way to promote the medium-term economic development of the island, given its non-intensive capital requirements and lower marketing costs (TransAfrica Forum, 2000).

Such a directive, however, also calls into question government's support for a strategy based on deliberate alternative tourism. Aside from the escalation of excursionists, cruise ship tourism in regions such as the Caribbean has been affiliated with water pollution, coral reef damage, spatial and temporal congestion and the consumption of imported luxury (i.e. duty-free) and other goods that curtail the multiplier effect (Allen, 1992; Riley, 1992). At the very least, some localized disruption of the marine environment is probably an unavoidable concomitant of cruise ship transit and docking. Furthermore, the standardized and temporally confined nature of land tours taken by cruise ship passengers often results in high levels of site congestion. For example, these passengers account for a substantial proportion of the 10–15,000 visits that occur each year to the Emerald Pool, an idyllic waterhole located at the base of a waterfall in Morne Trois Pitons National Park (WCMC, 2001). This level of visitation has been associated with the loss of ground vegetation, littering, crowding, soil erosion and damage to trees. Some of these negative impacts, moreover, may occur because cruise ship excursionists are less likely than stayover ecotourists to be sensitive to the environmental consequences of their actions (Christian, 2001).

However, the fact that cruise ship passengers are typically confined to a handful of high-profile sites such as the Emerald Pool also has positive implications. First, the vast majority of the Dominican landscape experiences virtually no impact from cruise ship passengers. Second, increasing levels of visitation have prompted appropriate site-hardening initiatives, including path upgrades and the construction of a viewing platform. The cost of these initiatives, moreover, have been largely met through the 1997 introduction of a user fee applicable to several of the island's major attractions. An added consideration when assessing the impact of cruise ship tourism is that high visitor numbers disguise a relatively small number of visitor days – that is, 250,000 as opposed to the 525,000 generated by the 75,000 overnight visitors. Because the focus of these excursionists is clearly focused on Dominica's natural assets and because guides commonly accompany these excursions, the argument can be made that many if not all cruise ship visitors qualify as 'soft ecotourists'.

Nature-based and other attractions

Along with the Emerald Pool, Trafalgar Falls (between Roseau and Morne Trois Pitons National Park) is the most popular natural attraction of Dominica, drawing a comparable level of visitation because of its accessibility to Roseau. In contrast, the Boiling Lake attracts an estimated 1500 to 2000 visitors per year (WCMC, 2001). In this case, the site is exceptional but requires a gruelling 12-km walk over extremely rugged terrain. The walk to the Boiling Lake is a litmus test for the 'hard ecotourist' and hence these visitation figures indicate the importance in Dominica of this ecotourist segment. Within the relatively small segment of visitors that is motivated primarily by recreational rather than business or visiting friends or relatives (VFR) considerations, scuba diving is an increasingly popular activity due to the relatively unspoiled nature of Dominica's marine environment as well as the novelty effect of a new destination. Among others, Cater and Cater (2001) argue that scuba diving generally qualifies as a form of ecotourism. However, this perspective is not universally held. Whether scuba diving is accepted or rejected as a form of ecotourism is an increasingly significant consideration in the assessment of Dominica's status as an ecotourism destination.

While focused on the natural environment, Dominica's tourism product also includes a significant cultural 'add-on' component that emphasizes (a) the alleged retention of 'traditional' or 'old-fashioned' Caribbean Creole culture and (b) the residual indigenous presence centred around the Carib Reserve on the eastern coast. As with the island's natural assets, promotional campaigns tout these as being unique in the region, hence providing an additional competitive advantage over other Caribbean islands. From an ecotourism perspective, such cultural attributes are widely accepted as a legitimate component of ecotourism provided that they are secondary and do not take priority over the natural environment in which they occur (e.g. Blamey, 2001). The same may be said of historical attractions. In Dominica, these include the military ruins at Fort Cabrits National Park (a major site for cruise ship visitors), parish churches and ruins associated with the old plantation economy.

Current dynamics within the external (non-tourism) environment

Tourism cannot be examined in isolation when assessing the status and prospects of ecotourism, given the fundamental influence on the latter of various 'external' or non-tourism environments. Crucial among these is the public policy and planning arena, including considerations of security, politics and administration, infrastructure, fiscal policy and financial incentives (Parker, 2001). It is important to stress that government policy and planning in Dominica since World War II, which includes the unsuccessful pursuit of mass 3S tourism before 1971 and the current emphasis on large-scale cruise ship tourism, has been focused above all on the imperative of economic growth, given the island's underdeveloped status relative to most other Caribbean islands. In this light, the promotion of proto-ecotourism can be seen as a default option necessitated by resource realities, rather than a reflection of government's fundamental commitment to 'small is beautiful' macroeconomic principles or deliberate alternative tourism. Similarly, the policy of not expanding the island's two international airstrips, while ostensibly consistent with and reflective of such principles, is motivated more by cost and low demand than by any conscious government desire to maintain the island as an alternative tourism destination.

Other external developments and events within the past several decades corroborate this idea of ecotourism as expediency and illuminate the shadow reputation of Dominica as a land of questionable and sometimes bizarre schemes that belie its repute as an ecotourism model. These include 1975 and 1979 attempts by government to create large-scale free port zones and oil refineries in the north of the island. Negative publicity and concerted local opposition thwarted each of these initiatives (Honychurch, 1984). More successful has been the conversion of Dominica into an offshore banking and finance centre since the early 1990s and its associated emergence as a major online gaming jurisdiction. A related development is the controversial 1991 Economic Citizen Programme, which provides Dominican citizenship to foreign investors for a one-time payment of US$50,000 (Main, 1999). The programme is alleged to have attracted Russian gangsters and others wishing to obtain visa-free access to other Commonwealth countries. Concerns over this programme prompted the Canadian government to impose visa restrictions on all Dominican citizens in 2001 (Canada Gazette, 2001).

These developments have indirectly hindered the evolution of ecotourism by their inconsistency with the latter and by calling into question Dominica's broader national repute. Other external developments, however, have had a more direct potential negative impact. In 1996 the multinational mining conglomerate BHP was granted prospecting licences covering about 10% of the island, including fragile mountainous areas upstream from the Carib Reserve. The Mines and Minerals Act of 1996, which opened the door for the licences, provided for discretionary rather than mandatory environmental assessments. Partially in response to public opposition, BHP abandoned its activity in Dominica the following year. However, government subsequently stated its willingness to consider future prospecting and mining proposals. Equally contentious and embarrassing have been Dominica's recent actions as a member of the International Whaling Commission (IWC). Although whale watching is becoming increasingly important in Dominica as a specialized form of ecotourism-related activity, the island voted with Japan in the 2001 IWC conference to defeat a proposal to establish a Southern Whale Sanctuary in the South Pacific. This behaviour was subsequently attributed to the Japanese strategy of using aid to secure the votes of vulnerable, aid-dependent microstates (Pattullo, 2001).

Enhancive external developments

Not all external developments within Dominica have undermined the evolution of ecotourism. Along with the formation of forest preserves in the 1950s, legislation, such as the Forestry and Wildlife Act, Fisheries Act and Beach Control Act, has helped to protect the island's natural environment and hence its suitability as an ecotourism destination. Since the establishment of Morne Trois Pitons National Park in 1975, two additional high-order nature-based protected areas have been created: the 34 km² Morne Diablotin National Park, which protects habitat of the island's endemic parrots; in 2000 and the Soufriere/ Scott's Head Marine Reserve, which extends for five kilometres along the southern coast in 2001. Morne Diablotin National Park was established through the initiative of the Rare Species Conservatory Foundation, a US-based NGO that allocated US$750,000 for associated land acquisitions. The Dominican government contributed an additional US$366,000. Local conservation groups, such as the Dominica Conservation Association, have also contributed to the well-being of Dominica's environment through their public opposition to the threatening external developments described earlier.

Conclusion

Two related observations summarize the 'ecotourism' situation in contemporary Dominica. First, the island's nature-based tourism sector shows some superficial adherence to ecotourism but is at best an example of 'proto-ecotourism' due to the continued absence of formal accreditation and education components that fulfill core ecotourism criteria. The probability that this will eventually evolve into full-fledged ecotourism is eroded by the second factor, which is that proto-ecotourism emerged and continues to serve as an expedient that is continuously threatened by other opportunistic and potentially incompatible internal and external environments. The tenacious but futile pursuit of mass tourism prior to 1971 is but one early indication of governmental priorities focused elsewhere. Tourism-related government actions since then, including the successful pursuit of cruise ship passengers and recent support for a proposed cableway that would provide a large number of tourists with direct access to Morne Trois Pitons National Park, suggest that this policy environment has not fundamentally changed despite the apparent shift towards a nature-based alternative tourism strategy. While Weaver (2001b) argues that high-capacity cableways and cruise ships are not inherently inconsistent with ecotourism, there is scant evidence of government action to mitigate the possible social and environmental effects of these higher intensity developments. In the case of the national park, which was designated a World Heritage Site in the late 1990s, the cableway proposal prompted an official statement of concern from UNESCO's World Heritage Committee (UNESCO, 1999). Developments within the external environment, such as the pursuit of offshore finance status, the issuance of economic passports and the willingness to accommodate large mining conglomerates, corroborate the contention that the Dominican government is not committed to pursuing an ecotourism-based tourism strategy and does not embrace broader principles of sustainability that are compatible with this. Dominica's reputation as a prototype of ecotourism and deliberate alternative tourism, therefore, is undeserved.

Dilemma of small island microstates

It is simplistic and counterproductive to dismiss the Dominican case study as a cynical example of the consequences of naive opportunism and political corruption, although undoubtedly these have influenced the country's post-World War II development. More insight is gained by focusing on the island's status as a chronically underdeveloped and vulnerable Third World microstate where successive governments have struggled to overcome severe resource limitations and, concomitantly, what Bertram and Watters (1985) have labelled the MIRAB syndrome (i.e. dependency on *mi*gration, *r*emittances, *a*id and *b*ureaucratic expansion). Ecotourism, or more accurately *proto*-ecotourism, may be seen in this light as just one of many different 'service output' opportunities pursued, often out of a sense of desperation, to stimulate economic growth as Dominica necessarily shifts away from a historical emphasis on 'product output' such as bananas. This desperation helps to account for Dominica's willingness to offer economic citizenship to questionable outsiders and harbour online gaming businesses and its submission to Japanese pro-whaling pressure in the IWF (being 'held to ransom', in the words of one critic).

This island microstate scenario of desperation cause and expediency effect, moreover, is not confined to Dominica. Votes to defeat the Southern Whale Sanctuary, for example, were also cast by Antigua & Barbuda, Grenada, St Kitts & Nevis, St Lucia and St Vincent. The Solomon Islands, another microstate, abstained. Similarly, Canada's imposition of visa requirements on Dominica was extended for similar reasons to Vanuatu, Kiribati, Nauru, Grenada and Tuvalu. Island microstates other than Dominica that are seeking offshore finance activity include Anguilla, Antigua & Barbuda, Bahamas, Bermuda, Cayman Islands, Cook Islands, Cyprus, Grenada, Marshall Islands, Mauritius, Montserrat, St Lucia, St Kitts & Nevis, St Vincent, Samoa, Seychelles, Turks & Caicos Islands and Vanuatu. Of these, St Vincent, the Solomon Islands, Montserrat and Samoa, like Dominica, ostensibly support a strategy of comprehensive ecotourism. Grenada, St Lucia, St Kitts & Nevis, Cayman Islands, Bahamas, Mauritius and Seychelles all include regional ecotourism within their broader tourism planning. All of these destinations, in reality, accommodate proto-ecotourism rather than ecotourism. Offshore medical schools and super-fluous postage stamp emissions are other strategies commonly used by island microstates to generate revenue.

What, therefore, is the likelihood that genuine ecotourism will emerge in Dominica and other island microstates? Despite the hostile policy milieu, Dominica and many other islands still have high-quality natural attractions, paper legislation that provides for a high level of environmental protection and many individuals as well as organizations committed to implementing the principles of alternative tourism and ecotourism. Furthermore, external aid agencies, both governmental and NGO based, are increasingly willing to fund ecotourism-related projects, while those wanting to pursue such initiatives are able to reference an expanding array of good practice prototypes, such as Australia's NEAP accreditation programme (Weaver, 2001a). But as long as the MIRAB syndrome and underdevelopment in general persist, genuine attempts to capitalize on these foundation ecotourism assets will be undermined by threatening parallel developments in the internal and external environment. The unsustainable logging of the Solomon Islands is one example. It is only through long-term prosperity and stability that a policy milieu conducive to genuine ecotourism will emerge. However, this will result in ecotourism only if the activities pursued to achieve prosperity and stability are not incompatible with ecotourism. This could, in theory, result from a strategy of mass tourism and offshore finance, as in the Cayman Islands, in which case ecotourism will likely become a locally important activity within the destination that serves as a diversionary add-on for the dominant tourism activity. The future scenario for ecotourism in a prosperous Dominica is similar, given the growth of the cruise ship and business tourism sectors, suggesting that this or any other island microstate is likely to emerge as, at best, a regional rather than a comprehensive ecotourism destination.

Questions

1 What is meant by 'proto-ecotourism' and what are its advantages and disadvantages?
2 Why do island microstates tend to possess 'proto-ecotourism' rather than genuine ecotourism?
3 How does the external or non-tourism environment potentially threaten the development of ecotourism in island microstates?
4 What can be done in island microstates to encourage the development of genuine ecotourism?

References

Allen, W. (1992) 'Increased dangers to Caribbean marine ecosystems: cruise ship anchors and intensified tourism threatens reefs', *BioScience*, 42, 330–35.

Bertram, I. and Watters, R. (1985) 'The MIRAB economy in South Pacific microstates', *Pacific Viewpoint*, 27, 497–520.

Blamey, R. (2001) 'Principles of ecotourism'. In Weaver, D. (ed.) *The Encyclopedia of Ecotourism*. Wallingford: CABI, 5–22.

Butler, R.W. (1980) 'The concept of a tourist area cycle of evolution: implications for management of resources', *Canadian Geographer*, 24, 5–12.

Canada Gazette (2001) Regulations amending the immigration regulations, 1978 (*http:// canada.gc.ca/gazette/part2/ascII/g2-13526 e.txt* (visited 18 April 2002)).

Cater, C. and Cater, E. (2001) 'Marine environments'. In Weaver, D. (ed.) *The Encyclopedia of Ecotourism*. Wallingford: CABI, 265–85.

Cazes, G. (1989) 'Alternative tourism: reflections on an ambiguous concept'. In Singh, T., Theuns, H. and Go, F. (eds) *Towards Appropriate Tourism: The Case of Developing Countries*. Frankfurt: Peter Lang, 93–116.

Christian, C. (2001) 'Morne Trois Pitons: Dominica's experience with ecotourism', World Heritage Review, No. 23 (http://www.worldheritagereview.org/news/ ful...:_Dominica's_experience_with_ecotourism.htm (visited 8 April 2002)).

Halpenny, E. (2001) 'Islands and coasts'. In Weaver, D. (ed.) *The Encyclopedia of Ecotourism*. Wallingford: CABI, 235–50.

Honychurch, L. (1984) *The Dominica Story: A History of the Island*. Roseau, Dominica: The Dominica Institute.

Jafari, J. (2001) 'The scientification of tourism'. In Smith, V. and Brent, M. (eds) *Hosts and Guests Revisited: Tourism Issues of the 21st Century*. New York: Cognizant Communications, 28–41.

Kastarlak, B. (1975) *Tourism and its Development Potential in Dominica*. Castries, Saint Lucia: United Nations Development Program.

Main, C. (1999) 'Dominica: encouraging investment . . . but not at any price' (*http:// www.escapeartist.com/efam11/Dominica_Investment.html* (visited 18 April 2002)).

Parker, S. (2001) 'The place of ecotourism in public policy and planning', In Weaver, D. (ed.) *The Encyclopedia of Ecotourism*. Wallingford: CABI, 509–20.

Pattullo, P. (2001) 'Dominica – a little fish with a big vote to cast', *The Guardian*, 23 July (*http:// www.guardian.co.uk/international/story/0,3604,525876,00.html* (visited 8 April 2002)).

Riley, C. (1992) 'The Atlantic-Caribbean cruise industry'. In Cooper, C. and Lockwood, A. (eds) *Progress in Tourism, Recreation and Hospitality Management*, Vol. 4. London: Belhaven Press, 245–51.

TransAfrica Forum (2000) *The Impact of Tourism in the Caribbean*. Washington, DC: TransAfrica Forum.

UNESCO (1999) Convention concerning the protection of the world cultural and natural heritage. 23rd session, World Heritage Committee (*http://www.unesco.org/whc/archive/ repcomx99.htm#sc814* (visited 16 April, 2002)).

WCMC (2001) 'Protected areas programme: World Heritage Sites' (*http://www.wcmc.org.uk/ protected_areas/data/wh/morne.html* (visited 15 April, 2002)).

Weaver, D.B. (1991) 'Alternative to mass tourism in Dominica', *Annals of Tourism Research*, 18, 414–32.

Weaver, D.B. (1993) 'Ecotourism in the small island Caribbean', *GeoJournal*, 31, 457–65.

Weaver, D.B. (2001a) *Ecotourism*. Brisbane, Australia: John Wiley & Sons.

Weaver, D.B. (2001b) 'Ecotourism as mass tourism: contradiction or reality?', *Cornell Hotel and Restaurant Administration Quarterly*, 42 (2), 104–112.

World Tourism Organization (1989) *Compendium of Tourism Statistics*, 10th edn. Madrid: World Tourism Organization.

Websites

Cakafete: a Dominican grassroots website that provides coverage of local politics and other developments. *http://www.cakafete.com/CAKAFETE_site_map.html*

Dominica – The Nature Island of the Caribbean: official website of the Commonwealth of Dominica, provides basic economic and tourism information from a government perspective. *http://www.ndcdominica.dm/index.htm*

VirtualDominica.com: one of the best websites that links with all aspects of Dominica, including local newspapers and descriptions of accommodations. *http://www.avirtualdominica.com/home.htm*

World Conservation Monitoring Centre: information on Morne Trois Pitons National Park, includes linkages with World Heritage Committee commentary. *http://www.wcmc.org.uk/protected_areas/data/wh/morne.html*

9 The Case for an Ecotourism Peace Park and Cultural Heritage Corridor in the Korean Demilitarized Zone

Ginger Smith and Alvin Rosenbaum

The four main objectives of this chapter are to:

- Discuss the theoretical framework and essential characteristics of peace park planning initiatives
- Provide the application of these principles to the peace park concept for preservation of the Korean Demilitarized Zone (DMZ) as a nature preserve
- Outline two case studies representing differing theoretical peace park frameworks – the Seattle Peace Park and Kgalagadi Transfrontier Conservation Area
- Elaborate on the jointly managed ecotourism peace park and cultural heritage corridor for the Korean DMZ

Introduction

Unfortunately, the term 'peace park' has been confusingly and loosely applied to a variety of constructs that have little to do with either park planning or post-conflict normalization. But there are two basic approaches to legitimate peace park planning that have been advanced in recent years.

The first is tied to the notion of a transfrontier conservation area. A transfrontier (as opposed to simply a frontier) is a regional borderland, where a remote boundary of one country fronts another. The idea is to create a bi- or trilateral compact to manage a large undeveloped area as a biosanctuary for habitat, environmental protection and low-impact recreation. The overarching mission of this kind of peace park is to gain the cooperation of two formerly antagonistic governments to invest in an environmentally friendly but an otherwise ideologically neutral initiative that demonstrates goodwill and collaborative enterprise.

The second concept rests on a contained war-ravaged site (rather than a large area), such as Nagasaki, Japan, My Lai in Vietnam, or a site commemorating such places, such as the Seattle Peace Park and its memorial to Sadako Sasaki, a child who died at Hiroshima (see later).

In theory, borderlands combining both war zone and natural wonders can be compatible since boundary disputes have been a typical rationale for centuries of armed conflict. From the ancient north–south divide between Scotland and England to the rural Nagorno-Karabakh region between Armenia and Azerbaijan, these places on the margin provide what Rob Shields calls 'alternative geographies . . . on the periphery of cultural systems of space' (Shields, 1991: 3). As such, they have tended to be portrayed by anarchistic and outlaw practices.

Another characteristic of these outback borderlands is that barriers, concertina wire, armed patrols and checkpoints are incompatible with peaceable cross-cultural coexistence. The reality may be that park rangers are law enforcement personnel who carry automatic weapons while patrolling the perimeter of their domain. The image, however, is more that of cowboys keeping the varmints at bay and the wildlife in check than that of soldiers controlling marauders, illegal immigrants and other troublesome human intruders.

The concept of peace parks began in Poland in 1925 with the Krakow Protocol in which twin national parks were established along the then disputed borders of Czechoslovakia and Poland. Conservationists today hope that the Bialowieza National Park on the Polish side and the Belovezhskaya Oushcha National Park on the Belarus side will become an international peace park that will unite these formerly mutually distrustful neighbours in common conservation projects. The ecological heart of this ancient landscape is a strict nature reserve in the inner sanctum of the Bialowieza National Park where visitors are allowed in only with park guides and the only vehicles permitted are bicycles and horse-drawn carts. Other park match-ups are under consideration for the Czech Republic–Germany, Greece–Turkey, and Russia–Finland (Richardson and Sochaczewski, 1999).

According to the IUCN–World Conservation Union, there are 136 trans-frontier 'protected area complexes' in 98 countries, 'many in areas where centuries-old enmities are deeply rooted in political and ethnic mistrust' (Richardson and Sochaczewski, 1999). The Jingpo Lake biological preserve borders China, North Korea and Russia. 'Transboundary initiatives have been very successful in situations similar to this' (Lee in Mayell, 1999).

Peace park initiatives of this nature are highly prominent in Sub-Saharan Africa. According to Nelson Mandela:

> I . . . know of no political movement, no philosophy, no ideology, which does not agree with the peace parks concept as we see it going into fruition today. It is a

concept that can be embraced by all ... In a world beset by conflict and division, peace is one of the cornerstones of the future. Peace parks are a building block in this process, not only in our region, but potentially in the entire world. (The *Johannesburg Star*, 10 December 2001)

A well-known transboundary refuge is Kruger National Park, shared by Mozambique, South Africa and Zimbabwe, a region about five times the size of the US state of New Jersey which in 1994 was separated by a no-man's land marked by an electric known locally as the 'fence of fire'. In Central American, successful transborder reserves such as La Amistad International Biosphere Reserve between Costa Rico and Panama and the Trifinio Trinational Conservation and Development Zone shared by Guatemala, El Salvador and Honduras allow sustainable use of natural resources in some areas. 'Meanwhile, ecotourism and the search for commercially and medicinally useful substances have greatly expanded the number and types of jobs. Such international parks have also diffused tensions by convincing rival neighbors to collaborate on protecting watersheds, curbing soil erosion, and slowing deforestation for their mutual benefit' (Drohan, 1996: 17). The Siapaz Park Complex established along the San Juan River Basin forms the border between Costa Rica and Nicaragua. The two countries had formerly argued over land and illegal trade and now share a package of 33 protected areas in Costa Rica and 18 in Nicaragua that has helped relieve tensions (Richardson and Sochaczewski, 1999).

The peace park concept for environmental preservation of the Korean DMZ

Established at the end of the Korean War in 1953 and untouched for nearly 50 years, the DMZ harbours many rare and endangered species including Amur leopards, Asiatic black bears, red-crowned cranes and Siberian tigers. A team of South Korean scientists, conducting a field survey in 1986 in the 3-mile-wide southern buffer zone below the DMZ, identified 41 native and 40 rare plant species and 16 native and 8 rare fish species. They also found 14 species not previously known to inhabit the area, including a relative of the timber wolf, and healthy populations of eight species that are threatened or endangered elsewhere, including the Manchurian tiger and Siberian bear.

K.C. Kim, Professor of Entomology and Director, Centre for Biodiversity Research at Pennsylvania State University formed a group known as the DMZ Forum in 1999, built on his own earlier proposal for a peace park as a nature preserve developed in 1995 while attending an international conference in Hokkaido. The DMZ Forum is a coalition of conservation groups working to turn the DMZ into a wildlife protection area of biosphere reserves before industrialization and urbanization encroach on the region, an idea first advanced by University of Hawaii Professor Glen Paige more than 20 years earlier.

The reserve long envisioned by Professor Kim would encompass the 4.8-mile-wide zone itself, which roughly straddles the 38th parallel for 148 miles across the Korean peninsula, plus the 3-mile-wide buffer zone that lies on each side of the zone. This 1600-square-mile habitat might eventually be extended further to include the Taebaek Mountains to the east and the forested plains and deltas of the Han-gang and Imjingang Rivers to the west (Drohan, 1996: 17). The DMZ Forum and other organizations have approached international organizations such as the World Conservation Union, UNESCO, United Nations Environment Programme, and World Wildlife Fund and international funding agencies including the GEF, UN Development Programme, the US-Japan Common Agenda, the Keidanren Nature Conservation Fund (Japan) and the Asia Foundation to stand behind efforts to recognize the unique, globally significant heritage of Korea's DMZ ecosystems and to provide assistance for activities towards developing a peace park for environmental preservation of the DMZ corridor. 'The political tension between the two Koreas is much stronger than that between Central American and African countries before they formed their transborder peace parks. The environment is a benign, seemingly apolitical issue on which the Koreans could possibly agree,' states Westing (in Drohan, 1996: 17). 'Environmental issues may be the least provocative way of breaking the ice.'

Peace park and sister city exchange as international relations – the Seattle Peace Park and Seattle–Tashkent sister city programme

On 6 August 1990 – the 45th anniversary of the bombing of Hiroshima during World War II – more than 100 people gathered at the University of Seattle District to dedicate Seattle's Peace Park. A statue by sculptor Daryl Smith commemorating the site is a life-size bronze of Sadako Sasaki, the young Japanese girl who survived the bombing at age two. She holds a small paper crane aloft towards the sky. Known all her life as a tomboy who could run very fast, Sadako became ill and died at age 12 of radiation sickness. A friend encouraged Sadako during her illness to start making 1000 small origami cranes out of gold paper to give away as symbols of hope, so that Sadako's hope would never die. She made over 600 cranes before her death. At the end of the peace park dedication ceremonies, dozens of schoolchildren took turns looping necklaces of multicoloured paper cranes around the neck and arm of the statue (Winfield, 1990: E3).

Dr Schmoe won the Hiroshima Peace Prize of $5000 in 1988 and used the award as seed money to mount support for the clearing of a small lot near the University of Seattle. In 1986, Schmoe wrote to Charles Royer, Mayor of the city of Seattle requesting that a site located at 7th Avenue NE be cleaned up and developed as a small park. From a half-acre site piled with wrecked cars, garbage and brush, Schmoe mobilized volunteers, city officials and local businesses to allocate the abandoned parcel to parkland and to the building of a beautiful park symbolizing world peace (Winfield, 1990: E3). The property, owned by the University of Friends Meeting of the Religious Society of Friends, was across the street from Schmoe's residence and the Friends Centre and easily accessible to Seattle's schoolchildren. The Park was created by a dedicated volunteer group of more than 100 local residents, who gave thousands of hours of manual labour and more than $6000 in private funds towards its development and $8000 community service grant from Fratelli's Ice Cream Corp. In 1986 Schmoe formed the non-profit Seattle Peace Park Associates which raised $15,000 to give to the Parks Department for future care and maintenance of the Park (Seattle Parks and Recreation, 1986–1997).

Schmoe had invited 9-year-old Dana and two other youngsters, and their adult adviser from Albuquerque, New Mexico, to Seattle for the dedication. For many months, Dana and 41 other young students worked on a 'Children's Statue of Peace' project after hearing the story of 'Sadako and the 1000 Cranes' and deciding they wanted to do something to change the world. Their project was raising money and support to build a peace statue in Los Alamos, NM. Without the vision of Schmoe and the Seattle community to buoy the initiative, in 1994 Los Alamos city officials and citizens rejected the plea of children from around the world to build a statue and peace park in the city, the birthplace of the atomic bomb: 'Council members feared the park would become a rallying point for peace activists and be seen as an indictment of Los Alamos' role. Several Albuquerque children said they had signatures and about $20,000 in donations from more than 41,000 youngsters in every state and 53 countries' (*Denver Rocky Mountain News*, 1994: 26A).

The Seattle Peace Park was built by Dr Floyd Schmoe when he was 93 years old, whose lifetime courage and efforts in support of world peace parallel that of Sadako. A conscientious objector in two world wars and a relief and refugee volunteer in Europe, Asia and Africa, in 1948 Schmoe led a group to Hiroshima on a mission to build 'houses for Hiroshima'. Over the next three years they built more than 30 homes in Hiroshima and Nagasaki. The project was eventually underwritten by the United Nations. In 1953 Schmoe moved to Korea, helping to build more than 100 homes as project director of 'Houses for Korea, Inc.'. Later he went to the Sinai Desert to help resettle refugees from the Arab–Israeli war (Angelos, 1990: C2).

Parallel to Schmoe's actions was another strong international movement in the 1970s in Seattle begun by the far-sightedness of then Mayor, Wes Uhlman, city officials and actively engaged citizenry. An entourage of Soviet mayors touring the USA in 1972 had dinner in the Seattle Space Needle with Mayor Uhlman which led to discussions of developing a sister city relationship. Undaunted by a period of extremely poor US–Soviet political relations, Seattle forged a sister city relationship with Tashkent in Uzbekistan, which helped to lead the way to over two decades of trade and economic growth.

The initiative expanded through the efforts of numerous Seattle and Tashkent citizens and government groups to include three exchanges of representatives from Seattle's legal community and the construction and dedication of Tashkent Park in Seattle during the late 1970s and early 1980s (Furlong, 2002). A powerful earthquake hit Uzbekistan in early 1988 and Seattle responded to the dire needs of its sister city's home country with an outpouring in relief efforts which included the activities of Gary Furlong, president of the Seattle–Tashkent Sister City Association and the establishment of an exchange network of Seattle doctors. Following the fall of the Soviet Union, relations between the two cities broadened, led, in part, by Furlong. Furlong, in 1991–1992, participated in 'Russia Winter Campaign' in which the entire state of Washington organized to collect used medical equipment for shipment to Tashkent on Soviet commercial and cargo planes which landed by special permit at McCord Military Base. The campaign included the shipment of medical equipment, supplies and the exchange of US doctors and nurses (Furlong, 2002).

Cultural interaction during the 1980s and early 1990s included education and sports exchanges of schoolchildren between Seattle and Tashkent through the 'Peach Child' play-writing and performing exchanges. Sports team exchanges included amputee soccer for Uzbekistani children injured by landmines. The Seattle–Tashkent agreement expanded during this period to also include economic cooperation for Washington State with all of Uzbekistan and has grown over the years to include continued exchanges among business people, schoolchildren, legal and medical communities and healthcare service providers focusing on programmes reducing domestic violence (Furlong, 2002).

In the 1990s Uzbekistan saw tremendous growth in its tourism infrastructure including the construction of Intercontinental and Sheraton hotels. Uzbekistan has been able to look ahead to promotion of its Silk Route cities and the development of student exchanges between the University of Washington and Tashkent University, including distance-training links through the University of Maryland and a university in Canada. Uzbekistan also developed a national airline with international routes between Tashkent, Kiev and New York City. In May 2002 a conference in Washington, DC, took place through the auspices of the American Uzbekistani Chamber of Commerce, promoting exchanges incorporating cultural as well as academic and agricultural products and healthcare services among non-government and government organizations including the Ministry of Higher Education (Furlong, 2002).

Early 1970s opposition from the US Department of State and the lowest point in US–Soviet relations during the Reagan administration did not stop the flourishing relationship between the sister cities. The nearly 30-year-old Seattle–Tashkent partnership provides an active, visible model of the value and accomplishments of a US–Soviet sister city programme centring on peace promotion, sustainable destination management and economic development based on cultural heritage tourism exchange, health and human welfare services, education and agribusiness, among many others. Seattle and Tashkent overcame significant political barriers adding depth and meaning to the 1970s' 'ping pong' diplomacy between the USA and China and to the value of the Good Will Games, enhancing international relations with and acceptance of the citizens of the former Soviet Union into a democratizing world. Since the 1970s Seattle has taken the lead in US sister city relationships building cultural and economic cooperation on a long history of exchanges which today include cities in South Korea, China, Indonesia, Taiwan, Japan, Europe and Africa, among many others. The Seattle Peace Park today stands in testament to Seattle's stalwart commitment to remain relevant in its relationship with the 'new' Uzbekistan and 'the challenge for understanding differing cultures and socioeconomic and political systems through peaceful exchange' (Furlong, 2002).

In 1999 Akiko Matsumoto, a 12-year-old from Ube, Japan, brought 4000 paper cranes collected from Japanese children to the Peace Park to present to the 102-year-old Floyd Schmoe. 'Together the two of them hung the cranes, braided in long colorful streamers, on the bronze statue of Sadado Sasaki' (Tizon, 1997). The Seattle Peace Park has been incorporated as a non-profit, public service, tax-free recreation area, open to the public at all hours, 'a visible reminder of the need to strive for a warless world' (Schmoe in Angelos, 1990: C2).

Transfrontier conservation areas take a new direction – the Kgalagadi Transfrontier Park

Transfrontier conservation areas (TFCAs) have become 'a worldwide phenomenon, albeit under various names and guises ... The environment does not recognize national boundaries, and solutions to environmental problems may require a multilateral and multidimensional approach ... Even the most advanced form of TFCA originated in most cases from *ad hoc* and spontaneously coordinated projects that led in time to formal institutions supported by legal arrangements.'
(Villiers, 1999: 93)

Much as the Seattle Peace Park and Seattle–Tashkent sister city relationship fostered long-range cultural exchange and economic development, the Kgalagadi Transfrontier Park has assisted in the establishment of formal consultative institutions engaged in joint decision making and recommendation authority. In this process, governments took the lead in setting national priorities and strategies for implementation and management (Villiers, 1999: 110). No sector creates more jobs in Africa than tourism. The creation of transfrontier peace parks can generate new jobs and opportunities, linking together game parks in different but adjoining countries through interstate agreements to development common conservation programmes and ecotourism. A Peace Park Foundation was established in 1998 and parks involving Zimbabwe, Namibia, South Africa, Mozambique, Botswana, Swaziland and Lesotho were identified. By the time all the current projects in southern Africa have been completed, a total of 300,000 square kilometres will become natural conservation areas (*African Business*, 2002: 8), yielding through ecotourism and hunting more than five times the income from cattle or crop farming. Priority tasks include community consultations, fencing, demining exercises and the training of game guards.

Proposed peace parks are often difficult to access and poorly mapped. 'Human settlements and their agricultural impacts are particularly difficult to pinpoint, yet are critical in planning conservation and tourism strategies for wildlife management areas' (Peace Park Foundation, 2000). A partnership between PS Publishing and South Africa Airways helped establish a geographical information system (GIS) laboratory to assist in the management of transfrontier conservation area (TFCA) projects. For a TFCA to become a reality, however, a Development Bank of South Africa report states that 'local communities would have to be adequately compensated for any loss of land and persuaded that peace parks are beneficial' (Morris, 1998).

The Kgalagadi Transfrontier Park is Africa's first formally declared TFCA, with shared borders between South Africa and Botswana. Its launch on 5 December 2000, at the culmination of nearly a decade of joint management, was characterized by the negotiation of pioneering bilateral legal treaties and by the restoration of access rights for indigenous communities to southern portions of the park to establish camps and rekindle ancient cultural practices. In its first year visitors to the Botswana side doubled, strengthening the conviction that peace parks can stimulate economic growth while expanding environmental protection (Kgalagadi Transfrontier Parks, 2002).

The Kgalagadi Transfrontier Park (KTP) has been in de facto existence for over 50 years, enabling South Africa and Botswana to manage this vast area as a single ecological unit. Its newly unified structure will strengthen the basis for joint promotion of tourism. No barriers to wildlife movement exist along the international boundary that separates the 9591-km^2 Kalahari Gemsbok National Park in South Africa and the 28,400-km^2 Gemsbok National Park in

Botswana – about the size of Massachusetts, Connecticut and Rhode Island. The name Kgalagadi is an attempt to get closer than 'Kalahari' to the original word for 'place of thirst' used by the San people, or bushmen. Each park will still run its own affairs and build its own tourist facilities, but they will adhere to a master plan. They will share entrance fees equally but keep the money they earn from renting out chalets and campsites (McNeil, 1999: p. 3). The Kalahari Conservation Society proposes that while, on the one hand, shared natural resources have partly been the cause of some of the regional conflicts in the world, the KTP, on the other hand, can provide an opportunity for regional countries to establish peace initiatives through the use of shared natural resources. Objectives include:

- increased regional stability, cooperation and peace through the sustainable utilization of resources, expanded tourism and economic growth
- respect for national sovereignty while at the same time developing models for cross-border cooperation and sharing resources
- accruing benefits to local communities adjacent to conservation areas through activities such as cultural tourism, training, and economic empowerment
- the establishment of natural systems to be managed as functional ecosystems for species conservation and sustainable development through bioregional planning (Tema, 2000).

In 2001 the World Bank approved grant funding worth $15.24 million to the governments of South Africa and Lesotho for the five-year Maloti-Drakensberg Transfrontier Conservation and Development Project to protect the exceptional biodiversity of the region through conservation, sustainable resource and landuse and development planning (Warner, 2001). Funded by the Global Environmental Facility as the single largest ever approved, the project's key objectives parallel those of potential and crucial interest to the two Koreas relative to the DMZ. These include partnership among governments and NGOs for the development of small businesses involved in ecotourism and job creation flowing from conservation. The Peace Park Foundation's newest endeavour opened in April 2002, known as GKG (Gaza/Kruger/Gonarezhou) Transfrontier Park and TFCA, involves signed international agreements among the ministries of Mozambique, South Africa and Zimbabwe. International funding sources include the German government, USAID (RCSA), the IUCN and Global Environment Facility through the World Bank. Promising tremendous benefits for wildlife and tourism alike, the sheer size of the GKG requires development of a whole series of protocols associated with immigration, security, agriculture and animal disease control, which require agreement by all three countries (Peace Park Foundation, 2000).

The case for an ecotourism peace park and cultural heritage corridor in the Korean DMZ

An increasing number of powerful examples are now in place illustrating the long-term viability of cultural heritage tourism and socioeconomic exchanges through such projects as the Seattle Peace Park and Seattle–Tashkent sister city programme. Furthermore, the advent of new transfrontier parks and conservation areas worldwide such as Kgalagadi, links multinational partnerships with the governance of biodiversity and preservation of environmental sustainability and serves as models for conservation in the 21st century. The time, then, appears brighter than in the past – and in light of South Korea's 'Sunshine Policy', which is South Korean President Kim Dao Jung's engagement policy with North Korea, a tacit extension of the earlier government's National Commonwealth Unification Formula – for the consideration of an ecotourism peace park and heritage corridor in the Korean DMZ.

Setting

Environmental issues given the stamp of approval of tourism may help build lasting international and interorganizational institutions dedicated to preserving biodiversity as well as economic development in the DMZ. Hostility between North and South Korea may be eased by fostering mutually sustainable tourism-related economic growth and development of the park's natural and cultural resources. Consideration of these issues came to the fore in 2000 when South Korean President Kim Dao Jung won the Nobel Peace Prize for his reconciliation efforts towards North Korea. This recognition and other signals led to increased interest in the USA by then President Clinton to engage North Korea in meaningful dialogue that could result in a lessening of tensions and, ultimately, in the reunification of the two Koreas. During the summer of 2000 the Korea National Tourism Organization invited the School of Business and Public Management at The George Washington University to consider a tourism initiative responsive to South Korea President Kim's efforts. To this end, the idea of a Korean DMZ Peace Park, first suggested more than two decades earlier by Professor Paige and endorsed by President Kim, was discussed and elaborated into a tourism-based initiative.

By the autumn of 2000 Secretary of State Madeline Albright had travelled to North Korea to toast future rapprochement on the Korean peninsula, clearing the path for a visit by the then President Clinton after the presidential elections in November. Secretary Albright's words to North Korean Chairman Kim Jung II emphasize cultural heritage and sports tourism as elements in diplomacy:

Mr Chairman, there are many dimensions to diplomacy, from intense discussions on security, to the establishment of diplomatic posts, to show in respect for cultural heritage, to the challenge of international athletic competition. Sometimes, sports can serve as a mirror reflecting improvement in relations or as a springboard to further gains. For example, the world was delighted this past month to see Koreans from the North and South march together in Sydney under one flag. In the same spirit that has taken hold since the North–South Summit earlier this year, I invite you all to join me in a toast to friendship between our peoples, and to a new era of opportunity and promise-through the Land of the Morning Calm. (US DoS, 2000)

President Clinton's trip never materialized and the election of George W. Bush as president and his labelling of North Korea as an 'evil empire' in the fight against terrorism stymied any new initiative that relied on United States' facilitation of the peace process. Recent signs indicate a return of rapprochement on the part of North Korea towards South Korea and other nations in the region without significant US engagement.

Management considerations

The DMZ of the Korean peninsula may be characterized as a Cold War relic, a shallow strip of land that serves as the inter-Korean border and as a painful symbol of a divided Korean people. The area, extending from the South China Sea to the Gulf of Korea, is patrolled by 30,000 US soldiers among many others along the southern border of the Democratic People's Republic of Korea. Regarding peace, the border between the two Koreas today is the most heavily armed in the world. It keeps several countries on military alert and costs money that could be invested in environmental protection and economic growth.

The DMZ is also a place of tremendous significance as a natural and cultural reserve, frozen in time for half a century. While discussions were proceeding in the waning days of the Clinton administration, a proposal was advanced by a cross-disciplinary faculty team organized by the International Institute of Tourism Studies in The George Washington University's School of Business and Public Management in the USA (including the authors of this chapter). The GW Institute for Peacebuilding and Development also played a role. Counterparts at Hyang Hee University in Seoul, Korea, also joined this team.

Because of the sensitive nature of any negotiations between the two Koreas, it was thought that a confidence-building and conflict-management measure such as a ecotourism peace park and cultural heritage plan would provide a neutral, mutually beneficial and apolitical component to reconciliation discussions. A key purpose of this chapter is to identify how this proposal went beyond other Korean peace park proposals in a number of respects.

The George Washington University (GW) Ecotourism Peace Park and Heritage Corridor long-term objectives include reconciliation and reunification, cultural and educational exchange and economic opportunity and environmental preservation. As a distinct feature, the foundation of the GW initiative is to create economic incentives through environmental and cultural heritage tourism that would bring North Korea into active participation in these discussions. The GW initiative seeks to address what appears to be a significant imbalance in the application of the concept of sustainable tourism within the natural and cultural environments (Egloff and Newby, 2000). In the short term, the effort seeks to organize and conduct consultations – among North and South Korea, US and Chinese experts – to assist in the development of a joint commission to advance this initiative and to develop a feasibility study and promote sponsorship for these efforts.

The stated principles are to:

- facilitate Korean family reunification, reunion, recreation and pilgrimage
- create numerous opportunities for business development
- be dedicated to peaceful reconciliation among the Korean people
- project a sense of celebration and hospitality to inbound visitors to Korea
- maintain authentic Korean cultural heritage and conserve the natural resources of the DMZ
- manifest a sense of peaceful reconciliation in both theme and programme content
- serve as a venue for peaceful reconciliation between the two governments
- contribute to heritage education
- provide for the management of special events that advance reconciliation efforts
- support all these points with financial and physical infrastructure, visitor and hospitality services, educational programming and information technology.

The reality of everyday life in North Korea is a broken economy in a country populated by starving and isolated people. The DMZ itself, its buildings and wildlife essentially undisturbed for half a century, harbours an untold number of landmines and unexploded ordinance that must be removed.

A new George Washington University ecotourism peace park and heritage corridor proposal developed a strategy that would produce investment, jobs and wide-ranging opportunities in North Korea as a leavening for advances in reconciliation and family reunification. The idea is not to style a peace park as a result of a peace treaty or as a symbol, but rather as an actual working component of the peace-seeking process.

Professor Kim had focused the DMZ Forum on the Korean ecosystem. 'After North–South relationships are resolved, the next challenge is the environment,' he declared at a July 2001 DMZ Forum meeting at New York University. Except for the environmental clean-up to take place, massive investment must be made to resolve the problems between the two Koreas. At the same conference, former US Ambassador to South Korea Stephen W. Bosworth observed that:

We must be patient with North Korea and not try to control their decision-making. North Korea's behavior is sometimes bizarre, but they are not crazy. Experience shows we can deal with them; it also shows they will observe agreements once reached. We must be willing to take 'yes' for an answer. We should not approach representatives of North Korea with an assumption it will not succeed. (http://www.dmzforum.org)

Villiers (1999: 28–41) points out potential difficulties in establishing transfrontier conservation areas, such as lack of political support, sub-regional instability and uncompleted democratization, lack of clearly defined benefits, predominance of national pride, differences in institutional and other capacity, differences in landuse and object of protection, incomplete management and institutional structures, absence of a regional framework and, finally, lack of sustained funding. These are serious issues no less important when considering an ecotourism peace park and heritage corridor in the Korean DMZ.

As The George Washington University team organized a feasibility study, it established criteria that could be useful in other ecotourism peace park and cultural heritage planning efforts:

1 As a 375-square-mile heritage corridor, comprehensive planning will feature tourism as the one of the highest and best returns-on-investment for an environmentally protected area.
2 Development alternatives will highlight mixed-use projects, from housing to commercial enterprises to nature-based tourism.
3 The attractions and programming within the corridor should benefit the Korean people through multiple channels.
4 The corridor should be developed as sacred ground: well-regulated visitation with limited and controlled vehicular traffic; four-season accommodation; frequent motor coach and light rail service from north and south and within the corridor; a range of accommodation amenities and prices, including hostel and camping, low-cost and luxury hotels; and facilitation for day trips and special sport and tourism events.
5 The benefits of development should accrue to all Korean people, regardless of the sources of investment.
6 There should be a strong reliance on packages for international visitors that can be placed into retail channels.
7 The planning should include sophisticated e-commerce components for prospecting sales and data mining, tied to passport ticketing and other dynamic packaging.
8 The planning should include special event programming and management tied to corridor themes and programme content.
9 Consideration should be given to the development of residential and commercial zones within the corridor and/or integrated into its adjacencies.
10 Programming content must be managed to permit creativity and enterprise within the context of peace and reconciliation and sustainable development.
11 Public–private partnerships in governance, ownership and management of corridor enterprises are desirable.
12 A strong intra-Korean preference for development employment and import substitution should be respected.

Beyond the obvious peace dividends earned from tourism development as a lubricant for international trade and understanding, there are strategic benefits from tourism development that can be deployed in the peace process itself. The issue rests within the definition of tourism and how tourism planning in sustainable development can be integrated in geopolitical policy processes.

Conclusion

Peace through tourism is an interesting concept. Hilton Hotels' motto, 'world peace through world travel', is countered by the concept of 'leakage', that is, the amount of money that flows through a country but does not remain to benefit the local economy. The problem with the subject of tourism in these discussions among many otherwise knowledgeable officials and the popular press are their use of egregious examples of massive, eco-destructive sun, sea and sand developments of the 1980s and early 1990s which are considered and presented out of balance with the significant parallel growth in numbers and market share in cultural heritage and nature-based travel.

The fear is that the world's distinctive cultures and indigenous peoples will be absorbed into one great mass of transnational business, a fragmented, packaged corporate culture that looks the same all over the world. For some, the issues of wealth and freedom gained in market economies take precedence over the social pleasures and agreeable pastimes of distinctive locality. Yet as tourism and travel becomes a primary contributor to a national or regional economy and balance of payments, the selection of factors for success becomes critical.

When tourism development is organized from the start to enhance and protect cultural distinctiveness and interpreted landscapes, both the planning processes and the results they produce can become remarkable new strains of cooperation and mutual benefit. Gerson (2001: 110–11) states that in complex and complicated settings of post-conflict reconstructions, the private sector in partnership with governments can help link disparate and less flexible institutional approaches, providing a 'rule of law' catalyzing peacemaking activities and 'reducing the avoidable risks of investment'. Few cooperative arrangements involving the private sector in the work of international institutions exist today for the purposes of instilling peace through tourism's significant role in the preservation of environmental and cultural heritage. As pressures mount from adjacent populations to develop the Korean DMZ, its preservation will be accepted only if local citizens and both Korean governments realize that the land is worth more if developed for long-term sustainable use. In this light, the case for the establishment of an ecotourism peace park and cultural heritage corridor for the Korean Demilitarized Zone can point the two Koreas and many other parts of the world towards a new way forward.

Acknowledgments

The authors express their deep appreciation to Ms Angelica King, graduate assistant and master of tourism administration candidate, Department of Tourism and Hospitality Management, The George Washington University, for her assistance with the research for this chapter.

Questions

1 Examine the different kinds of peace park framework.
2 Describe the potential for cultural exchange and heritage development within the peace park framework.
3 What issues are important in balancing conservation with development practices in The George Washington University Korea DMZ ecotourism peace park and cultural heritage corridor concept?
4 Discuss how a peace park may be best managed and governed.

References

African Business (2002) 'Daimler-Chrysler Support Peace-Parks', 8 January.

Angelos, C. (1990) 'At 94, he's busy building a peace park – many join his effort', *Seattle Times*, 12 July, C2.

Denver Rocky Mountain News (1994) 'City rejects peace park', 23 November, 26A.

Drohan, J. (1996) 'Sustainably developing the DMZ', *Technology Review*, 99 (6), 17.

Egloff, B. and Newby, P. (2000) Sustainable cultural tourism: is it a concept that can be made to work? Sustainable Heritage Conference, Environmental Protection Agency, 2–3 June, Queensland Government, Australia.

Furlong, G. (2002) President, Seattle – Tashkent Sister City Association. Personal telephone interview, 15 April.

Gerson, A. (2001) 'Peace building: the private sector's role', *The American Journal of International Law*, 95 (102), 102–119.

Kgalagadi Transfrontier Parks (2002) Fact Sheet, 25 March, *www.parks-sa.za/media_releases*.

Mandela, N. (2001) *The (Johannesburg) Star*, 10 December.

Mayell, H. (1999) 'Korea's DMZ: from war zone to park?', *National Geographic*.

McNeil, D. (1999) 'In Africa, a small step to bigger game parks', *New York Times*, 15 August, 3.

Morris, A. (1998) 'South Africa: national parks take on a new direction', Interpress Service, Global Information Network, 22 May.

Pearce, P. L., Moscardo, G.M. and Ross, G. F. (1996) *Tourism Community Relationships*. Tarrytown, NY: Elsevier Science.

Peace Park Foundation (2000) 'The Peace Parks Foundation at Work', Annual review (*www.peaceparks.org*).

Richardson, L. and Sochaczewski, P.S. (1999) 'Make parks, not war', in 'Across a divide', *International Wildlife*, July/August.

Seattle Parks and Recreation (1986–1997) Peace Park-related letters and memoranda courtesy of David Takami, Strategic Advisor, Seattle, WA.

Shields, R. (1991) *Places on the Margin: Alternative Geographies of Modernity*. London: Routledge.

Tema, W. (2000) 'A press release from the Kalahari Conservation Society on the occasion to the launching of the Kgalagadi Transfrontier Park (KTP)', Kalagari Conservation Society, 12 May.

Tizon, A. (1997) 'Sharing hope for peace', *Seattle Times*, 30 March.

US Department of State (2000) Remarks by Secretary of State Madeleine K. Albright. Pyongyan, Democratic People's Republic of Korea, 24 October.

Villiers, B. (1999) *Peace Parks – The Way Ahead: International Experience and Indicators for Southern Africa*. Pretoria: HSRC.

Warner, C. (2001) 'Lesotho and South Africa: World Bank Approves GEF Grant for Biodiversity and Sustainable Development Project', Peace Park Foundation Newsletter, 13 September.

Winfield, P. (1990) 'A peaceful idea takes flight', 7 August, E3.

Websites

www.parks-sa.za/media_releases
www.peaceparks.org
www.secretary.state.gov/www/statements/2000
www.secretary.state.gov/background_notes/n-korea

179

10 The State of Nature Tourism in Texas: Sustaining the Rural Agricultural Family Enterprise

Tazim Jamal, Andy Skadberg and Kim Williams

The four main objectives of this chapter are to:

- Discuss the land relationships and land ethic of rural ranchers and farmers in Texas, their issues and concerns and how this knowledge can contribute to a sustainable approach to nature tourism development and management
- Illustrate the importance of considering socio-cultural factors in nature tourism development in this rural agricultural domain and in conceptualizing ecotourism and its guiding principles
- Examine the complex domain of nature tourism in Texas and the role of scientific information and information technology
- Present the importance of the key scientific or technical personnel in overcoming knowledge and communication barriers

Introduction

This chapter examines the state itself and state of nature tourism in Texas, with respect to (1) the challenges facing family-based agricultural enterprises, (2) the experience of these rural farmers and ranchers with the land and their relationships with the land and (3) the role of scientific/technical experts and information technology in the successful development of nature tourism. A case study of farmers and ranchers in Calhoun County, Texas, is presented, which examines the issues and concerns of these producers, and identifies an agricultural land ethic. Implications for nature tourism development, planning and impact management are discussed.

Generally speaking, the 'green consumer' is an increasingly important and growing market segment and a new worldview, a 'green paradigm', is slowly replacing old paradigms of research and management (Weaver, 1998). In this new green paradigm lies possibilities for making mass tourism a little more sustainable and for new forms of tourism (such as ecotourism) to bridge the gap between environmental concerns and tourism development. However, the hope offered by ecotourism continues to be hindered by a lack of understanding of what ecotourism is, what role it plays in the everyday lives of those who engage in it and the ways in which regional and global political, financial and cultural factors impact a local ecotourism operation (Chapter 1).

Ecotourism is ostensibly based on a set of ethical principles that guide its development, management and delivery. These principles are not merely a 'code of ethics for visitors', they must clarify and enable the development of codes of conduct for nature tourism service providers and managers, including policy-makers, developers, marketers and business operators. It is therefore imperative to also clarify, define and understand what ecotourism is, in order to determine what principles should guide its development and practice. A review of the literature shows some of the confusion in the field. Note, for instance, the difference between the following two definitions of ecotourism:

> Ecotourism is responsible travel to natural areas which conserves the environment and improves the welfare of the local. (Lindberg and Hawkins, 1993)

> Instead, ecotourism can be broadly defined as travel oriented towards the natural environment or indigenous cultures of a region and it is generally expected to respect and protect the environment and culture of the host country or region. (Lawrence et al., 1997)

The second definition includes visits to indigenous cultures as part of ecotourism, while the first focuses on natural areas. Both contain an expectation of some type of benefit to the host region and local people, as do many other definitions. The following definition contains a more explicit emphasis of this being a low-impact activity that contributes to conservation directly and indirectly:

> Low impact nature tourism which contributes to the maintenance of species and habitats either directly through a contribution to conservation and/or indirectly by providing revenue to the local community sufficient for people to value, and therefore protect, their wildlife heritage areas as a source of income. (Goodwin, 1996, in Roe et al., 1997)

An examination of the multitude of definitions and descriptions of eco-tourism show that these generally hold a few common premises hinging on a nature-based experience, environmental education and sustainability of biodiversity and local communities (Orams, 1995; Diamantis, 1999; Sirakaya et al.,

2001). But a number of important elements are omitted in the ensuing discussions, for instance, with respect to values and perceptions of 'Nature'. *What* Nature is being represented in the destination site by the researcher, nature tourism operator, landowner, or how and why, is hardly questioned. Also ignored or poorly covered are the relationships between Nature and the nature tourism enterprise owner or manager, particularly with respect to the social and cultural barriers to and impacts of diversifying into nature tourism from other forms of livelihood based on the land (e.g. farming).

Regardless of whether to call it 'ecotourism' or 'nature tourism', nature-based tourism that purports to follow a sustainable tourism approach must advocate respect, ethical conduct and consideration of both natural and human communities. So, if ecotourism is to live up to its promise of being a (golden) green bridge between these two dimensions, then policymakers, developers and others in the tourism industry require a very clear understanding of at least (a) the first principles on which a nature-based tourism ethic is based, (b) the socio-cultural (human) factors that might sustain or impede attempts at responsible tourism development and (c) the spectrum of nature tourism activities that can be circumscribed by the nature tourism ethic. The Texas-based case study presented here offers some insights into these aspects and also discusses key planning and management issues related to the complex and fragmented nature tourism domain in Texas. The case offers insights for nature-based tourism scholars, as well as public agencies and nature tourism operators in similar agricultural domains.

In the next section, a historical overview of nature tourism in Texas is provided. This is followed by an exploratory study of the experience of rural, family-based, farming and ranching in Calhoun County, Texas. An agricultural land ethic can be identified from this analysis, which holds implications for a nature tourism ethic. The subsequent section discusses the implications of this case for nature tourism development, focusing on information communication, sustainability and socio-cultural as well as heritage impacts.

It should be noted that 'Nature-based Tourism' (also referred to as 'nature tourism') is used here as an umbrella term encompassing ecotourism, farm-based tourism, (outdoor) adventure tourism, etc (Chapter 1). So while this chapter is based on nature tourism in relation to farmers and ranchers in Texas, this term is synonymous with agricultural tourism (Hawaii) and ecotourism in other US states and countries. The case study described here therefore holds insights for ecotourism businesses and policymakers elsewhere where similar issues and concerns may be present.

Nature tourism in Texas

Impacts, particularly the social and cultural ones, are not always easy to identify and manage. They may, for instance, be intangible or difficult to 'measure'. The task is made even more difficult by the number of stakeholders involved in producing and providing the nature tourism experience, to say nothing of the individual and cumulative environmental impacts that also have to be factored into the decision making. Since the nature tourism 'product' is a combination of the nature-based experience and the goods and services that accompany the provision of this experience, these impacts also range over a number of different economic, environmental and socio-cultural domains. In addition, the impacts range from local to regional and global. This interrelated micro-macro domain is one that is often omitted in the study of nature tourism and its impacts. We therefore start this section with a look at the larger setting of nature tourism in Texas, followed by a location-based study of agricultural enterprises in Calhoun County, Texas, where a family tradition of farming and ranching is now threatened by economic conditions.

Texas covers 266,027 square miles. It is ranked as the second largest state in the USA, both in geographical size and population (20,851,820 in the year 2000, US Census Bureau, 2002). The state measures 801 miles from north to south and 773 miles from east to west and has 624 miles of coastline on the Gulf of Mexico. As Table 10.1 shows, tourism is a major contributor to the economic well-being of Texas. Eubanks and Stoll (1999) note that the state tourism agency, Texas Economic Development, describe the most popular activities for US travellers (non-Texan) to Texas in 1997 as follows: nature based (13%), cultural (22%) and attractions based (18%). Preeminent in valuable wetlands, Texas is considered to be the premier birdwatching destination in the USA, according to the results of a 1993 American Birding Association survey (Texas Parks and Wildlife Department, 2001b).

Nature Tourism has seen a steady evolution in Texas, in that the concept,

Table 10.1 Tourism in Texas

- Domestic and international visitors spent $40.4 billion in 2000, equivalent to $110 million spent in Texas businesses every day
- Travel spending in Texas has increased at an average annual rate of 6.5% since 1990
- Texas ranks third among all states in its share (6%) of domestic spending. Only California and Florida have greater market shares
- International visitors accounted for 11% of all travel spending in Texas in 2000. Residents accounted for 50%, while other domestic travellers accounted for 39%
- Local tax revenues were $676 million in 2000. State tax revenues were $2.2 billion. Federal tax revenues were $3.0 billion (estimates of local tax revenues do not include property taxes)
- The total tax impact (local, state and federal) of visitor spending in Texas was $5.9 billion in 2000
- During 2000, visitor spending in Texas directly supported 485,000 jobs (an increase of 2.4% over 1999) with earnings of $11.2 billion (an increase of 7.8%)

implementation and practice have been extensively developed and in use here for well over a decade. Recognizing the agricultural crisis and other factors impacting landowners and operators in the state of Texas over the last couple of decades, various public and private sector agencies and organizations commenced a series of initiatives designed to assist these rural businesses. However, at the public agency level, it is difficult to separate efforts to promote general tourism from those intended specifically for nature tourism. The department associated with transportation (TxDOT) and the Department of Economic Development, two of the major agencies involved with supporting nature tourism development, do not specifically have programmes aimed at nature tourism development. Their efforts focus on general tourism development.

Key among the public sector stakeholders (Table 10.2) is the Texas Cooperative Extension (TCE), associated with Texas A&M University in College Station, Texas. One of the main roles of TCE is to implement the land grant mandate of Texas A&M, which advocates outreach and improving the well-being of local communities and businesses in the state. TCE, in concert with other state agencies, hoped to soften the economic hardships that farmers and ranchers were facing by introducing the producers to nature tourism as a means of earning additional income. As such, this Extension arm of the university has played a vital role in the public sector for establishing nature-based tourism as an important means of economic diversification in Texas.

Table 10.2 Major stakeholders in the public sector domain

- Southwest Texas State University
- State Task Force on Texas Nature Tourism
- Texas A&M University
- Texas Commission on the Arts
- Texas Department of Agriculture
- Texas Department of Public Safety
- Texas Department of Transportation
- Texas Economic Development
- Texas General Land Office
- Texas Historical Commission
- Texas Nature Tourism Association
- Texas Parks and Wildlife Department
- Texas State Agency Tourism Council
- Texas Travel Industry Association

Table 10.3 provides an overview of programmes that are currently in place in the agencies involved in nature tourism development. The Parks and Wildlife Department has had the most significant impact since about 1991. Hence, as a concept and a 'quasi' industry, nature tourism has been recognized in Texas for a number of years, but public sector efforts to support and promote it continue to be hampered by a number of institutional and structural barriers. However,

Table 10.3 Overview of programmes being implemented by various agencies

Agency	Programmes/services	Characteristics
Parks and Wildlife Dept	Great Texas Coastal Birding Trail (with TxDOT)	Trail developed as a marketing platform to benefit communities and enhance habitat protection (L. Campbell, Texas, 1999, personal communication). Trail consists of 300+ birding 'sites' located along public roadways. Map provides directions, local information and interpretation (TPWD (a))
	Great Texas Birding Classic	Birdwatching competition held along the birding trail to promote it and raise money to establish more wildlife habitat (TPWD (a))
	Technical assistance	Staff training to be initiated in Spring 2000 (TPWD (c))
	World Birding Center	Currently under development and international in scope, the mission of the birding centre is to 'significantly increase the appreciation, understanding and conservation of birds, wildlife, habitat and Texas' natural heritage' (TPWD (d))
	Texas Conservation Passport	Park users get free or reduced rates on park fees, camping and programmes. Additionally, programmes are held at state parks, state historical parks and other cooperating areas (TPWD (b))
Dept of Economic Development	Community workshop series for tourism development	Workshops held in each of the seven tourism regions of the state. Designed to assist rural areas with tourism development. Participants include chambers of commerce, councils of government, tourism councils, city managers, etc.
	Market research	Tourism division captures tourism data and is beginning to track statistics about nature-related activities (C. Jackson, Texas, 1999, personal communication)

the formation of the State Taskforce on Texas Nature Tourism was the first officially mandated effort to evaluate and coordinate nature tourism development in the state.

State taskforce on Texas Nature Tourism

The State Taskforce on Nature Tourism was a 21-member committee co-chaired by the Executive Director of the Texas Parks and Wildlife Department and the Executive Director of the Department of Economic Development (Texas Parks and Wildlife Department, 2001a). This taskforce defined nature tourism as 'discretionary travel to natural areas that conserves the environmental, social and cultural values while generating an economic benefit to the local community' (State Taskforce on Texas Nature Tourism, 1994: 2). Nature tourists were defined as 'travelers who spend their time and money enjoying and appreciating a broad range of outdoor activities that have minimal impact on the environment'. The following was the mission given to the State Taskforce by Governor Ann Richards (State Taskforce on Texas Nature Tourism, 1994: 2):

1 Examine the potential of nature tourism in Texas.
2 Recommend opportunities for developing and promoting it.
3 Build on local efforts already under way.
4 Preserve local, social and cultural values.
5 Promote sustainable economic growth, restorative economic development and environmental conservation through nature tourism.

Given this mission statement, the State Taskforce made recommendations under four categories: conservation, legislation, promotion and education. Various actions have occurred as a result of these recommendations, for example, a wildlife management tax exemption and a landowner incentive programme (under the Parks and Wildlife Department) were set up (conservation related), a cap on landowner liability was instilled at the legislative level and a marketing campaign featuring natural attractions was also implemented. The State Taskforce clearly recognized the need to provide training to rural community leaders involved with tourism and a number of educational recommendations addressing direct 'in the field' activities for developing nature tourism emerged (State Taskforce on Texas Nature Tourism, 1994: 19):

1 Develop a step-by-step nature tourism handbook targeted to communities and private landowners.
2 Provide training and outreach for local communities, individuals and companies to nurture and enhance nature tourism in their areas.
3 Enable the development of local tourism infrastructure to support the nature consumer's needs.
4 Provide training for public and private sector employees who interact with the public concerning basic hospitality skills and nature tourism opportunities in their areas.
5 Identify and coordinate public and private organizations with the financial resources and expertise to help communities and individuals in their nature tourism efforts.
6 Identify nature tourism products and infrastructure that are both available and needed to promote sustainable growth and environmental conservation.
7 Develop programmes to communicate the importance of protecting and managing the state's nature resources.

Var (1997) noted that while these recommendations emphasize the importance of cooperation and coordination among various public and private institutions, no leadership or responsibility to implement these suggestions was assigned. This may be one possible reason why, despite the recognition of nature tourism's importance and the work that has gone into it so far, greater progress has not been made on accomplishing these objectives. Lack of coordination may be a primary contributing factor, for the nature tourism domain in Texas is a complex one, with numerous stakeholders and a predominance of private land ownership, as well as a rural agricultural crisis that policymakers are grappling with.

Calhoun County, Texas

In the USA, the globalization of agriculture through the globalization of trade, technology and finance, commodity prices and markets, has exerted a major effect on agrarian landowners. Among other factors, falling commodity prices and increasing competition have contributed to deepening the agricultural crisis facing these rural producers. This has driven a sustained effort by public agencies and policymakers in Texas to facilitate the development of nature tourism opportunities as a means of supplementing declining rural agricultural incomes. While it is a unique setting for nature tourism in that over 95% of the land in Texas is privately owned, the public sector's responses to challenges facing small nature tourism operators, ranchers and farmers here may be informative for nature tourism managers and policymakers in rural agricultural settings elsewhere.

How does an agriculturalist interested in supplementing declining revenues view nature tourism opportunities? What principles guide the development and management of nature-based attractions in rural agricultural domains? A few scholars have suggested that the ethical overlay of tourists and operators determines 'ecotourism' (e.g. Wight, 1993; Acott et al., 1998; Herremans and Welsh, 1999). Fennell's (1999) introductory text to ecotourism, is to be commended in the depth and breadth of topics covered, including one whole chapter on ethics. And Weaver (1998) offers a comprehensive set of case studies of ecotourism in lesser developed countries. Lacking are studies that richly explore the experience of being a rural landowner, farmer, rancher, how different activities and actions impact them and how these can inform or be informed by a well-structured definition and description of ecotourism and ecotourism ethics.

For example, how does getting involved in nature tourism affect their relationship with the land and with Nature? What is 'Nature' to these people who live so closely to the land? A study of rural producers in Calhoun County, located in southeast Texas and bordering the Gulf of Mexico offers some preliminary insights into these questions.

Case methodology

A series of interviews and detailed examination of reports, documents and academic literature informed this case study. The interview format consisted of in-depth, semi-structured questions (both open and close ended) using an interpretive approach to the data gathering and analysis. A qualitative software package (NU*DIST 4) was utilized for coding the data and recording the themes and sub-themes that emerged through careful paragraph and line-by-line analysis. The analysis of the transcribed data was an interactive and iterative process of the researcher moving between the transcriptions, the literature and the respondents. Each interview built on the previous one by asking questions on aspects that emerged during the meetings. Questions focused primarily on two areas: (1) participants' involvement and experience with ranching and farming and (2) their understanding and views about nature tourism.

In total, 14 rural agricultural producers were interviewed. Thirteen respondents were landowners who engaged in farming or ranching at least 50% of the time (one was a land manager). While landholdings varied in size from 500–2000+ acres, all the participants came from a tradition of farming or ranching. All except one couple had inherited the land through family relationships and were very concerned about their being able to hold onto the land. Several mentioned not passing the land onto their children due to the difficulty of making a living from it. The enterprises in this study are referred to as family-based enterprises, owned or operated as family businesses, although many supplemented their livelihood with outside jobs. The experience and concerns identified in the study (see Williams, 2000) are drawn on and examined in the context of nature tourism planning and development in Texas. Quotes from the interview transcripts are included so that the reader can see how the participants' voices inform the analysis conducted here (pseudonyms are used to ensure participant confidentiality).

Views and questions about nature tourism

How often do rural landowners contemplating nature tourism wonder what their product is and how they should position it relative to other nature tourism activities going on in their area and what 'the market' wants? (See Meador, 2001, a ranch owner's perspective on Nature Tourism.)

Twelve of the individuals interviewed were familiar with the term nature tourism; the remaining two had either not heard of nature tourism or were uncertain about its meaning. To those familiar with the term there was variation in what it meant to them. To John, ecotourism and nature tourism were interchangeable since both had something to do with 'the natural environment'.

This 'something' included hunting, fishing and birding. Ecotourism, then, was seen as an 'economic situation based on dollars generated by tourism'. Jake's understanding of nature tourism was similar to John's in that he defined nature tourism as 'giving the public access to nature', as well as 'making money off it'. While some of these individuals' definitions included money, others focused on what the attraction might be. For example, Tom described nature tourism as: 'Nature is the land we got out here and then people interested in coming out birding or . . . to see what is going on.' These agricultural producers generally view Nature in terms of land and the forces of weather. Cattle are seen as part of Nature and Nature is also associated with the unpredictable weather that creates challenges for agricultural production.

Two other definitions included an aspect of interest on the part of an outside visitor (see Table 10.4). After stating his definition, Kevin replied: 'We live in it everyday and . . . there are many people that never see it.' Al shared this sentiment when he explained that nature tourists will have to be someone from 'outside' the local area or not part of the agricultural community. Moreover, to other interviewees nature tourism was also associated with movement or touring. Roy and Mark described nature tourism by providing examples of their own experiences of it. For example, Roy discussed a well-known regional attraction, Aransas Park and Wildlife Refuge, as being a great nature tourism place. In his view the refuge at one time had whooping cranes and deer, however, in recent years the wildlife numbers have diminished. Nature tourism to Roy is an active experience, for although 'I don't want to go sit on a post and look at some birds and all', it was neat to be able 'to ride through there'.

Table 10.4 Nature tourism definitions provided by various respondents

Al: Tourism to me is somebody outside coming in

Roy: Years ago you had Aransas Park and Wildlife Refuge down here . . . That was a fantastic place to drive through and look at wildlife okay . . . We would rattle horns, certain type of deer, certain time of year. Bucks would come up. We would take our kids over there and picnic. That is what I would call nature tourism . . . I don't want to go sit on a, because I don't call that touring . . . sit on a post and look at some birds and all

Mark: He created artificial wetlands. He has leased that land out to hunting . . . your bird people probably the best area . . . for them to come and look at birds, bird sightings and that kind of thing

Shane: Bird sanctuaries and things like that where you have folks come and observe the birds and the nature in general

Jake: Giving public access to nature. Capitilize on it, I believe, make some money out of it

Tom: I guess nature tourism. Out here is the nature . . . nature is the land we got out here and then people interested in coming out birding, or what have you. See what is going on

Anne: Wanting the birdwatchers to come out

Kevin: My definition would be just people [who] want to come out and see nature. Nature on your farm whether it's birds or whatever, wildlife and have an interest enough to come out and see it

John: Ecotourism and nature tourism same thing, something to do with the natural environment

While they discussed nature tourism, these producers also described a number of needs and concerns about it as a potential enterprise. All the interviewees shared many of the needs and concerns listed in Table 10.5. From their responses, it became apparent that to assist those starting a nature tourism enterprise requires understanding their views about Nature (rather than taking this for granted as something common to tourists and locals alike) and also being able to identify and address a number of very different concerns. These issues related directly to starting an unfamiliar enterprise involving people rather than crops or cattle and other concerns and values related to the historical, social and cultural conditions in this rural Texas setting. Examining these individuals' relationship with the land provided insights into understanding how nature tourism might fit into this rural agricultural context.

Table 10.5 Information needs and concerns of farmers and ranchers with regards to nature tourism

Need for information – sample of questions commonly asked
- What can I offer?
- What do people want to see?
- How do I market spur-of-the-moment and infrequent happenings?
- How do I start a business?
- What type of infrastructure is required? Roads? Port-a-potties? Birding trails?
- Where do we find an investor to back such an enterprise?
- Can I see an example of a successful nature tourism enterprise?
- How can I get wildlife started?

Commonly mentioned concerns about starting and maintaining a nature tourism enterprise
- Destruction of property by hunters and general public
- [Visitors] Leaving trash
- Trespassing on the individual's own property and that of others
- Liability is a problem, regardless of proof of negligence, due to legal fees
- Giving tours is not appealing. Public demand may not be steady
- Seasonal enterprise
- We're in an economic downturn; public demand may not be there
- Public demand may not be enough to make it worthwhile
- Birders do not pay
- Birding is a fad

Relationship with the land

How do the farmers and ranchers fulfil their livelihood and conduct their daily activities, i.e. what is their relationship with the land? Three major, interrelated themes emerged from this analysis. They make a living from the land and they tend to it, but the act of being on the land is itself integral to their heritage and identity.

Making a living

Agricultural production is a livelihood that depends on being able to make the land produce economic commodities. Part of the production activities performed by these farmers/ranchers includes the use of fertilizer and pesticides for crops and growth hormones to enhance cattle productivity. These activities are performed to increase the economic returns from the land. Such activities may be viewed by some visitors as incompatible with nature tourism, but they are common practices in the majority of agricultural settings and would not necessarily exclude quality nature-based experiences for visitors.

Inherent in this livelihood is being able to make independent decisions, meet challenges and enjoy being faced by something new everyday – a new challenge, some new event. A supervised, predictable day job was not considered ideal by any of the individuals who participated in this research, although most of the participants had jobs to supplement their income. A key concern for these farmers and ranchers was being able to maintain ownership of the land, even it meant just getting a marginal income on which to live. This appeared to be a constant concern for many of these individuals.

Being on the land

These farmers/ranchers face daily changes, ranging from pests to weather, which present new challenges that they must face in order to raise livestock and/or grow crops. To address these challenges they must be on the land and be ready to deal with each new situation that may arise. The hands-on experience gained from this close relationship with the land was perceived by participants as being crucial to the successful management of the farm/ranch. This is also what distinguishes these individuals from 'those from the outside', like biologists. These outsiders were not always well regarded because their approach to managing Nature might identify potential environmental problems on these interviewees' property, which could result in them losing that piece of land. This was land passed down through generations in a frontier history where possession of land was crucial to survival and a sign of freedom from authority. Land ownership thus symbolized a long historical tradition of settling 'the West' through rugged individualism and an entrepreneurial spirit.

Taking care of the land

A recurrent theme was how the farmers and ranchers treated the land by actively 'taking care of things' (e.g. walking out to the field to pull a weed that is overtaking a crop plant or stopping to fix a fence). This point highlights the paradoxical situation for these rural agricultural producers. On the one hand, they know every part of their land intimately, where the birds nest, which trees are healthy and which are not, etc. But, on the other hand, they worry about the possibility of discovering an endangered species on their land. This is because they perceive a risk of losing control of that piece of land due to environmental regulations such the Endangered Species Act.

Furthermore, some participants felt that the biologist's perception of Nature was different from their own, i.e. it was a threatening, alienating one. Their own experience was one of intimate familiarity through hands-on presence, a pragmatic relationship of care and recognition of the unpredictable forces of Nature.

Further examination of the data and related documents reveals that these three primary categories of experience with the land are influenced by three interrelated sets of guiding principles or environmental ethics (see Williams, 2000, for more details). These are now summarized briefly, showing where each ethic fits its previously mentioned counterpart, i.e. the productionist ethic guides making a living, the being on the land ethic is an existential and experiential one and the agrarian stewardship ethic guides taking care of the land.

The productionist ethic

The productionist ethic requires farmers and ranchers to improve the land in order to produce various foods and make a living. The level of production is reliant on their ability to work hard, long and, at times, unpredictable hours. The land has to be used or made to provide some benefit (unless required to leave fallow for specific reasons). Control over the land is essential, since weather and Nature are unpredictable and can potentially impede agricultural production.

The being on the land ethic

This is an existential ethic that requires a daily presence of living on the land and emphasizes the practical knowledge gained from direct involvement with the land. This knowledge is local (specific to the area) and experiential (the result of daily interactions with the land). In this ethic there is a sense of historic identity and belonging to the land where cattle are as natural to the landscape as are the birds.

The agrarian stewardship ethic

The agrarian stewardship ethic is a pragmatic one, bestowing a responsibility to tend to the land (Nature) as something that sustains the well-being of human societies. It is related to the ethic of being on the land since direct involvement and attachment to the land results in practical knowledge and wisdom that can be utilized to take care of it.

It is important to understand that these three ethical dimensions are not to be treated in isolation from one another, but, rather, as integral aspects of a complex, rich and paradoxical lived experience with the land. The agricultural land ethic is embedded historically in a social and cultural ethic that influences how these rural Texan producers use and view the land. Diversifying into nature tourism presents a considerable challenge not only with respect to being an unfamiliar activity, but also with respect to accommodating the values associated with their entrepreneurial agrarian lifestyle and their agricultural land ethic. In addition, there were other issues and concerns to consider.

Issues and concerns of the landowners

Hours of discussion with the ranchers and farmers of Calhoun County, Texas, revealed a number of issues and concerns, as well as a number of factors related to their relationship with the land that require consideration when assessing the merits of diversifying into nature tourism.

The serious challenges posed by having to compete with large-scale producers in increasingly competitive global markets and amid declining commodity prices were further exacerbated for these rural producers by interrelated environmental and socio-political issues. A contentious inheritance tax in Texas has particularly worsened the crisis for rural producers, many of whom have had to sell off pieces of land to pay the tax. The result is smaller landholdings with decreased economies of scale and poorer possibilities for economic viability, plus increased habitat fragmentation and conservation problems.

Another noticeable impact has been the resulting outmigration from rural areas into urban centres in Texas, as a number of these landowners and producers have reluctantly sold their family dwellings and sought sustenance in towns and cities. This results in significant consequences not only for the sustainability of rural and urban spaces, but also for the heritage and identity of these Texans. As highlighted in the discussion on land relationships and the agricultural land ethic, the land holds important cultural and symbolic value for these rural entrepreneurs.

Understanding these participants' relationship with the land provides insights into potential conflicts with nature tourism activities. For example, tourists reacting to pesticides or spotting an endangered species were cited as important concerns. Hosting tourists meant incurring the risk of increased liability and potential lawsuits (e.g. getting injured while on the producer's land). Although some of these concerns are often times the result of misunderstanding or misinformation and do not present 'real' threats, the *perception* of their being real threats poses serious barriers to the adoption of alternative nature-based opportunities. Also, making a living in agriculture is already a difficult process without having the additional pressure of learning new skills and becoming distracted with running a nature tourism enterprise.

Maintaining control and focus over the agricultural sides of the business emerged as important concerns that would need to be considered carefully in any proposal to start a nature tourism enterprise.

Barriers and bridges to nature tourism

After examining the context of nature tourism in Texas and the case study of rural landowners in Calhoun County, Texas, it is clear that the family-based farmers and ranchers are experiencing what amounts to an agricultural crisis in Texas. The choices they make in dealing with the issues they face impact not only their financial and economic conditions, but also their quality of life and their sense of identity and belonging, i.e. their heritage. The development of nature tourism as an enterprise to supplement or replace declining incomes must address some of the barriers and constraints identified earlier. In this section, key issues that need to be considered in impact management are considered, particularly the strategic importance of information technology and the role of scientific and technical experts. The chapter concludes with several recommendations and a set of discussion questions.

Interrelated impacts in agriculture and tourism

This case study holds several insights for agricultural operators interested or involved in the nature-based tourism enterprise. World commodity prices, like international visitation trends, have a strong influence on the sustainability of the local agriculturalist and nature tourism operator. Unfortunately, both the agricultural and the tourism domains are part of large global economic and political systems, so that entering a nature tourism enterprise that attracts international visitors may mean that the producer is not escaping globalization's effects, but rather replacing one type of globalization with another.

For local landowners, farmers and ranchers exploring the possibility of diversifying into nature-based tourism, the interrelationship between agriculture and nature tourism is a critical one to understand from this micro–macro perspective. Only then does it also become evident that the impacts themselves are interrelated with respect to the type of impact (e.g. social and environmental impacts stemming from the inheritance tax) and also range from tangible (visible or measurable) to the intangible (e.g. impact on personal identity and heritage). Therefore, as our examined case suggests, it would be important for tourism feasibility and impact assessment studies in this agrarian-based domain to include:

- an economic perspective (e.g. the impacts of declining commodity prices and increasing large-scale agriculture production on rural sustainability and diversification into nature tourism)
- a service experience perspective (working with cattle and grain is very different from providing a satisfactory tourist experience; hence, need to understand service, hospitality and characteristics of tourism service provision, the 'nature' of attractions (what if 'nature' is absent that morning, e.g. no birds migrating through?))
- an environmental and political perspective (e.g. the impact of inheritance tax in Texas on land fragmentation and biodiversity conservation)
- a heritage and socio-cultural perspective (the loss of rural sustainability and traditional lifestyles relationships with the land; the historical distrust between the independent, pioneering spirit of the landowner and the public sector with respect to control over private property (land))
- a technological perspective, for this is a key factor in ensuring that rural farmers and landowners are able to access and obtain information they require for risk assessment, marketing and operating a sustainable nature tourism business (Texas is a very large state and much of it is rural with a few large urban cities). The technological dimension therefore needs to be included as a 'critical success factor' (CSF) in any strategic planning and management process.

Overcoming barriers through science and technology

The land relationships and associated socio-cultural conditions identified in the Calhoun County case study, as well as the concerns and questions raised by respondents reveal a number of constraints and barriers to the evaluation and adoption of nature tourism as an alternative source of income. Similar issues and barriers were identified during a two-day nature tourism workshop held in Kerrville, Texas, in 1998. The workshop was conducted by Texas Cooperative Extension (based in the Department of Recreation, Park and Tourism Sciences at Texas A&M University). An invited group of Texas landowners attended the workshop. Consistently, information needs related to marketing, liability, operations, education, training about service and hospitality and visitor management arose.

The needs of the landowners evaluating the potential of nature tourism is very similar to what has been identified through facilitated workshops conducted over the last 15 years by the Texas travel industry. A comparison of the results of these workshops (state, regional and local) reveal the following information need categories: (1) Market information (demographics, psychographics, customer profiles); (2) product development information (how-tos, management practices, guidelines, financial requirements); (3) impact assessment (economic impact, impact on community residents, environmental impacts); (4) trends, forecasting (market trends, projections), and (5) partnerships (cooperation and coordination in marketing, promotion, product management). In all the workshops mentioned earlier, market information was consistently the number one need identified by participants (Skadberg, 2002).

When considering the challenges of developing nature tourism in rural areas, two major issues arise that can create a significant obstacle: (1) distance from markets and methods to reach those markets and (2) the cost of marketing. In a recent study of nature tourism businesses around the USA, marketing and its cost were two of their greatest concerns (see Skadberg, 2002). However, survey participants also strongly believed that the Internet was a vehicle that helped them address both issues – it was one of the most cost-effective ways to market their businesses. Of the businesses surveyed, 87% indicated that they spent less than $100 a month to maintain their websites. When asked whether their websites had helped their businesses:

- 85% of these business owners felt that their website had helped their businesses to grow
- 94% of the respondents saw their websites as a cost-effective way to promote their businesses
- 99% of these respondents indicated they wanted to keep their websites online.

Many of the programme areas in Texas, including tourism/recreation, have limited resources to deliver information to a very large geographical area. Getting information to rural enterprises and to the Extension agents who work with community outreach and development can be greatly enhanced by using the Internet. Publications, marketing information and assistance and educational programmes can all be delivered with ease and at very low cost. However, there are a number of barriers that need to be overcome if the Internet is to become an effective tool for assisting the nature tourism domain. Lack of Internet access, slow access speed, lack of understanding of the utility of the Internet and resistance to adopting information technology and using computers still exists in much of the state. Nonetheless, progress is being made by the public sector in developing web-based projects that specifically address the information and assistance needs of people looking at nature tourism as a potential enterprise.

Texas Cooperative Extension (TCE) at Texas A&M University sees the Internet as a very important tool for delivering market data, other technical and scientific information, as well as management tools and resources to nature tourism interests in rural areas. Many projects currently underway with TCE aim to answer the questions and concerns that landowners and rural citizens have raised (see earlier). Among the web-based products being developed are tourism toolkits, inventory assessment databases, marketing information and educational programs. Web resources are also being used to develop networks of communication between various stakeholders (both public and private) in order to deal with the lack of coordination and the fragmented information flows within the nature tourism domain in Texas.

The Extension experts involved in the development and transfer of this technology to rural farmers and ranchers in Texas play two vital roles as communicative bridges. First, they act as technology facilitators, i.e. facilitating the diffusion of the technology, communicating and interpreting the scientific/technical information in a way that is understandable and considered useful by non-technical recipients at the local homestead. Second, they act as liaisons between other university-based scientific domains (e.g. agricultural economists, tourism researchers) and the rural homestead, again bridging the domain of scientific/technical expertise and local practical interests.

Conclusion

The domain of nature-based tourism in the 21st century is very different from what it was three decades ago, when the environmental movement first started gaining a little momentum with key markers such as *Silent Spring* (Carson, 1962) and the establishment of Earth Day on 22 April, 1970. Today, we argue, no call for environmentally sustainable tourism development (World Tourism Organization, 1997) can be addressed effectively without considering the role of information technology and the role of scientific/technical experts (including environmental scientists, community planners, county agents and university Extension specialists) as key stakeholders for transferring the technology and communicating relevant information to tourism enterprises and other small operators engaged in nature-based tourism development.

Today, also, no longer can ecotourism sustain its credibility without closely examining and clearly delineating the ethical and socio-cultural dimensions governing the use and protection of the natural environment (Proctor, 1996). New institutional and governance structures are also required to address these emerging factors (Westley, 1995). A number of recommendations and considerations for a responsible and responsive approach to nature-based tourism development and management can be derived from the examination in this chapter.

Assessing impacts

The case study described points to an important characteristic of tourism generally and nature tourism specifically. Along with agriculture, tourism is best viewed as being part of interrelated systems and sub-systems, ranging from the local to the regional, national and international. Moreover, its impacts are diverse and wide ranging in scope; socio-cultural impacts are particularly important to consider in nature-based tourism decision making and especially how land and nature are valued and treated by the individual. A rural land-owner's decision to diversify into tourism, or nature tourism in this case, has to made through a comprehensive evaluation of the economic and socio-cultural costs and benefits of this choice compared with other choices, such as using technology to improve production yields and marketing logistics. As shown in Figure 10.1, the decision also has to take into consideration wider systemic factors, such as global commodity prices in the agricultural domain and the effect of the global tourism system in the nature tourism domain: for example, sources of international visitors, political factors, financing, access and trans-portation, as well as intermediaries such as tour packagers and promoters.

Environmentally sustainable planning

The case study and examination of nature-based tourism and family-based agricultural enterprises in Texas conducted in this chapter suggest that the role of information technology in shaping the development and management of nature tourism in Texas will continue to grow in importance. This is not unique to Texas. Web-based initiatives and program development are also being undertaken by Extension specialists at other major US universities, aimed towards assisting landowners to (1) evaluate the merit of nature tourism as a tool for economic diversification and (2) implement nature tourism in a way that effectively sustains their agrarian-based lifestyle, heritage and identity (see the Community Tourism Development website referenced and Nickerson et al., 2001).

The planning and impact management models and modules in tourism planning textbooks (e.g. Gunn, 1989; Inskeep, 1991) and workbooks (e.g. Texas Agricultural Extension Service and Texas Department of Economic Deveopment, 1999) therefore will need to focus strategically on information technology and the Internet as vital conduits to effective nature tourism development in rural agricultural domains. Here, it is important to address both the *process* and the *content* aspects of strategic planning carefully, ensuring that attention is being paid not only to the content, but also to the process of delivering scientific and technical information to rural participants. An evolving role that deserves greater attention is that of the intermediaries through whom technology and learning is transferred to rural players in the nature tourism system.

Scientific and technical specialists

While the information technology tools described earlier relate to the substantive content of how nature tourism development and management can be facilitated for rural participants, the process of how these tools and technologies

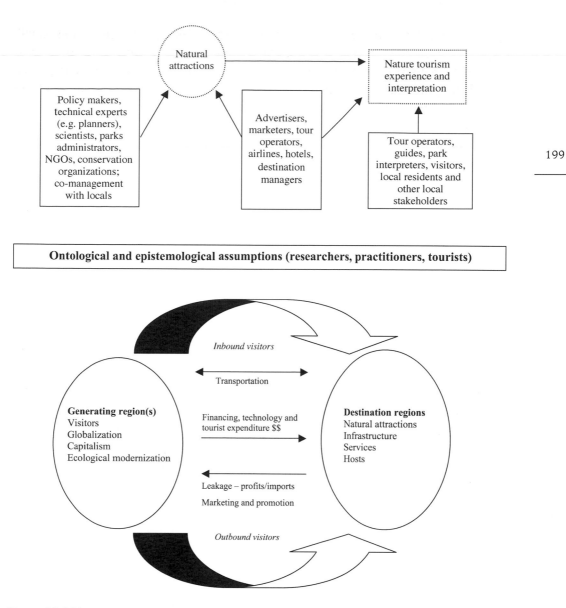

Figure 10.1 The nature tourism production system

are diffused into the rural agricultural domain is a crucial consideration. Process-related issues for consideration include who the scientific and technical people are in the overall nature tourism stakeholder domain and what role they play (or should play) in ensuring that information is communicated and transferred in a manner that is useable and helpful to rural landowners. This requires also that the information is perceived to be legitimate and trustworthy (hence requiring a consideration of the data gathering and storage procedure and process).

Identifying and involving intermediaries who can be respected and trusted by the rural producers is therefore an important aspect for legitimizing as well as communicating information. This is especially important in domains of historic distrust (or suspicion) and conflict (tension). Consider, for instance, the uneasy relationship between local landowners/private enterprises and the public sector/scientific experts in the rural agricultural sector in Texas. The case analysis here suggests that Extension agents have a vital role to play in transferring web-based technology and learning to rural areas and bridging some of the historical and socio-political barriers in the process. Organizing the intertwined agricultural and nature tourism domain of rural Texas will require new and innovative approaches to stakeholder management and sustainable development (see Westley, 1995).

Resisting eco-imperialism

A sustainability-oriented ethic would warn that care must be exercised in implementing these modules and models is in lesser industrialized countries and settings where the western development models are not dominant. 'Sustainable tourism' and 'ecotourism' if not implemented with sensitivity to the different political and cultural contexts can reproduce modes of western domination (Mowforth and Munt, 1998) and ecological imperialism (Hall, 1994), even while the surface characteristics of sustainability and ethics are being adhered to. Criteria for recognizing and addressing adverse economic and financial impacts related to such concerns are fairly well identified under the impact topic 'neocolonialism'. But as this case study shows, it is very important to consider nature tourism diversification and development in light of not only financial and economic impacts, but also its social, cultural and heritage impacts, along with a keen awareness of the interrelated local to global scope of the impacts.

A socio-culturally sustainable ethic for nature tourism

This brings us back to a consideration of land (Nature) and ethics, both of which are integral aspects of ecotourism. The term ecotourism is generally associated with a set of ethical principles and practices, while nature tourism, because it is a broader term, tends to be not as well defined with respect to ecological principles. However, as our case shows, this does not mean that a sustainable ethic towards land and Nature does not exist at the level of the rural agriculturalist. The case is particularly useful in showing the presence of a complex agricultural ethic that is both productionist and stewardship oriented, in addition to containing a strong component of an ethic grounded in living on the land, i.e. being-with-the-land in a very experiential manner. The challenge now becomes understanding how the agricultural land ethic comports with the ethical principles that guide sustainable tourism and ecotourism development.

Hence, one crucial issue that has yet to be tackled is as follows: under the set of ecotourism principles that guide tourists, operators, developers and other enterprises (e.g. rural agricultural landowners, indigenous groups, village tourism efforts), can one set of guidelines under 'environmental ethics/ principles' steer every stakeholder and interest group in managing nature-based activities? Or do we need carefully to revisit the concept of 'ecotourism' and test its rigour for guiding policymakers and enterprise owners, when it comes to the ethics of sustainability, society, land and 'Nature'? What environmentally based principles enable a policymaker or landowner to determine whether they can justify fishing as part of ecotourism or hunting as part of nature tourism? In states such as Texas, where hunting is a key part of heritage and identity, as well as a critical economic revenue generator, this aspect cannot be ignored any longer!

Redefining ecotourism?

And so we come back full circle to the beginning of the chapter, but hopefully with a better understanding of the interrelationships between the agricultural and nature tourism domains in rural Texas. To raise the question again: What is ecotourism and what are the first principles on which an ecotourism ethic should be based? This study of family-based farming and ranching enterprises in Texas suggests that this ethic has to be a multidimensional one that includes consideration of interrelated local to global impacts, as well as understanding of the rural agriculturalist's rich and complex land ethic and socio-cultural context.

The case study therefore supports the recommendation made by a number of scholars who suggest that 'nature based' rather than 'natural' is a more appropriate criterion for describing an ecotourism experience, as it allows for a wider array of options in the planning and conservation of ecotourism areas and experiences (see Higham and Lück, 2002).

Questions

1 What is the difference between 'ecotourism' and 'nature tourism'? (List at least four differences.)
2 In light of response to your Question 1, do rural agricultural landowners who practise nature tourism have an ethic of care and responsibility as is required for ecotourism operators? What does the case suggest?
3 What are the main advantages and disadvantages of diversifying into nature tourism for

landowners in Calhoun County, Texas? (Consider positive and negative impacts and the interrelated character of these impacts.)

4 What role do Extension agents play in nature tourism development in Texas? What lessons does this provide for structuring the role of technical experts (e.g. planners) and scientists in nature tourism settings elsewhere?

References

Acott, T.G., La Trobe, H.L. and Howard, S.H. (1998) 'An evaluation of deep ecotourism and shallow ecotourism', *The Journal of Sustainable Tourism*, 6, 238–53.

Carson, R. (1962) *Silent Spring*. Boston: Houghton Mifflin.

Diamantis, D. (1999) 'The characteristics of UK's ecotourists', *Tourism Recreation Research*, 24, 99–102.

Eubanks, T. and Stoll, J.R. (1999) *Avitourism in Texas: Two Studies of Birders in Texas and Their Potential Support for the Proposed World Birding Center* (Report). Austin, TX: Fermata, Inc.

Fennell, D. (1999) *Ecotourism: An Introduction*. London and New York: Routledge.

Gunn, C.A. (1989) *Tourism Planning*, 2nd edn. New York: Taylor & Francis.

Hall, C.M. (1994) 'Ecotourism in Australia, New Zealand and the South Pacific: appropriate tourism or a new form of ecological imperialism?', In Carter, E. and Lowman, G. (eds) *Ecotourism: A Sustainable Option?* Chichester: John Wiley & Sons.

Herremans, I.M. and Welsh, C. (1999) 'Developing and implementing a company's ecotourism mission statement', *Journal of Sustainable Tourism*, 7, 48–76.

Higham, J. and Lück, M. (2002) 'Urban ecotourism: a contradiction in terms', *Journal of Ecotourism*, 1, 36–51.

Inskeep, E. (1991) *Tourism Planning: An Integrated and Sustainable Development Approach*. New York: Van Nostrand Reinhold, 508.

Lawrence, T.B., Wickins, D. and Phillips, N. (1997) 'Managing legitimacy in ecotourism', *Tourism Management*, 18, 307–316.

Lindberg, K. and Hawkins, D.E. (eds) (1993) *Ecotourism: A Guide for Planners and Managers*. Vermont: The Ecotourism Society.

Meador, S. (2001) 'What is nature tourism? Defining an industry and identifying a market niche', *Texas Explorer*.

Mowforth, M. and Munt, I. (1998) *Tourism and Sustainability in the Third World*. London: Routledge.

Nickerson, N.P., Black, R.J. and McCool, S.F. (2001) 'Agritourism: motivations behind farm/ranch business diversification', *Journal of Travel Research*, 40, 19–26.

Orams, M.B. (1995) 'Towards a more desirable form of ecotourism', *Tourism Management*, 16, 3–8.

Proctor, J.D. (1996) 'Whose nature? The contested moral terrain of ancient forests', In Cronon, W. (ed.) *Uncommon Ground: Rethinking the Human Place in Nature*. New York: W.W. Norton & Company.

Roe, D., Leader-Williams, N. and Dalal Clayton, D. (1997) *Take Only Photographs, Leave Only Footprints: The Environmental Impacts of Wildlife Tourism*. London: International Institute for Environment and Development.

Sirakaya, E., Jamal, T.B. and Choi, H.-S. (2001) 'Developing ecotourism indicators for destination sustainability'. In Weaver, D.B. (ed.) *The Encyclopedia of Ecotourism*. New York: CABI, 411–32.

Skadberg, A.N. (2002) Nature Tourism in Cyberspace: An Examination of its Geography and Character in the Network. PhD Dissertation, Southwest Texas State University, San Marcos, TX.

State Taskforce on Texas Nature Tourism (1994) *Nature Tourism in the Lone Star State: Economic Opportunities in Nature* (Report). Austin, TX: Texas Parks and Wildlife Department.

Texas Agricultural Extension Service and Texas Department of Economic Development (1999) *Developing Tourism in Your Community* (Report). Austin, TX: Texas Agricultural Extension Service.

Texas Parks and Wildlife Department. (2001a) Making Nature Your Business (retrieved 27 May 2002 from http://www.tpwd.stat.tx.us/nature/tourism/yourbusiness/).

Texas Parks and Wildlife Department (2001b) *Nature Tourism in the Lone Star State* (Report). Austin, TX: Texas Parks and Wildlife Department.

US Census Bureau (2002) *State and County QuickFacts, Texas* (retrieved 10 May 2002 from http://quickfacts.census.gov/qfd/states/48000.html).

Var, T. (1997) 'Nature tourism development: private property and public use', In Wahab, S. and Pigram, J.J. (eds) *Tourism Development and Growth: The Challenge of Sustainability*. London and New York: Routledge, 199–209.

Weaver, D.B. (1998) *Ecotourism in the Less Developed World*. New York: CAB International.

Westley, F. (1995) 'Governing design: the management of social systems and ecosystems design'. In Holling, L.H. and Light, S.S. (eds) *Barriers and Bridges to the Renewal of Ecosystems and Institutions*. New York: Columbia University Press.

Wight, P. (1993) 'Ecotourism: ethic or eco-sell?', *Journal of Travel Research*, 21, 3–9.

Williams, K. (2000) Farmers and Ranchers in Calhoun County, TX: Their Land Ethic and Their Interest in Nature Tourism. Masters Thesis, Texas A&M University, College Station, TX.

World Tourism Organization (1997) *Agenda 21 for the Travel and Tourism Industry: Towards Environmentally Sustainable Development*. World Tourism Organization, World Travel and Tourism Council and the Earth Council.

Websites

Community Tourism Development – Illinois Tourism Network: http://www.tourism.uiuc.edu/itn/index.htm

Liability aspects addressed by the Texas Real Estate Center: http://recenter.tamu.edu/pubs/catlanl.html

Nature tourism website, TCE, Texas A&M University: http://naturetourism.tamu.edu

Texas Economic Development: http://www.tded.state.tx.us/

203

11 Canadian Aboriginal Ecotourism in the North

Atsuko Hashimoto and David J. Telfer

The four main objectives of this chapter are to:

- Identify the trends of tourism development among the indigenous/aboriginal population in Canada's north
- Analyze the issues and challenges of aboriginal ecotourism
- Present a conceptual framework for entrepreneurs going into ecotourism
- Examine future considerations for aboriginal ecotourism

Introduction

Canada has long been using images of aboriginal peoples and their culture as tourist attractions. The idea of creating aboriginal tourism products was examined in the late 1980s by various aboriginal associations and government agencies (Hinch, 1995). The demand for aboriginal tourism linked with culture and outdoor adventure was strong in certain major market segments to Canada such as Britain, France, Germany and Japan (Hinch, 1995). Meanwhile, in the 1980s, ecotourism's claim to be sensitive to local culture and natural systems also become attractive to governments, native populations, tourists and tourism marketers (Addison, 1996). Ecotourism, by definition, albeit that variations of definition exist (see Jaakson, 1997), promotes non-destructive, aesthetic and spiritual values based on a 'code of ethics that grants rights of continued existence of other species. It also provides a means of empowerment to disadvantaged groups such as Aboriginals by opening an economic and management role for them' (Gauthier, 1995: 216). It is no wonder many governments embrace the idea of ecotourism development and the governments of Canada's Northern Territories are no exception (see Chapter 1). Ecotourism defined by a Québec 'Adventure, Outdoor and Eco-Tourism Product Club' reads like this:

> **Ecotourism**, a kind of tourism whose goal is the discovery of a natural setting while preserving its integrity, which includes interpretation activities of natural

and cultural components within these surroundings, and fosters an attitude of respect towards the environment, calling for a long-lasting development that will result in socio-economic benefits for local and regional communities. (www.aventure-ecotourisme.qc.ca)

In this particular definition, ecotourism includes a cultural component; nonetheless it must be remembered that the emphasis on cultural aspects and local control is rather recent (Hinch and Butler, 1996; Johnston, 2000). Beeton (1998) points out that many Maori in New Zealand and Aboriginal communities in Australia see ecotourism as an appropriate form of tourism, since ecotourism is perceived to foster environmental and cultural understanding and appreciation. The Canadian Environmental Advisory Council defines ecotourism as 'an enlightening nature travel experience that contributes to conservation of the ecosystem while respecting the integrity of host communities' in which the importance of integrity of host communities is recognised (Scace et al., 1992, cited in Weaver, 1998: 17). Kanahele (1997) wrote on Canadian aboriginal tourism when he was invited to the Yukon's First Nations Cultural Ecotourism conference. He realized the dilemma in using 'ecotourism' to encompass the magnitude of cultural aspects in aboriginal tourism. He wrote:

> In putting 'cultural' before 'eco,' the indigenous sponsors of the conference recognized that the essence of tourism is found in the cultural distinctiveness of a place – its art forms, music, dance, history, languages, monuments and lifestyle unique to the place and its people. This is no way diminishes the importance of the natural environment. In fact, 'culture' and 'eco' are so closely intertwined in the Native mind, that they really are inseparable. (Kanahele, 1997: 4)

Some researchers suggest with the primary focus on the natural environment the term 'ecotourism' is quite limiting. An International Conference in Berlin in 1997 of environment ministers produced the Berlin Declaration on Biological Diversity and Sustainable Tourism. What is interesting about this declaration is that 'ecotourism' is not even mentioned, rather the focus is on 'sustainable tourism' (www.podi.com/ecosource/ecotour). The recognition of the limitations with the term 'ecotourism' is evident in the recent decision of the Canadian Tourism Commission's Ecotourism Product Club to change its name to the Sustainable Tourism Association of Canada (STAC) as sustainable tourism encompasses a wider spectrum of tourism (J. Sipkens, Alberta, 2002, personal communication). This may indicate a change in direction with respect to the use of the term ecotourism.

In a critical discussion of 'indigenous people and ecotourism', Johnston (2000) advocates that many governments take on 'ecotourism' and capitalize on a market image of ecotourism without proper dialogue or participation of indigenous population. For her argument, Johnston defined ecotourism as 'any form of industry monopolized tourism that commercializes indigenous bio-cultural heritage, including collective property and/or the homeland of the "host" people' (2000: 90). Arguments are also raised that ecotourism is derived from Euro-American urbanite environmentalism, which does not recognize indigenous peoples' ecological knowledge and lifestyle. Wenzel's study on Inuit and seal hunting (1991) and Colton and Hinch's (1999) discussion on Inuit's trapline-based tours highlight the differences in environmental values between aboriginal people and ecotourists in terms of consumptive-versus-non-consumptive activities that are difficult to reconcile.

The purpose of this chapter is to examine the background, recent initiatives and challenges facing aboriginal ecotourism in Canada's north. It will look at Canada's Arctic and Subarctic regions, which have unique natural environments with very low biological productivity. The recent creation of the territory of Nunavut has spurred other areas of Canada like Nunavik (northern Québec) to follow the movement towards self-governance and self-sufficiency, influencing tourism development in the Far North. Aboriginal people living in a subsistence economy are keen to develop their own ecotourism products with minimal intervention from the outside tourism industry.

In this chapter, the term 'aboriginal' will be used throughout, as it is the term Canadian native people (First Nations/Amerindian, Inuit, Métis and multiple aboriginal) use, although bodies such as the United Nations suggest an umbrella term 'indigenous' (Hinch and Butler, 1996). Canada is a vast country and while the entire area of 'northern Canada' is too wide to cover in one chapter, a number of case studies on aboriginal tourism development will be presented. Most of the cases will be drawn from Nunavut, Northwest Territories (NWT) and Yukon Territory. Mention will also be made of similar cases in Northern British Columbia, Alberta, Saskatchewan, Manitoba, Ontario and Nunavik/Québec, where aboriginal people are actively involved in tourism development.

Background of Northern Canada and its inhabitants

There are four major physiographic regions in Canada. A large part of Canada comprises the Canadian Shield; the west coast is covered by cordillera; between the west coast and the Canadian Shield lie the Interior Plains; and the far north is Arctic (Usher, 1987). The territorial North (Yukon Territory, Northwest Territories and Nunavut) is distinct from the rest of Canada (often referred to as the South) in many ways. The territorial North contains over 36% of Canada's landmass (9,980,000 km^2). Yukon covers 483,450 km^2, which is 4.8% of

206

Canada's landmass (www.btc.gov.yk.ca); Northwest Territories (NWT) covers 1,171,918 km^2 (www.gov.nt.ca), which is 11.7% of Canada; and Nunavut covers 1,994,000 km^2 (www.nunavut.com), which is 20% of Canada. The Arctic coastline is longer than the sum of the Atlantic and Pacific coastlines and so is the area of Arctic territorial waters, however, the year-round presence of ice and icebergs in the sea poses difficulties for use of the Arctic seas (Usher, 1987).

Northern Canada is classified as the 'Arctic' which is treeless and covered by permafrost and the 'Subarctic' is a northern forest zone with a range of closed crown forests in the south to open woodland of tundra vegetation in the north. In the Subarctic, permafrost is not as universal as in the Arctic and conifers are the predominant species. The Arctic includes a small part of northern Yukon, northern and eastern parts of NWT, Nunavut, parts of northern Manitoba, Ontario, Québec and Labrador. The Subarctic includes the rest of the territorial North and parts of British Columbia, Alberta, Saskatchewan, Manitoba, Ontario and Québec (Usher, 1987).

The North is characterized as an area of low temperature, low precipitation, poor soil, permafrost, low biological productivity, slow vegetative recovery and low species diversity. The Arctic has relatively simple food and energy chains, instability of populations (migration) and slow growth rate. Mammals in the Arctic cover larger areas for a longer cycle, resulting in seasonal migration. Natural fire in the Subarctic forests determines and changes the distribution of ecotypes. The fragile northern environment restricts human use of wildlife and permafrost creates challenges in construction for buildings, airfields, roads and pipelines which require a thermal regime at depth (Usher, 1987). However, Usher (1987) suggests that some geologists estimate the North holds up to 50% of Canada's potentially recoverable oil and gas and 40% of its potential mineral wealth.

The Arctic is the home of the Inuit. The Inuit (the Cree word *Eskimo* is no longer used) inhabit an area from Chukotka in Russia (www.nunavut.com) to Greenland and approximately 20% live in Canada (Usher, 1987). Inuit share a common language (Inuktitut) with dialectic variations. In the past century Inuit in Canada who were traditionally nomadic hunter-gatherers have gone to living in permanent settlements with a new language (English and French), Internet technology and 9-to-5 salaried jobs (www.nunavut.com). In order to preserve Inuit culture and the Inuktitut language, the territory of Nunavut that earned independence and autonomy in 1999 employs different regimes. For example, it set Inuktitut as a working language, Nunavut's civil service (which targets 85% Inuit participation) will adopt flexible working hours to accommodate hunting schedules and *Inuit Qaujimajatuqangit* (traditional knowledge) is expected to play a role in developing government policies (www.nunavut.com). In Nunavut, the population was estimated at 27,039 residents in 1999 and it is projected to be 29,885 in 2003, of which 85% is Inuit (www.gov.nu.ca). In 1996 83% of the population was Inuit, while other aboriginal groups represented less than 1% and the non-aboriginal population was at 16% (www.nunavut.com). The population of the main 28 communities varies from 51 (Umingmaktuuq) to 4405 (Iqualuit) (Nunavut Tourism, n.d.).

In contrast, in the Subarctic, various First Nations/Amerindian people inhabit the area. They belong to two major linguistic groups, namely the Athapaskan in the west and the Algonkian in the east (Usher, 1987). However, there are many distinctive peoples and languages. NWT had a population of 42,083 people in July 2000 with approximately half the population aboriginal (www.gov.nt.ca). Before Nunavut's separation from NWT, the 1996 census found the total aboriginal population was 48% of total population, of which the Inuit population was at 10% of the total population, Dene at 28%, Métis at 9% and other aboriginal population less than 1% (www.stats.gov.nt.ca/Statinfo). Thirty-two communities (including one city – Yellowknife) have a range of population from 55 (Jean Marie River) to 17,195 (Yellowknife) (www.stats. gov.nt.ca/Statinfo). NWT is the first territory/province in Canada in 2002 to mark 21 June as National Aboriginal Day, as a statutory holiday. Yukon, another Subarctic territory, had a population of 31,070 in December 1999. According to the 1996 population census, 21% of the total population has aboriginal (single or multiple) origins and 79% non-aboriginal origin. There are 31 communities (including one city – Whitehorse) whose population sizes are from 45 (Destruction Bay) to 22,879 (Whitehorse) (www.btc.gov.yk.ca).

History of colonialism and recent independence

Northern Canada has a history of colonization and economic exploitation. The Montréal-based Northwest Company established in 1770s engaged aggressively in the fur trade with Amerindians in the Subarctic and it reached the Yukon in the 19th century. When the Inuit got involved in fur trapping in the early part of 20th century it led to permanent settlements with fixed trading posts and new services for the Inuit (Addison, 1996). In 1920s when oil was discovered in the North, the government hastily created Northwest Territories and the Yukon Branch of the Department of the Interior to deal exclusively with the territorial North. The government also arranged a treaty with Dene First Nation. With the fur trade well established, First Nations people and the Inuit adopted Euro-American technology, dress and food, the English language and some observed Christian rites (Usher, 1987). Despite these changes, the aboriginal people still continued their traditional mode of production: hunting and fishing for subsistence and trapping/fishing for exchange (Usher, 1987; Wenzel, 1991). Collapse of the fur trade in the post-war years and the feeling against traditional colonialism led the Keewatin Inuit to demand action in the 1950s, media highlighted incidents of suffering in the North forcing the government to intervene. However, provision of services, schooling, housing, healthcare and welfare brought profound changes to aboriginal life. Compulsory education and relocation were enforced; their traditional mode of production was weakened; and they became dependent on the government for shelter, heat, power and education (Usher, 1987).

Shultis and Browne (1999) argue that the legacy of colonization likely caused challenges to tourism development. Displacement/relocation from traditional land, loss of territorial rights such as hunting, fishing, gathering, extinction of existing treaty rights and loss of self-determination are what Shultis and Browne cite as the most significant effects of colonialism. However, the Canadian government and various First Nations are negotiating agreements to reinstate self-determination, self-governance, settle land claims and establishing necessary restructuring to help stimulate economic and social development (Grekin and Milne, 1996; Shultis and Browne, 1999; www.ainc-inac.gc.ca). The legacy of colonialism prevented the aboriginal population from participating in or controlling economic initiatives, but rather, economic initiatives were planned and implemented by non-aboriginal planners (Brandon, 1993, cited in Shultis and Browne, 1999). Nonetheless, the introduction of tourism, as a means of economic development has the potential to affirm aboriginal cultural values and traditions, to empower the community, to restore community pride, create jobs, provide training and education and to generate revenue (Hinch and Butler, 1996; Shultis and Browne, 1999).

Interests in developing tourism

The aboriginal tourism industry in Canada is estimated at $CDN270 million employing 14,000–16,000 people. The challenge is that this is less that one-half of 1% of the Canadian tourism industry and half of those employed are seasonal or part time (Doucett, 2000). The main attractions in the Yukon and the NWT are wildlife and adventure experiences (Smith, 1996; www.btc.gov.yk.ca; www.gov.nt.ca; www.nwttravel.nt.ca). The native economy consists of a commodity/exchange sector and a subsistence sector, which required alternative means such as tourism to support self-sufficiency. When the government of NWT initiated a community-based tourism strategy in 1981, the government clearly favoured the development of non-consumptive ecotourism with focus on adventure, naturalist and arts/culture tours (Grekin and Milne, 1996). The Baffin Regional Tourism Planning Project in the North was one of the first Canadian planning initiatives in 'ecotourism' (Addison, 1996). Although both Yukon and NWT tourism websites have seemed to have dropped the 'ecotourism' label (www.btc.gov.yk.ca; www.nwttravel.nt.ca), their emphasis is still on naturalist and cultural tours and adventure travel, with reference to the native people and their cultures in the territories as attraction. The Government of Québec also openly embraces ecotourism. As Arctic Québec, known as Nunavik (507,000 km^2) is a region inhabited by the Inuit, the Naskapi and the Cree (www.nunavik-tourism.com), development of aboriginal tourism in connection to ecotourism seems to be a favoured strategy. As seen in the following exerts from the Québec Tourism website, it lures the potential tourists by casting Québec as a premium eco, adventure and cultural tourism experience:

> More and more, Quebecers are looking for ways to preserve and promote a deeper understanding of their vast natural heritage ... Many businesses specialized in ecotourism and adventure travel welcome you on your discovery of Québec's natural wonders, on foot, in a canoe or by sea kayak. In small groups, you'll be taken off the beaten track and learn about the complexities of various ecosystems as well as the mysteries of powerful natural phenomena that have shaped the geography, the people and the wildlife of Québec ... As you can see, Québec has left no stone unturned in its effort to make respect and understanding of its environment second nature for visitors and hosts alike! (www.tourisme.gouv.qc.ca/anglais)

In the early 1970s, mainly local non-aboriginal interests developed tourism in the North and development was unstructured, without local involvement or benefits to the local communities. This continued until 1981 when the government of NWT with Canadian Department of Economy, Development and Tourism, started a community-based tourism development strategy (Addison, 1996; Grekin and Milne, 1996; Swarbrooke, 1999). However, tourism activities or benefits from tourism activities were not evenly distributed despite the community-based tourism development strategy (Hinch, 1995). In the case of NWT, aboriginal peoples' share of tourism businesses increased from 18% in 1979 to 35% in 1988, but aboriginal tourism ownership at the same time still counts for 35% while 61% of the NWT population was aboriginal (Hinch, 1995).

With Nunavut becoming an autonomous territory in 1999, Nunavik is also looking to negotiate autonomy. Yukon Territory and NWT are also involved with native peoples' land claims and self-government negotiations. Although tourism development is not the only route these aboriginal nations opted for their own economic development and there are clear signs of interests in developing aboriginal tourism. Indian and Northern Affairs Canada (INAC) invested $CDN350 million on aboriginal tourism business development as of 1990 and it is also estimated other federal and provincial ministries made matching investment (Parker, 1993). This chapter now looks at two signs of interests in aboriginal tourism development: the roles of Aboriginal Tourism Team Canada and Aboriginal Tourism in Canadian Tourism Commission's Product Clubs.

Aboriginal Tourism Team Canada

Prior to the formation of Aboriginal Tourism Team Canada, the Canadian Tourism Commission (CTC) established the Aboriginal Tourism Programme in 1994, intended to undertake consultations to invite 'aboriginal communities to participate in tourism in a more formal way' (Ieria, 1997: 3). The Aboriginal Tourism Programme was officially introduced internationally at Rendez-vous Canada '97 (Travel Mart), with a centrepiece of *Live the Legacy* Travel Guide.

Aboriginal Tourism Team Canada (ATTC) was founded in 1996 and its vision is to 'represent Aboriginal people as world leaders in tourism in harmony with our culture', as shown in its philosophy statements:

- We believe that through partnerships we can create opportunities.
- We are committed to the protection and preservation of aboriginal traditions and way of life as well as the protection and preservation of the environment.
- We are committed to the stewardship of our renewable resources.
- We are committed to the authenticity of aboriginal products, art and experiences.
- We respect the importance of the individual in aboriginal tourism and the part the individual plays in the community.
- We work together to communicate our cultural pride in and through aboriginal tourism and products.
- We respect every aspect of aboriginal life and the caring and sharing that are part of our experience.
- We honour our spirituality and the strength of our people to be self-reliant.
- We value honesty in our communication and in our business. (www.attc.ca)

The ATTC's idea of aboriginal tourism is heavily inclined to cultural aspects of aboriginal life and harmony with nature. A strict definition of ecotourism with more emphasis on natural environment impacts rather than on cultural impacts does not fully reflect the aboriginal tourism's foci. The conflict in definition of ecotourism (non-consumptive) with aboriginal lifestyle, which includes hunting and fishing (consumptive) leads to another conflict. The environmentalism aspect of ecotourism is exogenous and it is not in full harmony with the environmental concepts of aboriginal people who see hunting and fishing as important parts of their natural world. With such a narrow definition of ecotourism and the various debates over definitions of ecotourism, tourism products aboriginal people would like to offer cannot always be described as 'ecotourism' products. Therefore, an 'ecotourism' label is rarely seen in regional ATTC product samples and on the ATTC's website 'ecotourism' is included under the category of 'adventure tourism activities' in addition to fishing, hunting and wildlife viewing (www.attc.ca). There is a suggestion that when the cultural component becomes a primary source of attraction, such is the case in aboriginal/indigenous tourism, it is more appropriate to talk about 'sociocultural alternative tourism' rather than 'ecotourism' (Weaver, 1998).

Some are even preferred to categorize aboriginal/indigenous tourism as 'resource-based' tourism (Ewart, 1997; Shultis and Browne, 1999).

Aboriginal Tourism Product Clubs

Aboriginal tourism development in Canada has also been supported through the Canadian Tourism Commission's (CTC) Product Club programme. The CTC Tourism Product Club exists for the purpose of developing new products or enhancing the quality of existing products, through partnerships composed of tourism industry stakeholders (www.canadatourism.com). The CTC Product Club promotes Canada as a four-season destination of nature, diverse cultures and communities. An example of the Aboriginal Tourism Product Club in Québec, with extracts from its website follows:

Aboriginal Tourism Product Club (Current 1999–2002)
The Quebec Aboriginal Tourism Corporation (STAQ)

Mission and Objectives:

The main objective of STAQ is to create, through tourism, activities that favour the social and economic development of Aboriginal communities.

For this purpose, the Corporation strives to bring together the mutual and complementary interests of Quebec's Aboriginal tourism entrepreneurs in a solid administrative structure dedicated to the development and promotion of their products. From the very beginning, STAQ drafted a strict code of ethics and a rigorous list of norms to guarantee the quality, safety and reliability of the operations, so as to meet the highest possible standards and to satisfy the stringent requirements of an international clientele.

Corporate Structure and Services

... With the backing of the Assembly of the First Nations of Quebec and Labrador, of Tourisme Québec and of the Canadian Tourism Commission, STAQ brings together Aboriginal enterprises involved in tourism in order to provide them with a structure, to position them on the market, and to encourage product diversification and coherence.

STAQ centralizes tourism activities and expertise for increased efficiency and professionalism and is responsible for assigning the label of quality and authenticity to accredited products. (http://www.staq.net/english/index.htm)

Another example, although currently inactive, is the *Aboriginal Waterways Product Club*, which focused on areas and corridors along the Saskatchewan and Qu'Appelle Valley River systems with a focus on the pre-contact and fur trade eras (www.sasktourism.com). The Saskatchewan Tourism Board's website (www.sasktourism.com) offered some 'aboriginal tourism packages' for summer

2002 including 'Experience, Embrace and be Enlightened by Métis Culture', which included visiting an interpretative centre, historic site and a boreal forest.

Issues and challenges with tourism development in the Canadian North

Canada's North is a vast area with various aboriginal peoples who have different cultural values, practices, community sizes and views on tourism development. As a result, tourism development issues need to be understood in different situational contexts. The issues that will be discussed in this section may not be specific to Canadian aboriginal people, but may also be shared with various aboriginal/indigenous groups all over the world. This section attempts to identify the common issues aboriginal communities in the Canadian North may face or have been facing in the process of developing aboriginal tourism. The issues are discussed under the subheadings of (1) differences in concept, (2) government control versus indigenous management and (3) resources issues. While this is not an exhaustive list, nonetheless these items are considered the most common challenges in the Canadian North.

Differences in concept

Physical difficulties in developing 'touristic' resources for ecotourism

As described previously, the Canadian North is very fragile. Such a fragile natural environment limits human use of natural resources. Construction of tourist facilities and infrastructure, including roads and airports for tourist and local use, is severely limited. Such a fragile environment also poses limitations on the choice of tourism activities and hence target markets. The severe seasonality of Arctic tourism is another challenge. Not all areas enjoy the short window of summer and northwest of the Arctic Islands, the sea is permanently covered with ice and the Central and High Arctic still have the icepack during summer. The window for offering popular ecotourism activities such as whale watching or sea kayaking in the North is much shorter than that in southern provinces. Accessibility to destination by road networks available in Yukon and NWT or by air, as is only available for the most part in Nunavut, can become a major problem during winter weather. Even in the south where winters are much milder, selling winter products is always a challenge. In the Far North where winter is much longer and harsher, it is a serious management challenge.

The stereotypical image of the North in the eyes of potential tourists from the south can also be an obstacle. It is a romantic and mythical but simultaneously fragile and frigid harsh environment. Many also believe that aboriginal communities share similar natural and built environments. Except for a short window of summertime when the landscape drastically changes in some Sub-arctic areas, the image of the North is snow, ice and frozen sea throughout the year. Such images are not necessarily a true reflection of reality, nonetheless they attracts die-hard outdoor lovers, e.g. hunters, anglers, winter sports lovers, to name a few, but may distance the types of market such as family, high-spending escape/relaxation holiday makers who are not ready to face the stereotypical image of the Far North. The type of activities people are attracted to are more likely to be consumptive (hunting and angling), while more passive, less consumptive ecotourism activities such as natural sightseeing (e.g. whale watching, birdwatching, caribou watching, etc.) are gaining popularity.

Lack of accessibility

The construction of the 2400 km Alaska Highway from Dawson Creek (Yukon) to Fairbanks (Alaska) during World War II and the 730 km Dempster Highway from Dawson Creek to Inuvik (Yukon) affected tourism development in the Yukon (Smith, 1996). These highways enable tourists to reach the Arctic by private car. Meanwhile, the major mode of transportation to NWT and Nunavut is aeroplane, as described in the *Explorers' Guide to Canada's Northwest Territories* (2001): 'Northerners fly just about everywhere.' There are no road links between these northern territories and southern metropolitans in Canada (Smith, 1996). Even in the Yukon, areas away from the highways have to be reached by aeroplane. Another mode of transportation in the North is the snowmobile (Colton and Hinch, 1999).

Dispersed communities with small populations in the Far North is, in a way, ideal for small-scale, community-based, lower impact ecotourism. However, the lack of accessibility or the impossibility of using public transportation to link communities (unless private small planes can be considered public transportation) is far from environmentally friendly. As suggested in the Berlin Declaration 1997 (www.podi.com/ecosource/ecotour), the use of public transportation to reach the destination is a key issue. There is, however, limited competition in the Canadian airline market. A passenger can fly on a discount carrier from Ottawa to Vancouver for as little as $CDN300 while a flight from Ottawa to Yellowknife is approximately $1300 based, on the lowest economy class fare posted on the Internet.

Different expectations of tourists' experience

The difference between ecotourists' expectations and what aboriginal communities would like to offer as a tourism product can be a most significant difference. In ecotourism today, from the non-aboriginal view, a shift from consumptive activities to non-consumptive activities is an important breakthrough to distinguish ecotourism from other forms of tourism, i.e. adventure tourism. Colton (Colton and Hinch, 1999) describes his unpleasant experience with harvesting game as a tourist attraction. Colton, as an experienced ecotourist, could not completely agree with or enjoy witnessing the guide's hunting on the trapline tour circuit. He concludes that the average ecotourist is not expecting to see trapped animals being killed. However, he also observes that birdwatching, which the average ecotourists expects to do in the natural setting, is not something aboriginal people enjoy or are willing to sell as a tourist attraction, based on differences in the views of wildlife and hunting as a means of survival.

The cultural focus has somewhat become less essential in comparison to the impacts on the natural environment in ecotourism today. This is rather concerning for the aboriginal communities as their emphasis is culture and tradition. According to Hinch (1995), there are four variations of aboriginal tourism experiences available: (1) visiting attractions such as heritage village and interpretative centres, (2) shopping for native arts and crafts, (3) specific experiences such as traditional wilderness outings, visiting native communities, attending dance performances and/or powwows and (4) guided native hunting and fishing experiences. Activities of category (1) and (3) could be accepted as non-consumptive ecotourism activities, while (2) and (4) might not. Yet, these are important aspects of aboriginal life, non-consumptive or not, and the aboriginal communities are willing to share them with non-aboriginal tourists.

Notzke's visitor survey with 70 visitors to Inuvik in 1995 found that 60% of the respondents are repeaters to the North, 41% had a postgraduate degree and 28% post-secondary education; 44% travelled by vehicle, 27% came for outdoor activities, 77% of respondents are most interested in named peoples' everyday life (Notzke, 1999). In comparison, the Travel Activities & Motivation Survey (Lang Research, 2001), a mailback survey of 11,892 Canadian and American respondents, identified types of tourists who are/will be interested in aboriginal tourism. Based on this report, the mature, well-educated market segment will seek outdoor accommodation (e.g. camping, wilderness lodge), enjoy natural sightseeing (e.g. birdwatching, wild fauna and flora viewing, etc.) and exploration (e.g. visiting museum, historical sites and natural wonders). It is indeed a groundbreaking survey for the aboriginal tourism developers, however, how much this survey result will help developing aboriginal tourism products in Canada's Far North is dubious for the following reasons. Although a fair percentage of those respondents who have already participated in aboriginal tourism in the past two years show relatively high interest in hunting and extreme sports, this report did not highlight this even as a separate market niche. This report also used a variable: 'An aboriginal or native Canadian attraction like the Indian Museum of North America in Arizona or the Polynesian Cultural Center in Hawaii ... would make them "a lot more interested" in taking a trip to Ontario' in this survey and the research institution considered this variable specifically associated with aboriginal tourism (Lang Research, 2001: 2). Even though the Polynesian Center is often a target of debate of cultural commercialization and staged authenticity and conditions (locations, accessibility, tourism expertise, etc.), aboriginal communities in Ontario are unlikely to be generalized and applied to other parts of Canada, yet this research institution used this variable to identify the potential tourist. Contrariwise, this report may have caused the aboriginal tourism developers to realize that the average potential tourists who are interested in aboriginal tourism may still have perhaps an unknowing mentality of 'coming to see the romantic savages'.

The differences in concept perhaps explain reasons why the term aboriginal tourism is preferred to ecotourism in the Far North. First of all, the natural environment in the North is far too fragile. A strict definition of ecotourism could not be satisfied as even low-impact outdoor activities identified with ecotourism can create serious impacts in the fragile North. Second, accessibility to the destinations is not easy and requires unusual modes of transportation, e.g. aeroplanes and snowmobiles, which are not environmentally friendly. Third, the difference between what the aboriginal communities would like to offer as products and the expectation of non-aboriginal tourists causes a serious dilemma. According to the Aboriginal Tourism report 2001, the expectations of non-aboriginal potential tourists, who are not even ecotourists, are outdoor activities and cultural entertainment oriented. It is also reported that some northern aboriginal people are not talkative and storytelling does not happen naturally every night in spite of the tourists' expectation to be entertained by stories (Colton and Hinch, 1999). Aboriginal tourism in the North may not be able to satisfy these tourists' expectations due to the physical constraints and philosophy of pure cultural experience, rather than modified cultural entertainment.

Government control versus indigenous management

Concept of co-management, more indigenous control oriented

The changes in aboriginal life began, as explorers, whalers and traders, then missionaries, mounted police, teachers and other outsiders came to the North (Nunavut Tourism n.d.; Usher, 1987). Researchers such as Shultis and Browne (1999) advocate that history of colonialism and recent independence of aboriginal peoples in Canada affects the lingering mistrust among the aboriginal people towards government and non-aboriginal people/institutions. Parker (1993) clearly indicates the fact that federal and provincial governments consider aboriginal people and lands as their jurisdiction and cause problems when aboriginal people try to conduct tourism business. He also suggests that government, as a support mechanism for developing aboriginal tourism, is not necessarily doing any favours to aboriginal communities. This implies that development of aboriginal tourism should also take a cautious approach with the involvement of aboriginal peoples a top priority and government or non-aboriginal agencies should not force tourism on the aboriginal people. One of the criticisms of current ecotourism is that the sustainability criteria of ecotourism are determined without appropriate dialogue with the involved aboriginal people (Johnston, 2000). As a result, ecotourism could be a threatening challenge to aboriginal culture, lifestyle and environment. The definition of aboriginal tourism, by way of contrast, clearly states the direct involvement of aboriginal people either through control and/or having their culture serve as a centre of attraction (Hinch and Butler, 1996). Parker (1993) defined aboriginal tourism as any tourism product or service owned and operated by aboriginal people, so that the aboriginal people can ensure that they and their culture are not exploited by the non-aboriginal tourism sector. Johnston (2000) also points out that most in the non-aboriginal tourism sector do not even obtain informed consent from aboriginal people for using their images in marketing or even selling cultural performances. As declared by the UN and ILO, self-determination of aboriginal people is a key. Johnston (2000: 91) advocates the indigenous models of tourism that is 'based on indigenous knowledge systems and values, promoting customary practices and livelihoods. Such tourism is viewed as a way to regain rights to access, use and manage traditional land and resources and cultural property'.

In response to this mistrust, the Canadian Royal Commission on Aboriginal Peoples and First Nation agreed to focus the dialogue by using four touchstones:

1 **new relationship** – bridging the gap between aboriginal and non-aboriginal people, understanding each other, and aboriginal people can share their culture with dignity and respect.

2 **self-determination** – when self-government is recognised, government-to-government agreements will be developed.
3 **self-reliance/self-sufficiency** – developing human resources and sustainable economies for aboriginal communities, competitive edge in the world market.
4 **healing** – recovering from low-self esteem, respects for aboriginal culture, and development of by-products to support tourism such as education. (Parker, 1993)

These guidelines were drawn from the needs for greater self-determination among aboriginal people, who perceive tourism as a catalyst for various social-political issues created by the colonial past. In order to rectify mistrust and a loathing towards external forces and non-indigenous agencies that colonial history has created (Shultis and Browne, 1999), the concept of co-management is emphasized as a way to foster new 'equal' partnerships between aboriginal peoples and the public and private sectors. Co-management regimes which involves sharing power and responsibility between government and local resource users for renewable resources is being established all over Canada (Notzke, 1999). In line with the movement of independence and land claims of native Canadians in recent decades, the federal, territorial and provincial governments recognize the rights of aboriginal people and many provincial jurisdictions have special considerations in the management of wildlife in order to maintain aboriginal peoples' traditional way of life. Wildlife co-management boards consists of aboriginal and government representatives and are present in Yukon and NWT (before the separation of Nunavut). Researchers and managers must include aboriginal people in proposed research, from design to implementation. The results also need to be communicated to them when dealing with administrations regarding aboriginal rights and concerns (Gauthier, 1995). This also applies to development of aboriginal tourism. The settlement of aboriginal peoples' comprehensive land claims spell out complex co-management regimes, which includes tourism development. In Notzke's example, licensing and operation of tourism enterprises in the western Arctic, the applicant must satisfy many aboriginal people and local boards, committees and community organizations in addition to meeting government regulations and this consultation process may take months (see Notzke, 1999, for details). This community-led consultation is warranted in aboriginal communities, although some non-aboriginal parties may find it an unusual business practice (Shultis and Browne, 1999).

Resources issues

Before discussing resource issues, a conceptual framework on entrepreneurial considerations for ecotourism is presented in Figure 11.1. A set of entrepreneurial characteristics (Morrison, Rimmington and Williams, 1999) along with

ENTREPRENEUR

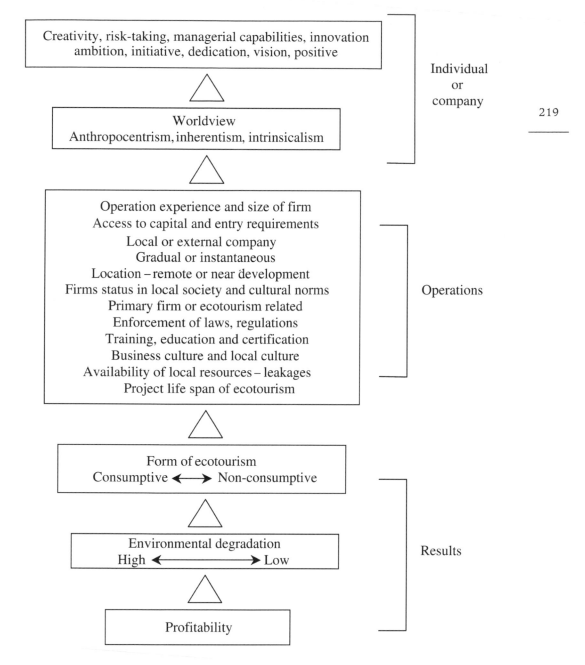

Figure 11.1 Entrepeneurial considerations for ecotourism: a conceptual framework

three paradigms on values and attitudes towards the environment is presented (Simmon, 1993). An operator would need to consider what skills they have what their beliefs are about the environment. Simmons (1993) believes that anthropcentrism is the dominant paradigm today, however, it could be argued that perhaps an aboriginal tour operator with stronger links to the land may be closer to inherentism or intrinsicalism. The operator must consider a range of operational issues such as level of experience, which is explored in more detail later. A form of ecotourism will be selected and offered which can be placed on a continuum from consumptive to non-consumptive and resulting in a continuum from high to low environmental degradation. Finally, a central question which all businesses must answer is what degree of profitability they are after and at what cost.

Inexperienced in tourism business

In comparison to some First Nations groups in the southern regions who have been involved in development of tourism in the province, aboriginal people in the North are less experienced in the business of tourism. Partly because of the remoteness of the territories, the number of tourists in the North is relatively small. To illustrate this, 280, 500 non-residential visitors came to Yukon in 1999 (www.btc.gov.yk.ca) and an estimated 18,000 people visited Nunavut (of which three-quarters are business visitors) in 1999 (www.gov.nu.ca).

As part of the inexperience in the business of tourism, lack of training facilities and/or opportunities is an oft-voiced concern. For example, as the majority of tourism products in the North are aboriginal culture and lifestyle based and there is a need for guides and interpreters who can provide the link between aboriginal culture and tourist culture. Therefore, the existence of guides who are knowledgeable about both cultures and have an ability to satisfy the needs of both parties is vital. It is illustrated in Colton and Hinch (1999) that the skilled guide Colton had was primarily a hunter and the guest was treated as a friend who was familiar with outdoor life. This approach itself is fine, however, the guide is not there to teach the know-how of outdoor life and the guest has to master how to operate the snowmobile alone, without help. The guide in this case was also not an interpreter and thus few interpretative chats and little storytelling took place. There is clearly a gap in the approach to guests' needs and wants and the guide's (or hosts') needs and wants.

Similarly, in a report on 'experimental ecotourism', a familialization tour to Baffin Island describes potential guides as local hunters. Many hunters/guides who joined the tour were monolingual speakers of Inuktitut and those who are helping with the camp and kitchen were wives, relatives and friends of the guides (Rauber, 1998). As aboriginal people look at tourism businesses as an employment opportunity for skilled and unskilled people (Parker, 1993), small-scale culture-oriented products like this one will hire unskilled staff in tourism establishments. Meanwhile, Parker (1993) is aware that it is the main challenge to prepare the aboriginal people who enter the business of tourism to be culturally oriented business people.

Some communities are sceptical about how tourism will affect their traditional lifestyle while there are cases of vigorous efforts to encourage local employment in tourism-related businesses (Hinch, 1995). Aboriginal associations are hoping to develop their own human resources, as described in one of the four touchstones, in the hope that aboriginal tourism businesses will hire aboriginal people with pride and knowledge in the tourism and hospitality industry (Parker, 1993). The ATTC has also taken an initiative with support from federal agencies to develop the First Host hospitality training programme and a comprehensive accreditation system for cultural tourism (Johnston, 2000).

Lack of capital/funding

Canadian aboriginal tourism has had some success. According to Johnston (2000), four out of 14 successful profiles in the CTC's list to the UN Commission on Sustainable Development in April 1999 were aboriginal tourism enterprises. The Canadian government also launched Gathering Strength – Canada's Aboriginal Action Plan in 1998, which highlighted a sizeable budget to support community economic development. Indian and Northern Affairs Canada spent $CDN350 million on aboriginal tourism business development by 1990, of which $180 million was spent on capital costs and $170 million on feasibility studies and business plans (Parker, 1993).

In the North, it is difficult to obtain financing through standard financial institutions mainly due to the lack of a local financial outlet in or near the communities, let alone finding ones that are knowledgeable and supportive of tourism business (Hinch, 1995; Doucett, 2000). Territorial governments such as in NWT have economic development programmes including business loans, investment contributions, joint venture opportunities with government, business advice and venture capital contributions. These programmes favour applications from small aboriginal communities (Hinch, 1995). There are also federal government-level financial programmes. The ATTC listed its financial links to Aboriginal Business Canada, Accessing Government Funding, Business Development Bank of Canada, Heritage Canada Museums Assistance Programme, Indian and Northern Affairs Canada, Human Resources Development Canada and Strategies Industry Canada: Financing for the Growing Business (www.attc.ca). Yet, the lack of long-term guaranteed funding is seriously affecting the development of aboriginal tourism (Parker, 1993). For example,

Aboriginal Business Canada provided a three-year funding term which ended in 2002 (ATTC, 2000).

Conclusion

In this brief overview of tourism development in the Canadian North, several issues became clear that need further attention. First, aboriginal knowledge on ecology was rarely utilized in tourism such indigenous knowledge that *has* been recognized by the western industrial world notwithstanding. For example, the native inhabitants of the place understand and express themselves in relationship to land (its unique environment) and animals they relied on for survival (Cajete, 1999). Yet the aboriginal views on sustainable development or minimizing environmental impacts were not incorporated when definitions and evaluation methods of ecotourism were developed. When aboriginal people are developing their own tourism products, this exogenous concept of ecotourism may be too foreign to apply to their products. In the case of Inuit culture, hunting and fishing are important aspects of their survival and these activities do not mean to destroy the balance of nature. If Inuit want to share that aspect of their lives with tourists, the question is whether it should be considered as an educational element for the ecotourist. At a recent industry meeting in NWT and in Saskatchewan, hunters and outfitters called for more marketing support from the CTC. They argue that the hunting sector is a significant revenue generator and with the hunting sector reaching new international markets, more aboriginal people are involved in the sector (Doucett, 2000).

Second, there is a question of how much and to what extent training and education should be provided to the aboriginal people who enter the business of tourism (see Figure 11.1). It is important that the employees in the tourism business are knowledgeable, however, tourism and hospitality education and training currently available are primarily developed out of the western industrial world. Language, for instance, is the first barrier. If the Inuit are putting efforts to revive the Inuktitut language, does the introduction of a foreign tongue such as English or French revert to cultural colonialism? Dealing with international tourists and domestic tourists from the southern provinces may mean joining the forces of globalization, which is often criticized as a new form of colonialism. The business of tourism is typical western consumerism and it is beyond the traditional hospitality which aboriginal people have experienced. Tourism is notorious for cultural assimilation and even imperialism. It will be a challenge for the aboriginal people to maintain their identity, lifestyle and tradition while immersing themselves in western business practices. It will also be a challenge to maintain the tourism products in the 'aboriginal' way when tourists and the non-aboriginal tourism industry demand changes in the host side to suit their needs.

Third, the ecotourism philosophies of raising awareness in public can be brought into the debate. From the results of the consumer survey in 2001, the respondents who are 'potential tourists' to the Far North were identified as culturally oriented people. Nevertheless, due to the research criteria used, there is ambiguity whether those people are seeking cultural entertainment rather than immersing themselves in a real cultural environment. It is a planning challenge for the aboriginal tourism developers and operators whether or not they would like to target this market segment. It is also a management challenge as to how to promote and educate potential tourists with a rather limited budget.

Fourth, the tourism development situation in the Far North is similar in some ways to the development of island tourism. Almost everything required for the operation of tourism has to be flown in, including tourists. There is no other means of public transportation, except for very limited motor vehicle access. It is also possible that the tourism expertise may have to be imported due to the lack of experience among the aboriginal staff. Economic impacts, i.e. leakage, therefore are considerable and how the aboriginal tourism developers and operators will justify the economic feasibility of small-scale, special-interest tourism products is another challenge. Although non-aboriginal ecotourism operators' profit margin is estimated for 200% (Johnston, 2000), it is questionable if the aboriginal tourism operators are able to price the packages at such a rate. It is necessary to consider if the economic benefits of aboriginal tourism development in the North are justified. Is it worth pursuing tourism as a means of economic development? If it is necessary to work with the exogenous tourism industry it may mean unequal partnerships. Should the type of tourism products the aboriginal tourism offers be modified in order to attract tourists?

This chapter has illustrated the complex relationship between aboriginal and ecotourism in Canada's North. The four main points discussed are far from comprehensive as aboriginal tourism development contains many complex issues and not all aboriginal groups in Canada are dealt with in this chapter. Working independently as an aboriginal tourism industry is not a simple question of independence as it contains many social, cultural and psychological issues. Geography and the physical environment also affect future potential developments. The use of the ecotourism label developed from the ethnocentric exogenous tourism industry may clash with the social and cultural values of the aboriginal communities. Returning to the comments by Kanahele (1997: 4) earlier: ' "culture" and "eco" are so closely intertwined in the Native mind that they really are inseparable'.

Questions

1 What is the difference between ecotourism and aboriginal tourism in Canada's North?
2 How can aboriginal peoples ensure that they are able to maintain control over the ecotourism industry in Canada's North?
3 To what extent has the history of colonization had an impact on ecotourism in northern Canada?
4 What are the main difficulties facing aboriginal ecotour operators in Canada's North?

References

Addison, L. (1996) 'An approach to community-based tourism planning in the Baffin Region, Canada's Far North: a retrospective'. In Harrison, L.C. and Husbands, W. (eds) *Practicing Responsible Tourism: International Case Studies in Tourism Planning, Policy and Development*. New York: John Wiley & Sons, 298–312.

ATTC (2000) 'Tourism highlights'. Newsletter, 2000 July/August.

ATTC (2002) 'ABC reviewing its investment'. Newsletter, Spring 2002. (Available at www.attc.ca.)

Beeton, S. (1998) *Ecotourism: A Practical Guide for Rural Communities*. Collingwood, Australia: Landlinks Press.

Cajete, G. (1999) ' "Look to the mountain": reflections on indigenous ecology'. In Cajete, G. (ed.) *A People's Ecology: Exploration in Sustainable Living*. Santa Fe: Clear Light, 1–20.

Colton, J.W. and Hinch, T.D. (1999) 'Trap-line-based tours as indigenous tourism products in Northern Canada', *Pacific Tourism Review*, 3, 1–10.

Doucett, V. (2000) 'The Aboriginal tourism challenge: managing for growth', *Communiqué*, 4 (11)1, 3.

Ewart, A. (1997) 'Resource-based tourism: introduction and overview', *Journal of Applied Recreation Research*, 22 (1), 3–7.

Gauthier, D.A. (1995) 'The sustainability of wildlife'. In Mitchell, B. (ed.) *Resource and Environmental Management in Canada: Addressing Conflict and Uncertainty*, 2nd edn. Toronto: Oxford University Press, 207–35.

Grekin, J. and Milne, S. (1996) 'Toward sustainable tourism development: the case of Pond Inlet, NWT'. In Butler, R. and Hinch, T., *Tourism and Indigenous Peoples*. London: International Thomson Business Press, 76–106.

Hinch, T.D. (1995) 'Aboriginal people in the tourism economy of Canada's Northwest Territories'. In Hall, C.M. and Johnston, M.E. (eds) *Polar Tourism: Tourism in the Arctic and Antarctic Regions*. Chichester: John Wiley & Sons, 115–30.

Hinch T. and Butler, R. (1996) 'Indigenous tourism: a common ground for discussion'. In In Butler, R. and Hinch, T., *Tourism and Indigenous Peoples*. London: International Thomson Business Press, 3–19.

Ieria, S. (1997) 'Why an aboriginal tourism program?', *Canada Communiqué*, May 3.

Jaakson, R. (1997) 'Exploring the epistemology of ecotourism', *Journal of Applied Recreation Research*, 22 (1), 33–47.

Johnston, A. (2000) 'Indigenous peoples and ecotourism: bringing indigenous knowledge and rights into the sustainability equation', *Tourism Recreation Research*, 25 (2), 89–96.

Kanahele, G. (1997) 'What is Aboriginal tourism?', *Canada Communiqué*, May, 4.

Lang Research (2001) *Travel Activities & Motivation Survey: Aboriginal Tourism Report September 2001*. ISBN-Print: 0–7794–2134–5, ISBN-Internet: 0–7794–2135–3.

Morrison, A., Rimmington, M. and Williams, C. (1999) *Entrepreneurship in the Hospitality, Tourism and Leisure Industries*. Oxford: Butterworth-Heinemann.

Notzke, C. (1999) 'Indigenous tourism development in the Arctic', *Annals of Tourism Research*, 26 (1), 55–76.

Nunavut Tourism (n.d.) *The Arctic Traveller: Nunavut Vacation Planner 2000 Edition*. Iqaluit: Nunavut Tourism.

Parker, B. (1993) 'Developing aboriginal tourism – opportunities and threats', *Tourism Management*, October, 400–404.

Rauber, P. (1998) 'On top of the world', *Sierra*, March/April 1998, 83 (2), 56–63, 100.

Shultis, J.D. and Browne, A.J. (1999) 'Aboriginal collaboration', *Parks & Recreation*, September, 34 (9), 108 (received by email via Academic Search Elite Database).

Simmon, I.G. (1993) *Environmental History: A Concise Introduction, New Perspectives on the Past*. Oxford: Blackwell.

Smith, V.L. (1996) 'The Inuit as hosts: heritage and wilderness tourism in Nunavut'. In Price, M.F. (ed.) *People and Tourism in Fragile Environment*. Chichester: John Wiley & Sons, 33–50.

Swarbrooke, J. (1999) *Sustainable Tourism Management*. Wallingford: CABI.

Usher, P.J. (1987) 'The north: one land, two ways of life'. In McCann, L.D. (ed.) *Heartland and Hinterland: A Geography of Canada*, 2nd edn. Scarborough, Ontario: Prentice Hall Canada Inc., 483–529.

Weaver, D.B. (1998) *Ecotourism in the Less Developed World*. Wallingford: CABI.

Wenzel, G. (1991) *Animal Rights, Human Rights: Ecology, Economy and Ideology in the Canadian Arctic*. Toronto: University of Toronto Press.

Websites

www.aventure-ecotourisme.qc.ca
www.btc.gov.yk.ca
www.gov.nt.ca
www.gov.nu.ca
www.nunavut.com
www.podi.com/ecosource/ecotour
www.sasktourism.com.
www.staq.net/english/index.htm
www.stats.gov.nt.ca/Statinfo
www.tourisme.gouv.qc.ca/anglais

12 Marketing Ecotourism: A Focus on Chile

Tim Knowles and Christian Felzensztein

The four main objectives of this chapter are to:

- Introduce the status of ecotourism in Chile
- Analyze the impacts of ecotourism in Chile
- Discuss the branding strategies of ecotourism in Chile
- Assess the success and failure of branding in ecotourism in Chile

Introduction

This chapter considers branding in international tourism markets and specifically marketing strategies as applied to the Chilean ecotourism industry. In the first part, the central arguments of selected writers about global brands, their standardization, adaptation and customization processes will be reviewed.

The second part of this chapter will illustrate the changes in the global ecotourism industry, the general situation of Chile in this sector, analyzing the main characteristics of this market. Additionally, the chapter will exemplify what firms should be doing in the marketplace and examine the factors affecting the possible scenarios for the creation of global/international brands for this tourism sector within Chile.

Finally, the chapter will argue that it is the combination of product brand recognition as well as the country effect (Brand Chile) that together could be strong marketing tools for Chilean ecotourism along with greater emphasis on a public–private sector partnership.

Setting the scene

Ecotourism is often associated with other forms of non-consumptive tourism based on natural history, such as nature tourism, wildlife tourism and adventure tourism (see Chapter 1). More conceptual definitions formulated by environmental organizations include a requirement for a contribution to the conservation of ecosystems at tourist destinations and emphasis on links between ecotourism and alternative as well as sustainable tourism (Brandon, 1996).

Industry and governments, contrariwise, concentrate more on ecotourism as a product, whereby the image of a unique or pristine natural environment appeals to a growing sector of the international tourism market. From a marketing perspective, ecotourism is sold as a speciality product, appealing largely to the upmarket, highly educated and affluent traveller. Ecotourism, thus interpreted, may be ecologically based but is not always ecologically sound and quite often expensive (Brandon, 1996). This category of tourism is not new; there is a long history of travel to natural areas. The establishment of national parks in the USA was based on a policy of achieving harmony between resource protection and public use. The traditional African game safaris were a consumptive form of tourism based on hunting and otherwise exploiting natural wildlife resources. However, ecotourism usually refers to non-consumptive recreation activities that are closely linked to natural history and that may also be related to wildlife, such as birdwatching, wildlife watching, nature photography, botanical study and wildlife treks and safaris.

The growth of ecotourism in Chile has resulted from two major factors. First of all, tourists have become more interested in a learning experience in natural environments and have grown dissatisfied with traditional, crowded tourist centres and resorts. Second, ecotourism in Chile has been assisted by slowly improving infrastructure, an increased number of specialist tour companies, widespread publicity and recognition of its importance by many government and non-government organizations within South America and their US and European feeder markets.

During the 1990s there was a growing acceptance in Chile of links that exist between protection of ecosystems and economic opportunities emerging through tourism. Increased interest in natural areas provided the authorities with a powerful incentive to protect the environment, as well as with the income from tourism to pay for conservation projects. Many environmentalists and managers of national parks and nature reserves within the country turned to ecotourism as a source of revenue for protected areas. This was part of a general realization of the need to improve the sustainability of all tourism throughout the country.

Chilean ecotourism has grown from a niche product, representing an extreme, idealized form of nature tourism, into a 'buzzword' used to promote a whole variety of tourism products. The popularization of the concept in Chile has resulted in a rapid expansion of ecotourism operators, specialist eco-travel tour organizers and agents, eco-lodges and in a significant advance in the government's ecotourism policies.

This tourism sector continues to evolve throughout the country but with increased tensions, as growing numbers of tourists lead to environmental problems and conflicts arise with other industries. However, certain factors remain constant – that ecotourism is bound to nature; that it should be educational; and that it needs to be sustainable. The contradictory combination of meanings occurring in various definitions of ecotourism and in the areas of resource protection and mass travel constitutes both a paradox and a planning challenge for the country (Diamantis and Ladkin, 1999).

The protection of the environment is an essential part of ecotourism development. Ecotourism is not substantially different from conventional tourism unless it is carefully planned and managed. In fact, remote, wilderness ecotourism destinations are more vulnerable to negative impacts of tourism, as the natural environment and local communities tend to be relatively untouched, with little experience of visitors. Damage through disturbance from even the most environmentally friendly tourists can occur in addition to the impact that developing the necessary infrastructure inevitably has on visited communities (Diamantis and Ladkin, 1999).

Successful, sustainable forms of ecotourism in Chile depend greatly on integrated planning between public and private sectors, the latter tending to be small or medium sized enterprises. Factors such as local community consultation and environmental impact assessments, enforcing codes of practice for developers and codes of conduct for tourists and continual monitoring and re-adjustment of policies are all essential in order to maintain biodiversity, cultural integrity and long-term economic benefits from tourism. Preserving and enhancing the natural and cultural qualities of the destination is absolutely critical in ecotourism as these attractions are often rare, if not unique, as well as extremely fragile.

Management considerations

During the last two decades, globalization of business activities has emerged as an important subject for academics and governments as well as private sector companies, with the last searching for new markets. This has been particularly the case with tourism and, in the case of this chapter, ecotourism (Knowles et al., 2001).

In this theoretical review, a number of academics (Levitt, 1983; Kogut, 1985; Yip, 1989) make a distinction between the different kinds of global strategies applicable for foreign markets. Levitt (1983) argues that different characteristics are apparent in a multinational as opposed to a global corporation: 'The multinational corporation operates in a number of countries, and adjusts its products and practices in each, while a global corporation operates with resolute constancy as if the entire world, or major regions of it, was a single entity' (Svensson, 2001). In simple terms, this means that the global corporation sells its products without local adaptations. A contrast here can be made between mass package tourists and the niche bespoke ecotourism traveller.

In a competitive and global business environment, both large and small tourism firms need to consider whether they can develop a national or multinational or global strategy in order to attract domestic and foreign tourism markets. For some authors (Kogut, 1985; Yip, 1989) an unadulterated multi-domestic strategy is appropriate for the full customization in each market: 'The location of value-added activities are restricted to each country, the marketing approach is local and the competitive moves are stand-alone by country' (Svensson, 2001). By the same token, the pure global strategy is related with some specific features like a standardized product around the world, high-share market participation in some major markets and a uniform market strategy worldwide. It is rare to see such an approach within tourism and unheard of with ecotourism.

Some authors (Svensson, 2001) have introduced the terms 'global strategy' and 'globalization' to refer to the needs for a global strategy to be aware of the local adaptations of business activities in some markets. However, this not only refers to a foreign market entry strategy, but also to the standardization of marketing activities and the advertising process. At this juncture, the following quotation is pertinent as it explains the definition of standardization in marketing and highlights the dilemma for mass tourism versus ecotourism: 'the offering of identical product lines at identical prices, through identical distribution systems, supported by identical promotional programs, in several countries' (Buzzel, 1968).

This quotation advances the view that the existence of only one global market, without consumer behaviour differences and without any modification in different target markets, may be possible for certain manufactured goods but is impossible for ecotourism. On this issue tourism companies within Chile should be aware of the distinction between customization and adaptation strategies, which are quite similar. There are, however, some important differences: 'Adaptation relates to changes attributed to mandatory requirements, whereas changes in customisation are optional to the firm' (Levitt, 1983). This means that adaptations can refer to changes in the physical characteristics of the product/service mix. Contrariwise, customization refers to changing some intangible aspects or in the communication mix, focusing on the customer's physiological differences. In this context it is important to consider that the international marketing of tourism brands should reflect the needs, interests, beliefs and way of thinking of the target customers.

Branding strategies

A standardization strategy, suitable for mass packaged tourism, can use the domestic market for testing marketing plans and the attributes of the product and brand name, in order to apply these local strategies in cross-national markets. Medina and Duffy (1998) argue: 'The domestic target market constitutes the sole authority in establishing the benefit-generating attribute-standard in the resulting brand.'

It is important to consider that, in some international markets, product adaptations are mandatory, as a result of demands from the local environment. As Medina and Duffy (1998) note: 'These adoptions translate into the adoption of new products standards, which will become useful to the firm in applying these same standards to similar environments elsewhere.' In contrast, brand customization, more apparent within tourism, represents the most intense example of brand adaptation, which involves specific and important changes for the foreign market. These changes are a result of the awareness of local differences in consumer behaviour and values of this specific market. To put it another way: 'Negative perception of the product category in taste, style and product quality can in fact kill the market for brands which might otherwise be adaptable – meet mandatory requirements' (Terpstra, 1981).

In the final stage, the brand global strategy is concerned with reaching 'global customers' around the world; a 'brand Chile' approach to tourism, perhaps implemented at government level. This is applying global standards and not a domestic one – an approach of little relevance in tourism niche products, although perhaps vital in promoting a country's tourism industry. In other words, differences in the product and brand attributes cannot be recognized in the diverse markets in which the company is operating. In this context, De Mooij (1998) states:

> A global brand is one which shares the same strategic principles, positioning and marketing in every market throughout the world, although the marketing mix can vary. It carries the same brand name or logo. Its values are identical in all countries. It has substantial market share in all countries and comparable brand loyalty. The distribution channels are similar.

This view implies similar niche segments in every country around the world, but it is well known that culture, language and values are different in each market (Hofstede, 1997). Having said that, products like the famous region of Patagonia or indeed the Atacama Desert in Chile are well known worldwide for specific attributes, thus attracting high-spending tourists each year.

The ecotourism industry of Chile: segmenting the market

McKinna's criteria for segmentation (Edwards and Spawton, 1990), presents diverse kinds of tourism consumers. Each one represents a different consumer behaviour and the reasons why people buy tourism products and how they make their decision.

According to this viewpoint, it is important to say that there may be new opportunities to market the product, the place and, in addition, the region as a positioning strategy for Chilean ecotourism. In support of this idea, Thode and Maskuta (1998) state: 'A place-based strategy provides the firm with the opportunity to establish a sustainable competitive advantage.' In other words, this strategy can differentiate products on the basis of characteristic geographic origin, which can be a strong marketing tool in foreign markets.

Chile's non-traditional exports,[1] such as fish oil, salmon, bottled wines, etc., have increased substantially during the last 20 years, especially because of the Government Promotion Programme made by ProChile as well as by the efforts of private companies (Central Bank of Chile, 1999). Within these non-traditional products, the tourism industry and its subsector, ecotourism, operate in a competitive international environment.

Over the past decade, Chilean tourism can be characterized as a 'country ambassador' in international markets, competing and adopting, improving quality and implementing an effective segmentation strategy. At the same time, the industry has entered into strategic alliances with other international companies around the world (ProChile, 2001). This great export push took place in the 1980s starting with an aggressive promotion campaign overseas. The reasons for this success are price-quality relationship, health factors and the climatic conditions, which are to be found in Chile, generating new waves of high-spending consumers. However, while Chilean tourism has broken international barriers, it is still recognized as a small country compared with the major worldwide tourism destinations. This implies that Chile must improve its search in finding a specific positioning strategy or niche.

Chilean ecotourism: developing a global brand?

During the last two decades, Chilean tourism has begun to be an important player in international markets (ProChile, 2001). In fact, one of the country's

---

[1] Traditional exports are mining (copper and iron), fresh fruit and fishmeal.

most important marketing tools has been the positioning of ecotourism as a product with high-quality value, although certainly not the cheapest.

The three most important tourist regions in Chile for international markets are Patagonia, Isla de Pascua and the Atacama Desert. Taking the last example and, specifically, San Pedro de Atacama, tourism has been growing at over 7% a year over the past five years. Turning to the Chilean Patagonia, this area has a direct connection with the Argentinean Patagonia which represents a clear opportunity for joint marketing activities between the two countries with respect to ecotourism. The key international markets being France, Germany, Italy, Spain, UK and the USA and, at a regional level, Argentina and Brazil (www.gochile.cl).

The importance of ecotourism can be highlighted by considering the Aysen Region (southern part of Chile) which generates 7.7% of the total employment and 10% of regional GDP. The area contains more than 30% of the natural resources protected by government policy. However, the central problem for the ecotourism industry in this part of Chile is that the majority of businesses are SMEs. The region has vast natural resources yet entrepreneurs working in the ecotourism sector have a low level of managerial capability. The way forward it would seem is for government and educational institutions to establish a net-working and consultative approach to developing the sector – a public–private partnership to developing ecotourism in the region. Such a cluster approach to development would need to address the low levels of infrastructure in the region and particularly the exploitation of the Internet as a means to promote ecotourism.

At present Chilean ecotourism is now without much generic marketing support to develop strategies in overseas markets. As a result of this, it is questionable if it is the right time to attempt to create a global brand for the Chilean tourism industry. Also it is important to know if an individual firm can create a successful label abroad, what the right positioning strategy for the market is and whether reliance should be placed on intermediaries. These are only a few issues without an easy answer for the Chilean ecotourism industry and which merit further study.

Management considerations: a practitioner's perspective

One of the main problems for Chilean tourism is the lack of a strong identity as a tourism country, in contrast to, say, Spain, Greece or, indeed, Brazil. It could be argued that some tourism firms should build a strong image as a quality des-tination, using a place-based marketing strategy as an important tool. This means having a 'link between the product's place of origin and presumed quality of these products' (Thode and Maskuta, 1998). Clearly this strategy is not an easy one without international promotion. Consequently, 2000–2002 saw almost no generic marketing activity of Chilean tourism. However, to carry out this generic strategy it is necessary to have good marketing and public relations systems. Subsequently, one important question related to this lack of generic strategy is what the next step will be in attempting to increase market share for Chilean ecotourism in the international tourism market.

The fundamental problem for Chilean ecotourism is that the current economic model is one of the principal causes of the appalling environmental conditions in the country. Public involvement on environmental issues must be increased, because only by involving people can sustainable development be achieved. Environmental NGOs argue that social and environmental sustainability should be seen as integrated entities.

When NGOs in Chile refer to the contemporary economic model they refer to the overall control the market has over everything. The model was introduced in the mid-1970s during the dictatorship and has, apparently, not changed radically since. It is still based on neoliberal principles and its strategy is to remove as many obstacles to trade as possible. Because of this, there has been no effective control of the over exploitation of natural resources, such as native forests, seafood and minerals. As well as that, the model has accentuated social stratification. Chilean culture has changed, contemporary society has been socially split and people are very self-centred. It would seem that everything is decided according to economic interest.

The government should introduce reforms to create more possibilities and encourage the public to take advantage of them. This could be achieved through better education programmes organized by both state and private organizations.

However, the impression can be gained that some changes are going to be made soon within the Chilean 'environmental movement'. The majority of these changes will come from below, from activists and smaller groups, such as residential pressure groups. It would seem that they would prefer to concentrate on human resources rather than economic management.

Many NGO members agree that the main objective for all of them in the next few years is to increase public participation in national issues and reduce the amount of in-fighting between NGOs. They all depend on outside help for their very survival but that does not mean they cannot work together to achieve it. Many of the bigger NGOs depend on the smaller ones for information and vice versa.

The outlook for stopping four of the most damaging projects ever to be proposed in Chile did not appear very promising for environmentalists at the end of 2000. All figures and reports seem to indicate that Chile's natural resources are being destroyed faster than ever. Major investment projects that threaten the environment are constantly receiving government support and environmental considerations seem to get swept aside. For instance, the Cascada-Chile project in Region X is a joint venture between the US company Boise Cascade and the Chilean wood company Condor designed to make medium-density fibreboard. The plant will consume some 600,000 cubic meters of wood from native evergreen trees a year (that is, 2.4 million trees a year). This is equivalent to one-quarter of all the wood that is processed in Region X each year.

The Ecological Policy Institute believes Cascada-Chile is the most absurd project in the country. It will destroy native forests and the environmental impact study only concentrated on the area directly surrounding the wood plant.

Another example is forestry project plans to cut some 103,000 hectares of native trees out of a total of 272,000 hectares owned by the company on Tierra del Fuego island. On 25 October 1999 the National Environment Commission, Conama, approved the environmental guarantee which was the last of the 100 conditions the company has to meet in order to go ahead with the project. The guarantee binds the company to pay compensation if it withdraws from the project early or cuts more than its quota of trees.

A further example is Ralco Dam project in the Alto Bio Bio where the outlook is poor. Work is continuing on the dam despite the fact that the contracted organization Endesa still has not resolved the situation with the seven indigenous families opposed to it. The Ralco project is plagued with ambiguities. For example, the NGO Grupo de Accion por el Bio Bio says Endesa does not have the water rights to the river. The Economy Ministry has indicated it intends to grant the electricity concession to the project.

Ralco is without a shadow of a doubt one of the worst government decisions as it proved the National Environment Commission was not autonomous and demonstrated the official line on sustainability and social and environmental issues. The decision-making powers of the National Indigenous Development Council were completely overriden over the issue. Former President Eduardo Frei forced the council's director, Domingo Namuncura, to resign and several other members followed suit, such as Dr Cristian Vives and Milene Valenzuela.

Finally, there is the example of the Northeast Access Highway project which threatens to go through one of the most important park areas in Santiago. There is a very low level of green area in Santiago with an average of 2.5 square metres per capita and the metropolitan region has been officially declared as saturated with pollution so it cannot afford to lose any more.

The project, which is designed to link Vitacura, in northeast Santiago, and the northern suburb of Colina requires a new 20.5-kilometre road, which includes four tunnels, will require an estimated investment of US$170 million and take six years to build. Up to 16,000 vehicles are expected to travel the route daily.

Conclusion

Generally speaking, the ecotourism industry in Chile is an immature industry, but is growing very fast in importance as well as in contribution to the local economic development of some remote regions, far away from the metropolitan economic concentration in Santiago. However, people, institutions and entrepreneurs involved in this industry need to change from an individualistic style in terms of marketing to a more collaborative networking approach. Thus only in this way will the industry create more competitive advantages. This means closer collaboration with universities, local research bodies and a private–public approach to development. This approach will assist in creating packaging, brand building and brand recognition of the sector. As mentioned in the chapter, this can only be achieved by knowing and positively responding to the behaviour of ecotourists visiting Chile.

Finally, this marketing strategy must focus on a long-term vision of the ecotourism market. Such a strategy would require effective public relations and positioning the country as well as individual products all of which are key marketing tools.

Questions

1 Critically analyze the opportunities for joint marketing of Chile's ecotourism industry.
2 Discuss the barriers to entry and the expansion of ecotourism in Chile.
3 Should ecotourism be regarded as part of a global or multinational marketing strategy for Chilean tourism? Discuss.
4 Explore the problems and opportunities in implementing a country-wide marketing strategy on ecotourism for Chile as opposed to focusing on individual products and destinations.

References

Brandon, K. (1996) 'Ecotourism and conservation: a review of key issues', Environment Department Paper No. 33, Washington: World Bank.

Buzzell, R., (1968) 'Can you standardize multinational marketing?', *Harvard Business Review*, 46, 102–13.

Central Bank of Chile (1999) Export division (www.bcentral.cl (Accessed on 1 July 2001)).

De Mooij, M. (1998) *Global Marketing and Advertising – Understanding Cultural Paradoxes*. London: Sage Publications.

Diamantis, D. and Ladkin, A. (1999) 'Green strategies in the tourism and hospitality industries'. In Vellas, F. and Becherel, L. (eds) *The International Marketing of Travel and Tourism*. London: Macmillan.

Edwards, F. and Spawton, T. (1990) 'Pricing in the Australian wine industry', *European Journal of Marketing*, 24 (4).

Hofstede, G. (1997) *Cultures and Organisations. The Software of the Mind*. New York: McGraw Hill.

Knowles, T., Diamantis, D. and Mourhabi, J. (2001) *The Globalisation of Tourism and Hospitality*. London: Continuum.

Kogut, B. (1985) 'Designing global strategies: profiting from operational flexibility', *Sloan Management Review*, 27 (1), 27–38.

Levitt, T., (1983) 'The globalization of markets', *Harvard Business Review*, 61 (3), 92–102.

Medina, J. and Duffy, M. (1998) 'Standardization vs globalisation: a new perspective of brand strategies', *Journal of Product & Brand Management*, 7 (3), 223–43.

ProChile (2001) Available at *http://www.prochile.cl*

Svensson, G. (2001) ' "Glocalization" of business activities: a "glocal strategy" approach', *Management Decision*, 29 (1), 6–18.

Terpstra, V. (1981) 'On marketing appropriate products in developing countries', *Journal of International Marketing*, 1 (1), 3–15.

Thode, S. and Maskuta, J. (1998) 'Place-based marketing strategies brand equity and vineyard valuation', *Journal of Product & Brand Management*, 7 (5) 379–99.

Yip, G.S. (1989) 'Global strategy . . . in a world of nations?', *Sloan Management Review*, 29–41.

236

13 Management of the Ecotourism Destination through Policies of Investment: The Case of the Peneda-Geres National Park, Portugal

Carlos Costa

The four main objectives of this chapter are to:

- Describe how tourism has evolved in Portugal
- Discuss the way in which the Portuguese government is planning to boost and organize the tourism sector in the future
- Analyze how tourism activities may be placed alongside the protection of the environment
- Present a tourism strategy for Portugal's most important natural park

Introduction

Portugal is the world's 16th largest tourist destination. In spite of its small size the country benefits from a privileged geographical position. Located right in the south of Europe, and on the shores of the Mediterranean, the most southern regions, Algarve and Alentejo, benefit from the influence of the Mediterranean climate, while the western coastline profits from the warm influence of the Atlantic Ocean. As a result of these two different types of weather, Portugal offers a wide diversity of temperature, ecosystem, ethnography, gastronomy, wine, heritage and cultural events.

The position of Portugal in the world's travel and tourism market may also be explained as a result of several important initiatives and events that took place during the 20th century. The Republican Government that emerged in the beginning of the 20th century, in a revolution that put an end to the monarchy, gave a tremendous boost to tourism. The first governmental tourism organizations, comprising national and local level authorities, were created in 1911; the first fully planned resort was launched during the 1920s; a number of new laws specifically concerned with tourism were passed during the 1920s and 1930s.

The years that followed the arrival of Salazar's dictatorship (1926–74) were characterized by a great step backwards in the dynamics introduced in the beginning of the century. During this phase tourism was regarded as a threat to the stability of the regime, the reason why the government decided to enact legislation aimed at preventing and controlling the movement of visitors in the country (Pina, 1988). This policy was not exclusive to Portugal, since Mussolini's dictatorship in Italy was also supported on similar premises. Nevertheless, and in spite of several initiatives launched by the government to stop tourism from expanding, the number of international arrivals never stopped rising during this period. Initially, this was due to Portugal's neutrality during World War II, which made the country a safe haven for refugees running away from the war. Furthermore, during the 1960s and 1970s, Portugal profited greatly from the expansion of mass tourism. Between 1950 and 1970 the number of international arrivals rose by 4297%, compared with 556% in the rest of the world, while the percentage of international receipts climbed by 1572% (752% in the rest of the world).

As in other countries, in the early years of the 21st century, tourism is, undoubtedly, one of the main social and economic activities in Portugal. With a population of about 10 million inhabitants Portugal attracts 28 million international visitors and 12.5 million tourists every year. International tourists spend 80,000 nights and generate an annual receipt of €6.5 billion every year. Hence, tourism accounts for 8% of the GDP and 6% of the working population. Moreover, domestic tourism is also booming. The number of Portuguese spending holidays more than doubled in a short 3 years, from 3.5 million in 1996 to 7.2 million in 1999.

As a result of its impact on the economy, society and environment, tourism is assuming growing importance among government's priorities. The conclusions put forward by the 1994 report on Portugal by Michael Porter (Porter, 1994), where tourism is singled out as a key cluster for the economy, have been re-evaluated and relaunched by a recently created intergovernmental board. During the second half of the 1990s many other initiatives were launched: the restructuring of several NTOs; the involvement of Portuguese universities and other research centres in the study of tourism; the creation of MSc and PhD scholarships designed for the first time for tourism; the beginning of the first joint MSc programme run in a partnership involving the Aveiro and Algarve Universities; the creation of a tourism observatory with regional offices at the seven Portuguese planning regions. All may be cited as examples of the growing importance paid to tourism during the second half of the 1990s.

Portuguese tourism policy

Alongside the initiatives introduced during the 1990s, the government decided to launch a comprehensive research project aimed at analyzing and discussing the efficiency and effectiveness of the tourism policies and investments that took place under the umbrella of the Second Framework of Support (1994–99). The study was conducted by a research team headed by the Aveiro University and involved several national and international consultants (Costa, 2003). A 1000-page report, organized into six thematic volumes (recommendations, policy, investment, education, legislation and Portugal's position in the international market), has become available.

As far as the policy and the funding of the tourism sector are concerned the conclusions brought about by the study draw attention to two main groups of issues. A number of somewhat negative areas that overshadow the economic performance and the quantitative evolution of tourism in Portugal are discussed in the first group of conclusions. It is remarked that, in spite of the benefits produced by tourism to the national economy, in terms of receipts, balance of payments, employment and income, the number of international arrivals is still increasing whereas receipts in real terms have gone down. In addition to this, the excessively seasonal characteristics, the dominance of the tourism sector by a few international markets and the geographical concentration of tourism at few places in the country are singled out as negative developments of the Portuguese tourism sector. In demand mainly because of its warm white-sand beaches and fine landscapes (holidays spent mainly on the beach represent more than 90% of total tourist motivation), Portugal's tourism is too concentrated at three regions on the western and southern coasts. Algarve, Lisbon and Madeira account for 80% of the total employment and 80% of the total 200,000 registered tourism beds.

The second group of conclusions highlight the fact that, despite the efficiency observed in the operation of most NTOs, national policies have failed to deliver forms of self-sustained development. In other words, tourism funding has been channelled towards mainly small individual projects, which have proved to be unable to boost, sustain and bind the development process.

Based on this evidence the national government decided to create a new funding programme. Alongside with the 'classical' forms of investment available for the funding of individual projects (hotels, restaurants, environmental protection, preservation of heritage, etc.) the government implemented a new funding programme called PITER (Projectos Integrados Turisticos Estruturantes de Base Regional), that may be translated into integrated tourism projects (Despacho Normativo no 35/98, 28/05).

When compared with the 'classical' forms of investment the policy that supports the new funding programme contains major differences. To start with, under the new programme individual projects may not be submitted for funding, since they must be put together and justified in a pack of projects. This set must be worth a minimum of €10 million, of which 50% of the investment has to come from private sector organizations. Second, projects must prove to be feasible from an economic point of view and demonstrate that they will not be harmful to the natural environment.

A justification regarding the indirect and induced economic benefits created by the project must also be included, since one of the government's major objectives is to stimulate the generation of value-added chains and self-sustained clusters of projects. Moreover, the pack of projects has to identify clearly what is labelled as the group of 'anchor projects', that is, projects responsible for being at the core of the development process and, thus, act as honeypots and stimulators of the development process. The idea is to boost the creation of organized and profitable tourism partnerships and networks. In fact, evidence collected in Portugal shows that the Portuguese regional tourism boards are supported on fragile structures since their informal connections and work relationships with their members are infrequent, not intense and do not involve the exchange of technical information (Costa, 1996). The implication of such a situation to the profitability and effectiveness of the tourism sector are enormous: while benefiting from the direct impacts created by tourism, the industry has failed to take full advantage from the indirect and induced development produced by tourism.

In order to avoid the presentation of simple lists of projects without a clear orientation, the programme has also made the inclusion of a tourism strategy compulsory. In order to justify why projects are included in the programme, and why some of them will head it with the label of 'anchor projects', the government demands the presentation of a tourism strategy that has to include, among other matters, objectives, directions, investment priorities, environmental concerns and a justification about how tourism will be able to improve the living conditions of the local population.

The experience from the first PITER programme (1998–2001) proved to be very positive. More than 20 projects were submitted to the national government, covering a variety of regions and tourism products. As a result of the success achieved by the first programme, the Portuguese government decided to relaunch the programme since 2002.

The Peneda-Geres National Park

The Peneda-Geres National Park (PGNP) is located in the north of Portugal and was created in 1971. The park is the largest and more emblematic Portuguese natural area: every year an estimated 2.5 million visitors, mainly excursionists, travel into the region. The PGNP comprises five municipalities, Melgaco, Ponte da Barca, Arcos de Valdevez, Terras de Bouro and Montalegre, that cover an area of 1952 km². Eighty-four percent of this area is fully protected land. The park accounts for 9.2% of the northern part of Portugal (21,194 km²) and represents 2.2% of Portugal's territory (91,985 km²). The density of population living in this land is very low. It varies from eight inhabitants per square kilometre in Montalegre up to 60 in Montalegre. Conversely, in northern Portugal the average density reaches 162 inhabitants per square kilometre.

One-third of the natural area includes very sensitive ecosystems with unique, and thus internationally protected, fauna and flora. This portion of the territory is fully protected and, thus, no human activities are permitted. In the remaining area, designated as an 'area of rural environment', human activities are allowed but within tight regulations that were enacted in strict accordance with the park master plan.

Disputes between the park authority and the five local mayors, involving development versus conservation issues, are common, since the pressure for building is very strong. Despite these conflicting points of view a unique and well-balanced relationship between nature and man-made activities has been achieved. The area offers unique landscapes in a land where a few, very small and scattered industries may be found: 22% of the area is used for agricultural purposes, 39% is occupied by forests, 36% comprises rivers, lakes and dams and 3% encompasses built environment.

The strict environmental standards set up for the area and its peripheral location in relation to the more developed coastline have contributed to the region's social and economic underdevelopment. While the population is still growing slowly in northern Portugal, permanent and significant losses of the mainly young working population are recorded in PGNP during the last three decades. In spite of the two motorways that make road accessibility to the outskirts of the region easy, the accessibility within the area is, for obvious reasons, problematic. In addition to this, the region is very poor in facilities such as schools, hospitals and health centres. Employment opportunities are also an issue, since there are a few jobs in the local industries. Most services are also very small and are restricted to a few vacancies offered by the small local authorities. In addition to all these shortcomings, local authorities' budgets are very small. This means that the capacity of the local public sector organizations to attract private investment and compete with their neighbouring munici-palities is greatly reduced.

The tourism sector

Dominated by outstanding landscapes, rich habitats and relaxing sites the PGNP has become one of Portugal's main visitor attractions. According to some estimates provided by the park, more than 2.5 million visitors descend on the region every year. Visitors look for natural ecosystems, traditional religious events and spas. Hence, the area has become Portugal's largest ecotourism destination.

In the absence of other prospectus of development, and aware of the potential created by the national park, the five local mayors and the national park director decided to create a tourism policy and strategy for the region. The project aims at boosting tourism in the surroundings of the protected area, regulating its operation within the protected area where tourism activities may take place and capturing for the local population the social, economic and environmental benefits produced by tourism. The project, designed by a team from the Aveiro University, was submitted in 1999 to the national government under the umbrella of the PITER programme (Costa et al., 1999).

The tourism policy and strategy was prepared based on several models frequently cited in tourism literature. Among them Inskeep's planning model (Inskeep, 1991: 39), Mill and Morrison's tourism matrix for the inventorying of tourism resources (Mill and Morrison, 1985: 300–302); the supply side tourism definitions recommended by the Tourism Satellite Account (WTO, 2000), Mathieson and Wall's conceptualization of the tourism sector (1982: 15) and Costa's approach on tourism networks and partnerships for Portugal (Costa, 1996) may be cited.

The project confirms that the ecotourism potential offered by the PGNP is enormous, since the region contains some of the world's unique ecosystems. Moreover, the balance reached between nature and man-made agricultural activities is outstanding and is the reason why the British Airways Tourism for Tomorrow Awards prized the area in 1999 among the world's 12 best eco-tourism projects. Symbiotic relationships between man and nature have also been achieved in a number of traditional, mostly religious, events as well as in the utilization of waters, streams and dams.

Bearing in mind the resources available in the region, it is not difficult to guess what the main characteristics of the local tourism industry are. Among the tourists' main motivations ecotourism, scenery, religious events, gastro-nomy and water-based activities, including water sports and spa tourism, are cited. The average length of stay in the region is very short (1.8 days), since most tourists travel into the area to enjoy nature. More than 90% of the visitors are nationals whereas less than 10% come from abroad, mainly from the France, Germany, Spain and UK. Most tourists are young, with ages ranging between 20 and 45 and hold an academic degree (polytechnic and university degrees).

The findings brought about by the project are also confirmed by another study conducted in the territory regarding the tourists' perception of the region (Kastenholz, 2000). Among the most common tourists' images 'nature', 'green', 'mountains', 'landscapes' and 'scenery' are cited. Adjectives such as 'peaceful', 'beautiful', 'pure' and 'wild' are also frequently used to describe the region. Not surprisingly, the same study reveals that word of mouth is the most often cited source of information mentioned by tourists when asked why they had chosen PGNP for a holiday.

Bearing in mind this description it should come as no surprise that some of the most important features that describe the supply side of this ecotourism destination are mentioned. Campsites and some typical houses, used by the park wardens decades ago (*casas abrigo*), are among the most frequently demanded forms of accommodation. The number and quality of most cheap guesthouses (*pensoes*) is very poor. They account for some 46,500 bednights per year, with an average occupancy rate that varies between 21% and 24%. Conversely, the larger tourism region, that includes the PGNP and the developed coastline (Alto Minho Regional Tourist Board), can boast 380,000 bednights (240,000 nationals and 140,000 foreigners). Indeed, most of the three, four and five star hotels are located along the more developed coastline and thus outside the park's direct area of influence.

The pressure created by tourists on the park's fragile ecosystems is also very high. In Mata de Albergaria, one of the most sensitive sections of the park, an average 1000 people descend on the place every day. At several places tourists have been known to move into sensitive areas in search of 'exotic' species. Hence, the pressure on some fragile areas is a big issue. The absence of a tourism master plan nicely articulated with an environmental strategy alongside the absence of tourism information centres may also be blamed as being responsible for fuelling this situation.

As far as the local tourism administration is concerned the situation is also complicated. Other studies have already described its inefficiency and ineffectiveness (Costa, 1996). Nineteen regional tourism boards and 27 local tourism organizations complicate the regional and local tourism administration. Within the boundaries of the protected area the full authority rests in the hands of the Ministry of Environment. This means that tourist organizations do not have too many chances of intervening in such high places. Again, disputes are found between environmental protection and the use of the land for leisure purposes.

Current environmental initiatives

The tourism policy and strategy for PGNP was designed in eight months by a team of five professionals with a background in tourism (two), environmental engineering (one) and agriculture-related areas (two), three supervisors (a tourism expert from the Aveiro University, the park director and the president of the PGNP development association), and an advisory board made up of representatives from two NTOs; the five local mayors; two RTBs; a local polytechnic and two technical schools; the regional planning authority for north Portugal (CCRN); and five local development associations that operate in the region. The study included the preparation of a tourism policy and strategy and the presentation of a list of 147 projects that amounted to €70 million: 76 were submitted by local investors while 71 were proposed by public sector organizations.

The study concluded that while PGNP is one of the most important Portuguese tourist honeypots a few other economic benefits are left in the area. As described earlier, from the total trips that take place to the region only some 46,500 bednights happen in the area. Moreover, most tourists stay on cheap campsites and for very short periods of time.

The local tourism industry is also too fragmented and geographically dispersed, which makes its profitability a problem. While travelling to enjoy landscapes and to contact nature, tourists move freely and easily from one place to another by car, bicycle or hiking. In the absence of a coordinated tourism strategy there has been a tendency for small businesses to emerge. Hence, the number of places where tourists may stop and potentially consume products are increasing, with obvious implications in terms of cost. In spite of not being frequently cited in literature it should not be forgotten that tourism brings about not only economic benefits but also costs in infrastructure, equipment and services such as water supply, sewage treatment plants, collection of solid wastes, accessibility, healthcare services, security, safety, etc.

In addition to all this, it should also be contended that the argument for developing tourism must not be accepted unless it is supported by clear advantages. In spite of its undeniable importance for the world's pacification and for a better understanding between different cultures, how much tourism will benefit and cost the local populations are among the critical issues that must be considered carefully. Local communities are increasingly aware of the full dimension and benefits created by the tourism industry. They do not wish to be burdened with rubbish left behind by tourists, nor do they wish to pay costs towards infrastructure and equipment provided for tourists from their own taxes, while the big operators keep most benefits.

Local communities are aware that most profits are generated through expenses on accommodation, food and beverage, shopping and entertainments. Nevertheless, they are also sensitive to the fact that such businesses do not represent an end in themselves. Tourists spend on such items, but their travelling triggers are the social, cultural and environmental assets that they want to experience at the destiny. In short, shared benefits between operators and local communities must necessarily happen.

It was based on these premises that the PGNP tourism policy and strategy was designed. The main objectives underpinning the strategy may be summed up as follows: (1) to promote and enhance environmental conservation; (2) to give private and public sector investment a strategic orientation; (3) to increase and complement the relationship between public and private sector investment; (4) to reorient tourism flows within the park, and direct them into particular pockets of development; (5) to concentrate tourism businesses in particular areas of the territory; (6) to create interdependent business clusters and chains of projects; (7) to improve the indirect and induced economic effects produced by tourism; and (8) to introduce tighter links between tourism and local economic development, thus, improving the living conditions of the local population.

In order to increase the revenue generated by tourism and make tourists stay longer, a strategy for tourism investment was produced based on the following principles. First, investment should be oriented towards the expansion of the number of beds. The idea is to attract and retain larger numbers of visitors to the area. Second, the area must also expand the range of quality restaurants and other establishments offering food and beverages. Research conducted in the area also demonstrates that, after accommodation, food and drink is the second most important source of expenditure by tourists. Besides, the region is very rich in traditional agricultural products and gastronomy. Hence, a greater pressure on the local economic basis will lead to the improvement of the local farmers' income and, generally speaking, to an increased demand for traditional products.

Third, tourism investment should also be oriented towards types of entertainment that will induce tourists to stay longer and make their visit more memorable. In particular, new investments in water-based facilities, river and dam beaches, sport activities, small operators responsible for hiking routes, and fitness centres were stimulated and included in the project.

Furthermore, the strategy aims at promoting a closer liaison between private and public sector investment. Public sector spending in areas such as training, preservation of heritage, TICs, water supply, sewage treatment plants, tourist guides, preservation of heritage and road accessibility, was stimulated to complement private sector investment. The idea is to create quality tourism products.

Bearing in mind the fragmented characteristics of tourism within the area and the low level of commercialization of most local tourism products, a new tour operator responsible for organizing and trading local tourism products was also proposed. The project is due to operate under the umbrella of the local development association (ADERE-PG), and will be owned by the five local municipalities and the park authority. Tourist and non-tourist information about the park and a booking centre where customers can make their own searches and reservations will also be available 24 hours a day from the Internet.

A master plan seeking to zone the expansion of the tourism industry was also produced. The strategy is based on a network of 5+5+5 spots, and seeks to: (1) circumscribe the tourism development process to the urban centres of the five local villages; (2) avoid the dispersion of tourism flows throughout the protect area; (3) concentrate tourism investment in some particular areas in order to increase the internal liaison within the local economic basis and to speed up the development process by taking advantage of scale economies and indirect and induced economic impacts; and (4) create a cluster-based economy supported by a network of investment, attractions and themes.

Most tourism investment in infrastructure, equipment and leisure and recreation activities was concentrated at the five urban centres of the five local municipalities. It is also within these areas that most of the population live. Hence, tourism investment will benefit from the already urban facilities and new spending will also revert in benefits to the local population.

There are five small villages located within the protected area. These villages portray the living styles of the region and are the reason why they are at the top of the motivation list of visitors travelling into the area. For these small five villages, investment mainly in the improvement of the local heritage, accessibility and infrastructure and equipment was considered.

For the 'border' that separates protected from non-protected land, five interpretation centres were projected. The idea is to introduce a new concept of the 'park door', that aims at 'filtering' and educating tourist flows before entering into the protected area. Such centres will operate as tourist gateways and distributors into the national park. Visitors will have the opportunity to learn more about the environmental characteristics of the region and will be taught how to conduct themselves in the protected area. The diffusion of information and commercial objectives are also among the guidelines set up for those five interpretation centres.

Conclusion

Ecotourism is becoming big business all around the world, but it is also becoming a big issue for national parks. While seeking to preserve fragile ecosystems, most park authorities now also have to face the 'invasion' of large numbers of consumers lured by fashionable tourist brochures. Located outside the most developed areas, and in the absence of many development options, ecotourism destinations feel tempted to embark on development strategies where tourism is viewed as the opportunity to improve the living conditions of the local communities. The relationship between conservation and utilization then becomes a critical issue.

The policy designed for the largest national park in Portugal is based on the idea that the improvement of the living conditions for the local communities and environmental preservation and enhancement are not enemies of one another. Both objectives may be placed together, provided that a very strict zoning and a clear economic orientation is set up for the private sector. Recent legislation passed by the Portuguese governments is aimed at achieving that end. Nevertheless, it will be critical to evaluate in the future whether such objectives will be achieved in accordance with the objectives set up in the legislation.

Questions

1 Discuss ecotourism practices used in Portugal.
2 Undertake a SWOT analysis of the national park.
3 Analyze how the national park can be managed and governed.
4 Apply the POLAR framework to the national park. (See also Chapter 6.)

References

Costa, C.M.M. (1996) Towards the Improvement of the Efficiency and Effectiveness of Tourism Planning and Development at the Regional Level: Planning, Organisations and Networks. The Case of Portugal, PhD thesis (unpublished) University of Surrey, England.

Costa, C.M.M. (2001) 'Towards a new tourism policy for Portugal – the role of private sector organisations' ('O papel e a posição do sector privado na construção de uma nova política para o turismo em Portugal'). In Associação Empresarial de Portugal (eds), Novas Estratégias para o Turismo. Porto: Associação Empresarial de Portugal, 65–87.

Costa, C.M.M. (2003) 'Evaluation of the second framework of support' ('Avaliação do II Quadro Comunitário de Apoio – Componente Turismo'), Secretaria de Estado do Turismo, Lisbon.

Costa, C. M. M., Castro, P. V. and Portela, A. (1999) 'Integrated tourism project for the Peneda-Gerês National Park' ('Projecto Integrado Turístico Estruturante de Base Regional (PITER) para a Região do Parque Nacional da Penêda-Gerês'), Parque Nacional da Penêda-Gerês (PNPG), Associação de Desenvolvimento das Regiões do Parque Nacional da Penêda-Gerês (ADERE-PG), Braga.

Inskeep, E. (1991) Tourism Planning: An Integrated and Sustainable Development Approach. New York: Van Nostrand Reinhold.

Kastenholz, E. (2000) Rural Tourism in North Portugal (O Mercado do Turismo em Espaço Rural no Norte de Portugal–Relatório Final). Porto: ISEE/ CCRN.

Mathieson, A. and Wall, G. (1982) Tourism: Economic, Physical and Social Impacts. Harlow: Longman.

Mill, R. C. and Morrison, A. M. (1985) The Tourism System: An Introductory Text. New Jersey: Prentice Hall.

Pina, P. (1988) Portugal: Tourism in the Twentieth Century (Portugal: O Turismo no Século XX). Lisbon: Lucidus.

Porter, M. (1994) *Building the Competitive Advantages for Portugal* (*Construir as Vantagens Competitivas de Portugal*). Lisbon: Monitor Company.
WTO (2000) 'Tourism satellite account', Madrid: WTO.

248
_____

14 Ecotourism Planning Considerations in Eastern Central Europe

Colin Johnson

The four main objectives of this chapter are to:

• Introduce the development of tourism in Eastern Central Europe (ECE)
• Assess the current ecotourism practices in the region
• Evaluate the application of ecotourism projects in the ECE
• Examine the concept of biosphere reserves with examples of three countries

Introduction

Eastern Central Europe has emerged over the years as an important tourism region. Although there are different geographical groupings described as 'Eastern Central Europe', this chapter uses Kostecki's (1994) definition of the region as including Hungary, Poland and the Czech and Slovak Republics, together with another country that has a border with the west, Slovenia. These five countries are at a comparable stage of economic transformation, are all seeking speedy integration into the European Union and constitute the study region.

Looking at the area of ecotourism, there are similarly different definitions and uses of the term 'ecotourism', the two-tier definition from the World Tourism Organization (WTO, 2002) is considered the most appropriate here:

1. Nature tourism is a form of tourism in which the main motivation of the tourist is the observation and appreciation of nature.
2. Ecotourism a form of tourism with the following characteristics:
   1. All nature-based forms of tourism in which the main motivation of the tourists is the observation and appreciation of nature as well as the traditional cultures prevailing in natural areas.
   2. It contains educational and interpretation features.
3. It is generally but not exclusively organised for small groups by specialised and small, locally owned businesses. Foreign operators of varying sizes also organize, operate and/or market ecotourism tours, generally for small groups.

4. It minimises negative impacts upon the natural and socio-cultural environment.
5. It supports the protection of natural areas by:
   i. generating economic benefits for host communities, organizations and authorities that are responsible for conserving natural areas;
   ii. creating jobs and income opportunities for local communities; and
   iii. Increasing awareness, both among locals and tourists, of the need to conserve natural and cultural assets. (WTO, 2002: 4–5)

The chapter is structured into three main sections. The first describes the major issues relating to the development of tourism in the region; the second discusses specific factors relating to sustainability and tourism policies, the third section gives examples of ecotourism practices in selected biosphere reserves.

General tourism development

In terms of international arrivals, Europe, although losing market share, is still the main tourist destination worldwide (WTO, 2001). Within Europe there are, however, important regional differences in terms of international arrivals (see Table 14.1).

Table 14.1 International tourist arrivals in Europe by sub-region (millions), 1990–1998

Year	Northern Europe	Western Europe	Central/East Europe	Southern Europe	East Med. Europe	Total
1990	29.1	113.8	43.8	88.6	7.4	282.7
1995	37.6	116.7	78.9	93.7	11.4	338.4
1998	43.9	161.4	83.4	111.9	13.1	383.8
Average annual growth rate						
1990–1995	5.3	0.5	12.5	1.1	9.0	3.7
1995–1998	5.2	4.0	1.9	6.1	4.8	4.3
1990–1998	5.3	1.8	8.4	3.0	7.4	3.9

(Source: WTO, 2000)

As the table shows, there are wide variations in growth rates. Although in absolute terms western Europe is still dominant, there are stronger growth increases in all other areas. Specifically, it can be seen that the market share of Eastern Central Europe, within European tourist arrivals as a whole, rises from 15.5% in 1990 to 24.1% in 1996, although, due mainly to the Kosovo crisis, this had dropped back in 1999 to 21.4% (WTO, 2000).

Development and peculiarities of tourism in Eastern Central Europe

The momentous events of the 1980s, from the unfurling of the banners of Solidarity in Poland to the velvet revolution in Prague and the fall of the Berlin Wall, resulting in the collapse of communism in the former centrally planned economies of Eastern Central Europe, are common knowledge. One of the major consequences for tourism was the re-evaluation of the its role within the economies in the region. Governments became more aware of the value of travel and tourism in generating hard currency earnings and in creating employment and investment opportunities. For the whole of the Eastern Central Europe (not merely the five countries designated in the introduction) in 2002 the travel and tourism industry is forecast to generate US$109.3 billion of economic activity. It is estimated this will grow to US$265.6 billion by 2012. Travel and tourism is also an important employer, responsible for 10.3% of the total workforce, which is expected to grow to 13.3% over the same period (World Travel and Tourism Council/WTTC, 2002).

The key difference between tourism in western Europe and in Eastern Central Europe was the importance of the Marxist ideological legacy, which considered the service sector, and therefore tourism as a whole, as 'non-productive', and so relatively unimportant among the economic priorities of national governments (Hall, 1992; Williams and Balaz, 2000). The main role of tourism was to rejuvenate the workforce and to provide collective holiday and recreation facilities, especially for trade union members. The result was a vast network of vacation centres, often of considerable size but of low quality. Owing to strict visa regulations high levels of security, regimented tours and restrictive currency regulations (Business Central Europe, July/August 1993), the region was not considered particularly attractive to foreign tourists. Consequently in 1987 only 3% of international arrivals to Eastern Central Europe came from outside the continent and over 60% from within that region (Hall, 1999). There were also severe limitations on the local population who might wish to travel outside the Comecon states, while western visitors were often regarded with deep suspicion. With the exception of business trips or visiting friends and relatives (VFR), western visitors were 'welcomed' only as part of an organized group (Kerpal, 1990).

As a result, perhaps ironically for the safeguarding of the natural environment, the region missed the opportunity of providing mass holidays in the 1970s (Hall, 1991), which were subsequently exploited by Mediterranean destinations such as Spain and Greece.

Towards the late 1970s and early 1980s, there was a reassessment of the role of tourism, however, and governments began to realize its potential, especially in earning foreign exchange. The priorities of the XVth Communist Party Meeting in Czechoslovakia in 1981, for example, set out the following aims for tourism:

1 development of mass sport and tourist activities, with the aim of regenerating the labour force
2 promotion of friendship between nations
3 generation of foreign exchange, particularly in the spa and transit tourism sectors
4 improved utilization of hotel, restaurant and spa facilities
5 development of more sophisticated tourism services (Williams and Balaz, 2000: 21).

It is evident from the list, therefore, that tourism was beginning to be seen in a more positive light and that the government had recognized the importance not only of the domestic market, but also of the different niches which had already proved popular with foreign tourists. There was already an awareness of the need to upgrade quality. Also evident in point 1 was the emphasis on transporting large numbers of tourists, through 'mass' activities.

Despite the role that tourism has played in restructuring the economies of Eastern Central Europe, there are few explanatory models for tourism development in the region (Hall, 1998b; Williams and Balaz, 2002). Tourism was identified as an attractive sector for investment and development very quickly after the fall of the Berlin Wall (Franck, 1990; Harrop, 1994) with a wide range of natural and cultural attractions that were in many ways superior to those of western Europe (Hall, 1995). Eastern Central Europe did indeed have vast areas of untouched natural countryside, some countries having well-established, well-organized structures for the management of tourism (Williams and Balaz, 2000), albeit within the communist framework.

In the early 1990s construction companies predicted that the first move in the rebuilding of eastern Europe would take place in tourism and services. It was noted at the time that Czechoslovakia possessed all the attractions of neighboring Austria, but that Austria derived 150 times more revenue from them. The journey to a market economy was evidently not going to be easy for tourism and hotel enterprises, however. On the one hand there were still frequent examples of extreme bureaucracy, backward technology, obsolete equipment and under-utilized maintenance and service departments and, on the other, there was an urgent need to develop a more effective framework for market regulation (Williams and Balaz, 2000). Quality control in the area is still often outmoded and there are major skills shortages, especially at the senior management level, in marketing, finance and change management.

As well as disadvantages, however, there are also significant advantages for international enterprises of doing business in Eastern Central Europe, which include prospects of strong economic growth, a well-educated and relatively

cheap labour force, proximity to the major tourist-generating markets of western Europe (important also in terms of cultural affinity), combined with policies
from national governments to attract foreign direct investment (Johnson and
Kunz, 1995; TTI, 2000). Finally, tourism is an excellent mechanism for the
development of small and medium sized enterprises, allowing easy access to
many thousands of the working population, as shown by Szivas and Riley
(1999), either working in the industry traditionally or switching to it from other
sectors (Hall, 1999). It could also have a significant role to play in establishing
a more equitable role for women, especially within rural society.

Changes in supply and demand in the tourism industry in Eastern Central Europe

While there have been monumental changes in the tourism industry in the area,
growth has been uneven and although the WTO (2000) and WTTC (2001)
forecast growth above the European average, the rate of growth has varied
significantly from country to country. Tourism does now play an increasingly
important role in the economies of the region and six countries receive over $1
billion per annum from tourist revenues (Hall, 1999). In 1985 there were 36
million tourist arrivals, which doubled within a decade, and which are forecast
to grow six-fold from the original figure by 2020 (Paci, 1995; WTO, 2000). It was
estimated that by 2020 one tourist in every three coming to Europe would
choose a central or eastern European destination and average annual growth in
the region would be 4.4%, 1.3% above that of Europe as a whole (TTI, 2000).

Reasons for these upbeat forecasts include both internal developments,
such as major economic growth in GDPs, together with increased disposable
income and less restrictive regulatory controls, with the easing of entry, exit and
currency regulations and the mobility of many eastern Europeans themselves,
thereby stimulating domestic demand for tourism products. Externally, there
has been increasing western involvement in aspects of tourism development,
including improvements to infrastructure and financial support, often through
the European Union (EU).

International arrivals in ECE

Table 14.2 shows the evolution and projections of tourist arrivals in Eastern
Central European countries from 1988.

As shown in the table, while there is strong growth in Poland, the Czech
Republic and Hungary, international tourism in the region started from an

Table 14.2 Tourist arrivals in Eastern Central Europe (thousands) 1988–2004

	1988	1989	1991	1993	1995	1997	1999	2004	%growth 1999/ 2004
Czech Republic		7079	7565	11,500	16,500	17,400	16,410	17,435	6.2
Hungary	10,563	14,490	21,860	22,804	20,690	17,248	18,357	18,727	2
Poland	2495	3293	11,350	16,930	19,215	19,514	17,940	18,647	3.9
Slovakia		957	623	653	903	808	942	1280	35.9
Slovenia			250	624	732	974	884	n.k.	

(Source: Euromonitor 1995, 2000; WTO, 2000)

extremely low base; additionally, the figures should be regarded with some caution, as arrivals contain a significant number of low-spending day trippers/ excursionists, especially from other Eastern Central European countries,[1] as well as cross-border traders and local cross-border customers for many services ranging from medical care to prostitution, reflecting differences (and availability) of goods and services across borders (Hall, 1995). Despite these caveats, however, progress is impressive. By 1994 Hungary, Poland and the Czech Republic were in the top ten rankings of the WTO, in 4th, 7th and 8th positions respectively. The change was the most dramatic for Poland, which had been ranked 16th in 1984.

Tourist receipts

Table 14.3 shows the details of receipts obtained from tourism by country.

Table 14.3 International tourism receipts (excluding international transport, US$ million)

	1988	1989	1991	1993	1995	1997	1999	2004	%growth 1999/ 2004
Czech Republic	608	492	714	1559	2875	3700	4121	4292	4.1
Hungary	532	542	1002	1181	1723	2570	2936	3945	34.3
Poland	206	202	2800	4400	6600	8700	8185	8739	6.8
Slovakia		89	135	390	620	535	714	836	2.9
Slovenia			275	734	1082	1275	1005		

(Source: Euromonitor 1995, 2000; WTO, 2000)

As seen in this table, the three major tourism markets of Hungary, the Czech Republic and Poland record the most impressive growth in tourism receipts during this period. The first two both increased them by a factor of

[1] For example, in Poland the average daily spend of Czech and Slovakian tourists in 2001 was US$12 and US$13 respectively. (Polish Tourism Institute (*www.intur.com.pl/itenglish/expendit*). Data obtained 22.01.02.)

seven, while in comparison with 1988 Poland does so by a factor of 42. Again at a much lower overall level, Slovakia and Slovenia have nine times and 3.6 times more revenues, respectively. Also of note is that, despite relative stagnation in terms of tourist arrivals, within the last five years Slovakia and Slovenia had both managed to increase their receipts.

However, as with Table 14.2, Table 14.3 should be interpreted with some caution. Eastern Central Europe still lags behind the rest of Europe in terms of per capita levels of tourism income generated. Although the region takes 25% of all European arrivals, it receives only one-eighth of the revenues (WTO, 1999).

Another equally important trend is the potential of the domestic market, as discussed in the next section.

Domestic tourism in Eastern Central Europe

For many years it has been a criticism of international tourism circles that there is no domestic demand in Eastern Central Europe. However, closer examination of the data reveals that there are considerable intercountry differences, as shown in Figure 14.1.

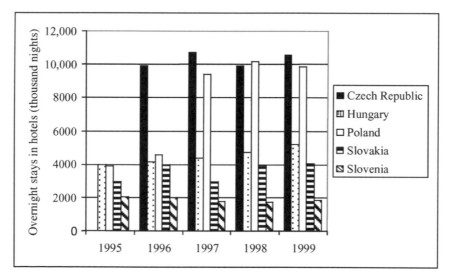

Figure 14.1 Trends in domestic tourism by country, 1995–1999

Evident from Figure 14.1 is the large share of Hungary's participation in domestic tourism, more than five times greater than that of the Czech Republic, which has a slightly larger population. Also clear is the major increase in Polish domestic tourism, with over 2.5 times the number of overnight stays in hotels in five years.

Image of ECE

The image of Eastern Central Europe is still associated with widespread environmental pollution, especially as a result of manufacturing and 'smoke stack industries', which have caused massive degradation of air and water and soil quality. While large areas, such as the summer holiday camps around Lake Balaton, in Hungary, were transformed under unimaginative socialist schemes, the region as a whole was in reality under-urbanized by western European standards. There are indeed wide tracts of unspoilt countryside, for example, in the West Transdanubian region in Hungary, which has remained unspoilt and undeveloped owing to the tightly controlled frontier between Austria and Hungary when there was an Iron Curtain. Additionally, in many countries a large proportion of the population still lives and works in rural areas.

Management considerations: an assessment perspective

Since the political transition and reforms of the late 1980s, environmental and sustainable practices in Eastern Central Europe have been given greater attention (Staddon, 1999) in parallel with the increased global awareness of sustainability issues (Hall, 1992; Smeral, 1993; Hall and Kinnaird, 1994; Yarnal, 1995; Fletcher and Cooper, 1996; Hall, 1998a; Diamantis and Johnson, 2003).

National decision-making structures and instruments

In assessing national decision-making structures and national instruments and programmes in the region, there are two indicators which reflect progress made towards sustainability and which show it in a generally positive light.

National decision-making structures

A survey shows that most of the countries do have 'national sustainable development coordination bodies' or are in the process of creating them. Similarly, countries score positively on other indicators, except in the case of the Local Regional Agenda 21 (WTTC, 1999; see Table 14.4).

Table 14.4 National decision-making structure with regards to sustainability

Country	National sustainable development coordination body	National sustainable development policy	National Agenda 21	Local Regional Agenda 21	Environmental impact assessment law
Bulgaria	In progress	In progress	In progress	Yes	Yes
Czech Republic	Yes	Yes	Yes	Yes	Yes
Federal Republic of Yugoslavia	No	No	Yes	No	Yes
Hungary	Yes	Yes	Yes	Yes	Yes
Poland	Yes	Yes	Yes	Few	Yes
Romania	Yes	Yes	In progress	No	Yes
Slovenia	Yes	No	Yes	No	Yes

(Source: WTTC, 1999)

257

Strategies and policies

With respect to the policies and strategies, the picture is rather more mixed (see Table 14.5). Most of the countries do have environmental educational systems in schools, as well as eco-labelling and recycle/reuse programmes, but at the other end of the performance scale, environmental indicator programmes and green accounting practices are not generally applied (WTTC, 1999).

Given this positive performance at the national level, the issue is the extent to which awareness of the need for sustainability has permeated to local levels of operation. Albeit on a somewhat anecdotal level, selected ecotourism projects illustrate progress made in the region, especially in the biosphere reserves.

Table 14.5 National instruments and programmes with regards to sustainability

Country	Environmental education in schools	Environmental indicators programme	Eco-label regulation	Recycle/reuse programme	Green accounting programme
Bulgaria	No	No	Yes	Yes	No
Czech Rep	Yes	Yes	No	No	No
Federal Rep of Yugoslavia	No	No	Yes	Yes	No
Hungary	Yes	No	Yes	Yes	No
Poland	Yes	In progress	In progress	Yes	No
Romania	Yes	No	No	Yes	No
Slovenia	No	In progress	Yes	Partial	No

(Source: WTTC, 1999)

Focus on biosphere reserves

Biosphere reserves are a special type of conservation area, which were created with the aim of achieving a sustainable balance between conserving biological diversity, promoting economic development and maintaining associated cultural values (UNESCO, 1996; Diamantis and Johnson, 2003). The remainder of this case study will examine the state of the environmental practices at biosphere reserves in Hungary and the Czech Republic where sustainable practices have been proposed.

Aggtelek biosphere reserve, Hungary

The *Aggtelek*, occupying 19,247 hectares in the northern part of Hungary (see Figure 14.2), was declared a biosphere reserve in 1979. Approximately two-thirds of it is covered by forest, while the remainder is attributed to other natural uses, such as grasslands (Toth, 1998; Diamantis and Johnson, 2003).

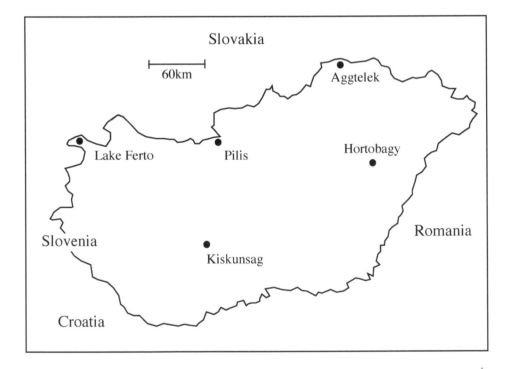

Figure 14.2 Biosphere reserves in Hungary

There are two main villages (Aggtelek and Josvafo) inside the biosphere reserve and 18 adjoining villages. The cultivated areas include croplands, old orchards and vineyards and tend to form an ecological buffer around the more urbanized section of the villages. One of the key problems in the Aggtelek reserve was the decline of traditional agricultural landuse, combined with a decline in the population. In particular, the following weaknesses were observed (Toth, 1998) for this region:

- The population has a disproportionately high number of elderly people.
- Economic circumstances have become more limited in the rural regions.
- The traditional source of income (i.e. agriculture) has become less viable.
- A high percentage of the cultivated area has been abandoned.
- The level of healthcare, education and other public services has declined.

One of the main challenges faced by the biosphere reserve was to preserve the traditional landuse patterns by maintaining the balance between natural areas and cultivated lands. In this respect, a management programme was formulated (Toth, 1998) with the following objectives:

- preservation of the so-called harmonic landscape
- preservation of diversity among both the human population and natural species
- involvement of the local population at all levels of the management programme
- development of partnerships among the communities
- preservation of the cultural heritage through promotion of traditional handicrafts
- promotion of rural tourism in the region.

Each of these objectives was divided into three different planning levels, especially in the case of nature conservation, community development and tourism. Regarding the last, emphasis was placed on the infrastructure of rural tourism development and identifying appropriate accommodations. Results so far have indicated that local citizens are involved in the programme development and implementation, in particular through new local businesses such as selling traditional products. In addition, the biosphere reserve initiative has led to the opening of a number of guesthouses, which illustrates its positive effects.

Trebonsko biosphere reserve, the Czech Republic

The *Trebon Basin* or *Trebonsko* was declared a biosphere reserve in 1977 (Jelinkova, 1998; Diamantis and Johnson, 2003). It occupies an area of 700 km^2 in the southern part of the Czech Republic, adjacent to the Austrian border, with a total population of approximately 25,000 (see Figure 14.3).

At the centre of the biosphere reserve is the historic town of Trebon (population 9000), where the administration of the project is located. The medieval core of the town, with its unique architecture, was declared a national monument in 1976. Trebon also has a special status as a spa town with a tradition of medical treatment using peat from local deposits.

Since 1979 the core area of the reserve has the legal status of a protected

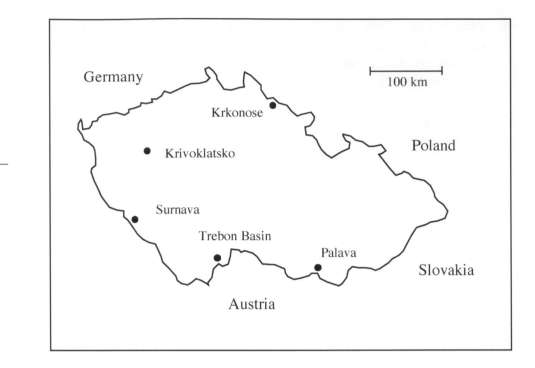

Figure 14.3 Biosphere reserves in the Czech Republic

landscape area according to Czech legislation. This region is also part of an important bird area of Europe (IBA) and incorporates 20 small-scale protected territories (nature reserves or monuments of national or regional importance). The western part of the Trebon region was also declared as a protected area of natural accumulation of water, in order to preserve the quality of its ground-water, which is accumulated in the thick sedimental strata of the Trebon Basin (Jelinkova, 1998).

Although the region is partly a man-made landscape, its natural potential and values are very high. The concentration of numerous animal and plant species living in a relatively small area is unique to this type of countryside in central Europe. Species native to both the northern tundra and to the warm continental lowlands grow in close proximity, together with other species associated with both extremely wet and extremely dry biotopes.

The most important ecosystems are protected within the core area of wetlands, fishponds, floodplains and wet meadows, as well as specific biotopes of old sand dunes, which are among the most valuable ecosystems of the reserve (Jelinkova, 1998).

Unfortunately, it suffered during the last 20 years from serious tourism development impacts and other human activities. Some of its traditional activities (agriculture, forestry and fish farming) have been practised very intensively and with modern technologies that did not respect natural ecological limits or the the carrying capacity of the landscape. Negative changes have occurred in the fragile ecosystems, such as eutrophication and loss of bio-diversity, as well as visual degradation of the countryside. In addition, the improper dumping of waste and intensive hiking by visitors have disturbed the legally protected core zone of the reserve.

Ecotourism and sustainable practices are carried out in the form of tours, mainly for the purpose of observing the flora and fauna of endemic and natural species. Adventure tours, as well as bio-gardening (the cultivation and pro-cessing of medicinal herbs and species), are also offered to visitors. Contra-riwise, no guidelines for the development of ecotourism and no frameworks have been developed for maintaining its attractions.

Owing to the increasing number of initiatives being developed in the reserve, a programme to estimate the carrying capacity of the area as a whole was initiated. The results indicate that:

- Potential tourists have no information about the tourism attractions or the facilities of the region.
- The biosphere reserve has only limited opportunities to influence the turnover of ventures operating in the area.
- There is a lack of data with regards to tourism arrivals.
- There is a lack of programmes to monitor the effects of tourism throughout the reserve.

Overall, sustainable ecotourism practice is still at the initial, planning stages. Until there is a comprehensive management framework for ecotourism, the threat of negative effects, both direct and indirect, spreading to the core zone will remain high.

An assessment of ecotourism biosphere projects in ECE

The sustainable and ecotourism practices in the biosphere reserves cited earlier have been demonstrated in different ways. Such initiatives reflect the range of perspectives and paradigms applied. Ecotourism may be practised in a con-tinuum from an active pole (actions of protecting the environment) to a passive pole (ecotourism development actions which do not create negative impacts). The priorities and objectives of ecotourism also differ considerably among authorities on the subject and may range from the welfare of the local com-munity to the sustainable management of natural resources (see Chapter 1). All ecotourism concepts, however, seem to contain three common components: a natural-based component; a sustainability component; and an educational component (Diamantis, 1999).

Within these, most ecotourism projects throughout the region are in the form of rural or nature tourism. This was a significant feature of Eastern Central European tourism even before communism, especially in Hungary, where rural tourism accounted for between 35–40% of all tourism (Suli-Zakar, 1993).

Otherwise, cross-country skiing also has potential, in contrast to its more destructive and energy- and capital-intensive Alpine cousin, classified as 'hard tourism'. The 'softer' cross-country form is far less damaging and makes good use of environmental assets (Hall, 1995).

Such developments can complement and diversify rural enterprises, transforming them into tourism and leisure SMEs offering accommodation, food, local crafts and other services (Hall, 1998a), bringing improved incomes and standards of living and the lessening of urban attractiveness and rural decline (Hall, 1995). Ecotourism is potentially a very lucrative market, when ecotourists typically spend more per capita than the package tour 'mass tourist'. It is estimated that at present, however, the ecotourist market represents only some 2–4% of all travel expenditure (Travelmole, 29.01.02). Generally speaking, in the post-communist era, certain countries (Czech Republic and Slovakia) have adopted tourism policies that have been partly laissez-faire (Williams and Balaz, 2002). Other countries have been more directive, but in all of them there are still inherent contradictions and paradoxes in terms of planning ecotourism projects, owing to the history of communist decision making and the legacy of centrally controlled planning. These include the legacy of almost half a century of centralized, top-down, civil administration, which gave local people few opportunities to experience bottom-up development or participate in meaningful decision making. There is, therefore, a connotation with collective action of the communist era. Although ecotourism stresses the importance of 'community involvement', in this context there is a distinct lack of homogeneity among communities with an ambivalence of community as a concept often with mistaken assumptions of shared values (Hall, 2000).

It should also be remembered that, somewhat paradoxically, ecology-based restrictions on such personal freedoms as hunting are seen in the light of communist impositions and are therefore often met with resistance (Hall, 2000: 449).

Implicit in the evolution of sustainability in Eastern Central Europe are the efforts made to transform the negative environmental image into policies that embody sustainable principles. Although sustainable tourism and ecotourism are emerging as important products, there still remain a number of key challenges at both national and local levels, for example, various local and national political problems that have arisen in establishing transboundary biosphere reserves.

Tourism markets in Eastern Central Europe are likely to become more polarized between the high added-value, postmodern, environmentally aware niche markets for (mainly) western tourists and the mass market demands of tourists from within the region, reminiscent of tourism development in western Europe 50 years ago (Hall, 1998a). It will not be easy to reconcile the different demands for these two kinds of market. Additionally, the notion of pristine countryside is the major attraction for most western tourists. As tourism increases, however, this will have a profound impact on the environment, as well as on the local population, who will expect improved standards of living from tourism earnings, directly or indirectly. The trend in most countries in the region has also been towards increasing urbanization (Hall, 1998b). Training and behaviours of the local communities will be extremely important and there are already signs that without effective educational programmes, rural communities are not automatically receptive to tourists (Verbole, 1995).

Furthermore, bureaucracies may still be powerful and sluggish, as in Slovakia (Williams and Balaz, 2000), and there is a desperate need for greater investment in the tourism sector in all countries. Although environmental concerns are well known, understood and promoted by various governments in the region, the emphasis on economic development means that in many cases, sustainability or ecological interests are at best in second place. Recently, however, there has been more rigorous analysis of the costs of industrial development and the expected benefits of ecotourism. Ecotourism development was seen to be more attractive not just environmentally, but also economically. A full analysis was also made of the expected revenue in the case of the large carnivores project, with revenues generated of over €315,000, over 40% of which remained in the local community (Annual Report, 2000). Although modest for a region of over 27,000 inhabitants, and one suffering from severe economic and social problems, it is nevertheless a promising beginning in providing alternative sources of employment.

It is also encouraging to see the introduction of public participation, in contrast to closed planning processes, as part of a wider restructuring and democratization process. In some instances this has been tied into environmental impact assessment (EIA) exercises, for example the use of parallel public participation (PPP) within the framework of an EIA had a significantly positive outcome on a proposed major tourism project in the Rajcherov Nature Park in southern Bohemia. This type of intervention against economic development was also successful in the case of the Romanian city of Zarneati, with the vision for its development that serves as a template for good practice:

Vision of the city of Zarneati for the year 2020

The economy of the community consists of tourism, traditional activities in the field of agroforestry, trade with local products and sustainable industry. Tourism is based on local family businesses, respecting ecological aspects, and is well organized and promoted. A landuse plan is designed, which considers the specific local architectural character and protects those zones adjacent to the nature park that have high ecological value.

Zarneati is internationally recognized for its Piatra Craiului Nature Park, for the presence of large carnivores and as an ecological sustainable model area. The local population and the visitors have a high degree of conservation education. Adopted unanimously by the Council of Zarneati, 16 December 1999. (From Carpathian Large Carnivore Project, Annual Report, 2000: 58)

The extent of the environmental challenges facing countries in the region is formidable and should not be underestimated; the Czech Republic estimates, for example, that the cost of a clean-up of 2500 polluted industrial sites would exceed US$1 billion. In the case of Poland this has been predicted to cost €30 billion, to come up to EU environmental requirements, and at current spending will take 20 years (Serafin, Tatum and Heydel, 2000).

Nevertheless, sustainability and ecotourism are now very much on the political agendas of all countries in the region, as may be seen from the examples cited in this chapter, in adopting the concept of biosphere reserves to raise awareness and to identify the challenges faced at a local level.

It is evident from the cases cited that there is already a certain level of awareness towards sustainability as well as strategies which provide a backbone to the daily management of the reserves. Although all of them are at their initial planning stages with regards to tourism, a trend shared by most is that they do not approach sustainability from an exclusively tourism perspective. For instance in the Tatras Biosphere Reserve, the sustainable and ecotourism practices are not applied to enhance the needs and and wants of the tourism industry and so do not create a so-called 'tourism-centric' situation.

One key element in the successful management of all three reserves is the development of concepts such as tourism carrying capacity and saturation levels. Due to a combination of inadequate resources, skill shortages and political indifference and in-fighting, however (Hall, 1999), declared intentions do not always translate into actual applications. A further serious hindrance in some countries (e.g. the Czech Republic) is the lack of formalized tourism strategies (TTI, 2000).

Conclusion

The inequalities that exist in the Eastern Central Europe require the adoption of very carefully planned crisis strategies and overall policies for sustainable development (Hall, 1998a). Undoubtedly, there is a base for creating ecotourism products in the region and for the tarnished image of environmental degradation to be replaced by that of unspoilt nature. There is, however, an urgent need for a harmonization of environmental regulations and agendas, all of which must be supported by training and management development programmes (Iunius and Johnson, 2000); central governmental functions and responsibilities must be better integrated with regionally based partnership schemes (Hall, 2000).

Further, the development of sustainability in tourism, and the growth of ecotourism, face a number of contradictory forces which, one way or another, have to be reconciled. These include the need for government intervention versus the desire to reduce centralized planning, spatial and environmental planning dilemmas, niche tourism versus mass tourism, increasing competition from MNEs and the role of women in the ecotourism industry. There is a need to create the right investment environment for FDI, but at the same time there are low levels of training and the natural environment may be said in some countries to be regarded by the authorities as clients were by service workers, with 'a studied indifference'. There are signs, however, that certain initiatives in the region are helping it gradually to shed this image.

Tourism has played an increasingly important role in the economies of the countries in Eastern Central Europe. As a major service industry, it has had an economic and social impact by exposing domestic enterprises to national and international market forces and encouraging FDI in tourist-related facilities. It has stimulated comparative market advantage and niche specialization and, finally, encouraged greater and closer interaction between formerly restricted host populations and the outside world (Hall, 1999: 228).

Questions

1 Discuss ecotourism practices in Eastern Central Europe.
2 Suggest four factors that destinations can use to improve their image. Pick a case from the book.
3 Undertake a SWOT analysis of the selected reserves.
4 What are the benefits of applying an ecotourism strategy in the selected biosphere reserves?

References

Business Central Europe (1993) July/August.
Diamantis, D. (1999) 'The concept of ecotourism: evolution and trends', *Current Issues in Tourism*, 2 (2/3), 93–122.
Diamantis, D. and Johnson, C. (2003) 'Ecotourism management in Europe: lessons from the biosphere reserves in Central and Eastern Europe'. In Fennell, D.A. and Dowling, R.K. (eds) *Ecotourism Policy and Planning*. Oxford: CABI, 275–92.
Euromonitor (1985, 2000) *Travel and Tourism in Eastern Europe*. London: Euromonitor.
Fletcher, J. and Cooper, C. (1996) 'Tourism strategy planning: Szolnok County, Hungary', *Annals of Tourism Research*, 23 (1), 181–200.
Franck, C. (1990) 'Tourism investment in Central and Eastern Europe: preconditions and opportunities', *Tourism Management*, December, 333–8.
Hall, D.R. (1991) *Tourism and Economic Development in Eastern Europe and the Soviet Union*. London and New York: Belhaven.
Hall, D.R. (1992) 'The challenge of international tourism in Eastern Europe', *Tourism Management*, 13, 41–44.
Hall, D.R. (1995) 'Tourism change in Central and Eastern Europe'. In Montanari, A. and Williams, A.M., *European Tourism: Regions, Spaces and Restructuring*. Chichester: John Wiley & Sons.
Hall, D.R. (1998a) 'Central and Eastern Europe: tourism, development and transformation'. In Williams, A.M. and Shaw, G. (eds) *Tourism and Economic Development*, 3rd ed. Chichester: John Wiley & Sons, 345–73.
Hall, D.R. (1998b) 'Tourism development and sustainability issues in Central and South-Eastern Europe', *Tourism Management*, 19 (5), 423–31.
Hall, D.R. (1999) 'Destination branding, niche marketing and national image projection in Central and Eastern Europe', *Journal of Vacation Marketing*, 5 (3), 227–37.

Hall, D.R. (2000) 'Tourism as sustainable development? The Albanian experience of "transition"', *International Journal of Tourism Research*, 2, 31–46.

Hall, D.R. and Kinnaird, V. (1994) 'Ecotourism in Eastern Europe'. In Cater, E. and Lowman, G. (eds) *Ecotourism: A Sustainable Option?* Chichester: John Wiley & Sons, 111–36.

Harrop, J. (1994) 'The role of tourism in the EC and prospects for Eastern Europe', *European Business Review*, 94 (2), 20–25.

Hunter, C. (1995) 'On the need to re-conceptualize sustainable tourism development', *Journal of Sustainable Tourism*, 3 (3), 155–65.

Hunter, C. (1997) 'Sustainable tourism as an adaptive paradigm', *Annals of Tourism Research*, 24 (4), 850–67.

Iunius, R. and Johnson, C. (2000) 'Romania: en route to capitalism', *International Human Resource Management in the Hospitality Industry*, 255–66.

Jelinkova, E. (1998) Science supporting local development from Czech point of view. Paper presented in the III Biosphere Reserves Coordinators Meeting, Joensuu, Finland, September.

Johnson, C.B. and Kunz, R. (1995) 'Eastern Central Europe – an opaque window of opportunity for western hospitality enterprises'. In Armistead, C. and Teare. R. (eds) *Services Management – New Directions and Perspectives*. London: Cassell.

Kerpal, E. (1990) 'Tourism potential in Eastern Europe', *EIU Travel and Tourism Analyst*, 1, 68–86.

Kostecki, M.M. (ed.) (1994) 'Strategies for global service markets'. In *Marketing Strategies for Services*. Oxford: Pergamon Press.

Kotler, P. and Armstrong, G. (1994) *Principles of Marketing for Hospitality*. Englewood Cliffs, NJ: Prentice Hall International.

Paci, E. (1995) 'Importance de tourism dans les économies des pays de l'Europe de l'Est', The Tourist Revue. The International Association of Scientific Experts in Tourism, Vol. 1, 4–10.

Serafin, R., Tatum, G. and Heydel, W. (2000) 'ISO 14001 as an opportunity for engaging SMEs in Poland's environmental reforms.' In Hilary R. (ed.) *ISO 14001, Case Studies and Practical Experiences*. Sheffield: Greenleaf.

Smeral, E. (1993) 'Emerging Eastern European tourism markets', *Tourism Management*, 14 (6), 411–18.

Staddon, C. (1999) 'Localities, natural resources and transition in Eastern Europe', *The Geographical Journal*, 165 (2), 200–208.

Suli-Zakar, I. (1993) 'The positive impact of rural tourism on the regional development of East-Hungary', *Communications from the Geographical Institute of Debrecen Lajos Kossuth University*, Hungary.

Szivas, E. and Riley, M. (1999) 'Tourism employment during economic transition', *Annals of Tourism Research*, 26 (1), 747–71.

Toth, E. (1998) Local community involvement in the management of cultural landscape in the transitional zone in Aggtelek national park and biosphere reserve. Paper presented in the III Biosphere Reserves Coordinators Meeting, Joensuu, Finland, September.

Tourism in Central and Eastern Europe (2000) London: Travel and Tourism Intelligence.

Travelmole (2002) 'Statement and briefing on Year of Ecotourism'. (Available at *http://www.travelmole.com/cgi-bin/item.cgi*.)

UNESCO (1996) *Biosphere Reserves: The Seville Strategy and the Statutory Framework of the World Network*. Paris: UNESCO.

Verbole, A. (1995) Pros and cons of Rural Tourism Development: Sustainability – A Possible Way Out. Joint ECA-ECE Symposium on Rural Tourism, 2–7 April, Galilee, Israel.

Williams, A.M. and Balaz, V. (2000) *Tourism in Transition*. London: I.B. Tauris & Co.

Williams, A.M. and Balaz, V. (2002) 'The Czech and Slovak republics: conceptual issues in the economic analysis of tourism in transition', *Tourism Management*, 23 (1), 37–45.

World Tourism Organization (1999) *Tourism: 2020 Vision Executive Summary* (updated).

World Tourism Organization (2000) *Tourism Market Trends: Europe*. Madrid: WTO.

World Tourism Organization (2001) *Compendium of Tourism Statistics*. Madrid: WTO.

World Tourism Organization (2002) *Tourism Highlights 2001*. Madrid: WTO. (Available at www.world-tourism.org.)

World Travel and Tourism Council (1999) *Millennium Vision Competitiveness Report*. London: WTTC.

World Travel and Tourism Council (2001) 'Tourism satellite accounting research: world'. (Available at *http://www.wttc.org*.)

WTTC (2002) Available at *http://www.wttc.org*.

Yarnal, B. (1995) 'Bulgaria at a crossroads', *Environment*, 37 (10), 6–15, 29–33.

15 Responsible Nature-based Tourism Planning in South Africa and the Commercialization of Kruger National Park

Anna Spenceley

The four main objectives of this chapter are to:

- Describe tourism planning policies and programmes in South Africa and how they have changed over time
- Illustrate responsible nature-based tourism (RNBT) planning through the example of Kruger National Park (KNP)
- Provide examples of how the environmental and social impacts of tourism may be assessed
- Address some of the implications of RNBT planning in South Africa

Introduction

This chapter describes how nature-based tourism planning takes place in South Africa in relation to the responsible tourism (RT) objectives laid out within the 1996 White Paper on The Development and Promotion of Tourism in South Africa (DEAT, 1996). Responsible nature-based tourism (RNBT) encompasses a number of the characteristics of ecotourism, but is less ambiguous in definition. The characteristics of RNBT incorporate (adapted from DEAT, 1996):

- a proactive approach by tourism industry partners to develop, market and manage the tourism industry in a responsible manner
- the development of environmentally based tourism activities (e.g. game viewing and diving) with responsibility to the environment (e.g. assessing environmental, social and economic impacts as a prerequisite of developing tourism; avoiding waste and overconsumption; using local resources sustainably)
- responsibility to involve the local communities that are in close proximity to the tourism

plant and attractions, through the development of meaningful economic linkages (e.g. the supply of agricultural produce to the lodges, outsourcing of laundry, etc.)

- responsibility to respect, invest in, maintain and encourage local cultures and protect them from over-commercialization and overexploitation
- responsibility of local communities to become actively involved in the tourism industry (e.g. in planning and decision making), to practise sustainable development and to ensure the safety and security of the visitors
- responsibility on the part of the tourists themselves to observe the norms and practices of South Africa, particularly with respect to the environment and culture of the country, and
- monitoring of the impacts of tourism and ensuring open disclosure of information.

This chapter focuses on the current status and implementation of RNBT planning in South Africa, in the light of the country's historically inequitable tourism development and land tenure policies that discriminated between people on the basis of race and gender.

National and provincial planning policies and programmes

National tourism policy

The 1996 Tourism White Paper set the agenda for RNBT planning and development in South Africa (DEAT, 1996). The government parastatal conservation agencies, such as South African National Parks (SANParks), are significant role players in nature-based tourism (NBT) and the government's Department for Environmental Affairs and Tourism (DEAT) defines their role in (DEAT, 1996):

- Ensuring the *protection of biological diversity* within the network of protected areas and other areas contributing towards conservation and tourism.
- Proactively integrating areas under their control into the *tourism resource base* by providing controlled access to and use of protected areas to the public and commercial operators.
- *Providing tourist facilities* and experiences in a responsible manner, where appropriate.
- Promoting the *diversity of tourism* offered within and adjacent to protected areas.
- Offering a range of tourism experiences *accessible* to the average South African.
- Facilitating and supporting the establishment of *biosphere reserves, conservancies and community-owned reserves*.
- Facilitating and supporting the establishment of *partnership tourism ventures* between communities, private operators and conservation agencies inside or adjacent to protected areas.
- *Contributing* to the development of policies and plans for the tourism industry.

Ecotourism policy and planning

South Africa does not currently have a national ecotourism plan or a national ecotourism policy. To remedy this, DEAT initiated a consultation process in 2001 to develop an ecotourism plan for South Africa. Part of the impetus to develop the ecotourism plan was the participation of South Africa at the International Year of Ecotourism Summit, hosted by the WTO and UNEP in Québec, Canada, in May 2002. It was proposed that the ecotourism plan would build on the national responsible tourism guidelines, the development of which included their fieldtesting on marine and terrestrial NBT operations (see Chapter 16) (DEAT, 2002; Spenceley et al., 2002).

Spatial tourism planning approaches

There are a number of spatial planning frameworks and programmes in South Africa that focus on NBT development, including transfrontier conservation areas (TFCAs) and strategic development initiatives (SDIs).

Transfrontier conservation areas (TFCAs)

TFCAs are described as relatively large areas encompassing one or more protected areas, which straddle frontiers between one or more countries (World Bank, 1996). TFCAs can enhance conservation potential as they provide larger areas in which greater populations of species can survive and they can provide a framework for ecosystem-based management spanning international boundaries. They can also provide stimulation for socioeconomic uplift and empowerment of marginalized, poor communities to participate in and obtain benefits from the sustainable utilization and management of wild resources (Wolmer, 2001). NBT is a key priority for proposed economic development within TFCAs and these areas have the potential to address a number of the RNBT issues outlined in the 1996 Tourism White Paper. The case study presented regarding KNP within this chapter falls within the Great Limpopo Transfrontier Park (GLTP).

Strategic development initiatives (SDIs)

SDIs are a government initiative aimed at drawing private sector investment into areas of underutilized economic potential, while promoting spatial and sectoral growth. They aim to reverse some of the economic damage that was incurred during apartheid while encouraging an export-oriented growth strategy (Kepe et al., 2001). SDIs have been used to mobilize private sector investment in parts of the country where there is a surfeit of natural beauty, landscapes and wildlife but historically little development (Koch et al., 2002). Some SDIs provide context for community control and empowerment in associated tourism projects, although there has been some concern that benefits should not be hijacked by the white-controlled tourist enterprises that currently dominate the national tourism economy (Koch et al., 1998; Mafisa, 1998; Elliffe, 1999; Rogerson, 2001). Community empowerment has been promoted through the development of community-based tourism projects (Leballo, 2000) and small, medium and micro enterprise (SMME) development among previously disadvantaged communities (Elliffe and Manning, 1996). The Lubombo SDI in KwaZulu-Natal and the Wild Coast SDI in the Eastern Cape have both included a tourism focus.

Tourism planning in conservation areas

The extent, quality and diversity of tourism infrastructure and facilities varies greatly between protected areas in South Africa. For example, there are national parks that have no accommodation facilities (e.g. Knysna National Park) while others have luxury and budget accommodation; extensive tar road networks; 4x4 routes; wilderness trails; bush barbecues; guided safari drives; swimming pools, and even golf courses and banking facilities (e.g. KNP) (Spenceley, 2001).

There is no national policy that deals specifically with the level or extent to which protected areas must be developed or how they should be conserved. This is left to the responsibility of SANParks and the Provincial Conservation Authorities. Many protected areas have management plans that utilize zoning systems to spatially plan varying degrees of tourism development. For example, KNP's master plan deals with the zonation of the park, providing for regions without any tourism activity that are to be retained for their conservation value and wilderness qualities. Meanwhile, other zones are devoted to tourism infrastructure and visitor activities. This system permits strategic management of the park to maximize its potential to capture revenue from tourism, without extending the potentially negative impacts of tourism development to all ubiquitously (ibid).

To illustrate advances in responsible nature-based tourism planning in South Africa, the following case study examines RNBT planning in SANParks in KNP.

Commercialization of nature-based tourism in Kruger National Park

Historical overview

In the past, commercial development in national parks was almost exclusively undertaken by the state and conservation agencies. The state therefore mono-polized commerce in most of the country's most valuable wildlife estate and private sector development was effectively confined to relatively small privately owned reserves (e.g. the Sabi Sands Game Reserve) (Koch et al., 2002). How-ever, since the post-apartheid democratic elections in 1994 the South African government's resources have increasingly been reallocated among many com-peting demands, with a bias towards the more immediate social needs of the electorate (SANParks, 2001a). The post-apartheid government has recognized that it should not operate commercial tourism operations itself, but that instead it should provide an enabling environment to stimulate private sector involve-ment in the tourism industry (Mahony and Van Zyl, 2001).

The basis of both the conservation *and* empowerment facets of the com-mercialization process have a historical grounding in the opinions of rural local communities. In the period between the promulgation of the National Parks Act in 1926 and the end of apartheid, SANParks perceived itself as purely respon-sible for nature conservation, rather than as a development agency for its neighbours. In the past many of South Africa's national and provincial parks were created by forcibly evicting the inhabitants and barring their access to the land. With the first multiracial democratic elections in 1994 many black com-munities assumed that the Mandela government would dismantle the parks and return their lands to them. Instead, the government decided to keep most of the parks but allowed communities to file land claims against the state, which would be adjudicated on a case-by-case basis. South Africa's post-apartheid land reform programme (see Chapter 16) has included cases where portions of the country's public wildlife estate have been conditionally transferred to people who were dispossessed under apartheid (Koch et al., 2002). Some reclaimed areas in national parks have given rural poor people access to land with sig-nificant NBT potential, but they have faced trade-offs in terms of livelihood options open to them – given their restricted access for agriculture and reset-tlement (for example, the Makuleke and Mdluli tribes, in Spenceley, 2003).

Neighbouring communities had increasingly negative perceptions towards KNP due to the law enforcement of illegal poaching and forced removals of tribal groups in order to enlarge the parks. Subsequent to the unbanning of the African National Congress (ANC) in 1990 there was scrutiny of KNP – in par-ticular by pressure groups and the media. They asked critical questions regarding why KNP had not been involved in improving livelihoods and reducing human suffering around the park (Marais, 1994). In 1993 Dr Derek Hanekom (who later became Minister of Land Affairs) accused the park of being irrelevant to an impoverished Africa and even suggested that it should be abolished to promote more productive landuses (Marais, 1996). A meeting was arranged between the top management of KNP and the media, in which SANParks invited comments regarding the public's perception of the park. The media reported to them that the park was seen as a playground for rich white people; that their employees were thought to consider animals more important than people; that it killed innocent people; and that it had chased people from their land (Marais, 1994). The following quote illustrates some of the perceptions of KNP:

> During the 60s Skukuza[1] people used to hit us and take away our curios. There was a ranger called Thyus, who used to call the police to hide in the bushes and then chase us away and hit us ... Our forefathers graves are now in Skukuza ... Skukuza destroyed our mango trees, because they wanted to stop people from knowing that anyone had lived there. (Nyongane community elders, quoted by Botha and Venter, 1994)

The severity of acrimonious feelings towards the park led to a paradigm shift within KNP and a difficult evolution from a protectionist attitude towards conservation, to a more inclusive stance out of self-preservation. For example, by the late 1980s SANParks Corporate Plan recommended that parks should (SANParks, 1998: 24):

> Establish relationships with local communities in order to encourage their participation in the provision of services which will be both socially and economically beneficial to the respective communities.

SANParks developed a social ecology unit, which aimed to develop and nurture good relationships with communities adjacent to the park, while accounting for local cultural values and resources in park development and management. The unit was to identify opportunities for commercial operations through franchising, subcontracting, developing community-driven enterprises, joint ventures, apprenticeships and employment (SANParks, 1998).

The commercialization process has also allowed SANParks to grant the private sector rights to use defined areas of land and infrastructure within national parks, in order to build and operate tourism facilities over specific time periods (SANParks, 2001a). The aim of SANParks commercialization was to increase the net revenue that commercial activities contributed towards nature conservation. Its major objectives included the application of SANPark's

---

[1] Skukuza is the main administrative centre, and also the largest tourist camp in KNP.

environmental regulations and global parameters to all concessions and the economic empowerment of formerly disadvantaged people through the promotion and provision of business opportunities to emerging entrepreneurs (and in particular, local communities adjacent to national parks) (SANParks, 2000a, 2000c). Therefore the objectives of SANParks' commercialization process fitted within the national social and environmental policy objectives of creating RNBT.

The first round of the commercialization programme took place during 2000 and 13 concessions were put out to tender in national parks. These included nine sites in KNP, two in Addo Elephant NP and in the Kalahari Gemsbok NP and one in the Golden Gate Highlands NP (SANParks, 2000a). Seven concession contracts were agreed in December 2000, which guaranteed SANParks a minimum income of R202 million[2] over a 20-year period. Three of the concessionaires were black-controlled consortia and all the others had significant percentages of shareholding by historically disadvantaged individuals (HDIs). The average percentage HDI shareholding between the concessionaires, either immediately or that was contractually bound to be in place within three years, was 53% (SANParks, 2001a).

The rights of occupation and commercial use were granted to the private sector in relation to an agreed set of obligations regarding financial terms (e.g. concession fees), environmental management, social objectives and empowerment. It was made clear that infringements of these rules would incur financial penalties and could ultimately result in termination of the contract with assets reverting to SANParks (SANParks, 2001a).

Local socioeconomic implications

The bidding criteria set out by SANParks specified the empowerment criteria that were used to evaluate offers they received.

Weighting of bids

In all, 20% of the points used to rate bids were allocated to the evaluation of empowerment plans, with the remaining 80% allocated to financial criteria (e.g. business planning and the financial offer) (SANParks, 2000a, 2001a, 2001b). Aspiring concessionaires were advised that their empowerment proposals would be weighted in relation to:

---

[2] In real net present value terms.

- shareholding by historically disadvantaged individuals or groups (HDI/HDG)[3] (40%)
- training and affirmative action in employment (20%)
- business and economic opportunities for local[4] communities (40%).

The contracts signed by successful bidders required that they would provide SANParks with annual reports that would quantifiably account for their empowerment achievements in relation to their bid objectives. SANParks reserved the right to impose financial penalties if concessionaires failed to meet their empowerment obligations and retained the option to terminate contracts (SANParks 2001b). The revenue from financial penalties were to be directed towards promoting the empowerment of HDGs living in the vicinity of the Park (SANParks, 2002). SANParks realized that not all empowerment goals might be feasible immediately and quantifiable goals with time targets were encouraged, with credit for initiatives occurring within five years (Spenceley et al., 2002).

Empowerment offers

HDI shareholding

A review of the HDI shareholdings that were proposed within the first round of the commercialization in KNP revealed proportions that ranged from 7.5% to an effective 68% (Spenceley et al., 2002). One of the bidders proposed that 26.4% of company equity would be placed within an empowerment investment trust. The aim of the trust was to enable empowerment shareholders to participate directly in establishing and managing empowerment initiatives and processes, with respect to human development, affirmative action and preferential procurement policies. It was proposed that the trust would be divided into three sections; an employee incentive trust (10.8%), a community empowerment trust (12%) and an ecotourism empowerment entity (3.6%) (ibid).

It should be noted that due to the definition of HDI utilized by SANParks, HDI shareholders were not necessarily the poor or disempowered (e.g. one shareholder was a previous government minister, while another was a director of a hotel chain) although there was a weighting favouring *local* HDIs. In other instances, shareholders were HDI staff working within the concession, while other concessionaires proposed equity for HDI community trusts or development

[3] Historically disadvantaged individuals or groups (HDI/HDG) were defined by SANParks as any organization or group where the majority ownership or membership is held by citizens of the Republic of South Africa and individuals who are citizens of the Republic of South Africa who, according to racial classification, did not have the right to vote or had restricted voting rights immediately prior to the 1994 elections.
[4] The term 'local' was not defined by SANParks. Within SANParks' guidelines for scoring the empowerment proposals 'communities adjacent to the national parks' were defined as 'historically disadvantaged individuals ordinarily resident within the economic sphere of the park'; although the range of the 'economic sphere' was not specified (SANParks, 2000b).

groups. It was also interesting that the commercialization process did not attract bids from any wholly community-owned or run tourism enterprises. It is not known to what extent this was a reflection of the lack of capacity of local communities to run a concession site; a lack of information regarding the process; a lack of interest by local community organizations and entrepreneurs; or an indication of the type of commercialization process applied by SANParks (ibid).

Training and affirmative action

In half of the eight bids put forward for concessions in KNP there were predictions that the general manager of the enterprise would be an HDI within five years. In addition, four of the bidders specified that middle management positions that would be staffed by HDIs within specific timescales. The bidders proposed a mixture of formal and informal on-the-job training for staff. Some of the training proposed was linked to established national programmes such as the Tourism Hospitality and Sport Education Training Authority's (THETA) national qualifications and the Field Guides Association of South Africa (FGASA) field guide training (Spenceley et al., 2002).

Business and economic opportunities for local communities

Four of the bidders in the first round of KNPs commercialization made quantified predictions regarding the amount of business that their operation would provide to local empowerment initiatives (Spenceley et al., 2002). These are shown in Table 15.1.

In addition, a number of the bidders detailed the empowerment and social responsibility initiatives that they would implement if they won their preferred concession. For example (ibid):

- **Food production**: One bidder proposed the development of an irrigated community garden from which they and other lodges could purchase fresh produce, if the quality and quantity were suitable. Another bidder proposed the development of a nursery and herb garden, in addition to a replanting scheme for tree species that were used to carve sculptures for tourists. Another proposal was made for a community fishing project, through which the community could obtain revenue from tourists wishing to camp and fish at a community dam.
- **Crafts**: A bidder proposed to enter a contract with a senior and disabled HDI woodcarver for branded products that would be sold at the concession enterprise.
- **Maintenance/transport**: There was a proposed joint venture company between a bidder and local community, which would service all staff transport while also maintaining buildings and roads. The company would also finance game drive vehicles and eventually take ownership of them.

- **Laundry**: One bidder proposed to develop a laundry that would provide jobs and salaries totalling around R500,000 for local community members. The laundry was proposed to be community based, with 10% of the equity held by the tribal authority.
- **Recycling**: A hopeful concessionaire entered negotiations with a national forestry company in order to set up a local recycling centre for recyclable paper and cardboard. It was proposed that waste from surrounding companies and villages would also be collected, packaged and sold.

Table 15.1 Annual anticipated revenue for proposed local community empowerment initiatives from four private sector operators bidding for KNP's concessions

Empowerment initiative	Range of revenue
Construction contract	R23,500–R3,200,000
Accommodation in local villages	R60,000–R900,000
Transport to and from lodging	R30,000–R350,000
Curios	R6,300–R240,000
Food supplies	R2,000–R300,000
Laundry services	R60,000–R200,000
Game drives	R50,000
Waste disposal	R60,000–R100,000
Maintenance	R4,800–R120,000
Catering	R160,000
Furniture	R115,000
Visits to local villages	R50,000
Recycling	R30,000
Crèche/aftercare	R20,000
Environmental education organization	R16,000
Printing	R2000
Theatre	R1500

(Source: Spenceley et al., 2002)

Environmental implications

SANParks' tender requirements heavily emphasized the sustainable use of the environment within concession areas and the most detailed criteria and targets were laid out within the environmental guidelines. Given that SANParks' primary objectives include the protection of biological diversity within the network of protected areas contributing towards conservation and tourism (DEAT, 1996) their focus is perhaps not surprising (Spenceley et al., 2002).

With respect to the conservation monitoring requirements of SANParks, the draft Concessions Operations Manual (COM) stated (SANParks, 2002: 25):

> SANParks as a statutory organisation has to comply with the National Environmental Management Act of 1998 (NEMA) as well as the Environment Conservation Act of 1989 and its regulations. This includes the Integrated Environmental Management (IEM) Procedure to guide the planning and implementation of development proposals. The Concessions had to do an Environmental Impact Assessment (EIA) for the proposed Concession developments

that included detailed Environmental Management Plan's (EMPs) for the Construction and Operational Phases on a Concession. The[re] ... is a legal agreement between the Concessionaire and DEAT which becomes the basis for monitoring compliance with the recommendations of the EIA during the Construction and Operational Phases. The EMP will form the basis of the environmental performance conditions in the Concession Contract between the Concessionaire and SANParks.

Quantifiable monitoring targets were specified for the following environmental aspects of concession sites (SANParks, 2000a, 2002c, 2002):

- *Road length*: maximum length of new road was defined in kilometres specifically for each concession area.
- *Carrying capacity*: the maximum number of beds was defined specifically for each concession area, which included both guests and staff.
- *Water consumption*: a limit of 350 litres per person, per day was specified, and water sources had to be detailed. Concessionaires were required to install and maintain water meters, which SANParks staff would consequently monitor.
- *Waste water production*: estimates of the volumes of waste water that would be produced daily were required and concessionaires were to provide SANParks with monitoring reports.
- *Waste production*: although the tenders were not required to include targets to *reduce* volumes waste annually, concessionaires submitted estimates of the *volumes* of waste that were likely to be produced, in addition to detailing proposed methods of disposal. Concessionaires were not permitted to create landfill sites within KNP.
- *Game drives and sightings*: The maximum distance that guests could venture from vehicles during a game drive was set at 50 metres, while the minimum approach distance to Big-5 wildlife[5] was 40 metres. Maximum drive speeds of 25 km/h were set on field tracks, with 40 km/h permitted on gravel roads.[6]
- *Monitoring*: SANParks retained the right to access concession areas and monitor the environment.

Each concessionaire was required to employ an environmental control officer (ECO) on their staff who would monitor and report on environmental impacts during construction and operation of the tourism development. Stiff penalties were specified, of R10,000 for every occurrence of non-compliance with the environmental regulations laid out in the concession contract, in addition to the potential for decreasing guest capacity at the camp (e.g. in relation to water consumption) or potential termination of the contract (Spenceley et al., 2002).

---

[5] The 'Big-5' is a term used to describe elephant, rhino, buffalo, lion and leopard.
[6] These quantitative figures were still in draft when this report was compiled and therefore may be different in the final version of the concession operations manual.

Conclusion

South African RNBT policies and programmes coupled with the recent responsible SANParks' commercialization process provide a very positive basis for sustainable development. The success of the implementation of socioeconomic and environmentally sensitive activities by the private sector within national parks will depend on the effectiveness of SANParks' monitoring and penalty application. At the time of writing, the monitoring had not yet taken place within KNP and the assessment framework is still in the process of development. Within a recent review of SANParks' commercialization, it was recommended that to enhance the likelihood of sustainable NBT, SANParks should (Spenceley et al., 2002):

- Pilot test their frameworks and monitoring methods (e.g. on non-private sector-run SANParks' camps). This would determine whether they were practical to apply; would produce comparable data; would report on all contractual requirements; would denote whether the ECOs had the skills to implement them; and would develop cost-effective assessment procedures.
- Ensure that reporting frameworks ensured explicit, unambiguous descriptions of data required to ensure that comparable information was collected.
- Provide training courses for ECOs and concession managers in monitoring and reporting.
- Provide each concessionaire with a specific definition of 'local' or allow concessionaires to devise their own.
- Introduce more performance and process targets and benchmarks where feasible (for example, in relation to electricity consumption).
- Create capacity and mechanisms for 'local' communities to report on concessionaire performance in terms of empowerment.
- Address the definition of HDI and report on whether HDI's shareholders and staff were marginalized, poor people.
- Produce a mechanism to determine whether the social costs of developments had been outweighed by social benefits.
- Provide incentives for improvements in empowerment over the full 20 years of concession tenure, rather than only within the first five years of operation.
- Be flexible in terms of adapting monitoring systems and contractual requirements in terms of environmental and social requirements, in line with concession-specific constraints and opportunities.

In terms of communicating the successes and limitations of the commercialization process, it was suggested that information regarding the process of commercialization and RNBT monitoring should be disseminated to stakeholders including TFCA technical committees, provincial conservation authorities, private game reserves and other interested parties. This would promote the application of similar empowerment and environmentally sensitive practices across and within South Africa and the rest of the world (ibid). It would show that the process of commercializing state assets can be designed in order to benefit the poor, uplift impacted neighbouring communities and avoid detrimental developmental impacts within biologically valuable protected areas.

Acknowledgements

The commercialization assessment portion of this paper reports on part of a technical assistance project funded by the Rural Livelihoods Department of the UK Department for International Development (DFID) to support the development of responsible tourism guidelines with the Department of Environment and Tourism in South Africa. The Enterprise, Trade and Finance Group at the Natural Resources Institute ran the project for responsible tourism through the International Centre at the University of Greenwich. Both DFID and DEAT provided resources for this assessment. The views and opinions expressed are those of the author alone.

Thanks to Peter Fearnhead and Hector Magombe of SANParks for facilitating the review of the SANParks' commercialization and also to Dr Harold Goodwin and Bill Maynard of the International Centre for Responsible Tourism for their contributions.

Questions

1 Describe ecotourism practices in South Africa.
2 What are the pros and cons of commercialization of ecotourism in KNP?
3 Discuss how KNP can be managed and governed.
4 Apply the POLAR framework in KNP (see Chapter 6).

References

Botha, J. and Venter, A.J. (1994) Nyongane Participative Rural Appraisal Workshop Proceedings. Report prepared for the Nyongane Art Association (c/o the Kruger National Park). In Marais, C. (1996) Kruger National Park: Managing for the Future: Integrating the Goals of Conservation and the Development of Neighbouring Communities. Unpublished report.

DEAT (1996) *The Development and Promotion of Tourism in South Africa*, White Paper, Department of Environmental Affairs and Tourism, Government of South Africa.

DEAT (2002) *Guidelines for Responsible Tourism*, Department for Environmental Affairs and Tourism, Government of South Africa.

Elliffe, S. (1999) Guidelines for the release/development of dormant state or community assets for ecotourism development in the context of community involvement, land issues and environmental requirements. Unpublished paper presented at the Community Public Private Partnerships Conference, 16–18 November, Johannesburg, cited in Rogerson, C.M. (2001).

Elliffe, S. and Manning, C. (1996) A generic framework for dealing with empowerment and SMME development in relation to potential opportunities at Dewsa/Cwebe/Nqabara, Mkambati and Coffee Bay. Unpublished paper, the South African Spatial Development Initiatives Programme, Midrand, cited in Rogerson, C.M. (2001).

Kepe, T., Ntsebeza, L. and Pithers, L. (2001) 'Agri-tourism spatial development initiatives in South Africa: Are they enhancing rural livelihoods?' ODI Natural Resource Perspectives, No. 65, March, Overseas Development Institute.

Koch, E., de Beer, G. and Elliffe, S. (1998) 'SDIs, tourism-led growth and the empowerment of local communities in South Africa', *Development Southern Africa*, 15, 809–26.

Koch, E., Massyn, P.J. and Spenceley. A (2002) 'Africa: getting started'. In Honey, M. (ed.) *Ecotourism and Certification: Setting Standards in Practice*. New York: Island.

Leballo, M. (2000) Study of best-practice in community-based tourism initiatives in South Africa, Unpublished paper prepared for the Land and Agriculture Policy Centre, Johannesburg, cited in Rogerson, C.M. (2001).

Mafisa (1998) Culture, tourism and the spatial development initiatives: opportunities to promote investment, jobs and people's livelihoods. Unpublished report prepared for the Department of Arts, Culture, Science and Technology, Pretoria.

Mahony, K. and Van Zyl, J. (2001) Practical Strategies for Pro-poor Tourism: Case Studies of Makuleke and Manyeleti Tourism Initiatives. Report to the Overseas Development Institute. (Available at *http://www.propoortourism.co.uk*.)

Marais, C. (1994) Community Liaison. Unpublished internal report to Kruger National Park.

Marais, C. (1996) Kruger National Park: Managing for the Future: Integrating the Goals of Conservation and the Development of Neighbouring Communities. Unpublished report to Kruger National Park.

Rogerson, C.M. (2001) 'Spatial development initiatives in Southern Africa: the Maputo Development Corridor, discourse and the making of marginalised people', *Journal of Economic and Social Geography*, 92 (3), 324–46.

SANParks (1998) Corporate Plan: A Framework for Action and Transformation. Report from South African National Parks.

SANParks (2000a) Preliminary notice to investors: concession opportunities under the SANP commercialisation programme, South African National Parks, 24 May 2000. (Downloaded from *www.parks-sa.co.za/Concession%20Opportunities/noticetoinvestors.htm*, 2 August 2000.)

SANParks (2000b) Bidding memorandum for the tender of concession sites, 2nd draft, South African National Parks, 25 September 2000.

SANParks (2000c) Concession contract for the [ ] Camp in the [ ] National Park, South African National Parks, draft of 26 September 2000.

SANParks (2001a) Information memorandum on the second round of concession opportunities, South African National Parks, 6 April 2001.

SANParks (2001b) Bidding memorandum (revised) for the tender of restaurant and retail facilities, South African National Parks, 30 June 2001.

SANParks (2002) Concessions operations manual, draft, 6 March 2002.

Spenceley, A. (2001) *Integrating biodiversity into the tourism sector: Case study of South Africa*. Report to United Nations Environment Programme – Biodiversity Planning Support Programme.

Spenceley, A. (2002) Overview report of three case studies: Pretoriuskop Camp, Jackalberry Lodge and Coral Divers. National Responsible Tourism Guidelines for the South African Tourism Sector, Application of the Guidelines to the nature-based tourism sector. Report to DFID/DEAT, March 2002 (*www.nri.org/NRET/nret.htm*).

Spenceley, A. (2003) Tourism, local livelihoods and the private sector in South Africa: case studies on the growing role of the private sector in natural resources management. Sustainable Livelihoods in South Africa Research Paper 8, Sustainable Livelihoods Southern Africa project, Institute of Development Studies, Brighton UK, February 2003 (*www.ids.ac.uk/env/slsa/index.html*).

Spenceley, A., Goodwin, H. and Maynard, W.B. (2002) Commercialisation of South African national parks and the National Responsible Tourism Guidelines. Report to DFID/SANParks, April 2002.

Wolmer, W. (2001) Transboundary natural resource management: politics, ecological integrity and economic integration in the Gaza-Kruger-Gonarezhou Transfrontier Conservation Area, SLSA Paper, October 2001, unpublished draft.

World Bank (1996) Mozambique, transfrontier conservation areas pilot and institutional strengthening project, Global Environment Facility Project Document.

16 Development of Responsible Tourism Guidelines for South Africa

Anna Spenceley, Harold Goodwin and Bill Maynard

The four main objectives of this chapter are to:

• Describe the international trend in the market demand for responsible and sustainable tourism
• Detail the socio-political context in South Africa that set the scene for developing national responsible tourism guidelines
• Explain the process by which the responsible tourism guidelines were established
• Make predictions regarding the evolution of responsible tourism through the development of industry codes of conduct and best practice, with measurable indicators and targets

Introduction

Responsible tourism emphasizes the importance of tourists, operators and people in destinations taking responsibility to make a better form of tourism. It is anticipated that in the future consumers, companies and destination communities will aspire to realize a better form of tourism and will take responsibility to achieve it (Goodwin, 2002).

This chapter describes the process by which responsible tourism guidelines (RTG) were developed for the South African tourism industry. The authors of this chapter represented the core project team that facilitated the development of the RTGs on behalf of the South African government's Department for Environmental Affairs and Tourism (DEAT), with support from the UK's Department for International Development (DFID). The RTGs were developed in South Africa and *are* South African. They reflect the particular experience of South Africa – both the place and the people who live there. The guidelines are based on some generic principles, but the details were designed through a multi-stakeholder process that took place in South Africa in order to be used there, to improve tourism, and to report transparently on progress nationally. The guidelines fit within the context of the World Tourism Organization's Global Code of Ethics on Travel and Tourism (WTO, 1997) and are designed to enable enterprises, government and consumers in South Africa to take responsibility for improving tourism and making it more sustainable.

International context for the responsible tourism guidelines

Tourism did not feature strongly on the agenda at the Rio Earth Summit in 1992. The World Tourism Organization/World Travel and Tourism Council Agenda 21 for the Travel and Tourism Industry was a plan that subsequently laid out an agenda for 'green' tourism. There have since been a series of initiatives designed to deliver environmentally sustainable tourism. Tourism was first discussed within the Commission for Sustainable Development (CSD) process at CSD7 in New York in 1999. There was considerable criticism of the heavy emphasis on the 'greening' of tourism from both developing country governments and non-governmental organizations (NGO), with a reassertion of the importance of the social and economic dimensions. DFID also launched its pro-poor tourism policy work at CSD7 (Goodwin, 1998). The focus of work shifted following CSD7 towards ways of achieving the triple bottom line of economic, social and environmental sustainability – rather than focusing primarily on the environment.

Krippendorf argued in *The Holiday Makers* (1987) that the world needed a new and less exploitative form of tourism that should be measured by its capacity to contribute to 'gross national happiness' – measured in terms of 'higher incomes, more satisfying jobs, social and cultural facilities and better housing'. Balanced tourism development had to meet the interests of both the host population *and* travellers. He argued passionately for a clear commitment to local culture and the celebration of local traditions in architecture, art, food and beverages.

Regarding the demand for responsible tourism, Tearfund commissioned research on the attitudes of UK holiday buyers on their self-assessed propensity to purchase holidays with companies holding written codes to guarantee good working conditions, protect the environment and support local charities in the tourist destination. In 2000 45% of consumers said that they would, but by 2002 when the identical question was asked, the proportion agreeing had increased to 52% (Tearfund, 2002). In the UK the Association of Independent Tour Operators (AITO), comprising some 150 independent companies, has committed to responsible tourism, with a set of responsible tourism guidelines (AITO, 2000) to which its members have committed. Since AITO members must account to the tourists who travel with them, they have an obligation to demonstrate that their ground handlers are operating in a responsible manner. A host of other independent companies have also made specific commitments. These developments in the UK and in other European travel markets (particularly Belgium, France and Germany) reflect a wider movement in the consumer market place, which range from ethical investment funds to fairly traded coffee. In South Africa, evidence from its most important originating markets (for example, the UK: SA Tourism, 2001b) is a significant factor driving increased emphasis on corporate social responsibility within the private sector.

No industry or sector works in isolation and it is important to recognize that however far one goes in identifying the links to conventions and initiatives that are clearly related to the growth of interest in the tourist sector, there are other less obvious links that bind thinking within the tourist sector to seemingly unrelated parts of the global market. It is not important here to go through the genealogy of how the Quaker movement in the 19th century influenced food policy and consumer thinking about trust and the importance of credibility in building up long-term business and market share. What it is important is to recognize that when developing guidelines, sources of information and experiences that help to build a stronger and more transparent process are not all going to come from within one sector or country. Any process to develop RT guidelines must be set within the national and international sector agenda. By breaking away from this, a singular vision of where standards may be derived, results are more robust and it is easier to see what systems might work, based on what has been shown to be practical (and more importantly *im*practical) elsewhere.

At the heart of the process of developing South Africa's RTGs has been the understanding that they must be market led and it is the perceived changes in demand that is driving adaptation in the originating markets. DEAT sought to develop specific guidance for enterprises on the implementation of the 1996 White Paper and to do so in a way that would require the industry to be specific about what had been achieved. Enterprises and entrepreneurs responding to the guidelines have called for tools to help them address the triple bottom-line issues that they face. The travel and tourism industry has sought to reduce its exposure to risk by identifying schemes that deliver clear messages, and within which they can secure commercial advantage. The imposition of RTGs without the participation and support of industry leaders in enterprises and trade associations would be pointless within a voluntary and market-driven strategy.

Enterprises in South Africa that can quantifiably report on their activities that responsibly promote triple bottom-line sustainability will secure market advantage by meeting the increasing demand for operating and demonstrating responsible business practice. Such operations can also access market advantage by advertising on responsible tourism websites, such as www.responsibletravel.com.

Framework for responsible tourism guidelines in South Africa

Historical context of South Africa

In 1948 the National Party came to power in South Africa, with a policy of race segregation and the country was alienated from the international community. A process of forced removals and the dispossession of African people under apartheid led to extreme land shortages and tenure insecurity for a major proportion of the black population (Lahiff, 2001). The unsustainable utilization of resources was a consequence of concentrating 8 million South Africans on 13% of the land area (DEAT, 1999a). Half of the population of South Africa lives under the international poverty line of US$2 per person per day and levels of poverty are highest among the black population at over 60% (ibid). People living in poor rural and urban areas experience multiple sources of deprivation including high unemployment, poor education, limited health services, few commercial opportunities, a lack of information and weak infrastructure.

In the mid-1980s and early 1990s internal dissent (including impending economic collapse and external pressure) forced change within the country (ibid). After the first South African democratic election in 1994, the Constitution of South Africa and the 1997 White Paper on South African Land Policy tackled the challenge of redressing the racial imbalance in landholding (Lahiff, 2001). Since many people were forcibly removed from land that had been used to create or expand protected areas, some reclaimed areas gave rural poor people access to land that had significant tourism potential, but there were trade-offs in terms of livelihood options, with restricted access to certain land uses (for example, agriculture: Spenceley, 2003).

White Paper on the development and promotion of tourism, 1996

The *vision* of the government's DEAT is to manage tourism in the interests of sustainable development in such a way that it contributes to the improvement of the quality of life of all South Africans (Matlou, 2001). In 1996 DEAT published the White Paper on the Development and Promotion of Tourism, which had been developed through a lengthy and inclusive public consultation process that explored the advantages and constraints of promoting tourism development.

The White Paper noted that tourism had largely been a missed opportunity for South Africa and stated that tourism planning had been inadequately resourced and funded, with inadequate environmental protection, infrastructure development and little integration of either local communities or previously neglected groups (DEAT, 1996).

The government considered that tourism could provide the nation with an 'engine of growth, capable of dynamising and rejuvenating other sectors of the economy'. This was due in part to the capacity of tourism to generate significant employment while providing considerable entrepreneurial opportunities and potential for linkages (ibid). Tourism could also bring development into rural areas (ibid) where the levels of poverty were highest. The White Paper laid out how the government perceived the roles and responsibilities of different stakeholders such as the private sector and communities. It also set out the division of labour between national, provincial and local government agencies in terms of tourism planning and development (Table 16.1).

Table 16.1 Governmental roles in tourism development

Stakeholder group	Functions
National government	• Development of integrated national tourism plans • Application of environmental management principles in landuse development proposals to facilitate sustainable use of resources • Formulation of development guidelines and regulations to facilitate sustainable and responsible development • Equitable development of destinations; promotion of community involvement • Promote the spread of responsible tourism
Provincial government	• Responsible for the formulation of tourism policies applicable to their areas • Partners in the implementation of national policies, strategies and objectives • More prominent than national government in tourism development, with the involvement of local communities, environmental management, safety and security of visitors, tourism plant development and infrastructure provision
Local government	• Responsible landuse planning and control over landuse and land allocation • Provision and maintenance of tourist services, sites and attractions • Facilitation of local community participation in the tourism industry

(Source: Adapted from DEAT, 1996)

The 1996 White Paper was foresighted in its declared commitment to develop and manage the South African tourism industry in a *responsible* and *sustainable* manner in order that the South African tourism industry would become a leader in responsible economic, social and environmental practices. It promoted key elements of (ibid):

• assessment of environmental, social and economic impacts of tourism developments

- monitoring of tourism impacts with open disclosure of information
- involvement of local communities in planning and decision making
- ensuring the involvement of communities that benefit from tourism
- maintenance and encouragement of natural, economic, social and cultural diversity
- sustainable use of local resources
- avoidance of waste and over-consumption.

Subsequently the government's Tourism in GEAR emphasized that tourism should be government led, private sector driven, community based and labour conscious (DEAT, 1997). However, the government was slow to convert the principles of the tourism White Paper into a formal system that could monitor and reward sustainable tourism practices. There have been some initiatives developed to address tourism-grading systems in relation to consistency in hospitality levels of quality, health and safety standards, as well as some ethical environmental and social standards. Some of the larger private sector tourism establishments subscribed to international certification programmes such as Green Globe 21 and ISO 14001-based programmes, but few applied for such certification (Koch et al., 2002).

A summary of the South African tourism industry can be seen in Box 16.1.

Box 16.1 Summary of the tourism industry in South Africa

The tourism sector is the fourth largest generator of foreign exchange in South Africa and lies third, after manufacturing (24.4%) and mining and quarrying (8.6%), in its contribution to the economy at 8.2%. Although South Africa attracted just 0.9% of the total world tourism arrivals internationally in 1998 it represents the economic sector of most significant growth in the country (DEAT, 1999b). Predictions from the World Travel and Tourism Council indicate that the travel and tourism industry will grow from an estimated R69.8 bn[1] industry in 1998 to R270.2 bn by 2010 (WTTC, 1998).

There was a 37% increase in foreign tourist arrivals to South Africa between 1994 and 1999 (SATOUR, 1999). During 2000 South Africa received 5.8 million visitors, of which 1.53 million were from overseas. This showed a growth of 2.7% over 1999. The UK is the top source market, which saw a 5% growth in 2000, with almost 350,000 visitors (SA Tourism, 2001b). Domestic tourism attributes around 67% of the South African tourism industry, contributing R16 bn of the R24 bn generated from the combined domestic and foreign tourism spend (SA Tourism, 2001c). Between April 2000 and May 2001 an estimated 34 million domestic trips were taken, during which 10.9 million people spent R4,520 million (SA Tourism, 2001a).

(from Spenceley, 2003)

---

[1] On 27 February 2003 £1 = R12.74; US$1 = R8.09 (www.x-rates.com).

Responsible tourism guidelines development process

The national responsible tourism guidelines were developed between 2001 and 2002 in order to provide national guidance and indicators that would enable the tourism sector to demonstrate progress towards the responsible tourism principles embodied in the 1996 White Paper. It was recognized that there would be market advantage to enterprises that could provide evidence that they were operating responsibly. In addition, companies might be able to decrease their overheads, while reducing both their environmental and social costs. The objectives of the responsible tourism guidelines were to:

- define a baseline of acceptable practice for the industry against which it could be judged
- avoid false claims of responsibility and the danger of 'greenwashing' which undermined the marketing utility of ecotourism
- achieve credibility for South African tourism internationally as a responsible tourism destination
- ensure that the guidelines were clear and accessible and would prompt action.

It was envisaged that the outputs would include both a paper document and a web-based information system, with an implementation strategy and monitoring framework. In addition, it was proposed that there would be a manual for responsible tourism available on the Internet. It was recognized from the outset that the manual would need to be regularly updated and that a web version would be more sustainable.

The process of development and the outputs is summarized in Table 16.2.

The key elements of the process just described were:

- Engaging official support from DEAT for the process of developing responsible tourism guidelines.
- Active participation by South African stakeholders.
- The development process: from the 1996 White Paper to provisional responsible tourism guidelines.
- Buy-in from tourism industry and trade associations.
- Case studies that tested application of the responsible tourism guidelines to operational tourism enterprises.
- Evaluation of SANParks' commercialization process in relation to the responsible tourism guidelines.

These six elements are now discussed separately.

Engaging official support from DEAT for the process of developing responsible tourism guidelines

The official support by DEAT for the responsible tourism guidelines development process was critical to the process. This was in terms of sourcing funding from

Table 16.2 Process of development of the responsible tourism guidelines and outputs

Timing	Activity
October 2000	• Initial identification of gaps in responsible tourism policy implementation and lack of consistency in application of sustainable tourism practices
April 2001	• Scoping workshop with representatives of DEAT, the Natural Resources Institute (NRI) and the Institute of Natural Resources (INR) • 31 attendees representing 30 institutions including government, conservation agencies, NGOs, IGOs, the tourism private sector and financing agencies • Official support from the South African Government for the process of developing national responsible tourism (RT) guidelines and endorsement to approach DfID to finance technical support for the process • Project proposal submitted to DFID (Goodwin and Maynard, 2001)
July 2001	• Funding agreed by DFID • Scoping meetings across South Africa with 39 stakeholders from 20 institutions including government, conservation agencies, NGOs, tourism private sector and financing agencies
August 2001	• Review of international best practice in sustainable and responsible tourism, including guidelines, codes of conduct and certification schemes (Spenceley, 2001b)
September 2001	• Technical working group convened to formulate a proposed guideline development process and terms of reference for South African consultants to draft the guidelines with respect to the triple bottom line • 13 participants from 8 institutions including DEAT, consultancies, financing institutions and civic society • Three South African consultants commissioned to develop draft responsible economic, social and environmental guidelines in relation to international best practice and the 1996 White Paper
October 2001	• Technical working group convened to oversee consultant progress, including UNDP and Development Bank of Southern Africa (DBSA) representatives • Consultants present draft guidelines (Elliffe, 2001; GTKF, 2001; INR, 2001) • Draft responsible tourism guidelines report produced for discussion (Spenceley, 2001c) • Workshop with the presentation of the draft guidelines • 37 attendees from 29 institutions, including government, conservation agencies, tourism trade associations, consultants, financial institutions, NGOs and civic society • Discussion of draft and potential targets/indicators of responsible tourism at the workshop • Guidelines redrafted in light of workshop discussions
November 2001	• DEAT distributed redrafted guidelines to stakeholders, including 253 individuals and 195 organizations. Comments received from 20 organizations in South Africa (10.3% sample) • Technical working group convened to develop draft indicators and targets, with representation from tourism education, community-based tourism, consultancies and World Summit company • Workshop to review consultation results, draft indicators and targets • 59 attendees representing 52 institutions including government, conservation agencies, tourism trade associations, consultants, financial institutions, NGOs and civic society • Presentation by the Open Africa Initiative on responsible tourism routes and Code for Responsible Tourism for the Wild Coast • Technical working group finalized national generic guidelines
January 2002	• Trade associations initiate development of sub-sectoral guidelines (e.g. Federated Hospitality Association of South Africa (FEDHASA); the Bed and

	Breakfast Association of South Africa (BABASA); Off Road-Tactix (4 × 4 group for Nissan); the DBSA
	• Development of methodology to test application of national RT guidelines to the nature-based tourism sub-sector, with review by representatives of SANParks and DEAT
	• Consultants commissioned to implement 3 case studies to address terrestrial and marine nature-based tourism and to practically test national targets and indicators
February 2002	• Consultants reports on case studies undertaken at Jackalberry Lodge in the Thornybush Game Reserve (Relly with Koch, 2002); Pretoriuskop Camp in Kruger National Park (Kalwa et al., 2002) and Coral Divers in Sodwana Bay (Spenceley, Roberts and Myeni, 2002)
March 2002	• Case study overview and implications report compiled (Spenceley, 2002)
	• Conference convened to present progress on trade association sub-sector guidelines (FEDHASA, BABASA, Off Road-Tactix, The Mountain Club of South Africa and the South African Boat-Based Whale Watching Association) and case study findings, with discussion of targets and indicators
	• 52 attendees representing 45 institutions including government, conservation agencies, tourism trade associations, consultants, financial institutions, tourism private sector and NGOs
	• Evaluation of commercialization of South African National Parks in relation to the responsible tourism guidelines and development of an assessment methodology (Spenceley, Goodwin and Maynard, 2002)
	• Peer review of guidelines by the World Tourism Organization
	• Provisional responsible tourism guidelines for South Africa produced (DEAT, 2002a)
May 2002	• Publication by DEAT of Guidelines for Responsible Tourism (DEAT, 2002b), with their launch by Minister of Environmental Affairs and Tourism, Valli Moosa, at the tourism Indaba in Durban.
	• Commissioning by DEAT of the development of a Manual for Responsible Tourism (Spenceley et al., 2002)

DFID to finance facilitation and technical support, and also in relation to key individuals who drove the process. Support from Moeketsi Mosola, the Chief Director of Tourism Development in DEAT,[2] was critical at the initiation of the process. DEAT was under pressure to present examples of sustainable development and poverty alleviation initiatives during the World Summit on Sustainable Development (WSSD) in August/September 2002 in Johannesburg.

Active participation by South African stakeholders

The process of development of the RT Guidelines included 27 scoping meetings, four technical working groups, three workshops, a stakeholder consultation incorporating 195 organizations and a dissemination conference. In all, 176 individuals representing 121 South African institutions participated in the development of the guidelines. They represented all sectors of the tourism industry: government (including DEAT, the Department of Arts, Culture Science

[2] He is now working at SA Tourism as Chief Operating Officer.

and Technology and the Department of Land Affairs); national and provincial conservation authorities; provincial and municipal tourism associations; tourism trade associations; the tourism private sector, community-based tourism; non-governmental organizations (NGO); civic society; committed individuals and consultants. Although there was some disappointment in the level of support from individual private sector enterprises and the hunting fraternity, their interests were represented by tourism trade associations.

The widespread and committed participation by a diversity of stakeholders, in addition to the continual support by key individuals throughout the process, was critical in providing an inclusive forum in which the unique issues of responsible tourism in South Africa could be addressed. The degree of buy-in from key stakeholders was not only critical to the development of the responsible tourism guidelines, but also vital to the continuation of the process and uptake by the tourism sector once the technical support for the development financed by DFID ceased.

Development process: from the 1996 White Paper to provisional responsible tourism guidelines

As described in Table 16.2, the guidelines were developed through a process of research, development, stakeholder consultation and review. The 1996 White Paper and the review of international best practice (Spenceley, 2001b) provided the basis for consultants to devise draft economic, social and environmental responsible tourism guidelines for discussion. Through a series of technical working groups and workshops this expertise was used to draw up a provisional set of 104 guidelines (DEAT, 2002a and b), addressing the triple bottom line of Rio in the context of South African social, economic and environmental issues and political objectives. Uniquely they create the basis for transparent, quantifiable monitoring reporting of responsible tourism practices. These provide a means of collating responsible tourism information at a regional or national level in order that DEAT can report on its progress towards implementing responsible tourism, as was envisaged in the 1996 White Paper.

Buy-in from tourism industry and trade associations

The guidelines were developed in order that marketing, trade and professional associations and geographically based groups could use the guidelines to guide the development of specific sectoral Codes of Conduct and Codes of Best Practice. It was envisaged that these codes would place commitments on association members, which the associations themselves would monitor and report annually on progress. It was not intended that associations would attempt to implement all 104 of the responsible tourism guidelines, but instead that they would select those that were most appropriate to their business, destination or sector. They would do this by proactively examining sectors in which they could showcase responsible business practice through economic, social and environment initiatives that demonstrate commitment within the specific markets operated in. Integral to the ethos of responsible business was the assumption that enterprises would comply with all relevant national legislation and regulations, in addition to addressing the principle that the 'polluter pays'.

Evidence of buy-in within the tourism industry and trade associations of South Africa came from initiatives that utilized the national responsible tourism guidelines to develop subsector codes: the Federated Hospitality Association of South Africa (FEDHASA); the Bed and Breakfast Association of South Africa (BABASA); Off Road-Tactix (4 × 4 group for Nissan); and the Development Bank of Southern Africa (DBSA), which all drafted specific guidelines for their use. In addition, FEDHASA modified an existing environmental award to create the Imvelo Responsible Tourism Award. Through a series of 22 forthcoming workshops with its private sector members, FEDHASA aimed to promote uptake of the responsible tourism guidelines and buy-in to the award. The winner of the Imvelo award, Phinda Resources Reserve, obtained considerable kudos as the winner through an award ceremony held during WSSD and subsequent media reports.

Case studies that tested application of the responsible tourism guidelines to operational tourism enterprises

Sixteen of the 104 economic, social and environmental guidelines were selected to assess application to the nature-based tourism subsector. These guidelines were highlighted for testing due to:

- their attractiveness and interest among consumers (tourists and tour operators)
- the fact that they were objectively and transparently measurable and declarable (rather than qualitative or intangible issues that were open to interpretation)
- the fact that they dealt with responsible tourism issues that could decrease costs for business and improve marketability.

The assessments were implemented using a previously prepared comparative methodological framework. This was provided to ensure consistency between the studies and the production of comparable data and reports, which would allow the performance of the operations to be transparently assessed and compared (Spenceley, 2002).

The nature-based tourism industry was chosen for the fieldtesting of the RTGs since it relied heavily on the integrity of an attractive environment to persist and occurs in rural areas, where the majority of South Africa's poor reside. The study sites were chosen to illustrate the application of the guidelines in national and provincial parks and on privately owned land within three of South Africa's provinces. They also illustrated terrestrial photographic safaris and marine scuba diving as different forms of nature-based tourism. The study sites were Jackalberry Lodge in the Thornybush Game Reserve (Relly with Koch, 2002); Pretoriuskop Camp in Kruger National Park (Kalwa et al., 2002) and Coral Divers in Sodwana Bay (Spenceley, Roberts and Myeni, 2002).

Comparison of the case studies revealed that the level of interests and participation by enterprise management staff had great implications for the level of success of the assessment. It was encouraging that the tests provided a stimulus for enterprises to consider ways in which the sustainable tourism agenda can be widened to reflect the triple bottom line rather than simply dealing with environmental issues (Spenceley, 2002).

Despite provision of a detailed methodological framework for assessment and reporting, it was also found that there were difficulties in collating comparable data across enterprises. This has implications for the collation of progress within trade associations and government in monitoring and reporting responsible tourism and clear assessment guidance would be required for future assessments. In addition, training in responsible tourism practices and evaluation would be valuable for assessors and businesses, as would the provision of a best practice manual. Such a manual would guide enterprises and assessors in designing and operating responsible tourism (Spenceley, 2002).

Evaluation of SANParks' commercialization process in relation to the RT guidelines

The application of the RTGs to the SANParks' commercialization process provided another opportunity to test the guidelines and also to determine whether the national RTGs provide a useful framework within which SANParks could manage the concessions programmed. The evaluation of the bidding process, in addition to concessionaires' empowerment and environmental proposals revealed that the commercialization process had incorporated a significant proportion of the responsible tourism guidelines. SANParks had also developed a system of applying penalties for concessionaires failing to comply with their empowerment and environmental targets, including the last resort of losing their contracts (Spenceley, Goodwin and Maynard, 2002). The commercialization of SANParks showed the use of RTGs as a planning tool. (This is discussed further in Chapter 15.)

Conclusion

For the guidelines to deliver to their full potential, the enabling framework and the market context in which they work must be supportive. In South Africa the guidelines were developed on the basis of an extensive consultation process undertaken for the earlier White Paper and they relate directly to the legislative structure that should prevail throughout the sector already. At this level they do not contradict current demands and the objective was always to make the aspirations within the stated government policy comprehendible, accessible and practical. The first purpose was relatively simple because the White Paper had gone through an extensive consultative process throughout the industry. This task has involved taking those aspirations off the shelf and making them relevant to the day-to-day running of tourism businesses. As such, the guidelines need to be of instantaneous appeal to a manager and of meaning to other members of the travel industry.

Although the aim of the guidelines has been to make them as accessible and transparent as possible they still need to go through a further iteration of simplification to make them truly applicable at field level where the impacts need to be felt. To this end, DEAT commissioned the formulation of a Manual on Responsible Tourism, in order to guide enterprises in strategies for responsible development and operation, and also mechanisms for associations to develop their own guidelines for members (Spenceley et al., 2002). The pre-WSSD conference Cape Town on Responsible Tourism in Destinations focused on the implementation of the guidelines, the manual and practical application to real commercial enterprises in the city's townships. Representatives of inbound and outbound tour operators, emerging entrepreneurs in the tourism industry, national parks, provincial conservation authorities, all spheres of government, tourism professionals, tourism authorities, NGOs and hotel groups and other tourism stakeholders, gathered together from 20 countries in Africa, North and South America, Europe and Asia to attend the conference, which culminated in the agreement of the Cape Town Declaration. At this time, Calvia (Spain) announced its intention to host the second conference on Responsible Tourism in Destinations in May 2004, in order to focus on the roles of local authorities and tour operators in working to achieve responsible tourism (Cape Town, 2002).

The future of the responsible tourism guidelines may lie in their being used as a tool for government or its appointed agency to measure the state of the industry or particular subset or individual organization against simple criteria with a common methodology, thus giving a means for comparison. In the meantime, the potential for the guidelines to be used on a voluntary basis by the private sector to police themselves is better than the likelihood of an enforced, government-regulated certification system: the 'carrot' rather than 'stick' approach.

Within the worldwide industry it is unlikely that one country's developing responsible tourism guidelines, however good they are, is going to be a powerful incentive to change behaviour. It may be that the RT guidelines are an excellent tool for those delivering the services on the ground and it will help them to identify weaknesses and improve their management, but that is not going to carry weight outside South Africa. For the system really to gain credibility in the wider marketplace it has to become a model that is picked up and replicated elsewhere, then it can become the basis for comparison and will gain greater recognition. For the authors the most satisfying means of transfer would be for operators who have interests in South Africa and elsewhere to recognize this as a useful enough tool to start applying it in other destinations.

Therefore, the wider movements within FEDHASA, AITO, the Association of British Travel Agents and the tour operators initiative to promote responsible tourism imply that the movement towards responsible tourism will gain momentum. Assuming that the issues of transparency, monitoring and reporting of activities remain central to claims of responsibility, then it is possible that the concept will progress and evolve with such synergies into the type of holiday experience that is expected and demanded by tourists globally.

Acknowledgements

This chapters reports on a technical assistance project funded by the Rural Livelihoods Department of the UK Department for International Development to support the development of responsible tourism guidelines by the Department of Environment and Tourism in South Africa. The project was run by the Enterprise, Trade and Finance Group at the Natural Resources Institute through the International Centre for Responsible Tourism, both at the University of Greenwich. DFID and DEAT provided resources for this project but the views and opinions expressed are those of the authors alone.

Thanks go to Dr Johann Kotzé, Deputy Director of DEAT, who was the national project leader and pushed the programme throughout its development through the various bureaucratic hurdles, institutional constraints and political processes within government. Also to Aphista Mataboge, for her work and support of the guidelines development process.

Questions

1 Evaluate the pros and cons of developing responsible tourism guidelines.

2 Discuss three factors that will influence the development of responsible tourism guidelines in South Africa.
3 How can the indicators discussed in Chapter 3 be applied in the South African setting?
4 Outline three factors that will determine the success of the responsible tourism guidelines in the next five years (and elaborate your answer).

References

Association of Independent Tour Operators (AITO) (2000) *Responsible Tourism Guidelines*. London: Association of Independent Tour Operators.
Cape Town (2002) The Cape Town Declaration of Responsible Tourism in Destinations, August 2002.
DEAT (1996) The Development and Promotion of Tourism in South Africa, White Paper, Department of Environmental Affairs and Tourism, Government of South Africa.
DEAT (1997) Tourism in GEAR: tourism development strategy, 1998–2000.
DEAT (1999a) The National State of the Environment Report, Department of Environmental Affairs and Tourism. (Available at www.ngo.grida.no/soesa/nsoer, updated February 2000.)
DEAT (1999b) Tourism Factsheet August 1999, Department of Environmental Affairs and Tourism. (Available at www.environment.gov.za/tourism/factsheet99/index.html.)
DEAT (2002a) National Responsible Tourism Guidelines for South Africa, Provisional Guidelines, March 2002.
DEAT (2002b) Guidelines for Responsible Tourism, Department for Environmental Affairs and Tourism, Government of South Africa.
Elliffe, S. (2001) Draft framework – Number two: Social guidelines for responsible tourism, 10 October 2001. Ballygrooby Investments & Business Solutions.
Grant Thornton Kessel Feinstein (2001) Framework for economic guidelines for sustainable tourism development, October 2001.
Goodwin, H. (1998) Sustainable Tourism and Poverty Elimination, A Discussion Paper for the Department for the Environment, Transport and the Regions and the Department for International Development, International Centre for Responsible Tourism, 7.
Goodwin, H. and Maynard, W. (2001) Rural Livelihoods and the Tourism Industry in South Africa, Proposal to DFID, 20 April 2001.
Goodwin, H. and Spenceley, A. (2001) Draft National Responsible Tourism Guidelines, DEAT.
Goodwin, H. (2002) 'The case for responsible tourism'. In *Ethical Tourism: Who Benefits?* London: Hodder & Stoughton.
Institute of Natural Resources (INR) (2001) Framework for the Environmental Guidelines for sustainable tourism, 8 September 2001 (*www.nri.org/NRET/nret.htm*).
Kalwa, R., van der Walt, W., Moreko, J. and Freitag-Ronaldson, S. (2002) Case Study Assessment of Pretoriuskop Camp, Kruger National Park, National Responsible Tourism Guidelines for the South African Tourism Sector, application of the Guidelines to the nature-based tourism sector. Report to DFID/DEAT (*www.nri.org/NRET/nret.htm*).
Koch, E., Massyn, P.J. and Spenceley, A. (2002) 'Africa: getting started'. In Honey, M. (ed.) *Ecotourism and Certification: Setting Standards in Practice*. New York: Island.
Krippendorf, J. (1987) *The Holiday Makers*. Oxford: Butterworth-Heinemann.
Lahiff, E. (2001) Land reform in South Africa: is it meeting the challenge? PLAAS Policy Brief: Debating land reform and rural development, No. 1, September 2001, Programme for Land and Agrarian Studies, School of Government, University of the Western Cape.
Matlou, P. (2001) The potential of ecotourism development and its partnership with spatial development initiatives (SDI). Seminar on Planning, Development and Management of Ecotourism in Africa, 5–6 March 2001, Regional Preparatory Meeting for the International Year of Ecotourism, 2002, Maputo, Mozambique.
Relly, P. with Koch, E. (2002) Sustainable Nature-Based Tourism Assessment Jackalberry Lodge, Thornybush Greater Game Reserve, National Responsible Tourism Guidelines for the South African Tourism Sector, application of the Guidelines to the nature-based tourism sector, Report to DFID/DEAT (*www.nri.org/NRET/nret.htm*).

SAIRR (South African Institute for Race Relations) (1998) *South Africa Survey 1997–1998*, Johannesburg, cited in DEAT (1999b).

SATOUR (1999) South African Tourism Statistics: Foreign Tourist Arrivals 1999, Tourism Factsheet 2000. (Available at www.environment.gov.za/tourism/factsheet2000/index.html.)

SA Tourism (2001a) SA Domestic travel and tourism survey, April-May 2001. (www.environment.gov.za/Documents/Audiovisual/DomesticTravelTourismSurvey, accessed on 12 January 2002.)

SA Tourism (2001b) South Africa – a destination in high demand, South African Tourism Media Release, Sandton, 16 November 2001. (http://satour.com/media/releases/messages/92.html, accessed on 12 January 2002.)

SA Tourism (2001c) New survey unlocks true value of domestic tourism, South African Tourism Media Release, Sandton, 18 September 2001. (http://satour.com/media/releases/messages/77.html, accessed on 12 January 2002.)

Seif, J.A. (2002) Facilitating market access for South Africa's disadvantaged communities through 'fair trade in tourism'. Paper prepared for Reispavilion Travel Fair, January 2002, Hanover, Germany.

Spenceley, A. (2003) Tourism, Local Livelihoods and the Private Sector in South Africa: Case studies on the growing role of the private sector in natural resources management, Sustainable Livelihoods in South Africa Research Paper 8, Sustainable Livelihoods Southern Africa project, Institute of Development Studies, Brighton UK, February 2003, (*www.ids.ac.uk/env/slsa/index.html*).

Spenceley, A. (2002) Overview report of three case studies: Pretoriuskop Camp, Jackalberry Lodge and Coral Divers. National Responsible Tourism Guidelines for the South African Tourism Sector, application of the Guidelines to the nature-based tourism sector. Report to DFID/DEAT, March 2002 (*www.nri.org/NRET/nret.htm*).

Spenceley, A., Roberts, S. and Myeni, C.M. (2002) Case Study Assessment of Coral Divers, Sodwana Bay. National Responsible Tourism Guidelines for the South African Tourism Sector, application of the Guidelines to the nature-based tourism sector. Report to DFID/DEAT. (*www.nri.org/NRET/nret.htm*).

Spenceley, A., Goodwin, H. and Maynard, W. (2002) Commercialisation of South African National Parks and the National Responsible Tourism Guidelines. Report to DFID/SANParks, April 2002.

Spenceley, A., Relly, P., Keyser, H., Warmeant, P., McKenzie, M., Mataboge, A., Norton, P., Mahlangu, S. and Seif, J. (2002) Responsible Tourism Manual for South Africa, Department for Environmental Affairs and Tourism, July 2002.

Spenceley, A. (2001a) Integrating Biodiversity into the Tourism Sector: Case Study of South Africa. Report to United Nations Environment Programme – Biodiversity Planning Support Programme.

Spenceley, A. (2001b) Development of National Responsible Tourism Guidelines and Indicators for South Africa: Literature Review: Principles, Codes, Guidelines, Indicators and Accreditation for Responsible and Sustainable Tourism. Report to the Department of Environmental Affairs and Tourism and the Department for International Development, August 2001 (*www.nri.org/NRET/nret.htm*).

Spenceley, A. (2001c) Responsible tourism guidelines for the South African Tourism Industry: Draft Guidelines for Discussion. Report to DFID/DEAT, October 2001 (*www.nri.org/NRET/nret.htm*).

Tearfund (2000) *Don't Forget Your Ethics*. London: Tearfund.

Tearfund (2002) *Worlds Apart: A Call to Responsible Global Tourism*. London: Tearfund.

WTO (1997) Global Code of Ethics for Tourism. Madrid: World Tourism Organization.

WTTC (1998) South Africa's Travel and Tourism: Economic Driver for the 21st Century. Travel and Tourism, Creating Jobs, World Travel and Tourism Council, September 1998.

Websites

www.environment.gov.za – DEAT's website, with links to the 1996 White Paper.

www.fairtourismsa.org.za – Fair Trade in Tourism South Africa.

www.fedhasa.co.za – information about the Imvelo Responsible Tourism awards.

www.theinternationalcentreofresponsibletourism.com – the Responsible Tourism Manual and guidelines, plus other information and literature on responsible tourism.

www.nri.org/NRET/nret.htm – reports from the responsible tourism guidelines development process.

www.offroadtactix.co.za – a 4 × 4 organization with responsible tourism guidelines and a manual of best practice.

www.propoortourism.org.uk – various case studies on pro-poor tourism.

www.responsibletravel.com – website advertising responsible holidays and community-based tourism enterprises.

17 Ecotourism in Thailand and Kenya: A Private Sector Perspective

Yvette Johansson and Dimitrios Diamantis

The four main objectives of this chapter are to:

- Discuss the ecotourism practices of the Lisu lodge in Northern Thailand
- Present the ecotourism practices of the Ngwesi Tourism Lodge, Laikipia District in Kenya
- Evaluate the marketing and management issues of these resorts
- Assess the economic, social and environmental impacts of these resorts

Introduction

The term ecotourism emerged in the late 1980s. Its popularity in recent years was claimed to be based on the demands of the tourist for a more unique natural environment or specialized tourism experience. Furthermore, the support from a number of government bodies, the tendency of achieving sustainable development by any means, the employment opportunities of natural areas and the shift to protected areas planning all enhance the profile of the concept (see Chapter 1).

In the late 1980s ecotourism was regarded as a small-based niche product in which it was a specialized form of nature-based or adventure tourism (Lindberg and McKercher, 1997). This niche concept changed in the early 1990s, with ecotourism becoming a popular term in terms of its definitions, application and evaluation, stemming from the viewpoint that ecotourism was a 'politically correct form of mass tourism' (Lindberg and McKercher, 1997). Much of its success nowadays is seen at the local level from small to medium sized ecotourism enterprises. To this effect, two eco resorts in Kenya and Thailand are discussed as they provide evidence of both the pros and cons of ecotourism development at the destination level. In addition, the case study sets the groundwork for what needs to be done by ecotourism operations so that they succeed in forthcoming years.

Thailand: Lisu Lodge, northern Thailand

The government in Thailand has realized the potential that ecotourism has for conserving the natural environment and has promoted ecotourism as a 'tool for biodiversity conservation and rural development' (Hvenegaard and Dearden, 2002). The principal objective of the Thai national parks is to safeguard the land in a natural condition, while offering the potential for education and leisure.

Lisu Lodge, which opened in 1992, is located 50 kilometres (30 miles) north of the city of Chiang Mai, in northern Thailand. The land has been leased from the village and is part of the Asian Oasis Collection, owned and managed by East West. The lodge resembles a typical hilltribe village home of the Lisu, one of Thailand's ethnic minorities, and consists of only six guest rooms, built in close collaboration with the Lisu villagers (Anonymous, 2002a).

The management team of Lisu Lodge works in close collaboration with the village elders to ensure the visitor experience is as authentic as possible. Seven Lisu tribe members are employed by the lodge, including the manager. Fact sheets educate guests and trained local people are engaged to act as guides in the village. Interaction between villagers and visitors is encouraged, for example, by family visits. Traditions are preserved and offered proudly to the visitors who come to stay at the lodge (Anonymous, 2002a).

The lodge provides not only employment and income to the families of the village but also serves as a role model for sustainable tourism. This is evident by the fact that Lisu Lodge has received several awards, for example, from Conservation International – Ecotourism Excellence Award 2000 for making extraordinary contributions towards preservation, social and cultural safeguarding and continuation. In 2001 Lisu Lodge received the prestigious Condé Nast *Traveler* magazine's (USA) Ecotourism Award. According to Condé Nast *Traveler*: 'This is the 5th international award for Lisu Lodge in the past 3 years. This again proves the natural world and the business world can indeed coexist and can, under the right management, even work to mutual benefit' (Karantzavelou, 2001; Anonymous 2001a).

The guests gain insights into several local diverse cultures by visiting different tribal villages. Tours and treks ranging from one to four days can be arranged elephant safaris, guided hikes, four-wheel-drive tours, mountain bike trips as well as white water rafting are other activities offered to the visitors of Lisu Lodge. A handicraft centre and shop, where villagers can display their proficiency in weaving, embroidery, silverware, jewellery and woodwork, have also been established (Anonymous, 2002a).

Management's belief is that by working closely with the hilltribes of northern Thailand this will help promote their distinctive and dynamic cultures. Also authentic ecotourism ventures like this can contribute towards the preservation of customs and traditions that might otherwise fade away as time goes by (Karantzavelou, 2001; Anonymous, 2001a; Anonymous, 2002a).

Kenya: Il Ngwesi Tourism Lodge, Laikipia District

Kenya is considered one of the global leaders in community-based ecotourism, working closely with local tribes to develop novel ways to safeguard the environment and local culture (Anonymous, 2002b).

In December 1996 Il Ngwesi Lodge opened its doors to the public, being Kenya's first community-owned and managed lodge. It is located nearby the Ngare Ndare River on the edge of the Mukogodo Hills and displays impressive panoramic views across northern Kenya (Anonymous, 2002c).

Il Ngwesi Lodge is a communally owned group ranch. A board of directors, consisting mostly of village elders representing over 6000 people, carries out the day-to-day management of the lodge and the surrounding community conservation area. This committee is elected once a year at an annual general meeting when matters such as revenue distribution, management policies and registration of new members are discussed (Anonymous, 2002d).

The lodge is constructed according to local building traditions and includes four individual double or family *bandas* (huts), accommodating up to 11 people all together. Practically all building material apart from the water pipes and showerheads comes from the land itself (Anonymous, 2002c).

The lodge employs 28 people from the local community, with 14 working in the lodge and the rest making up Il Ngwesi's ranger force, which provides security for the animals and people in the region. Profits are divided among the local community and help to support nearly 500 households as well as other group ranch operations, water supplies and cattle dips. Other improvements that have been made with the profits arising from the lodge include building schools, improving roads to attract more visitors and funding children of the community to attend university. The establishment of Il Ngwesi Lodge has meant that the prior dependence on livestock has been reduced (Anonymous, 2002e).

Visitors coming to the lodge are able to engage in a number of activities, for example, game drives, bush walks and camel rides along the river. Visits to a nearby Il Ngwesi Maasai *boma* (village) provide a special opportunity for visitors to gain an understanding of the history and traditions of the Maasai and to witness their cultural practices and daily living, including traditional hunting skills, rituals, rites and dances (Anonymous, 2002d).

In 1997, just one year after the opening of the lodge, it was awarded the British Airways' prestigious Tourism for Tomorrow Award (Anonymous, 2002d).

The community of Il Ngwesi have come to understand that wildlife is equal to tourism. A realization has set in that the local community is the key to conservation, unless wildlife can be turned into a profitable commodity the survival of the traditional lifestyle will face difficulties (Johnstone, 2001; Anonymous, 2002c; Anonymous, 2002d; Anonymous, 2002e; Anonymous, 2002f; Anonymous, 2002g).

Components of ecotourism

When identifying and analyzing the importance and effect of ecotourism one of the main areas to look into is the components of ecotourism: participation of the local community, sustainable tourism development and a learning process for visitors (see Chapter 1). These three components are also considered as the beginning of sustainability (Weaver, 2001; Anonymous, 2001b). In analyzing how the two eco-lodges conform to these components they will be looked at individually.

Participation of the local community

In order for the local community not to feel exploited and lose control over the community and situation, their involvement is a key issue. This involvement can come in several forms, however, the most important consideration is that locals are involved from the beginning of the planning and development of ecotourism. The best approach is if the control of the development is in the hands of the local community (Brandon, 1993; Wearing and Neil, 1999).

At Lisu Lodge in Thailand, this involvement is of high quality: seven members of the staff are Lisu tribe members, including the manager. Employment is also extended to several guides of Lisu origin. These employment opportunities offer an opportunity to the hilltribe to gain direct economic benefits from the visitors who come to the lodge (Karantzavelou, 2001).

Hilltribes in northern Thailand have long been restricted to outside visitors without a specific permit. As a result of this they have had to find ways to support themselves through the natural resources available. However, this 'new' open policy has made northern Thailand more accessible to all forms of travel and also the opportunity for the local communities to integrate with the overall economy of the country (Weaver, 1998). This has given the hilltribes of northern Thailand a better opportunity to gain financial advantages obtained through the increase of ecotourism.

The involvement of the local community at Il Ngwesi Lodge is complete; the lodge is the first community-owned and managed lodge of its kind in Kenya. The lodge employs 28 members of the local Maasai tribe. Seeing that the participation of the local community is as intended when it comes to ecotourism, it is clear why the lodge received the British Airway's Tourism for Tomorrow Award in 1997 (Anonymous, 2002c; Anonymous, 2002d).

Sustainable tourism development

There are different actions a management team can take in order to ensure a sustainable approach towards the development of an ecotourism lodge. Resource management, introducing carrying capacity limitations and involving all stakeholders in the planning and development process are a few examples available. Sustainability concerns not only the environment but also the culture and the traditions of the local communities so these are not forgotten as tourists move in on their communities (Gurung and De Coursey, 1994; Godfrey, 1996; Stadel, 1996).

Both Lisu Lodge in Thailand and Il Ngwesi Lodge in Kenya are very small; the former can accommodate 12 guests at any one time (six guest rooms are available) the latter 11 guests (four *bandas* or huts) (Karantzavelou, 2001; Anonymous, 2002g). The management function of resource management and carrying capacity has clearly been developed and implemented at both eco-lodges.

Providing a sustainable culture for future generations is something both lodges are working hard to achieve. Lisu Lodge has received several awards; one of them is the Conservation International – Ecotourism Excellence Award in 2000 for making extraordinary contributions concerning preservation, social and cultural safeguarding and continuation. Lisu Lodge has established a handicraft centre and shop where the hilltribe members produce and sell traditional goods, as a means of protecting their culture and traditions from being forgotten by the younger generations (Anonymous, 2002a). Both eco-lodges welcome visitors in order for them to learn more about the native culture, traditions and values. Interaction between villagers and tourists is encouraged so both can learn and benefit from one another's culture (Anonymous, 2001a). This approach works towards sustaining the culture of the native population while creating a learning process for the visitors and natives alike.

Local issues

When identifying the meaning of a learning process for visitors, both professionals and academics repeatedly mention two topics: education and interpretation (Black, 1999; Wearing and Neil, 1999; Black, 2001). It is very common for an ecotourism lodge to introduce an onsite educational programme for the visitor (Black, 2001). The education offered comes in several forms, for example, guided tours with a local guide, native family visits, environmental programmes on how the area is working towards maintaining and preserving its natural resources and booklets sent out to the visitors prior to a visit, containing information on the area, its history, the culture of the area and codes of practice (Hawkins, 1994; Lee, 1995; Black, 1999; Black, 2001).

These processes of learning to get the most effect need to include the native population as well. Before an ecotourism lodge is established the locals needs to be made aware of exactly what is included in the topic of ecotourism, what impacts are likely to be derived from having tourism coming to the area, both in positive and negative terms, and how to ensure a sustainable future for the local population in terms of natural resources, culture and traditional values (Black, 2001). All this can be achieved through a community organization programme. The two Mexican communities of San José and Alta Cimas both took part in a project regarding the impact of a community organization programme. The local inhabitants of Alta Cimas had a more in-depth knowledge of the effects of ecotourism after being involved in a programme for over two years (Walker, 1995; Addison, 1996).

Lisu Lodge offers several opportunities for visitors to be educated, which begin as the visitor arrives with a fact sheet of the lodge, the hilltribe and the culture and the environmental resources surrounding the area (Karantzavelou, 2001; Anonymous, 2001a). Through interaction between natives and visitors, learning experiences take place, as they exchange views and beliefs. This situation is the same for Il Ngwesi Lodge, where interaction is also encouraged. In both lodges the visitors are exposed to several diverse cultures through visits to neighbouring communities (Anonymous, 2002a; Anonymous 2002d; Anonymous, 2002g).

Management considerations: impacts perspective

When analyzing the effects of ecotourism on a destination, different types of impact are used to assess the consequence incurred on a community or area (see Chapter 1). A good working relationship between the local community and the planners and developers, who are usually outsiders, needs to be established. One very important point in this relationship is for the locals to raise awareness and build an understanding of what the potential benefits and costs of ecotourism are. The locals need to have this knowledge so they are able to contribute effectively in the planning process (Walker, 1995; Wood, 2002).

These potential benefits and costs are referred to as positive and negative impacts by both professionals and academics and it is not possible to indicate which of them are more important than others. There are three different types of impact, namely economic, environmental and social (Wall, 2002). For any tourism planning and development, however, especially for ecotourism, since it is usually operating in environmentally sensitive areas, is that the negative impacts are reduced while presenting economic incentives to the local community. Reducing or actually minimizing the negative impacts is the ultimate goal of ecotourism (Beeh, 1999).

One method of reducing negative impacts is by introducing different management functions such as carrying capacity limitations. Looking at the three different areas, economic, environmental and social, in general the environment accrues most damage from having visitors in the area. Therefore, it becomes very important to establish the capacity limit of all three areas and then follow the visitor number indicated by the lowest one (UNEP, 2003). By using this method, negative impacts are better controlled and the visitor experience is maintained at a high quality.

Economic impacts

Economic impacts come in different forms – direct, indirect and induced – all of which can be positive or negative in nature (Lindberg, 1996; UNEP, 2003). It is thus very important for a developer and the local community to know exactly what they can expect from having tourists coming to the area. Several areas fall under this category: employment, taxation, leakages and finance for conservation are but a few examples. The positive economic impacts ecotourism can have on a remote area are very important, as revenue gained can be used for the development of infrastructure, bettering the financial position of the local community and in the process ensuring long-term sustainability (Lindberg, 1996; Schaller, 2002).

Ecotourism operators, as mentioned in the discussion regarding marketing functions, need to find a balance between sustainability and profitability. Should an operator become too focused on profit, the likelihood is that carrying capacity limitations might be overlooked and more visitors entering the area is a possibility (Simmons, 2001; Wood, 2002). Leakages in the economy are another area that needs special attention. It becomes very important that the owner of the ecotourism lodge or resort does not take the revenue out of the area but reinvests it locally (Weaver, 1998).

Of the case studies presented, Il Ngwesi Lodge in Kenya is the one that has gained more economically, recognizably by identifying all the areas the community is able to maintain and contribute to. With the profits from the lodge the community has been able to pay for many social improvements, such as building nursery and primary schools, forming a fund for sending students to university, water maintenance and security of wildlife. Since the lodge is wholly community owned and managed, all the revenue from the lodge goes directly into the economy of the community (Johnstone, 2001; Anonymous, 2002d; Anonymous, 2002e; Anonymous, 2002g).

When Lisu Lodge received its award from Conservation International, Condé Nast *Traveller* magazine commented on the occasion, saying the Lisu Lodge was an example of how the natural and the business world can coexist to the mutual benefit of the two (Anonymous, 2002a). Ecotourism has provided an economic incentive to the country and region to maintain and preserve the natural surrounding in their existing state (Hvenegaard and Dearden, 2002).

Direct economic benefits for Lisu Lodge come in the form of employment and income to the tribe members. However, all the food for the lodge is bought locally, contributing to additional benefits for the community. The management team of the lodge is also encouraging the village to grow new crops to sell in local markets and to other hotels in the area as additional sources of income (Karantzavelou, 2001).

Environmental impacts

The environment is basically what all tourism thrives on and ecotourism is no exception; it may play an even greater role for the ecotourism operator. The environment needs to be managed properly and according to set guidelines so that no negative impacts occur, as this would undermine the whole concept of sustainability (Anonymous, 2002h). Taking into consideration the fact that ecotourism is normally concentrated on sensitive and unique environments around the world makes this even more important. Without proper management functions for protecting the environment, which is the ultimate goal of eco-tourism, sustainability will suffer, since ecotourism challenges the envir-onment's resource system (Simmons, 2001). The wildlife of areas surrounding an ecotourism operation also needs to be considered. Animals and birds are easily disturbed and it is vital to protect their natural settlements (Anonymous, 2001b; Anonymous, 2002i).

Luckily, nowadays both ecotourism operators and tourists recognize the value of sustainability and conservation. Operators are changing their business practices to support these goals and the tourists are being better educated on how to preserve the environment (The International Ecotourism Society, 2002). One very important factor when considering the growth in importance of eco-tourism: is that it is vital that all operators follow the same international guidelines. Those operators that take advantage of the environment and the natural resources available need to be made aware of the damage they may be causing for future generations.

One very positive effect of ecotourism is that it offers motivation and incentives for the preservation of natural areas and regions (Israngkura, 1996). The establishment of protected areas, such as national parks, should be something every country becomes involved in.

Both Lisu Lodge and Il Ngwesi Lodge are working towards maintaining and preserving the natural environment surrounding their areas and regions. One of the main goals of Lisu Lodge is to conserve the land in its natural state, while providing opportunities for education and recreation. This goal is in line with the primary goal of the Thai national parks. The government of Thailand has realized the importance of natural resources to the country and is striving towards preserving them (Hvenegaard and Dearden, 2002; Anonymous, 2002a). The management team of Il Ngwesi Lodge has come to the understanding that wildlife is equal to tourism. In order to protect and preserve the wildlife the Il Ngwesi community has a ranger force that ensures the safety and security of the wild animals found on the plains surrounding the community (Johnstone, 2001; Anonymous, 2002d).

Social impacts

Social and cultural impacts occur anywhere people of different cultures meet; it is not something that is exclusive to tourism (Zeppel, 1997; Honey, 1999; Rátz, 2002). The level of difference and how informed the visitors are of the host community's culture will influence how the visitors behave when they arrive at a destination. Looking at this fact it is apparent how vital it is for the visitor to be educated *prior to arriving* at a foreign destination. The impacts that occur are, however, generally not recognizable in the short term, they have long-term effects, such as changes of community norms and standards, cultural practice and social relationships. It is, in general, the older generations that recognize changes taking place within the community and once they have occurred it becomes difficult to change them back to the 'old' traditions and values of the community (Zeppel, 1997).

In areas where indigenous people live, they are commonly considered to be a main attraction. The issue of exploitation needs to be carefully handled, so the local community does not feel used but that preservation takes its place (Anton and Gines, 2002). This is one area that can be handled by involving the local community in the planning process and by educating them on the effects that tourism will have on the community. It is essential too that the negative impacts of tourism be discussed, so the local community knows the potential risks of having visitors coming to their community. Carrying capacity limitations are important here but also the ratio of visitors to the host community (Israngkura, 1996; Zeppel, 1997; Hvenegaard and Dearden, 2002). This last figure should not exceed the number of locals, otherwise negative impacts are likely to follow.

Looking at Lisu Lodge and Il Ngwesi Lodge, even though they are small communities, the visitor number at any one time is lower. By ensuring that visitors do not take over the area, it becomes easier to protect and safeguard the social structure and culture of the inhabitants. Both lodges enjoy a very rich culture, which is positively promoted and preserved through the use of eco-tourism (Anonymous, 2001a; Anonymous, 2002d). The management team of Lisu Lodge believes that genuine ecotourism can add to the continuance of customs and traditions that might otherwise fade away. In teaching visitors about the diverse cultures that exist in northern Thailand, they believe its survival is guaranteed for future generations to enjoy and learn about (Anonymous, 2002a).

Management considerations: a marketing perspective

One main argument concerning ecotourism is the two opposite poles of sustainability and profitability. All venues, in whatever industry, need a profit in order to survive and continue operations. To find a coexistence between these two functions is something ecotourism operations depend on. There is a fine line between the two, which needs to be maintained. If there is no sustainability, the natural resources will be used up and the tourism operator will move on to the next area to plan, develop and finally exploit (Wearing and Neil, 1999).

Another objective is whether to plan for short-term or long-term goals of the organization. Without planning for the future, the likelihood exists that the environment and local community will suffer (see Chapter 1). The tourism industry as a whole depends on the natural environment and the resources it has to offer and should these become degraded or extinct the world would lose a considerable part of its own heritage. It becomes increasingly important, therefore, to develop a more long-term approach and offer products and services that work with the environment in order to maintain sustainability (Eccles, 2002).

The marketing of an eco-lodge plays a vital role here; the image being promoted will influence the type of visitor attracted and the overall profitability of the operation. An operation will need to consider the different channels it uses in order to raise awareness and establish a contact with interested clients. It has been suggested by Wearing and Neil (1999) that ecotourism operators should focus their products and services on specialized travel agencies and operators. By doing this they are sure to receive only visitors who are truly interested in the environment. Placing advertisements in specialized interest magazines is another method available to the operators. The Internet is a further possibility and one which has gained credibility in the last few years (Wearing and Neil, 1999).

One of the best methods of advertising a product or service is through word of mouth (USDA, 2001). Il Ngwesi Lodge relied, very successfully, for the first year solely on marketing by word of mouth, with an average occupancy rate running at 60% (Anonymous, 2002g). One of the best methods of achieving positive word of mouth is through relationship marketing (Kotler and Andreasen, 1996). By establishing a relationship with the customer, the possibility is great that the visitor will talk to friends and relatives in their home community regarding their stay at the destination. However, one key factor of this statement is that the visitor has had a satisfactory experience, which exceeded their expectations prior to the visit. One technique of establishing a relationship with the visitor after the visit is to include them on a mailing list so visitors are kept updated on the news of the lodge. This also has the potential of raising the awareness of the destination for future visits (USDA, 2001).

It becomes increasingly important, in order to gain sustainability, that marketing takes on a supply-led approach rather than a demand-led approach (Wearing and Neil, 1999). Looking at the case studies presented it becomes obvious that the two eco-lodges have definitely taken on this approach. A supply-led approach is more common for a service industry since the operators are restricted in the number of rooms available at any one time. A demand-led approach is more the reality for the manufacturing industry given that they are able to increase of decrease production should the demand fluctuate (USDA, 2001).

Management considerations: a practitioner's perspective

There are no set standards, policies or practices as to how the running of an ecotourism lodge or resort should be undertaken. It relates largely to how the organization is set up and what its priorities are. Many countries around the world are establishing their own guidelines and practices, for example, Australia and Canada (Eagles, 1995; Office of National Tourism, 2002). Several tourism and ecotourism organizations around the world have also established guidelines and standards for ecotourism, the most well known being the International Ecotourism Society in Vermont, USA (The International Ecotourism Society, 2000). Both Thailand and Kenya have either ecotourism associations or environmental organizations dealing with tourism development: Network for Environmentally and Socially Sustainable Tourism (NESSThai) and Ecotourism Society of Kenya (ESOK) (ECoNETT, 2002; NESSThai, 2002).

Having set guidelines is considered to be a very cost-effective method of evaluating and monitoring an operation. They also have the ability to reduce visitor impacts (Blangy and Epler Wood, 1993). This should be regarded as an ongoing process by the management team in order to ensure that there are no negative impacts and, should there be, how they can be surmounted so the environment and local community is preserved and sustained (Masberg and Morales, 1999).

When the management team decides on the policies and practices they are to adhere to, it becomes important the three components of ecotourism are considered. They are a fundamental part of ecotourism and, should these not be followed, then the organization does not have 'the right' to call itself an eco-tourism operator. Local involvement is a key area to be taken into account, since with greater local involvement the benefits derived from tourism development increase significantly (Cater, 1994). This is the case for Il Ngwesi Lodge, which is wholly owned and managed by the community. Thus all benefits financial and social are to the advantage of the community as a whole. The members of the community have elected a board of directors who handle the day-to-day operations of the eco-lodge and, once a year, all members of the community gather in a formal meeting where different issues are discussed, such as revenue distribution, management policies, registration of new members and election of the management committee (Anonymous, 2002d).

There are certain other factors that need to be under management control in order to protect and conserve the area and ensure a quality experience for the visitor. Control over tourist infrastructure and development so the area does not become too 'touristy' is important (Wearing and Neil, 1999). Other areas falling under management control are carrying capacity limitations, access to the eco-lodge and resort as well as the different impacts of having visitors coming to the area (Wearing and Neil, 1999).

The management team of Lisu Lodge works very closely with the village elders in order to make sure the visitor experience is as authentic as possible. The fact that the manager is a Lisu tribe member further increases the possibility of visitors not seeing a false picture of the community and environment. One belief of the management team is that ecotourism projects, such as Lisu Lodge, managed with sensitivity and care, can be a factor in preserving and sustaining the delicate human ecology and environment (Anonymous, 2002a).

At Il Ngwesi Lodge the management team, being part of the community, has realized that wildlife is equal to tourism. The belief is that the local community is the key to conservation and unless wildlife can be turned into a profitable product the survival of the traditional lifestyle will undoubtedly face difficulties (Anonymous, 2002e).

Conclusion

The importance of ecotourism is increasing as governments and the tourism industry recognize the contribution it offers towards preservation, conservation and the ultimate goal of sustainability of the environment and its natural resources. Ecotourism, if implemented and managed properly, can generate vast benefits for the host community: increased financial position, development of infrastructure and social improvements. Thailand and Kenya are considered prominent when it comes to development of ecotourism and the two ecolodges provide evidence of how the private sector can contribute to the tourism development of a country.

Questions

1 Discuss the current eco-practices of the two resorts.
2 Suggest the objectives of a certification programme for the Lisu Lodge in northern Thailand (see also Chapter 5).
3 What are the most important risks associated with the ecotourism strategy of Ngwesi Tourism Lodge, Laikipia District in Kenya?
4 Design an ecotourism strategy for one of these resorts by using a management tool of your choice from Chapter 3.

References

Addison, L. (1996) 'An approach to community-based tourism planning in the Baffin Region, Canada's Far North'. In Harrison, L.C. and Husbands, W. (eds) *Practicing Responsible Tourism*. New York: John Wiley & Sons, 296–312.
Anonymous (2001a) 'Lisu Lodge tops list.' (Available at *http://www.bangkokpost.net*.)
Anonymous (2001b) 'What is ecotourism?' (Available at *http://www.mssrf.org.sg/aeis*.)
Anonymous (2002a) 'Lisu Lodge'. (Available at *http://www.lisulodge.com*.)
Anonymous (2002b) 'Kenya leads the way in eco-tourism'. (Available at *http://www.eco-resorts.com*.)
Anonymous (2002c) 'Il Ngwesi'. (Available at *http://responsibletravel.com*.)
Anonymous (2002d) 'Il Ngwesi Group Ranch'. (Available at *http://www.lewa.org*.)
Anonymous (2002e) 'Il Ngwesi Community Conservation – a success story?' (Available at *http://www.aeffonline.org*.)
Anonymous (2002f) 'Lewa & the community'. (Available at *http://www.lewa.org*.)
Anonymous (2002g) 'Il Ngwesi Lodge'. (Available at *http://www.lewa.org*.)
Anonymous (2002h) 'Opportunities and impacts of ecological tourism'. (Available at *http://www.tumennet.mn*.)
Anonymous (2002i) 'UN-NGLS Voices from Africa'. (Available at *http://www.unsystem.org*.)
Anton, D. and Gines, C. (2002) 'Tourism, biodiversity, and culture: toward a sustainable ecotourism strategy'. (Available at *http://www.idrc.ca*.)
Beeh, J.E. (1999) 'Adventure vs. ecotourism'. (Available at *http://www.findarticles.com*.)
Black, R. (1999) 'Ecotourism and education'. (Available at *http://lorenz.csu.edu.au*.)
Black, R. (2001) 'Ecotourism'. (Available at *http://lorenz.csu.edu.au*.)
Blangy, S. and Epler-Wood, M. (1993) 'Developing and implementing ecotourism guidelines for

wildlands and neighboring communities'. In Lindberg, K. and Hawkins, D.E. (eds) *Ecotourism: A Guide For Planners & Managers*. North Bennington, USA: The Ecotourism Society, 32–54.

Brandon, K. (1993) 'Basic steps towards encouraging local participation in nature tourism projects'. In, Lindberg K. and Hawkins, D.E. (eds) *Ecotourism: A Guide For Planners & Managers*. North Bennington, USA: The Ecotourism Society, 134–51.

Cater, E. (1994). 'Ecotourism in the third world – problems and prospects for sustainability'. In Cater, E. and Lowman, G. (eds) *Ecotourism A Sustainable Option?* Chichester: John Wiley & Sons, 69–86.

Eagles, P.F. (1995) Key issues in ecotourism management. Invited paper for State of Western Australia Annual Tourism Conference, Perth, Australia, June.

Eagles, P.F.J. (2001) 'Understanding the market for sustainable tourism'. (Available at *http://www.ecotourism.org*.)

Eccles, G. (2002) 'Marketing, sustainable development and international tourism'. (Available at *http://www.emeraldinsight.com*.)

ECoNETT (2002) 'The ecotourism society of Kenya – ESOK'. (Available at *http://www.greenglobe21.com*.)

Godfrey, K.B. (1996) 'Towards sustainability?' In Harrison, L.C. and Husbands, W. (eds) *Practicing Responsible Tourism*. New York: John Wiley & Sons, 58–79.

Gurung, C.P. and De Coursey, M. (1994) 'The Annapurna Conservation Area Project: a pioneering example of sustainable tourism?' In Cater, E. and Lowman, G. (eds) *Ecotourism a Sustainable Option?* Chichester: John Wiley & Sons, 177–94.

Hawkins, D.E. (1994) 'Ecotourism: opportunities for developing countries.' In Theobald, W. (ed.) *Global Tourism, The Next Decade*. Oxford: Butterworth-Heinemann, 261–73.

Honey, M. (1999) 'Definition of ecotourism: how to know ecotourism when you see it'. (Available at *http://www.lohasjournal.com*.)

Hvenegaard, G.T. and Dearden, P. (2002) 'Ecotourism in Northern Thailand'. (Available at *http://www.idrc.ca*.)

The International Ecotourism Society (2000) 'Ecotourism statistical fact sheet'. (Available at *http://www.ecotourism.org*.)

The International Ecotourism Society (2002) 'Environmental impacts of tourism'. (Available at *http://www.ecotourism.org*.)

Israngkura, A. (1996). 'Ecotourism'. (Available at *http://www.info.tdri.or.th*.)

Johnstone, R. (2001) 'Community conservation and tourism in Kenya'. (Available at *http://www.ecotourism.org*.)

Karantzavelou, V. (2001) 'Lisu Lodge receives Conde Nast Traveler's Ecotourism Award'. (Available at *http://www.traveldailynews.com*.)

Kotler, P. and Andreasen, A.R. (1996) *Strategic Marketing for Non-Profit Organization*. New Jersey: Prentice Hall.

Lee, M. (1995) 'Best practice ecotourism'. (Available at *http://www.isr.gov.au/sport_tourism/*.)

Lindberg, K. (1996) 'The economic impacts of ecotourism'. (Available at *http://ecotour.csu.edu.au*.)

Lindberg, K. and McKercher, B. (1997) 'Ecotourism: a critical overview', *Pacific Tourism Review*. 1 (1), 65–79.

Masberg, B.A. and Morales, N. (1999) 'A case analysis of strategies in ecotourism development', *Aquatic Ecosystem Health and Management*, 2, 289–300.

NESSThai (2002) 'Welcome to NESSThai Online'. (Available at *http://www.geocities.com*.)

Office of National Tourism (2002) 'Best practice ecotourism'. (Available at *http://www.isr.gov.au*.)

Rátz, T. (2002) 'The socio-cultural impacts of tourism'. (Available at *http://www.geocities.com*.)

Schaller, D.T. (2002) 'Indigenous ecotourism and sustainable development: the case of Río Blanco, Ecuador'. (Available at *http://www.eduweb.com*.)

Simmons, D.G. (2001) 'Eco-tourism: product or process'. (Available at *http://www.landcare.cri.nz/conferences/manaakiwhenua/*.)

Stadel, C. (1996) 'Divergence and conflict, or convergence and harmony?' In Harrison, L.C. and Husbands, W. (eds) *Practicing Responsible Tourism*. New York: John Wiley & Sons, 445–71.

UNEP (2003) 'About ecotourism'. (Available at *http://www.uneptie.org/pc/tourism/ecotourism*.)

USDA (2001) 'Tourism and natural resource management: a general overview of research and issues'. (Available at *http://www.fs.fed.us/pnw/pubs/gtr506.pdf*.)

Walker, S. (1995) 'Measuring ecotourism impact perceptions'. (Available at *http://www.mtnforum.org*.)

Wall, G. (2002) 'Ecotourism: change, impacts, and opportunities.' (Available at *http://www.yale.edu*.)

Wearing, S. and Neil, J. (1999) *Ecotourism Impacts, Potentials and Possibilities*. Oxford: Butterworth-Heinemann.

Weaver, D.B. (1998) *Ecotourism in the Less Developed World*. Oxford: CABI.

Weaver, D.B. (2001) 'Ecotourism as mass tourism: contradiction or reality?' (Available at *http://www.hotelschool.cornell.edu*.)

Wood, M.E. (2002) *Ecotourism: Principles, Practices and Policies for Sustainability*. Paris: UNEP/TIES.

Zeppel, H. (1997) 'Ecotourism and indigenous people'. (Available at *http://ecotour.csu.edu.au*.)

312

18 Ecotourism Planning and Destination Management in Vietnam

Ralf Buckley

The four main objectives of this chapter are to:

- Introduce ecotourism planning in Vietnam
- Analyze the pros and cons of ecotourism planning in Vietnam
- Discuss two case studies of national parks in Vietnam
- Evaluate the implications of ecotourism planning in a park setting

Introduction

Tourism is a significant and growing component of Vietnam's national economy, with large-scale tourism investment over US$100 million pa (Anonymous, 1999). When the country first opened its borders to international travellers after the 1970s' war, novelty alone was a sufficient attraction for many tourists. Now, however, the novelty has gone, and Vietnam must compete in an international tourism market against other countries in Southeast Asia and indeed worldwide. Military relics of the 1970s' war are still a significant part of the overall marketing mix, but no longer a dominant one. Vietnamese cultures both modern and ancient, urban and rural, are more important for most international visitors, as indicated, for example, by coverage in travel guides such as the *Lonely Planet* series. Equally important are Vietnam's natural environments, especially icon destinations such as World Heritage areas (Flora and Fauna International, n.d.; Ngo, 1997; Le, 1997, 1998, 1999; Cao, 1998; Dang, 1998; Davey, 1998; Koeman, 1998, 1999; Buckley, 1999; Fiditourist, 1999; Hoang, 1999; Koeman and Gregorio, 1999; Nguyen, 1999; Pham, 1999; Saigontourist, 1999; Son et al., 1999; Vu, 1999; Cresswell and Maclaren, 2000).

Increasingly, it appears that international tourists select destinations for their distinctive features, a phenomenon described in the 1990s as endemic tourism and currently known by the recently coined term, geotourism (National Geographic Society, 2002). As in many countries, Vietnam's natural environments are critical to the future health of its tourism industry. Equally, tourism may be critical to the long-term conservation of Vietnam's natural environments: both as an economic and political tool to promote protection and as a major source of environmental impacts within protected areas. As in most nations, the interactions between tourism and environment do not take place in isolation, but in the context of population pressures, other landuses such as farming and forestry and other environmental issues such as pollution and wildlife poaching. And in Vietnam as elsewhere, domestic tourists outnumber international tourists and any country's own citizens commonly view their own cultures, parks and wildlife rather differently from overseas visitors.

Vietnam has a wide range of natural attractions for international and domestic tourists alike. It has 3260 km of coastline, one kilometre for every 100 km^2 of land area (Jansen-Verbeke and Go, 1995). Despite logging and defoliants, it still has almost 20% of forest cover, although a further 1000–2000 km^2 is being cleared each year (Cresswell and Maclaren, 2000). These forests include some of Southeast Asia's richest remaining primary forest, although only 20,000 km^2 currently remain intact (Cresswell and Maclaren, 2000). Vietnam is home to about 275 species of mammal, including endangered species such as tiger and Javan rhinoceros. Most of the world's large mammal species have been known to western scientists since the early days of European exploration, but in the early 1990s two entirely new species, the giant muntjac and the saola or Vu Quang ox, were discovered in the Vu Quang area of northwestern Vietnam, close to the border with China (WWF Vietnam, 1996). While tourists, or indeed scientists, certainly cannot expect to see these endangered mammal species in the wild, Vietnam also has over 7000 named plant species and about 800 bird species (Cresswell and Maclaren, 2000), which are much more easily observed. The country has an established system of protected areas, including ten national parks and 61 nature reserves. These are visited by 30% of international tourists and 50% of domestic tourists (Pham, 1999). Both parks and wildlife, however, are under severe pressure at present, with agricultural settlements encroaching on park borders and illegal hunting for food and for the illegal international trade in body parts from endangered species, such as tiger paws and rhinoceros horn. For example, there are 30,000 local residents immediately around the Vu Quang conservation area. As of the early 1990s, 365 of the animal species in Vietnam's forests were endangered, including 28% of the mammals, 10% of the birds and 21% of reptiles and amphibia (WWF Vietnam, 1996).

Ecotourism planning in Vietnam

National tourism policy in Vietnam is largely the responsibility of the Vietnam National Administration for Tourism (VNAT). As in many other countries, VNAT's primary focus is on increasing inbound tourists to urban and beach destinations and increasing international investment in hotels and other mainstream tourism infrastructure.

Vietnam's *Ordinance on Tourism 1998-UVTVQH10*, a whole-of-government legislative document (VNAT, 1998), incorporates a number of provisions which could form a strong basis for ecotourism planning and destination development. Article 8 prohibits tourism adverse to the environment or cultures. Article 14 allows for fees and charges, so that parks and protected areas could charge visitor entrance fees and operator permit fees, for example. Article 15 appears to provide for environmental impact assessment (EIA) of tourism development proposals, albeit by VNAT rather than MOSTE, the Ministry of Science, Technology and Environment. In most countries, formal EIA is ultimately the responsibility of the environmental portfolio, irrespective of industry sector. Article 16 requires funding to be provided for research, presumably including research on environmental impacts and management and for restoration. And Article 32 requires that guides be trained and accredited. All these prescriptions, if actually followed, could assist in improving sustainability of tourism in Vietnam.

Vietnam's *State Tourism Action Program 2000*, in contrast (VNAT, 1999), barely mentions the natural environment. This is a significant and presumably deliberate omission and may reflect VNAT's own policies more accurately, since the document is essentially a VNAT marketing strategy.

VNAT has, however, co-sponsored two national workshops relevant to ecotourism planning. In 1997, VNAT held a conference on sustainable tourism in Hue (Smith, 1998) which included contributions on biodiversity (Dang, 1998), ecotourism (Cao, 1998; Koeman, 1998) and national parks (Le, 1998). Subsequently, the World Conservation Union (IUCN) funded a project to build capacity for sustainable tourism in Vietnam, which included a workshop on a possible national ecotourism strategy, co-sponsored by VNAT and held in Hanoi in 1999. This workshop took advantage of experience gained in developing the National Ecotourism Strategy for Australia (Australia, Commonwealth Department of Tourism, 1994; Buckley, 1999; Grant, 1999; Woodside, 1999) as well as ecotourism expertise within Vietnam (Hoang, 1999; Le, 1999; Nguyen, 1999; Pham, 1999; Vu, 1999). Major issues considered at those conferences and elsewhere (e.g. Cresswell and Maclaren, 2000) are outlined later in the chapter.

Ecotourism may be viewed as a strategic alliance between tourism and environment (Buckley, 2000). Tourism can support conservation and conservation supports tourism (Van Osterzee, 1999). This support may be political, economic or both (Driml and Common, 1995; Driml, 1997; Kinhill, 1998; Read Sturgess, 1999; Ward, 2000). To be effective, such alliances must typically include the public, private and voluntary sectors (Sweeting et al., 1999).

Effective ecotourism planning therefore needs an integrated whole-of-government strategy for tourism, landuse, conservation and investment; involving economic development agencies and land management agencies as well as tourism and conservation interests. Some key features are listed in Table 18.1. In Vietnam, the relevant agencies are the Ministry of Planning and Investment (MPI), the Ministry of Science Technology and Environment (MOSTE), the Ministry of Agriculture and Rural Development (MARD) and the

Table 18.1 Key features of ecotourism planning in Vietnam

- National approach to landuse planning, covering all landuses simultaneously, to ensure that adequate areas are set aside for conservation and tourism and protected from damage by other industry sectors
- Full conservation of core protected areas including all existing national parks, forests and reserves, with adequate management funding
- Establishment of new areas for tourism and conservation, with basic management funds
- Protection of water and sea, especially rivers and coastal waters, against industrial and agricultural pollution
- Protection of wildlife, including measures against poaching, and measures for rescue and conservation of the endangered species which form a primary tourist attraction
- Joint lobbying, information gathering, education and local community development projects by tourism and conservation interests, to overcome wildlife poaching and illegal trade in endangered species and body parts
- Community involvement in local tourism, to assist in conservation and reduce poaching
- International marketing of Vietnam's natural and cultural heritage as a basis for a globally competitive tourism sector
- Appropriate local marketing of natural and cultural attractions, to establish tourist expectations that can be satisfied
- Environmental management within the tourism industry, to minimize its impacts on the natural and cultural environment on which it depends
- Effective independent EIA, managed by the environment portfolio, for major tourism developments in any geographical area or land tenure
- A routine process and criteria, including environmental criteria, for screening investments in tourism development and infrastructure
- A routine system for public environmental reporting and performance monitoring of tourism operators
- Environmental performance screening, environmental accreditation and environmental audit of tourism developers, tourism operators and tour guides
- Best practice environmental design, technology and management for all forms of tourism
- Incentives, awards and perhaps tax concessions for tourism companies with high levels of environmental performance
- Penalties for poor environmental performance, such as fines, cancellation of operating permits or exclusion from national marketing programmes
- User charges to fund public costs of managing tourism, particularly in protected areas
- Independent environmental monitoring in protected areas used for tourism and independent audit of tourism EIA and corporate monitoring programmes
- Environmental education both by and within the tourism sector, to generate respect for nature and culture within domestic as well as international tourists

Ministry of Forests (MOF) as well as the Vietnam National Administration for Tourism (VNAT).

Most importantly, integrated landuse planning is required to ensure that other industry sectors do not destroy the natural assets on which the tourism industry is based, as has happened in many other countries. For example, the mountain forests and rivers of southwest China, immediately north of Vietnam, are a tourism asset of enormous potential value, but the forests are being logged and the rivers polluted by pulp mills and dammed for large-scale hydroelectricity generation, effectively destroying the economic opportunities for the tourism sector.

Similarly, the natural attractions that form the basis for Vietnam's future tourism industry are under increasing threat from other activities: forest clearance to the very boundaries of protected areas and even inside them (Gilmour and Nguyen, 1999); industrial pollution in the rivers and along the coast; and large-scale illegal wildlife poaching, even of highly endangered species such as tiger. In Vietnam, therefore, a strategic alliance between tourism and conservation is particularly urgent and significant for both. The tourism industry needs a national strategy to protect Vietnam's forests, wildlife and water; and its parks and protected areas need well-planned tourism to contribute funding for natural resource management.

The significance of watchable wildlife, and particularly rare species, to inbound international tourism needs particular emphasis. Wildlife tourism is a multi-billion dollar industry worldwide, yet tiger paws, turtle shells and other body parts from endangered animal species are still on sale in Vietnam and traded illegally to China in contravention of the Convention on International Trade in Endangered Species (CITES). This represents a major loss in future tourism revenue for the Vietnam economy and the tourism sector needs to become active in lobbying at central and local government levels for major education and enforcement campaigns to close down the illegal trade in endangered animal parts. Of course, tourism can also make a major contribution by providing alternative employment opportunities to local communities which form the first step in the endangered species trade. This alone, however, will not be enough. Worldwide, international trade in endangered species is a large-scale organized criminal business, which can only be eradicated by a concerted effort from central government, involving police action and customs enforcement.

National parks as ecotourism destinations – examples from Vietnam

Destination development can occur at a wide range of different scales. At a national level, for example, an approach for Vietnam was outlined by Jansen-Verbeke and Go (1995) in the form of nodes, corridors and tourist experiences. Destinations also develop at a more local level, through involvement of individual tourism entrepreneurs and local land management agencies. One common case in ecotourism is the development of national parks as nature tourism destinations. Two case studies are outlined here: Cat Ba Island in Halong Bay and Cuc Phuong National Park, near Hanoi. Except where otherwise noted, data are from field visits by the author in late 1999.

Cat Ba Island, Halong Bay

Halong Bay lies on the coast of northern Vietnam east of Hanoi. It is famous for its World Heritage limestone islands. The port of Halong City receives around one million visitors a year, of which about 350,000 take a boat into the bay and about 45,000 visit the island with the main caves. There are 24 caves in all, but only two are heavily visited. These have formed tracks, lighting, interpretive signs and guides. There are also jetties for tour boats to pull up, chemical toilets, a generator to power the cave lighting system and a kiosk selling food and drink. A small fee is charged to enter the caves. There is a Halong Bay Management Authority which includes staff responsible for managing the caves themselves. These caves are thus managed effectively for high visitation through a combination of infrastructure, hardening and fees, but this makes them a developed rather than a wilderness attraction.

Most of the islands in Halong Bay are relatively small, with steep limestone walls and are undeveloped. One, however, contains a large marine lagoon accessible to tour boats and is used for snorkeling. Another has been developed as a small beach resort by a Chinese joint venture. There is also one island with a private beach and house reserved for recreation by government officials. The Halong Bay Management Authority is considering importing sand to create artificial beaches closer to Halong City.

The best-known island within the Halong Bay area is Cat Ba, which has become a major tourism destination within Vietnam (Son et al., 1999). It receives around 45,000 visitors annually, of which 20,000 are foreigners. In late 1999 there were about 30 small hotels in the main port on Cat Ba, with more under construction (Buckley, 2003). Five years previously, apparently, there had been only three hotels. There is a government quango, the Environmental and Urban Company, responsible for municipal infrastructure such as drains, sewerage and street sweeping. This is funded in part by an environmental levy on tourist boats in Halong Bay.

Part of Cat Ba is reserved as a national park, but only about 800 ha still retains its original forest cover. The rest has been cut in the past for firewood and is currently regrowth. The park is known for whiteheaded monkeys, with a remaining population of about 100–150 individuals. Visitor access to the park is through a heavily fenced and gated road with guards and a military-style compound, but how far around the park this fence extends is not clear. The entrance area is effectively a small village with tourist shops and restaurants, staff accommodation, etc. It also incorporates an environmental education centre funded by overseas aid. There is an interpretive leaflet in French and Vietnamese, also funded by an international donor. There are two formed trails, a short one to the top of a limestone peak near the entrance area and a longer one which requires overnight backpacking (Buckley, 2003).

Cat Ba seems to have been subject to rapid and unplanned development of private tourism accommodation and facilities in the town area, relying on the national park as the primary tourist attraction but providing little or no support for conservation of the park and its wildlife. An increased entry fee to the park, to fund visitor management environment protection and education, would seem to be one obvious approach.

Cuc Phuong National Park

Destination management issues for tourism in Vietnam's mainland protected areas are exemplified by Cuc Phuong National Park, accessible from Hanoi. The park is 200 km^2 in area and receives around 50,000 visitors annually. As of 1999 it had an annual operating budget of US$600,000. Of this, $100,000 is from tourist fees, which according to the park's director is insufficient to cover the costs of managing tourists. The remainder is from a government budget allocation. Cuc Phuong National Park employs 36 staff specifically in tourism, ten as rangers and the rest in the park's three visitor guesthouses. There is a single vehicle access, a narrow paved road through the forest. There are a number of formed tracks and walks, including one to a cave with prehistoric human remains reputedly of considerable antiquity. There is a primate rescue centre within the park, which operates a veterinary care and rehabilitation programme for animals rescued from traps and poachers and also runs a captive breeding programme for civets.

The core area of the park is surrounded by an area with shallow rocky soils which is a buffer zone, but in practice is completely cleared. This area has apparently been occupied by people who formerly lived within the park and who have been unable to obtain agricultural land in the more fertile and heavily populated lowland valleys nearby. Hunting and poaching within the park are apparently widespread.

To manage Cuc Phuong as an ecotourism destination will require several major social shifts. To reduce hunting and poaching will require an alternative source of income for those currently dependent on it for food. Because of the very high prices paid by end users of endangered species body parts, however, non-subsistence poaching can only be cured by concerted police and customs action to halt illegal trade in such items, so as to remove the primary market for the poachers. Given the prevalence of wildlife markets within Vietnam itself, and the shared border with China, this will not be easy to achieve.

In addition to agricultural encroachment immediately outside the park's boundaries and wildlife poaching inside, there are also environmental impacts from tourism and recreation. The majority of the park's visitors are domestic rather than international tourists and, as in many developing nations, the former may not always appreciate or care about the ecological impacts of litter, noise, weeds and human waste. From a destination management perspective, therefore environmental education may be as important as infrastructure such as guesthouses and toilets.

Conclusion

Vietnam's forest plants and wildlife are of international conservation significance and important for Vietnam's future tourism economy. Many of them are highly endangered through logging, clearing and poaching. Ecotourism could assist in conserving them, but bringing visitors to national parks is not enough. Tourism also needs to provide funds for effective protection of parks and biodiversity. This may include providing an income for former residents of the areas concerned. In addition, other government portfolios need a strong involvement, to prevent damage to protected areas both by other industry sectors and by illegal poaching.

Questions

1 Discuss the current practices of ecotourism in Vietnam.
2 By using one of the strategies and tactics for managing wilderness, natural and protected areas from Chapter 3, design a strategy for the national parks.
3 What are the most important risks to the destination with which you are most familiar?
4 Critically appraise the factors that can influence Vietnam's ecotourism industry in the next five years.

References

Anonymous (1999) 'Investment update'. *Vietnam Investment Review*, 6–12 September, 18.

Australia, Commonwealth Department of Tourism (1994) National Ecotourism Strategy. Canberra: AGPS.

Buckley, R.C. (1999) 'Planning for a national ecotourism strategy in Vietnam'. In Pham, T.L., Koeman, A., Nguyen, T.L., Nguyen, D.H.C. and Hoang, D.C. (eds) Proceedings, National Workshop on a National Ecotourism Strategy for Vietnam. Hanoi: VNAT, 39–45.

Buckley, R.C. (2000) 'Tourism and wilderness: dancing with the messy monster'. In McCool, S.F., Cole, D.N., Borrie, W.T. and O'Loughlin, J. (eds) (comps) *Wilderness Science in a Time of Change*. US Forest Service Proceedings RMRS – P-O, Vol 2. Ogden, UT: USDA, 186–9.

Buckley, R.C. (2003) *Case Studies in Ecotourism*. Oxford: CABI.

Cao, B.S. (1998) Ecotourism potential in Vietnam. Proceedings, International Seminar on Sustainable Tourism Development in Vietnam. Hue: VNAT.

Cresswell, C. and Maclaren, F. (2000) 'Tourism and national parks in emerging tourism countries'. In Butler, R.W. and Boyd, S.W. *Tourism and National Parks*. Chichester: John Wiley & Sons, 281–99.

Dang, H.H. (1998) The role of biodiversity in ecotourism development in Vietnam. Proceedings, Workshop on Ecotourism in Sustainable Development in Vietnam. Hanoi: VNAT.

Davey, A.G. (1998) Vietnam Protected Area System Planning and Management. Report to MARD and IUCN, Hanoi. Canberra: University of Canberra.

Driml, S.M. (1997) 'Bringing ecological economics out of the wilderness', *Ecology Economics*, 23, 145–53.

Driml, S. and Common, M. (1995). 'Economic and financial benefits of tourism in major protected areas', *Australian Journal of Environmental Management*, 2, 19–29.

Fiditourist (1999) *Vietnam is Not a War, But a Country*. Ho Chi Minh City: Fiditourist.

Flora and Fauna International (undated) Welcome to Cuc Phuong Conservation Project. Information Leaflet. Cuc Phuong, Hanoi: FFI.

Gilmour, D.A. and Nguyen, V.S. (1999) *Buffer Zone Management in Vietnam*. Hanoi: IUCN Vietnam.

Grant, J. (1999) 'The development and implementation of Australia's national ecotourism strategy'. In Pham, T.L., Koeman, A., Nguyen, T.L., Nguyen, D.H.C. and Hoang, D.C. (eds) Proceedings, National Workshop on a National Ecotourism Strategy for Vietnam. Hanoi: VNAT, 86–93.

Hoang, P.T. (1999) 'Ecotourism in relation to biodiversity protection and conservation'. In Pham, T.L.; Koeman, A., Nguyen, T.L., Nguyen, D.H.C. and Hoang, D.C. (eds) Proceedings, National Workshop on a National Ecotourism Strategy for Vietnam. Hanoi: VNAT, 75–8.

Jansen-Verbeke, M. and Go, F. (1995) 'Tourism development in Vietnam', *Tourism Management*, 16, 315–25.

Kinhill Economics (1998) The Value of Protected Areas to Queensland. Report to Queensland Department of Environment, Kinhill, Brisbane.

Koeman, A. (1998) Ecotourism based on sustainable development. Proceedings, Workshop on Ecotourism in Sustainable Development in Vietnam. Hanoi: VNAT.

Koeman, A.L. (1999) Removing the blinkers: advocating for inclusion of biodiversity conservation and the environment into tourism planning in Vietnam. Proceedings, Workshop on Building Biodiversity into Sectoral Strategies and Action Plans. Montreal: Global Biodiversity Forum.

Koeman, A.L. and Gregorio, M. (1999) Culture and tourism, complex inter-relationships. Proceedings, Workshop on Culture and Development. Geneva: UNDP.

Le, V.L. (ed.) (1997) Proceedings, National Workshop on the Participation of Local Communities in Management of Protected Areas in Vietnam. Ho Chi Minh City: Vietnam Forestry Association.

Le, V.L. (1998) Ecotourism and management of the tourism environment in national parks in Vietnam. Proceedings, Workshop on Ecotourism in Sustainable Development in Vietnam. Hanoi: VNAT.

Le, V.L. (1999) 'Ecotourism in protected areas in Vietnam: potential, existing conditions, solutions and strategic for development'. In Pham, T.L., Koeman, A., Nguyen, T.L., Nguyen, D.H.C. and Hoang, D.C. (eds) Proceedings, National Workshop on Development of a National Ecotourism Strategy for Vietnam. Hanoi: VNAT, 63–74.

National Geographic Society (2002) www.nationalgeographic.com. (viewed 10 May 2002).

Ngo, D.T. (1997) Cultural diversity and community participation in management and protection of protected areas in Vietnam. Proceedings, National Workshop on Participation of Local Communities in Management of Protected Areas in Vietnam. Ho Chi Minh City: Vietnam Forestry Association.

321

Nguyen, V.L. (1999) 'Ecotourism development in the context of state management'. In Pham, T.L., Koeman, A., Nguyen, T.L., Nguyen, D.H.C. and Hoang, D.C. (eds) Proceedings, National Workshop on Development of a National Ecotourism Strategy for Vietnam. Hanoi: VNAT, 115–20.

Pham, T.L. (1999) Current situation, potential and orientation on ecotourism development in Vietnam. Proceedings, National Workshop on Development of a National Ecotourism Strategy for Vietnam. Hanoi: VNAT.

Read Sturgess & Associates (1999) *Economic Assessment of Recreation Values of Victorian Parks*. Melbourne: RSA.

Saigontourist (1999) 'Development experiences and orientation in the ecotourism programs'. In Pham, T.L., Koeman, A., Nguyen, T.L., Nguyen, D.H.C. and Hoang, D.C. (eds) Proceedings, National Workshop on Development of a National Ecotourism Strategy for Vietnam. Hanoi: VNAT, 56–62.

Smith, R.A. (1998) 'Sustainable tourism in Vietnam', *Annals of Tourism Research*, 25, 765–7.

Son, N.T., Pigram, J.J. and Rugendyke, B.A. (1999) 'Tourism development and national parks in the developing world: Cat Ba Island National Park, Vietnam'. In Pearce, D.G. and Butler, R.W. (eds) *Contemporary Issues in Tourism Development*. London: Routledge, 211–31.

Sweeting, J., Bruner, A. and Rosenfield, A. (1999) *The Green Host Effect: Sustainable Approaches to Large-Scale Tourism and Resort Development in Natural Areas*. Washington, DC: Conservation International.

Van Osterzee, P. (1999) Tourism and nature conservation: two-way track. Earth Alive Tourism Summit, 9 September, Sydney. Canberra: Environment Australia.

Vietnam, National Assembly Standing Committee (1998) Ordinance on Tourism 1998-UVTVQH10. National Assembly, Hanoi (English draft).

Vietnam, National Administration for Tourism (VNAT) (1999) State Tourism Action Program and Tourism Events for 2000. Hanoi: VNAT.

Vu, T.C. (1999) 'Development of a national ecotourism strategy for Vietnam'. In Pham, T.L. (eds) Proceedings, National Workshop on a National Ecotourism Strategy for Vietnam. Hanoi: VNAT, 121–7.

Ward, J. (2000) The Relative Net Economic Benefits of Logging and Tourism in Selected Australian Forests. PhD thesis, Griffith University, Gold Coast, Australia.

Woodside, D. (1999) 'Ecotourism: is it a sustainable use of wildlife?' In Pham, T.L. (eds) Proceedings, National Workshop on a National Ecotourism Strategy for Vietnam. Hanoi: VNAT, 94–102.

World Wide Fund for Nature, Vietnam (1996) *Vietnam Country Profile*. Gland: WWF.

322

19 An Ecotourism Development Plan for the Abrolhos Islands, Western Australia

Ross K. Dowling

The four main objectives of this chapter are to:

- Identify the location of the Abrolhos Islands
- Summarize the history of tourism in the region
- Describe the proposed tourism development strategy
- Outline specific management plans

Introduction

The Houtman Abrolhos Islands, commonly referred to simply as the Abrolhos Islands, lie off the coast of Geraldton, Western Australia (WA). They have long been of interest to the general public and visitors have been travelling there for centuries. The islands are a major commercial fishing ground vested in the WA Minister of Fisheries and managed by the Department of Fisheries so little organized tourism has occurred beyond that carried out by the fishers themselves together with their families and friends. However, increased interest in the area has put pressure on the government to examine the possibility of developing organized tourism and, in recent years, there have been several studies conducted on the potential for tourism development (Dowling and Kemp, 2000).

The Abrolhos Islands lie 60 km west of Geraldton. They comprise 122 islands low-lying islands and reefs clustered in three major groups, Wallabi, Easter and Pelsaert, extending 100 km from north to south. The islands lie in the stream of WA's warm, southward flowing Leeuwin Current and the surrounding marine environment is a meeting place for tropical and temperate marine life (Mann, 1990). The current maintains water temperatures throughout the winter enabling corals and tropical species of fish to thrive in latitudes in which they would not normally survive.

The Abrolhos coral reefs are the most southern living reefs in the Indian Ocean and contain the the world's best high-latitude examples of luxuriant and diverse coral growth. They are noted for their mixture of tropical and temperate corals and, in addition, the area comprises various whales, seals and reef fish of many kinds. The island landforms are of varied types and also have a high diversity of plants, animals and birds. Large breeding colonies of seabirds exist on many of the islands, some of which are of international significance (Storr et al. 1986).

The islands are also famous for their historic shipwrecks. The best known are the Dutch East India vessels Batavia (1629) and Zeewijk (1727). The Batavia shipwreck is one of the bloodiest episodes in Australia's history, with the shipwreck followed by the subsequent slaughter of 125 men, women and children by mutineers. Artefacts dating from the incident can still be seen on the islands. Eighteen other historic wrecks, mainly from the 19th century, have also been discovered in Abrolhos waters.

The Abrolhos Islands are also the focus of the most valuable rock lobster fishery in Australia generating $AUD300 million per annum in export earnings. Each year during the open fishing season from 15 March to 30 June, about 140

Figure 19.1 Fishers' camps on the 22 designated islands of the Houtman Abrolhos Islands, Western Australia

324

licensed fishers, deckhands and families live on the 22 islands designated as fishers' camps (see Figure 19.1).

Management considerations

There are concerns that increasing pressure on the ecosystem due to fishing (both amateur and professional), recreation and tourism is damaging the environment and that better management is needed. The islands collectively comprise an 'A class' reserve for the purposes of conservation of flora and fauna, tourism and for purposes associated with the fishing industry. They are vested in the Minister for Fisheries who has established the Abrolhos Islands Management Advisory Committee (AIMAC), to advise him about the planning and management of the islands and adjoining state territorial waters.

In 1994 the Abrolhos Islands Management Advisory Committee (AIMAC) was formed and they prepared a management plan for the area (AIMAC and Fisheries WA, 1997). The objective of the plan is to provide a sound mechanism for conserving the terrestrial and marine environment of the Abrolhos system for present and future generations, as viable ecosystems by protecting their natural diversity, cultural heritage and ensuring sustainable use. The waters of the Abrolhos Islands are managed to allow commercial rock lobster fishing to flourish while also fostering conservation. The waters comprise a fish habitat protection area and there is also a reef observation area in each island group where fishing for fin fish is not permitted.

In 1997 a further tourism survey was commissioned to develop a management plan for the islands based on sustainable tourism (AIMAC and Fisheries WA, 1998). This was subsequently updated and revised (Fisheries Western Australia, 2001) and now forms the subject of this chapter (see Figure 19.2)

Early tourism

In 1950 tourism began, when some vacant buildings on Pelsart Island which had been abandoned by the guano industry were rented out to tourists. However, the camp was spartan, there was little fresh water and the boat trip out from the mainland was generally rough, so within a relatively short period of time the venture failed. After several more proposals in the early 1960s the WA state government appointed a 'Tourist Survey Committee' to assess them. Over the past 20–30 years an increasing number of visitors have been attracted to the area by its rich fish life, unique coral formations, birdlife, shipwrecks and wild beauty. Visitors have mainly arrived by private yacht and pleasure boat.

In recent years 'carrier boats' have been introduced, operated by the

Figure 19.2 Sustainable tourism plan for the Houtman Abrolhos Islands

commercial fishers during the rock lobster season. The boats carry supplies out
to the islands returning with live rock lobster for processing on the mainland. In
the off-season some of these have been used extensively as charter vessels for
tourists.

In the late 1980s a major study of the islands concluded that in regard to tourism, there should be no tourist accommodation developed (AICC and AITF, 1989). However, it did recommend that permanent moorings be set aside in each island group for recreational users. It also suggested the opportunity of tours using fixed-wing aircraft or helicopters to access the islands in concert with boat-based tours in the islands. A fly/boat trial was conducted in the islands between June 1992 and June 1993. The trial was considered to be successful but interpretation of the results was hampered by the sale of the boat during the trial (AICC and AITF, 1993).

In the mid-1990s tourism was again investigated by a working party (AICC, 1995). The report concluded that large-scale developments on the islands would be ecologically damaging and probably not be economically viable. However, it did argue in favour of developing natural area tourism provided it were undertaken in a sustainable manner. The report also recommended the establishment and operation of tourist developments subject to strict environmental and management conditions. It suggested that, initially, there should be a limited number of permanent mooring sites and small land-based tourism sites, with access being by boat or air.

Tourism today

One of the major constraints in planning tourism in the Abrolhos is the lack of information on the actual number of visitors (AIMAC and Fisheries WA, 1998). During the fishing season, which occurs between mid-March and June, the 'permanent' population on the islands is about 1000 people. However, a controversial point is that friends of fishers visit during the season and tourism operators consider this to be 'de facto' tourism while the fishers argue that if a friend visits someone on the mainland it is not considered tourism. Fishers can use their huts during the off-season only for maintenance and repairs but it has been suggested that friends participate in some of these trips and they are treated as holidays (see Figure 19.3). Private yachts also visit the islands and during 1996 a total of 28 boats carrying 252 people officially 'registered' their visit. However, not all yachts register and thus the number of registered yachts and visitors is only an indicative amount on the lower end of the anticipated number.

It is estimated that the four commercial operators carried approximately 2000 visitors during the past year (2002–2003). Thus overall it is claimed that there are 1000 people living in camps on the islands during the season and an additional 7500 people during the year.

Figure 19.3 De facto tourism on the Houtman Abrolhas Islands

Regional ecotourism planning

A decade ago the environmentally based tourism (EBT) development planning model was devised, which essentially seeks to foster environmental protection and tourism development through a sustainable resource and development planning framework (see Figure 19.4) (Dowling, 1993). In essence, the major thrust of the EBT planning model is not towards the determination of land use sustainability or capability, carrying capacity, threshold analysis or pattern analysis. Instead, it is best summarized as determining environmentally compatible tourism through the identification of significant features, critical areas and compatible activities (Newsome et al., 2002).

Significant features are either environmental attributes that are valued according to their level of diversity, uniqueness or representativeness, or tourism features, valued for their resource value. Critical areas are those in which environmental and tourism features are in competition and possible conflict. Compatible activities are outdoor tourism recreational activities that are considered to be both environmentally and socially compatible.

The essential elements of the regional EBT planning model include its grounding in the sustainable development approach, that is, being based on environmental protection, community well-being, tourist satisfaction and economic integration in order to achieve environment-tourism compatibility (Page and Dowling, 2002). Other essential elements include its being strategic and iterative, regionally based, incorporating landuse zoning and environmentally

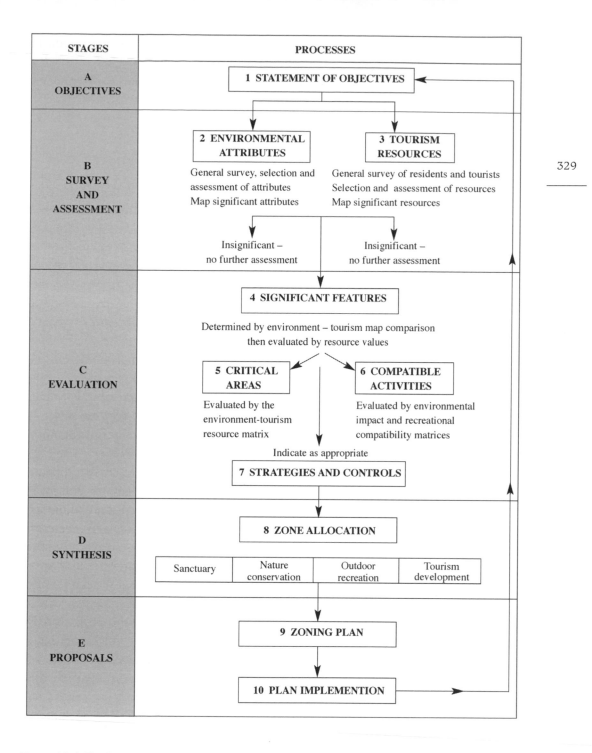

Figure 19.4 The EBT planning framework

educative, that is, fostering the environmental ethic. The EBT planning model is a strategic planning approach to environment-tourism planning in five stages: a statement of objectives, survey and assessment, evaluation, synthesis and proposals. This model was applied to the Abrolhos region.

³³⁰ The Abrolhos management plan

Any tourism development and management in the Abrolhos must conform to the goals of the overall management plan for the islands (Fisheries Western Australia, 1998). The overall objective of the plan is to 'provide a sound mechanism for conserving the terrestrial and marine environments of the Abrolhos system for present and future generations as viable ecosystems by protecting their natural diversity, cultural heritage and ensuring sustainable use' (Fisheries Western Australia, 1998: 8). The plan has a number of specific goals related to conservation, management, research and monitoring, community awareness and involvement, use and development, legislation and implementation and resources. Key goals relative to tourism include those of 'conservation', which aims to develop policies to conserve the ecosystem and cultural heritage values, as well as the 'community awareness and involvement' goal to raise the awareness, appreciation and understanding of the unique values of the Abrolhos.

The terrestrial environment of the Abrolhos is managed in two different ways according to whether or not they are inhabited. Uninhabited islands are managed as reserves intended to maintain the natural and cultural features of the region. Islands that are inhabited during the Abrolhos season have traditionally evolved on an ad hoc basis with little regard for usual planning procedures. The marine environment is one of the most important ones in WA and management of them is carried out in a manner that ensures the retention of their natural values while allowing fair and equitable access to the various resources of the region. One major development in managing the marine system of the Abrolhos is the introduction of reef observation areas which occurred in 1994. These areas have been declared in order to allow the recovery of fin fish populations towards their original state, providing divers with an area to observe large fish that were not frightened by their approach. Such areas will also allow the comparison with others where fishing is carried out so that scientific study of impacts can be made.

The tourism strategy

The overall thrust of the Abrolhos tourism management strategy is to 'manage environmentally sustainable nature-based tourism which is consistent with the protection of the natural and cultural values of the Abrolhos System and provides appropriate managed access to the area for the community' (Fisheries WA, 2001: 2). The basic goals of the plan are to make the islands more accessible to a variety of people from WA, interstate and overseas so they can enjoy the many attractions of the islands, while at the same time undertaking tourism in an environmentally sensitive way. Nature-based tourism is well established in the state with the current implementation of the WA Tourism Commission's Nature-Based Tourism Strategy (WA Tourism Commission, 1997) based on a set of 'eco-ethics' for tourism developments established by the Commission and the state's Environmental Protection Authority in the late 1980s (WATC and EPA, 1989).

Principal strategies for the development and management of tourism in the Abrolhos include:

1 protection of the marine and terrestrial environments of the Abrolhos Islands
2 development of environmentally sensitive nature-based tourism in the Abrolhos
3 establishment of sustainable and appropriate facilities to support nature-based tourism
4 incorporation of local communities into the decision-making processes for tourism development and management.

One of the major constraints in planning tourism in the Abrolhos is the lack of information on the numbers of people actually visiting the region. Planners recognize two major types of visitor – private recreational tourists who make their own way to the area and visitors who arrive through commercial tours operators.

Private recreational tourism

Little is known about the use, magnitude and impact of recreation on the Abrolhos Islands. There have been no systematic surveys undertaken and no records of visitor numbers maintained (AIMAC and Fisheries WA, 1998: 13). However, from anecdotal evidence it is known that recreational visitor use is highly seasonal, with weekends being very popular, and the numbers of visitors is increasing. Further, there are two known types of visitor: the people who visit on yachts and those who stay on camps as friends of fishers. Private visitors are required to conform to island regulations, which prohibit camping, fires and pets on the islands; the use of moorings and jetties without the written permission of their owner; and the necessity for boats to notify Fisheries WA before their visit to the islands when travelling outside the rock lobster season.

Commercial tourism operations

The key objective in regard to commercial tourism operations is to manage the development of environmentally sensitive nature-based tourism through licensed tourism operators. While the opportunities abound for such development, there are also a number of constraints for tourism development in the Abrolhos Islands including limitations of the environment, water, the weather, sanitary waste disposal and infrastructure. The environmental attractions for tourism in the Abrolhos are considerable. However, the fragile nature of the Abrolhos terrestrial and marine systems is also one of the major constraints for tourism. Many of the islands are susceptible to erosion as they have little or no vegetation cover. In addition, the seabird populations of the islands are of international significance but their colonies are very vulnerable to disturbance.

Other problems are the lack of fresh water and the hard limestone base of most of the islands. The harsh weather is another key constraint. The low-lying islands are very exposed, with little natural shelter from the winds and rain. The sea crossing from the mainland to the islands can be very rough and 'is uncomfortable to many people on all but the calmest of days' (AIMAC and Fisheries WA, 1998: 16).

There is virtually no public infrastructure on the Abrolhos. The few facilities that are present have been developed by fishers at their own expense to support the fishing industry. The jetties are all privately owned, either by individual fishers or small groups. There are no medical facilities except for a limited facility nursing station on one of the islands during the fishing season and there are no land or satellite lines.

Tourism development proposals

Several types of commercial tourism are recommended for the Abrolhos (see Table 19.1). These are charter boats, shore-based facilities and moored accommodation facilities. It is suggested that charter boat operations with up to 20 passengers will be permitted throughout the islands, subject to the needs for safety and minimization of adverse environmental impacts. The operator could tender for a shore-based jetty and shed to provide space to store equipment and could engage in fly/boat ventures. It is also recognized that the charter operator may need one or more mooring sites in the islands. Any tourism operations will be monitored and, if no damage occurs, larger operations may be permitted. Small-scale, low-impact shore-based facilities could be operated in several areas of the Abrolhos. It is recommended that it should not accommodate more that 40 people, a number considered large enough to be economically viable but small enough to minimize adverse environmental impacts. Areas recommended

332

Table 19.1 Overview of strategies for the development of tourism in the Houtman Abrolhos Islands, Western Australia

Tourism type	Period	Strategy
Independent	Immediate	Collect data on tourism – where, when, how and numbers of people Provide more information on attractions in the islands and areas to avoid Encourage visitors to utilize core areas by zoning and provision of facilities Avoid conflict between nature conservation, private tourism and fishers Provision of moorings, which can be rented through Fisheries WA Access to East Wallabi jetty for private flights
	Medium term	Progressively provide more facilities and control access to sensitive areas
Commercial	Immediate	Any tourism must be ecologically and economically sustainable Consider the development in each group for tourist ventures Provide access to the airstrips on East Wallabi Island Provide for establishment of common moorings
	Medium term	Ensure all tourism developments are environmentally sensitive and have a net environmental benefit to the Houtman Abrolhos If agreement can be achieved, possible mixing of fishers and tourism Any tourism development should use 'best practice' techniques Permanent moored facility near Leo's Island Assess the potential tourism opportunities at East Wallabi Island while maintaining the high conservation values of the island Other options for tourism facilities to be investigated, such as use of a large catamaran from shore

(Source: Fisheries WA, 2001)

for such an establishment include Long and Little Roma Islands. Medium-term development possibilities include the establishment of a tourist facility on East Wallabi Island. This is one of the more scenic islands in the Abrolhos group and it has an extensive sand beach backed by low, rolling dunes.

The possibility of providing a moored accommodation facility has been recommended within the Leo Island reef platform. The advantages of a moored accommodation facility are that it can be established in an area of interest while having minimal effect on the environment. The facility can be constructed elsewhere and towed to the Abrolhos, further decreasing environmental impact. There are, however, impacts that still occur including shading of the underlying bottom and concentration of wastes.

It is also recommended that there is a broadening of air services to the islands to allow their use for tourism. Commercial tourist operators will be allowed to establish moorings for their use, which in some cases would be used by the industry as a whole. Public moorings would be installed and rented for use by private boats.

Management strategies

To complement the proposed tourism developments there are a number of management strategies recommended. These include the introduction of visitor fees and licences. A fee will be required for all visitors to the islands to help recover part of the costs of managing the islands and providing facilities for visitors. The fee will apply to tourists, A zone fishers and private boats. For fishers the fee will be incorporated into an annual licence fee whereas private boat owners will be able to obtain either a single-trip or annual permit to visit the islands. Licences for commercial tourist operators will be granted for an initial period of seven years, with two renewals of seven years each being possible, for a total tenure of 21 years before new tenders will be called. The renewals will be subject to prescribed environmental and operational conditions being met.

Independent environmental monitoring of the effects of larger projects such as moored accommodation or shore-based facilities will be required. Such monitoring may also be required for smaller projects if there is concern over the potential effects of the operations. If permanent shore-based facilities or pontoons are established they must be decommissioned and removed by the proponent when the project is terminated or the permit expires.

Conclusion

The future development of the Abrolhos Islands is a sensitive issue from environmental, social and economic perspectives. To ensure that the Abrolhos system is maintained in an ecologically sound condition it will be essential that any form of tourism development is both low key and environmentally sensitive.

There are currently two types of visitor: private recreational visitors and commercial tourists. The proposed management plan focuses on commercial operators and recommends the introduction of charter boats, small-scale shore-based development, moored accommodation facilities and a medium-term development in Turtle Bay on East Wallabi Island. To facilitate this development further infrastructure will be required including an airstrip and boat moorings.

If tourism developments are given the go-ahead then visitor fees and licences for commercial tourist operators will be introduced. The current Minister of Fisheries is enthusiastic about low-key, nature-based tourism development in the region. He called the Abrolhos 'one of the most attractive environments on earth' and suggested that ecotourism development will complement the other marine industries in the area as well as provide a boost to the regional economy (McDonald, 2001). However, the WA Conservation Council does not agree and its coordinator states that 'this is a classic case where commercial exploitation is overriding sound conservation management' (McDonald, 2001).

Providing the recommendations outlined in the Abrolhos Tourism Management Plan are adhered to, it is envisaged that the development of tourism on the islands will bring further prosperity to the region. And last but not least, at the time of writing, expressions of interest have been called for and received from a dozen potential ecotour developers, all wishing to establish ecotourism operations in the Abrolhos Islands.

335

Acknowledgements

This chapter is based on a report carried out by the author for the Department of Fisheries, Western Australia. The original report was prepared in conjunction with Fred Wells and Jim Singleton of LeProvost Dames & Moore. Thanks are also due to the assistance given by Kim Nardi, Department of Fisheries, Geraldton.

Questions

1 Given that the Abrolhos Islands have a rich history and sensitive natural environment, should any tourism development at all be sanctioned?
2 Should tourism be allowed to coexist with the rock lobster industry or should the two industries be separated?
3 Given that there is virtually no public infrastructure on the islands, is tourism in the area safe?
4 Is the emphasis on commercial operations the right approach to tourism development or should there be more scope for independent travellers?

References

AICC and AITF (1989) Abrolhos Islands Planning Strategy: Final Report. Prepared for the Abrolhos Islands Consultative Committee, Geraldton, Australia.
AICC and AITF (1993) Houtman Abrolhos Islands Fly/Boat Visitor Trial. June 1992–June 1993: Final Report. Abrolhos Islands Consultative Council and the Abrolhos Islands Task Force, Geraldton, Australia.
AICC (1995) Tourism at the Abrolhos Islands: Final Report. Prepared for the Abrolhos Islands Consultative Committee. Abrolhos Islands Consultative Council, Western Australia.
AIMAC and Fisheries WA (1997) Draft Management Plan for the Houtman Abrolhos Systems. Abrolhos Islands Management Advisory Committee and Fisheries Western Australia, Perth, Australia.
AIMAC and Fisheries WA (1998) Management Plan for Sustainable Tourism at the Houtman Abrolhos Islands, Western Australia. Fisheries Management Paper No. 120. Abrolhos Islands Management Advisory Committee and Fisheries Western Australia, Perth, Australia.

Dowling, R.K. (1993) 'An environmentally based planning model for regional tourism development', *Journal of Sustainable Tourism*, 1 (1), 17–37.

Dowling, R.K. and Kemp, S. (2000) Nature-based tourism development in the Abrolhos Islands, Western Australia. Paper presented at the Tenth Council for Australian University Tourism and Hospitality Education (CAUTHE) Conference, Peak Performance in Tourism & Hospitality Research, 2–5 February, Mt Buller, Victoria, Australia.

Fisheries Western Australia (1998) Management of the Houtman Abrolhos System. Fisheries Management Paper No. 117, Fisheries Western Australia, Perth, Australia.

Fisheries Western Australia (2001) Sustainable Tourism Plan for the Houtman Abrolhos Islands. Fisheries Management Paper No. 146, Fisheries Western Australia, Perth, Australia.

Mann, P. (1990) 'The Houtman Abrolhos', *Australian Geographic*, 18, 74–97.

McDonald, K. (2001) 'Wind-swept treasures', *The West Australian*, 5 May.

Newsome, D., Moore, S.A. and Dowling, R.K. (2002) *Natural Area Tourism: Ecology, Impacts and Management*. Clevedon, UK: Channel View Publications.

Page, S.J. and Dowling, R.K. (2002) *Ecotourism*. Harlow: Pearson Education.

Storr, G.M., Johnstone, R.E. and Griffin, P. (1986) 'Birds of the Houtman Abrolhos Islands, Western Australia', *Records of the Western Australian Museum*, Supplement 24.

WATC and EPA (1989) *The Eco-Ethics of Tourism Development*. Perth, Australia: WA Tourism Commission and the Environmental Protection Authority.

WATC (1997) Nature-based tourism strategy for Western Australia. Report prepared by the Nature-Based Tourism Advisory Committee, WA Tourism Commission, Perth, Australia.

Websites

Maps and other figures relevant to the case study can be found at the following addresses (see also appendix):

Australian Tourism: *www.australia.com*

author's website: *www.business.ecu.edu.au/mtl/tourism/sustainable_tourism/index.htm*

Eco Abrolhos Company: *www.abrolhosislands.com.au*

the Ecotourism Association of Australia: *www.ecotourism.org.au*

Western Australia: *www.westernaustralia.net*

Appendix: Websites for Further Research

Main websites for research

The following websites can assist readers in their research. Specific chapters also provide various addresses for an additional investigation of the issues raised.

UK and worldwide sites

Audubon Nature Odysseys: *http://www.audubon.org/market/no/*
British Trust for Conservation Volunteers (BTCV): *http://www.btcv.org/*
Conservation International: *http://www.conservation.org*; *http://www.ecotour.org*
EARTHFOOT Programme: *http://www.earthfoot.org*
ECoNETT Project Office (WTTC), London: *http://www.wttc.org*
The Eco-Source Network – a sustainable tourism site: *http://www.ecosourcenetwork.com*
Eco-Source website: *http://www.podi.com/ecosource*
The Ecotourism Society (USA): *http://www.ecotourism.org*
Ecuadorian Ecotourism Association: *http://www.planeta.com/mader/ecotravel/south/ecuador*
Escape Artist site: *http://www.escapeartist.com*
Gentle Earth Walking – Australia: *http://ren.netconnect.com.au/~sueandon/*
Green Audit Kit (perform an environmental audit on your business. This UK site has a step-by-step guide): *http://www.greenauditkit.org/*
Green Travel: *http://www.greenbuilder.com*; *http://www.earthsystems.org/list/green-travel/*
Hawaii Ecotourism Association: *http://planet-hawaii.com/hea/url.html*
Kiskeya Alternative website (Spanish): *http://kiskeya-alternative.org*
MacLaren, Deborah – Evaluating Ecotourism Operators and Agents: *http://www2.planeta.com/ mader/planeta/1196/1196agents.html*
META (includes marine ecotourism reports): *http://www.tourism-research.org/reports/html*
National Audubon Society Travel Ethic For Environmental Responsible Travel: *http:// www.audubon.org/market/no/ethic/*
National Parks Conservation Association: *http://www.npca.org/*
National Parks Magazine: *http://www.npca.org/magazine/currentissue.html*
Nunavut Tourism – Arctic: *http://www.nunavut.com/tourism*
Parks in Jeopardy: *http://www.npca.org/whatshot/topten.html*
Planeta.com: *http://www2.planeta.com/mader/ecotravel*
The Regional Environment Centre for Central and Eastern Europe: *http://www.rec.org*
The Site for Adventure Travel: *http://www.iexplore.com/*
Terraquest Site: *http://www.terraquest.com*
Tourism Concern: Community Tourism Directory (UK): *http://www.gn.apc.org/tourismconcern/*; *http://www.oneworld.org/tourconcern*; *http://www.tourismconcern.org.uk*

The Tourism and Environment Forum: Sustaining Scotland's Natural Advantage: *http:// www.greentourism.org.uk/*
Travel Weekly Online: *http://www.traveler.net/two/*
UNESCO and UNESCO Environmental Education Directory: *http://www.unesco.org/whc/heritage.htm*; *http://www.unesco.org/education/educprog/environment/index.html*
United Nations Environment Programme: *http://www.unepie.org/contact.html*
World Conservation Union (Switzerland): *http://www.iucn.org*
World Heritage Committee: *http://www.unesco.org/whc*
World Travel Guide destination information: *http://www.wtgonline.com*

Australian sites

Australian Conservation Foundation: *www.acfonline.org.au/*
Bureau of Tourism Research: 1998 Ecotourism Conference Proceedings: *http://www.btr.gov.au/ conf_proc/ecotourism/ecotourism.html*
Commonwealth Department of Tourism: *http://tourism.gov.au/publications/BPE*
Department of the Environment, Sports and Territories, Australia: *http://kaos.erin.gov.au/life/ general_info/biodivser*
Environment Centre Northern Territory: *http://www1.octa4.net.au/ecnt*
Friends of the Earth, Australia: *http://www.metropolis.net.au/foe*
Great Barrier Reef Marine Park Authority (best environmental practices): *http://www.gbrmpa.gov.au/ corp_site/key_issues/tourism/best_environmental_practice.html*
International Centre for Ecotourism Research, Australia: *http://www.gu.edu.au/centre/icer*
Queensland Environmental Tourism: *http://www.tq.com.au/qep/qep.htm*
World Wide Fund For Nature – Australia: *http://www.wwf.org.au/master.htm*

New Zealand sites

Department of Conservation, New Zealand: *http://www.doc.govt.nz*
Ecotour Operators throughout New Zealand: *http://www.ecotours.co.nz*
Forest and Bird: *http://www.forest-bird.org.nz*
New Zealand Whale and Dolphin Trust: *http://nzwhaledolphintrust.tripod.com/home/*
Tourism Industry Association NZ: *http://www.tianz.org.nz*
Tourism New Zealand: *http://www.tourisminfo.govt.nz*
Tourism New Zealand 100% PURE marketing campaign: *http://www.purenz.com*

Other sites of interest

www.adventuretravelbusiness.com
www.adventuretraveltips.com
www.asiamarketresearch.com/columns/tourism-branding.htm
www.betterworldclub.com
www.centralamerica.com
www.costaricamap.com
www.costaricapressroom.com
www.ecotour.org
www.ecotourism-adventure.com/vidybook.htm
www.ecotour-iran.com/glance.htm
www.ecotourism.cc/
www.eduweb.com/schaller/
www.ee/ecotourism/ar-rio-2.htm
www.footprintseco-resort.com
www.geocities.com/Yosemite/Trails/7987/page5.html
www.gorp.com
www.ifg.org/un.html

www.infocostarica.com
www.longwoods-intl.com/Longwoods-Brochure.pdf
www.members.aol.com/jwvoelker2/english/thesis/chapter9.htm
www.odci.gov
www.qttc.com.au/qep/actions.htm
www.sidsnet.org/eco-tourism/footprints.html
www.spaef.com
www.travel.state.gov
www.un.org/esa/sustdev/agenda21chapter36.htm
www.unep.org/Documents
www.uneptie.org/pc/tourism/ecotourism/iye.htm
www.unepie.org/pc/tourism/sust-tourism/economic.htm
www.ursainternational.org/whatwedoecotourism.html
www.wetpaper.com.au/products/Videos/Ecotourism.html
www.wildernesstravel.com
www.wri.orgwww.wilderness.net/pubs
www.wttc.org/stratdev/agenda21.asp

339

Index